# Advance Praise

"This book is a must read for anyone who wants to truly understand the fish we love to hunt. Matt's unique writing style keeps a subject that could otherwise be pretty boring, interesting and fun to absorb. From tales of his childhood in Poland to the anecdotal tales of the trout, and the endless amount of intense historical data he has compiled. This book will definitely keep you interested and learning. The more you understand about the history and ways of the brown trout the better you will be equipped to outsmart the wiriest of all trout. Matt has a unique intimate style, and I feel I was right there in the tree house with him, and would have pushed him out if I were his cousin."—Kelly Galloup, author of *Modern Streamers for Trophy Trout* and editor-at-large, *Fly Fisherman*

"The sport of fly fishing and the recorded history of its pursuit and passion is much like a tapestry which has been woven by the fabric of its thoughtful and inquisitive participants over a period of thousands of years. Its fabric is spun from the intricacies of developments in its rods and reels, the tapers of its lines and leaders, and the intricate beauty of countless fly patterns thoughtfully crafted by its deans and disciples. It's a road much loved, explored, and traveled. In *Nexus*, one of the sports more passionate modern disciples takes us down a road far less traveled. While the writings of rivers, equipment, aquatic insect hatches, fly patterns, and tactics for fishing them have been well documented in our sports thousands of manuscripts, Matt Supinski takes us to a discussion of the core of our sport and a discussion of the fish themselves.

Matt Supinski's life-long love affair of civilization's founding fish *Salmo* begins with his boyhood observation of them and their behaviors from a tree house overhanging a river pool in his native Poland, to New York's famous Catskill rivers, to the rich limestone streams of Pennsylvania's Cumberland Valley, to his present day home rivers in Michigan, and to other places in the world where they now swim. *Nexus* takes readers from the origins of *Salmo* in Europe to its distribution around the world and discusses how its unique evolutionary adaptability has enabled it to survive and thrive in spite of climactic changes, the rise of civilizations, industrialization, and the destruction of wars which has allowed them to take root and thrive wherever they have been introduced.

While *Nexus* dives heavily into *Salmo*'s deeper biological and behavioral traits in both brown trout, *trutta*, and Atlantic salmon, *salar*, the book ultimately discusses why these gamefish have earned our respect, love and pursuit of them over the centuries. From the challenges of the chess-like game of cracking the code of selective feeding on a limestone stream to the thrill of a pursuing a predatory *"truttasaurus"* with giant articulated meat streamers; *Nexus* is a must read for anyone who enjoys *Salmo* and their pursuit with a fly."—Henry Ramsey, author of *Matching Major Eastern Hatches*

"I can't think of anyone better to write about our founding fish. Matt Supinski has studied brown trout and salmon for decades, and can explain their similarities and nuanced differences as fluently as a wine connoisseur can describe red wines from the Old World and the New."—Ross Purnell, editor and publisher at *Fly Fisherman*

"This is a special book; it takes me back to my youngest days fishing with my father through powerful memories of the early 1950s. Matt's skilled presentation also imparts fresh insight, intriguing theory, and practical application that even a geezer like me can absorb. His writing style is enthusiastic and passionate, and seasoned with stunning photography.

I fell in love with brown trout on a warm spring day in northern Michigan nearly seventy years ago. A brightly colored brown of about ten inches ate a small Adams and I asked my father if it was a "German brown." I had caught a brown the previous afternoon from a different creek and he had called it a German brown. This one looked similar but not the same. My father said he thought this fish might be a "Loch Leven" strain fish from Scotland. He told me about an article he had read that traced different plantings in Michigan to two different European sources. The article went on to say that the Loch Leven trout's black spots usually looked like a smudged, or blurred, letter X. I have looked closely at the spots on brown trout since that day so long ago.

Reading this book is like falling in love for the first time, all over again. It filled me with joy, excitement, and wonder. I am pretty sure you will like it."—Robert Linsenman, author of *Great Lakes Steelhead, Trout Streams of Michigan*, and others

"With an impressive breadth of knowledge, Matt Supinski takes his readers on the natal journey of his beloved *Salmo*, from the dawn of the age to the modern angling sport we now enjoy. Matt draws on his experience from a lifetime of fly fishing, but also shares the wisdom from many of the masters of our sport."—Jason Randall, author of *Moving Water-Fly Fisherman's Guide to Currents*, among others

"I've read and utilized all of Matt Supinski's books over many years, from the *Pere Marquette River Journal* to *Steelhead Dreams* and *Selectivity*. The collective knowledge, global talent, research, theory, and thought that is combined into *Nexus* is masterful and addicting. *Nexus* easily represents the passion of his life's pursuit of steelhead, salmon, and trout, and is Matt's finest work."—Greg Senyo, author of *Fusion Fly Tying*

"Matt Supinski's knowledge of trout and salmon is immense. Since boyhood, he has explored these species both in streams and rivers and in the pages of angling literature. His newest work displays not only his technical angling side, but his passion for the lore of trout and salmon. Whether you are a home-spun fisherman or a globe-trotting angler, this book will shed light on the fish we love and their impact worldwide."—Glen Blackwood, owner of Great Lakes Fly Fishing Company

In *Brown Trout-Atlantic Salmon-Nexus*, author and expert guide Matt Supinski takes fly anglers beyond the sport's latest trends and fads. Calling on more than four decades of experience chasing trout and salmon in the Western Hemisphere and Europe, Supinski imparts his extensive knowledge and angling skills and lays bare his failures to the serious fly angler. Devotees of the quiet sport need a copy for their personal library."—Beau Beasley, director of *Fly Fishing the Mid-Atlantic: A No Nonsense Guide to Top Waters*

"Being the spring creek sculpin founding father and designer on the hallowed Letort Spring Run, also an Atlantic salmon angler, I realize the importance of the aggressive prey-predator relationship that all *Salmo*'s have when targeting their food in an aggressive manner. Matt's *Nexus* book deals beautifully with the aggressive nature and journey with the role and importance the "big meat streamer game" has evolved to in its modern day! It is a must read for the leviathan brown trout and Atlantic salmon chaser."—Ed Shenk, author of *Ed Shenk's Fly Rod Trouting*

# THE BROWN TROUT–
# ATLANTIC SALMON
# NEXUS

▲ Michigan Ground Zero Brown. Credit: Author

# THE BROWN TROUT–ATLANTIC SALMON
# NEXUS

### Tactics, Fly Patterns, and the Passion for
### Catching *Salmo*, Our Most Prized Gamefish

## MATTHEW SUPINSKI

SKYHORSE PUBLISHING

Skyhorse Publishing books may be purchased in bulk at special discounts for sales promotion, corporate gifts, fund-raising, or educational purposes. Special editions can also be created to specifications. For details, contact the Special Sales Department, Skyhorse Publishing, 307 West 36th Street, 11th Floor, New York, NY 10018 or info@skyhorsepublishing.com.

Skyhorse® and Skyhorse Publishing® are registered trademarks of Skyhorse Publishing, Inc.®, a Delaware corporation.

Visit our website at www.skyhorsepublishing.com.

10 9 8 7 6 5 4 3 2 1

Library of Congress Cataloging-in-Publication Data is available on file.

Cover design by Tom Lau
Cover photo credit: Matthew Supinski

ISBN: 978-1-5107-3029-8
Ebook ISBN: 978-1-5107-3030-4

Printed in China

oremost to my father Antoni, who took me on weekend jaunts to our favorite brown trout streams, and who learned the fine art of gentlemanly fly fishing while a Polish Army officer refugee after World War II in the British Royal Army in England, where the Rivers Test and Avon gave him the strong *Salmo* sporting affection. Also to my mentors, who are too numerous to list. But I especially thank the ones I had personal contact with and tutelage from: the late Vince Marinaro, who I fished with on the Letort Spring Run; Carl Richards and the late-night streamside bourbon-fueled intense discussions along Carmichael Flats on my home Muskegon River; and to the true national treasure, Nick Lyons, who taught me how to write and got my first article published in *Fly Fisherman* back in the eighties. Also to the master Lee Wulff, the true "*Salmo* salar Buddha re-incarnate," who I have been blessed to have many a discussion and pick his salar inspired thoughts at the Atlantic Salmon Federation dinners and in the Catskills, where we have our summer home and his magnificent fly-fishing virtuoso wife, a true living salar legend, Joan Wulff, whom I have been blessed. And to Jay Cassell and Tony Lyons for believing in my Nexus concept, and Jay McCullough for the excellent editing.

To Bror Jonsson from Norway, the "Godfather of *Salmo*," whose *Ecology of Atlantic Salmon and Brown Trout: Habitat as a Template* is a must read for the modern ichthyologist. He was so kind to absorb/tolerate my adventurous and bold Freudian *Salmo* salar theories in my previous book, and be a constant scientific reality reference check and source of inspiration for this book. All in all, so many great minds have had tremendous influence on me and have taught me how to perceive and love these fish and the enigmatic chase the beguiling brown trout and Atlantic salmon will forever lead us on.

Finally to my supportive, tolerant, and loving wife Laurie, creative son Peter, and to all my supporters around the world that read my passionate ramblings, thank you!

# CONTENTS

# Preface

*I*n this beautifully romantic, sometimes anthropomorphic, and one might even call reverential compendium of historical, biological, and evolutionary information, Matt leads the reader through a seemingly endless array of diverse and frequently contradictory information. In his unique storytelling style, he skillfully captures the reader's attention and keeps the reader wondering what is coming next. Skimming or jumping ahead is no help. By doing so one is only compelled to go back to find what you missed. In the process, long-time anglers will be saying "Yeah, I remember seeing that," or "I never thought of it that way." And over and over one will think, "Is that who came up with that idea?" Inevitably Matt feeds the angler tidbits of tried-and-true angling tips mixed with the thoughts of innumerable angling greats that have helped and continue to goad the fly-angler to induce his quarry to make a mistake. After all, neither Atlantic salmon nor brown trout ever *eat* chunks of feathers, fur, hair, plastic or tinfoil wrapped around a piece of wire, jointed or not. Every time a trout or salmon takes a fly it has made a mistake.

This book goes beyond everything the reader will look for in a how-to book, a scientific treatise, everything *Salmo*. Regardless of how many useful tips or experiences, this very experienced angler and guide shares it all with the reader. Through his love of both brown trout and Atlantic salmon, Matt introduces the reader to the ever-perplexing "nexus" that connects these two animals. No doubt these fish have been evolving over a very long time and have one thing in common, a long relationship with people. I count myself among the many who have wondered just how much and what kind of selective pressure humans have had in developing the enormous varieties of the Genus *Salmo*. Is it contact with humans over millennia that have resulted in adaptive mutations that have molded the behavior of *Salmo* more than any other salmonid? Does this at least partially account for them to be thought of as being more cautious and hard to catch than perhaps any other salmonids? It appears that they may very well have been harassed by human beings over a longer period of time than any of the rest.

As a student in animal behavior I prefer to lump what the author of this book and many other writers on the subject refer to as selectivity, aggression, cannibalism, predation, territoriality, or even moodiness as "optimal foraging." That is, the animal is simply feeding in the most successful way it can to maximize energy intake from the food available in the environment, all the while minimizing its being eaten itself before it has a chance to get its genes into the next generation.

This in not to imply that Matt and previous writers got it all wrong. On the contrary, it shows how different but complementary things appear when viewed from the perspective of an angler trying to catch a fish on a fly than from the perspective of trying to understand what a fish does to get its genes into the next generation. One can learn a lot through both perspectives. In one case the trout is thought of as "biting." The hook and the anglers are both involved. On the other case, only the fish and its environment are involved.

Read on for a great adventure that has intrigued anglers for a long and fruitful nexus. Who hasn't ever seen a trout or salmon rise to a fly and at the last moment turn with a splashy "Oh shit!" refusal. No, it didn't think. But you did. The fish certainly realized that it almost made a mistake. Have you ever changed flies after a splashy rise only to hook that trout on the very next cast by simply tying on a different fly of the exact same size and pattern? That's how well a trout can detect the subtle difference of one fly from another. Call it selectivity or a "search image." Either way it shows how well the trout can see, and how quickly it can learn what is edible and what is not. After all, that is what they do all day long, day after day and year after year. And you wonder why they are at times so very selective? It's all about survival. Behavioral ecologists call it using a search image.

If there are a lot of bugs on the water, and some are easier to catch than others (cripples?) or some are more plentiful than others, what is the most efficient way to maximize energy intake with the least number of mistakes or waste of energy? If you wanted to pick out the greatest amount of energy in the least amount of time from a box of cracker jacks dumped on a conveyor belt what search image would you use? Wouldn't you concentrate on the peanuts and ignore the rest? Read on as Matt leads you through a Cracker Jack box full of experiences and memories.

—Dr. Robert Bachman
Lancaster, PA
February, 2018

# Foreword

This is pure poetry in text and magnificent images on how Atlantic salmon and brown trout evolved and behave in the always-changing climate of land and riverscapes. Few, if any, love these Atlantic trout more than Matt Supinski. Few, if any, spend more hours of the year watching and hunting these magnificent creatures with a similar degree of passion. Few, if any, seek new knowledge about the Atlantic salmonids with greater thirst. Few, if any, have a more intimate knowledge about their innate and flexible behaviors, all rooted in his early upbringing by the Wieprza River in Poland.

Matt shares his vast experience as the true storyteller he is, easily envisioned by readers while preparing for the next trip to a salmon river. With a text combined with over two hundred color images and twenty fly pattern plates by some of the best nature photographers of the world, readers are taken through the evolution of the Atlantic trouts and how they adapt to their variable environments. This is not just a science book, but a text for fly fishers and anglers that hold a special place for these fishes in their hearts. This is a book for those who hunger to become a more perfect angler. For all these, Matt Supinski's experience blended with scientific facts is a natural next step, an unbeatable recipe for success.

—Bror Jonsson
February 2018

# Introduction

**by Tom Rosenbauer**

*I* was a kid nurtured by the worldly tales of Al McClane and Ernest Schwiebert, and Matt Supinski's writing takes me back to those days, when I could quote entire paragraphs from Schwiebert's books verbatim because I had read them so many times. Somehow, these guys had the knack of making fishing holes, whether they were in the Catskills or in Bavaria, seem like mystical places, no matter where they were or what the fishing was really like. Matt's writing does the same things to me, unlike he works of any other modern fishing writer. Not only has he fished around the world in rivers I can only dream of visiting, he tells damn good stories about them, tying in history, geology, and culture. I don't think it is far-fetched to say he has inherited Schwiebert's mantle.

Or maybe I like his writing because we both were fly-fishing-obsessed teenagers in western New York at about the same time. And we both devoured that new book called *Selective Trout* as soon as it was published. In those days there were not many kids our age into fly fishing and I find it hard to believe that we never ran into each other on the Wiscoy or Caledonia Spring Creek. So perhaps we both inherited the same kind of fishing nature at an impressionable age because we fished the same waters. Or maybe it's not nurture, but perhaps nature. Half of my genes are Polish.

I was surprised by the depth of this book. I expected to enjoy the writing. I have never heard anyone speak of a brown trout as a bipolar predator but that description is perfect and a classic Supinski-ism. And only Supinski could quote Lee Wulff and Nietzsche in the same paragraph. And the book has lots more fishing technique and useful nuggets than I expected. I anticipated a philosophical or pop-science comparison of brown trout and Atlantic salmon, which to my taste would account for a pretty boring read. But what I found instead was a tour of the world of brown trout and Atlantic salmon, which is at times a travelogue of some of the most interesting rivers in the world and at times a modern history of flyfishing over the past half-century—something long overdue because it has been a rich and full history with plenty of innovation and a host of interesting characters. Such topics as in-depth discussions of favorite prey items of trout and detailed comparisons of the pros and cons of Euro nymphing (Matt calls it "Slavic nymphing," but we'll forgive his chauvinism), indicator nymphing, and sight-nymphing give Matt's book an unanticipated depth.

I have read many histories of the introduction of my favorite fish to North America, as I grew up fishing one of the first, Caledonia Spring Creek in New York State, but I never knew that the Michigan stocking, contrary to what has been written before, was not a single point-source stocking in Baldwin Creek, a tributary of the Pere Marquette, but in fact the trout were sprinkled over several spring creeks along the train's journey, including Bigelow Creek and the White River. Not many fly fishers would bother to get into such historical details, and maybe it only matters to nerds like myself (and Matt). But to some of us it matters.

I found his observations of the surface orientation of resident brown trout, Atlantic salmon, and sea-run brown trout all rising to inspect pieces of floating debris on his boyhood river in Poland fascinating. I had always considered brown trout to be the least surface-oriented of all the resident salmonid species, but after diving into this book I realize that it's more their simple reluctance to feed at times and not their lack of interest in the surface. Thanks, Matt, for sharing these insights with us.

I have always found writings on Atlantic salmon to be either overblown purple prose about the "king of fish" or fawning reminiscences of wealthy sports who thought they were great anglers because they could afford to go to salmon rivers at exclusive camps at the peak of the run. But I became entranced with Matt's thought-provoking observations of the behavior of these enigmatic fish and the outlandish behavior they exhibit when taking a fly. I still cannot figure out why these fish ever take a fly, especially a dry fly, and don't agree with Matt's attribution of playfulness and curiosity to salmon. But he's caught salmon in many more places than I have and I am willing to admit my ignorance after reading his observations.

And I can say for certain that in the future any Atlantic salmon fishing I attempt will be vastly different. Not only will I try more oddball flies and presentations, I will also apply my powers of observation to the same degree I do to brown trout fishing after reading his statement:

> This is a common approach the lethal brown trout angler will take in order to observe foraging predator profiles on clear waters. Unless you are employing a Euro nymphing/mine sweeping/dredge casting technique, especially on fast tannic waters where this technique is highly effective, observing your prey will allow you to notice many subtleties not revealed to sufferers of chronic casting syndrome. Just as you don't sit in a duck blind or big-game tree stand and

shoot your gun constantly to attract your victim, so also stalking and observing must be applied to the salmon game, especially in highly visible waters like the Bonaventure.

This would be a great volume even without visuals, but the amazing photography in here makes me drool uncontrollably. I dearly love photos of brown trout in their widely varying phases and the images here did not disappoint. I don't think I have ever seen so many brilliant brown trout images in one place, and to have these and those tasty photos of salmon and trout rivers from around the world makes we want to convince some wealthy benefactor to adopt me and set me up with a trust fund so I can see them in person.

▲ Credit: Dave Jensen

# 1. The Passion Begins: The Big Pool and the Tree House

It is nonsense to believe there is a color for every month (this was still a common notion, since the time of the *Treatise*)—it is not so—for in fishing three mill pools on the same stream, (Big Spring, Pa.) on the same day, I have found, that to be successful, I had to change my fly and the color of it at each pool; and in fishing in the same places a few days after, the only fly trout would rise to, was a small grey one, and to such a one they would rise freely in all the pools. In the early part of the season when the trout is poor, he will run at anything; but towards June he becomes a perfect epicure in his feeding at such time.

—George Gibson, *Turf Register* (1838)

The summer of 1968 seemed like an enchanted fairy tale that I will forever enshrine for the rest of my life. To this day, my most vivid dreams take me to that surreal period when the vibrancy and magic of the natural world coexisted with how pure and simple life was, and still can be. It was also the time I learned to see and observe wild trout and salmon in their most feral and fascinating state of existence, just as they were millions of years ago.

As a ten-year-old wide-eyed, bushy-tailed, white-haired *bialy* (Polish for whitey), I was always in search of thrill seeking adventures, forever asking "how come" and never knowing when to stop the chase. It was a summer when I spent time back on my dad's farm off the Baltic in northern Poland with my relatives, where our families were large land barons and farmers. My dad and mom, who lived through the dark period of World War II and its reign of demonic human terror like the Nazi's concentration camps and bloody partisan warfare, had made up their minds to go back and resume dad's master's degree education and relive the places and things that brought them so much pain and suffering, yet taught them the beauty and resilience of the human spirit. It taught them to forever enjoy the alluring gift of life we take for granted every day. We revisited my mother's Austria and my father's Poland to relive all the bedtime stories they told me about the fabulous and mesmerizing countryside, the pastoral farms and valleys, the rivers and mountains, the food and spirits—and most importantly, the gaiety of human life's celebration of nature and especially in this case, how my passion for *Salmo* began, which placed an addicting curse on me for life.

As a city boy in upstate New York, my dad had already introduced me to the finer points of fly fishing at the age of six, taking trips every weekend to the fabulous wild brown trout streams of southern New York's Allegany Mountains and foothills. He taught me how to tie a crude Sawyer's Pheasant Tail nymph with copper wire and tail fibers with my hands in the field. He also gave me his hand-me-down beater bamboo rod, one of several he acquired while learning to fly fish in England, where he served as a displaced Polish officer, then in the British Army. Fly fishing and bird hunting were his passions. Also, making home-made sausages, which I still seek out as a connoisseur wherever my travels take me. He taught me about wild mushrooms, how to tell a mayfly from a caddis (he called them sedges), and how to pick ripe juicy cherries without the white worms in them.

For me, a mischievous and somewhat cocky young lad, it was a humbling experience. The farm had thatched straw roof houses and barns, animals of all kinds, no running water or electricity—it was back to the medieval times I saw on TV—yup, no TV also! At that time there were no video games, cell phones, or Internet. It was only you and your family and all the fun and misadventures you could possibly muster up in a day. The deep starlit nights of the country, with the Milky Way staring at you like it was in front of your nose kept us star gazing all night, as we descended into sleep out in the meadows with the sheep and cows. Of course to scare the American city boy, my Polish cousins would tell me ghost and Nazi stories until we began to see and hear things that went bump in the night. We even played in old abandoned German Army concrete bunkers, and once came in contact with a land mine which almost took me and my cousins away to the big trout stream in the sky. The local *Policia* took the mine away live.

But the magic was in the *rzeka* (Polish for the stream) that ran near the pasture and down the valley from the farm. They were stunningly clean wooded little spring creek jewels and broader rivers adorned with huge European red oak and birch trees lining its banks. It had fast waters, long, slow meandering runs with beautiful vegetation, and one large, deep crystal-clear pool. Here, my little architecturally-minded cousins built a cool tree house over the pool with a swing rope to jump and swim from, but I soon found out how cold the water was, even in the extreme heat of summer. Here you could only do the skinny-dip dive-bombardier plunge on warm sunny days. Most of the time we skinny-dipped in the warmer ponds.

▲ My father's stories of the little streams and rivers near the family farm kept me awake at night with anticipation. He said they were full of colorful little red-dotted *Brazowy Pstragy* (Polish for brown trout) and how it was so tough to catch them. Credit: Arek Kubla

My first day up the tree house I was called an *Americanski coura*—an American chicken—because I was afraid of heights. But once up there, I was like a king at his throne. Always in search of fish, I noticed the big white mouths of the kype-jawed male brown trout, finning close to the surface near the pools overhanging banks. Bingo!—I'm on a farm with trout, how cool was that? But I had no tackle and started asking my many questions "How can I . . . blah, blah, blah? Go fishing now, Mom?"

My shining knight came to my rescue the very next day in a beat-up Soviet-issue pickup truck. It was my old retired Uncle Stasiek (Stanley). He was a local game warden who oversaw the *stave* (fish ponds and lakes), the wildlife, hunting, and of course, the rivers and streams. "So you must be the *rybak* (fisherman) your mother has been telling me about," Stanley said. After a warm embrace, he proceeded to show me his sporting cache: Three bamboo fly rods—one from Czechoslovakia, one he built himself, and the other his perennial favorite, an English Hardy. The three reels were all English, along with the leather and wool fly wallets. In these he kept his favorites like the Tup's Indispensable, Wickham's Fancy, Iron Blue, Pale Watery, and a leather wallet of gorgeous Atlantic Salmon flies.

"Hate to tell you, but those trout in that big pool are downright impossible to catch in the summer," he said. "In the spring, they are a lot easier when the water is higher and big *muchy*"— mayflies—"are on the water. That is when we get some big brown trout. But we can give it a go until the big fish come in."

Big fish? I wondered what he meant. Some of those Browns I saw in the pool were up to twenty inches long.

"*Wojeck*,"—uncle—"what do you mean by big fish?" I asked.

"Ahhh, those are the big *Losos*"—Atlantic salmon and sea trout—"that come to that pool after the strong rains of late August. They are monsters!"

He went on to mention that "the stream" (it really had no name other than that) ran into another river called the "Wieprza," which ran into the Baltic Sea. The salmon used the smaller stream that ran through the farm as a spawning place with all its very fine gravel. "Now when those first fish come in, you'll get a good crack at catching one of these. Once they settle into that pool, they have a nasty attitude and are downright impossible to catch. But they are fun to look at and watch swimming around; they are beautiful creatures."

To this day the Wieprza still has Atlantic salmon,

as well as colorful, native resident and sea-run brown trout, despite indigenous salmon in Poland becoming almost extirpated and the rivers heavily polluted by the Communist occupation. Their salmon restoration program has been slow and now is just starting to see some good runs come back with wild reproduction.

My uncle Stanley said if we want to catch lots of fish, there were much easier quarry than the salmon, in terms of fun, like the pike in the farm lakes—they were really easy and fought really hard. But I wasn't interested, thank you! I wanted the beautiful *Salmo.*

That first evening my uncle and I went down to his pool and he rigged up two rods and we had a go at it.

"Your mom tells me you are quite the caster."

"Yeah, I've been fly fishing for four years and we have these same brown trout at home."

"Yes, you Americans took them to the US from Europe—Germany I believe. But they are not as smart as the real European ones," he said, chuckling.

We threw every fly at the fish we saw without a touch. A few of the fish closely inspected the Iron Blue flies, but ultimately refused them.

"Do you have any smaller flies of the same blue-winged kind?" I asked.

"Nope, these are the smallest I've got," Stanley shot back.

Damn, if only I would have brought my fly tying kit—the trout have been looking the fly over that looks like a BWO, but the ones I saw were a lot smaller, most certainly *Baetis* or *Drunella.* At the end of the day, my uncle and I walked back to the farmhouse while he pulled out a big bottle of beer out of his leather sack.

"Want a sip?"

"Sure, why not?" I replied in the cavalier fashion of a ten-year-old. That was the first sip of alcohol I ever had and man did it taste good! I got a tingle in my toes and a funny feeling like I'll never forget. As we walked, the stars in the darkness of the valley seemed so close to you that you could touch them—it was a truly enchanted night. In

▲ My cousins and uncles always spoke about the brown trout and Atlantic salmon of their farm stream that ran into the Baltic with a reverence reserved for royalty, believing it was good luck to have these perfect specimens of the Almighty nearby. Credit: Dave Jensen

bed, that's all I could think about were those trout and the real monsters yet to come . . . *monsters*, mind you!

The next day I noticed my uncle left me one of his homemade cane rods and a wallet of flies, an English Hardy reel, a small net, and a worn-down spool of tippet material. He wrote me a note my mother interpreted, since I could speak fluent Polish but couldn't read it. He said good luck with those impossible trout and he'd be back in a few days to persuade me to go pike fishing and pheasant hunting.

Each morning and evening I'd do my best to try and catch those cunning rascals. I trimmed down a few flies to almost nothing, but the hook stood out like a sore thumb. No luck—just refusals. I ended up spending a good part of the time in the tree house watching the trout while lying on my belly—they were a fascinating lot. There were the larger trout that seemed to hold the best positions in the current, often near overhanging brush, along the foam line, and near an undercut grassy bank. The smaller trout tended to go all over and never attained a true lie like the big boys. They were very active, sipping tiny white flies off the surface—midges or Tricos. When the wind swept through the valley in late August, tons of flying ants were all over. The trout really relished them. One evening I did finally get a good fish to take a brown-bodied fly that I chopped to have an ant shape. I think the tippet material was old and brittle and the good brown broke off as it ran for the bank. Although it was an exhilarating moment, it left me in tears for days.

My uncle finally came back and we went pike fishing. We used long strands of rooster cock feathers tied to the hook—white, black, reds et cetera, and caught lots of pike. I think they were pickerel and Zander, a walleye/perch creature of some sort that tasted better than farm-raised carp.

Stanley had two handsome and well-trained German Short Hair pointers that knew how to hunt. His gun was his treasure—a well-polished German over/under 16 gauge. He let me shoot it with his arms wrapped around me to cushion the recoil. The grain-filled grassland farms and hedgerows had lots of *bazant*—pheasants. They were beautiful, large, fat birds that made for memorable dinners. I controlled the dogs while my uncle did the shooting. I wanted a gun, but my mother bought me a good bow and arrow from the town market vendor, and gave me instructions to "use this to shoot the birds." I liked it a ton, but trying to shoot a pheasant with a bow and arrow was very sporting. I did get one bird to have a brush of fate with the shaft of the arrow, but that was it. I did shoot a rabbit—and that was way too cool!

As my time in Poland drew short, I returned each day to watch the trout in the pool, hoping a rain storm would come soon to bring up the water for the "monsters."

Three days of rain finally came and like clockwork, Uncle Stanley showed up in what seemed like a Model-T version of a pickup truck. It was loud, smoky, and had a real creaky stick shift. Out he came with his bigger cane fly rod.

"Let's go see if the monsters came in," he said. I could hardly contain myself and I ran down to the stream well ahead of my uncle, who had a limp from a war injury.

"It's blown out! Crap!" I shouted.

"*Mieczyslaw*," he said, calling me by the Polish version of my name, "don't worry, this is what they need to come up—they'll be here, trust me! I'll be back when it's time."

Uncle Stanley made good on his promise and showed up one morning while I was still sleeping. Mom said "get dressed, Stanley is here."

"You don't want the water to be too clear," he told me, "it's perfect now." Again I ran to the pool, my uncle limping behind me.

They were there! I saw two humongous chrome-hued fish leap. That was the first time I saw an Atlantic salmon close up, and they were beautiful. My uncle loaded up the bigger rod and put on a large, stunning, green English fly.

"This should be the one they want. If not, I've got orange ones, and red and black ones. I'll go first and show you what to do if you get one on—they aren't little trout, after all."

After about what seemed like eternity of swinging the wet fly through the pool, he screamed *cholera*—damnit— as his rod bowed and a chrome silver missile launched out of the pool. We both held onto the rod, but after three jumps it was off—we both looked extremely dejected— me more so, because I'd screwed up by having my hand on the reel knob.

"*Szkoda*," he said. What a shame. Just then another strong thunderstorm came upon us. At least I knew they were there.

After a customary lunch of rye bread, *Krakowska* cold cuts, and my uncle having a shot or two of home distilled vodka-moonshine, he left me one of his old hand-me-down big cane rods and some flies. "Give these flies a try, but remember when they run, don't hold on to the line, let the drag on the reel do its work. When the salmon is finally tired, beach it and bring it back. They are pink colored in their flesh—the best for the table or smoker! *Dobrze?*" and he was off. I got it.

In the week or so before we were to depart for the US, I spent every waking moment on the pool and tree house. My cousins thought I'd gone mad and was possessed by the fish, and they were not far wrong. I could never get a salmon to take my fly, but had a few close swipes and good long looks. Mostly I was on my belly in the tree house looking down.

The Atlantic salmon had a definite pecking order and

▲ The Atlantic salmon were the main attraction in the pool. Like a bunch of aristocrats, they pushed the resident Browns to the fringes and tail-outs and took up residence in the current flow of the bubble foam right at the heart of the pool. Credit: Arni Baldurson-Lax-A

two of the largest ones were at or near the top of the pool. One had a green fly hanging off the side of its mouth—the one I broke off (I think it was a Green Highlander). At times they were completely listless—passive and dormant. Then out of the blue, they would get excited and chase each other. Usually one smaller male in the tail of the pool stirred up the pecking order pot. They seemed to become most restless before a thunderstorm or at evening. During the day they usually just laid there, finning motionless in the current. Their big white mouths and kypes would open wide like they were bored and yawning. When a *botchan* (European stork) flew by and casted a large shadow on the pool, the salmon would freak out. The same would happen if a hawk flew by. In time, the browns eventually got closer to the salmon and went about their day of selective feeding, almost as if the salmon weren't there.

When our time in Poland came to end and the families hugged at the train station where the trains would take us to Warsaw, and then a plane to Amsterdam and New York, our tears ran freely, and the memories of those special times still run through my mind. I felt for the first time in my young life the hypnotic spell and power that nature had on you when you carefully and quietly observed its perfect essence. I also learned how to yearn to be back in the freedom and democracy of America after experiencing a totalitarian communist rule of bullshit corruption, propaganda, and terror worthy of the Nazis.

From those memorable summers of my youth to my life today as a fly-fishing guide, I learned to respect the magnificence and awe of the magical world of selective brown trout and Atlantic salmon. Now, as then, observing patiently and precise presentations brings me as much joy and tranquility as the catching—quite often more.

That deeply affecting journey of my youth taught me to understand the crux and foundation of the selective process. Observation, inquisitive thinking, the unfolding empirical process—and most importantly, deductive reasoning were firmly instilled principles in my mind. Applying these key principles to solve the riddle of the "whys," "how comes," "did you see that?" and the "I bet

if I tried this," caused me not to overreact, but to spend much more time watching and less time fishing. When I was confronted with an angling problem, I chose to find the fundamental things I was doing wrong, or sought the advice and wisdom of the old timers—I stalked them on every trout stream I visited and drove them crazy with my questions.

Ironically, later in my life, that Polish tree house of my youth was transposed to the hallowed viewing benches alongside the Letort Spring Run along Fox's Meadow in the enchanting Cumberland Valley Limestone Country. Here, Marinaro, Fox, and their high court of astute Letort regulars would play the "game of nods." Trying to hook giant brown trout with 8x–10x Tortue French tippets, size 24 Jassids, and delicate bamboo rods in swirling back eddies of the limestone spring creeks was not easy stuff, but a highly technical game of puddle casts and hands-and-knees presentations. This "think tank" of Letort regulars would be entertained by the extremes of the unfolding selectivity process that continues to amaze me as a life-long theoretical fly fisher.

In the early 1980s a tree house of sorts played a major breakthrough to how brown trout behave, feed, and go about their daily routine. Dr. Robert Bachman, doing his dissertation at Penn State University, built a tree house tower along the very fertile and wild trout rich spring creek waters of Spruce Creek, Pennsylvania. Here he developed models explaining the behavior and movement of wild trout and how they interact with stocked trout. His research won "Best Paper Award" by the American Fisheries Society, and gave fisheries biologists and anglers around the world a better understanding of the complex world of trout and their environments. Bachman summed up the pool/structure dominance of aggressive browns by the following in his research:

The foraging behavior of wild brown trout in Spruce Creek reflects the profound effect that current has on the energy fish must expend while living in a lotic environment. The restricted home range of individual fish, the discrete nature of the foraging sites within these home ranges (pools), and the large proportion of time the fish spend feeding stationary in foraging sites suggests that energy expended by the wild brown trout may be a principal determinant of growth rate and population density.

My hope for this book is to take the novice and seasoned brown trout and Atlantic salmon lover and fly fisher into an appreciative thinking, theoretical world where the angler can enjoy watching and solving the multi-faceted task of understanding and stalking these two closely-related cousins that most people never associate as a nexus of one fish—*Salmo*. The predator/prey relationship with the fly fisher and his or her *Salmo* quarry is a bond that evolves by the constantly-changing ecological conditions and the evolutionary molding of a *Salmo*'s behavior through this interactive process of understanding the complex beasts they are and how to form a predator fly fisher's strategy for success.

A trout does not eat in the manner of humans, or even as animals do. Humans have worked out a very satisfactory way of eating. We sit in a comfortable chair before a solidly-positioned table on which are displayed, within easy reach, all the food that we may need for a full meal, and we do not need to spend much time at our eating. It is usually a very relaxing and pleasant affair. We do not go rushing about the dining room for endless hours, plucking a little bite here and there, tasting some, inspecting some, eating some; sometimes spitting out some that we do not like. A trout does all this and more. He is forever sorting out things, constantly bringing all possible food under close scrutiny; and he questions every bite that he gets. Eating, for him, is not a simple matter. His dinner table is always in motion, sometimes very fast, and heaving violently. The bits of food coming his way are moving just as fast as the table. Then there is the endless exertion to hold his place at the table. He is not allowed to remain there but must move his entire body, sometimes a distance of many feet, to obtain something from the moving table. And always, there is that recurring crisis of inspection and decision-making. All this is usually concluded by an amazing skill displayed in the act if interception, gracefully executed with consummate ease and precision. —Vincent Marinaro, *In the Ring of the Rise* (1974)

▲ As the Ice Age retreated, northern Europe and the Atlantic/Baltic corridor began to look a lot like it does today with stunning flowing rivers and forests.
Credit: Albert Pesendorfer

# 2. The Dawn of *Salmo*

The Eocene Ice Age was a time of volatile climactic change 33.9 to 55 million years ago that saw Mother Earth make her real big move toward the metamorphosis of a new world ecology. Taken from the Greek word *Eos*, or dawn, it is here that our infatuation with my subject matter's journey begins.

The greenhouse gases of carbon dioxide and methane we place so much focus on today, were at all-time highs, despite not having civilization's altered destructive influence, and played a significant role in the giant roller coaster from global warming to the icehouse cooling that took place once the carbon dioxide levels dropped. Much of what happened then and what is trending today makes us wonder and feel quite insignificant in the grand scheme of the earth's evolution over the millennia.

It was a time that saw the earth's tremendous warmth grow vast forests from the North Pole to the South Pole, as many climate change prophets today are predicting will occur. It was a balmy environment where palm trees grew in the northern hemisphere and the oceans were warm and teeming with all sorts of aquatic sea monsters. Once the Ice Age took place, we saw deciduous forests, more hearty and adaptable to the volatile weather extremes, replacing the tropical evergreens.

But as the Ice Age soon developed, large glaciers of snow and ice began to cover most of the northern hemisphere, as the Arctic and Antarctic polar caps began to take over. The global hot house turned eventually into a frigid icebox. Some flora and fauna species of the warm tropical earth became extinct. But Darwinian survival and adaptation created salmonids, a refined strain of organisms more masterful and fine-tuned to their environments than previously before.

In its forests and on the new wide open valleys, where mounting glaciers started to run their course, the new dawn saw the introduction of the modern hooved animals that became prototypes for modern cows, horses, bison, and elk. Creatures such as artiodactyls, though smaller in size, became the forerunners of the modern farmworking animal.

In the seas, Baltic amber and other precious gems where also created during this period, allowing today's jewel lovers to admire and collect them for their magnificent jewelry. My European mother Natalia had a special fondness for these amber stones and always proudly wore them when we went to formal events.

If there were ever a shrine to be built for a time that created good fortune and opportunity for us piscatorial angling addicts, it would be dedicated to this Eocene Ice Age era. It eventually resulted in the creation of millions of rivers, lakes, and seas that we have come to love and worship. These hallowed aquatic jewels were carved out by the compelling and energetic glaciers. The once-giant supercontinent of Laurasia started to break apart and give us a semblance of the new world geography, as Eurasia, Greenland, and North America started to shape into today's now-familiar shapes.

As if the master artist of creation didn't find these jeweled aquatic masterpieces perfect unto themselves, they were surrounded by a canopy of deep green forests, lichens and ferns, as they flowed through tall mountain coulees and ravines of boulder-strewn cascading runs, ultimately ending in smooth, long, serene pools and winding river valleys onward to the sea and oceans. It was here that the "dawn of *Salmo*" gained access to many evolutionary niches to exploit for superior zoological development.

Once brown trout established a dominant inland river and lake niche, their inquisitive migratory natures had oceans and seas at their disposal, which eventually developed a strong urge for them to be migratory nomadic wanderers, adapting an anadromous lifestyle, far away from the small gentle streams and brooks of their *Salmo* birth. Here they relished their newfound deep-sea environments to grow large and strong, and feed on the bounty of pelagic (Greek word for "open sea") baitfish and rich crustaceans. Their great swimming agility could reach thirty miles per hour as *Salmo salar*, though sea-run browns were slower homebodies.

They eventually crossed hemispheres to establish colonies in what would eventually become the Americas. Their mocha orange and colorful mosaic red and dark spotting gave way to a sleek sheen of silver, aqua blue with a gunmetal gray back. This deep ocean translucency attire gave them the predator cloaking that made them such proficient hunters of the seas.

But eventually the unyielding life force bond with the rivers brought them back to their natal river origins. Back to the waters of their blood kin, who never left and still had their colorful resident mosaic spotting attire. As if to celebrate their return, their spirit would give them super powers to leap tall waterfalls unimaginable to negotiate. It is through such magnificent feats of nature that the conquering Roman legions gave them the Latin name *salar*, or "leaper," along with primal man's awe and veneration, as expressed on artistic cave wall drawings and animal skins.

The magnificent flowing rivers that unites and evolved the salmonids has also influenced mankind in spiritual ways.

Throughout folklore we find the worship of rivers and powerful waterways. In my boyhood neighborhood of the mighty Niagara, local lore has it that a young Seneca Indian maiden, Lelawala, was a sacrifice to the gods of the river falls. Another telling indicates that she was saddened by her husband's death, and the strong hypnotic pull of the falls caused her to ride her canoe over the edge. As a boy playing and fishing near these roaring waters, we often found floating bodies of those that took the leap of death, for whatever reason, near the spinning trap of the whirlpool below the falls.

Thus rivers have forever been etched romantically into the dreams and piscatorial spirits of anglers and artists alike since the dawn of mankind. Many throughout history, including this author, have often found them to be a surreal experience. Whether by sitting next to babbling brook or thunderous waterfalls, or wading in a classic freestone river in pursuit of fly waters, we feel and become a part of their mystical nature.

In his masterpiece *A River Runs through It*, Norman Maclean wrote "I am haunted by waters." It is in this draw and addiction to the flowing river, with its soothing sound or a thunderous aquatic waterfall crescendo, that these waters unleash their hydro hypnosis. The emotional identity and bond that flowing waters brings to our trout and salmon, as well as humans, is spiritual, and perhaps relates us to our strong ties with cetacean whales on both an intelligence and mammalian bond. Simply put, all living organisms eventually evolved from the seas and oceans. That alone can explain our strong hermetical bond.

The further uplifting and fine tuning of the modern Alps, which originally began 650 million years earlier in Eurasia, along with the glacial and plate tectonic upheaval, gathered more and more rivers, lakes, streams and mountain ranges to the creator's artistic canopy. As the Eocene ice age eventually declined and the earth began to stabilize into its modern Holocene era, the stage was set for the dawn of primal mankind.

But quietly through all this cataclysm, emerging gloriously and serenely, was the masterpiece of the piscatorial wonders. With all the beauty and magnificence of nature, deep in the clear mysterious waters, the first quivering and swimming glimpses of them appeared. With their beautiful mosaic-like spotting and colors, streamlined bodies, and their unique facial kypes, they must have been a magnificent and mystical sight to witness. Here was the genesis and template of the new world order for the dawn and creation of the first trout and salmon to swim the earth.

Perhaps these hallowed creatures made their first appearance in the dense fog of the icy cold blue waters of a Nordic fjord, as they ambushed a school of herring for a meal. Perchance it occurred on a small glen side brook in Scotland, were the deep lichens, heather and mosses covered the grayish ancient Moine rocks that layered the brook's ravine.

But it is without doubt they loved the deep dark ecological setting of the sandy soiled, glacial till spring creeks in Germany's Black Forest and central Europe. Here the dense red European pines and white birches perfectly veil

▲ The dawn of *Salmo trutta* of the forested streams and brooks. Credit: Rich Felber

and cool its waters. Here they camouflaged themselves next to the tight, woody structure and gravel runs, like perfect sit-and-wait predators, as the dean of these fish, Norway's Dr. Bror Jonsson, describes them. Here, on these enigmatic capricious waters, where fly presentation is not always easy, their predator/prey relationships became refined.

These small streams were developmental laboratories where they precisely timed the energy and movements necessary to attack a sculpin like a kill artist, or daintily sip, their mayfly meals with a fine rhythmic staccato in the gentle-flowing, schnapps-clear waters. These spring creek waters were, as a Wyoming preacher once described them, "God's special brew." They had constant cold water temperatures from underground calcium carbonate caverns created millions of years before. The surrounding streamside garnish bouquet of bright green watercress were the marketplace shelves that housed the precious food of dainty nymphs and scuds. Its fallen wooded banks became shelter and ambush points for our subject to seek larger carnivore prey. Above all this was the dense pine canopy of the Schwarzwald, as the Germans call it, which veils its waters like a proud mother. All in all, it was the perfect evolutionary and adaptation ecology.

It was during these times as the ice ages receded, here for the first time the earth witnessed the birth of the modern trout and salmon nursery rivers that became the gravel cradles of their creation. These pristine, crystal-clear waters, which rippled and churned capriciously over and through fine gravel, rocks, boulders, and glacial till sand, anointed the fish with the blood bond of the natal river.

In hindsight, this habitat was the foundation of the beloved home waters of my youth, which took place from New York to Poland, Pennsylvania to Virginia, and finally in my adulthood, today in Michigan were they found their western hemisphere invasion. But wherever they mystically emerged, the fish were finally here. *Salmo*, for all practical purposes, were civilization's first founding fish, and since then we have come to love and enjoy these beautiful and enigmatic creatures. They are a very special creation that continue to captivate us, hopefully forever.

*Salmo fario* was the early name given to the brown trout of the forested brooks and rivers in Europe. *Fario*, in the Spanish Latin text means "everything." I often ask fellow trout bums to describe the perfect trout—the brown trout is always their unanimous reply. It has an unmistakable striking beauty that many an artist and musician has scored and painted. It has the delicious flesh that world-renowned chefs have come to relish. But, it is in its unique quality of a bipolar predator, simultaneously displaying savage aggression, or the elusive and enigmatic picky discriminator of minutiae, that has driven the fly fisher to tears on many occasion. Here adaption, migration, elusiveness,

and assimilation fuse together to form cunning, enigmatic behaviors that are forever ongoing in the "live knowledge" phase of fly fishing, as described by the British angling great G. E. M. Skues.

Eventually *Salmo* conquered and infiltrated the ecosystems where they were naturally or exotically introduced, and thus formed a strong bond with its admirers, but sometimes a love-hate relationship with those who eventually embraced and adored them, as we shall see in the historical chapter. My book is a journey into the enigmatic and mystical world of the *Salmo*—what makes them so unique and connected, and how to crack the code for ultimate fly-fishing enjoyment. It is a journey to discover how we can embrace these magnificent creatures from all facets of the cultural, historical, culinary, and artistic pursuits. Now and hopefully forever, *Salmo* will always be ours to enjoy, as they fuel the thoughts, hopes, and dreams of the often delightful, yet perplexing experiences with them that we have come to adore and appreciate, no matter where in the world we encounter them.

## The Blood Bond of The Rivers

From my boyhood onward, these magnificent *Salmo* beasts of perfection played a powerfully influencing role throughout my life. At first I thought it was a very nostalgic sentiment that had resonated and bonded this fish with me in such a serious and profound way, but as I traveled the world and fly fished in many inland rivers, lakes, streams, maritime tributaries, and exotic destinations, wherever I come in contact with anglers and artists of all kinds, almost everyone shares such a profound affinity and respect for *Salmo*.

The genetic and behavioral blood bond of the rivers in the *Salmo's* evolutionary process is perhaps what unites these fish. Carolus Linnaeus in his tenth edition of *Sytema Naturae* of 1758 simply broke out the *Salmo* group into stream or Brook trout (*fario*), river trout (*trutta*), sea trout (*eriox*), and anadromous salmon (*salar*). Back when Linnaeus started his monumental work, there were more than sixty synonyms for varieties of brown trout and more than twenty varieties of Atlantic salmon. *Salmo's* incredible ability to explore, infiltrate, and dominate different habitats throughout the world makes it difficult to classify them. Their colorations and markings, brightness of red dots or marbling, sometimes causes the layman to confuse them for brook trout and chars.

So the brown trout in Sweden and Norway are *Salmo microps/mistops*, and the in Italy and southern Europe are more probably *Salmo visovancensis*. One only needs to go to Facebook and to the "Brown Trout Nation" page started by good friend Ethan Cramer, to see the unique colorations and spotting in posts from all over the world. This variation exists more in *Salmo* than any other fish perhaps, thus making it difficult for ichthyologists to pinpoint their exact evolution and origin.

Take for instance the magnificent marble trout of Slovenia and in other Adriatic rivers in Albania, Croatia, and Italy. These aggressive carnivorous Browns can grow to very large sizes and are absolutely beautiful species endemic to that area. But due to the constant wars, agricultural runoff, and industrial pollution still haunting some territories since the Soviet occupation of Eastern Europe, their populations are declining. Fisheries managers often introduce Atlantic brown trout to these waters to provide larger trout populations, especially where fly fishing is popular, since the these trout are much more hearty and adaptive. Thus the reproductive barrier or divergence in Life Survival Strategy (LSS), does not isolate the two and allows hybrids to appear and grow faster than the purer, native marble trout strains.

Though the blood bond of the rivers is one strong constant in the formation of brown trout and Atlantic salmon populations, the intermixing with migratory ocean and sea/lake populations can evolve into different and uniquely separated lifestyles. In Italy's Po basin on the Garda Lake, *Salmo carpio*, known as *carpione*, have learned to adapt to deep lake or shoreline gravel-bar spawning, thus forgoing the need to migrate up river systems to accomplish procreation. It does not appear that the *Salmo carpio* interbred with Atlantic sea trout strains for lake- and sea-dwelling adaptation, and thus evolved all by itself. There are other similar species in the Black and Caspian Seas like *Salmo trutta caspius* and *trutta labrax*. Often when brown trout populations do not have favorable riverine spawning opportunities, they execute localized spawning and feeding adaptations.

Here on my Michigan home waters of the Torch Lake and its river systems, and on lake systems similar to the Rangeley Lake systems in Maine, landlocked Atlantic salmon and brown trout cohabit the ideal crystal-clear glacial waters. It is here on these waters that a client of mine, as I was guiding him, caught what is still today's IGFA world record landlocked Atlantic salmon, coming in at twenty-six pounds, twelve ounces. We chase these landlocked *salar* and browns during upriver or estuary spawning migrations, or while they feed close to shore in the spring.

But while the numbers of Atlantic salmon seem to be quite high during this time, we rarely see the large lake-dwelling brown trout that trolling anglers and charter captains catch on down-rigging at deep depths fifty to one

▲ The morphological beauty of *Salmo trutta*—this one showing marble trout markings. Credit: Albert Pesendorfer

hundred feet. Keep in mind that Torch Lake has depths to three hundred feet, and icy blue cold and warm waters make a perfect mix favoring excellent macro and micro vertebrates and invertebrates. Baitfish of all kinds, small perch, sticklebacks, and the nymphs of large *Hexagenia* mayfly make up a bulk of the diets, along with freshwater crustaceans. The incredible clarity of these waters also aid the rapid growth of phytoplankton and zooplankton, which fuel the entire food chain.

Despite the absence of large river systems feeding the lake, which would be conducive to natural reproduction, the lake-dwelling wild brown trout exist in excellent numbers and have been known to gain sizes of close to thirty pounds. Through further polling of lake charter fishermen, who continue to catch these larger lake brown trout through the fall in the open water or near rocky shoals with current, where they have learned to spawn, it is obvious that these brown trout are leading similar lifestyles as their cousins in the Po basin's Garda Lake. Though we have seen the strong bond with the rivers as the predominant lifestyle survival strategy unifier, these unique divergent adaptable populations that spawn in lakes continue to stump fishermen and biologists alike.

It is also interesting to note by all the tens of thousands of scientific studies featured in Bror and Nina Jonsson's scientific masterpiece *Ecology of Atlantic Salmon and brown trout*, the question of whether *Salmo* evolve from the sea or fresh water, or were anadromous and migratory right from the start, will never fully be concluded. But the overlying theme here is that the evolution of *Salmo* has momentum and direction and always projecting adaptation from a straight line. This sums up and conversely refutes Darwin's niche survival of the fittest and particulate inheritance theories. *Salmo* seem to abide no rules but their own.

Habitat and its variables influence evolutionary histories; *Salmo*'s physiology and uniquely adapted behaviors have led to its success. In addition to geographic, climatological, and ecological variables, *Salmo* have done very well to adapt and dominate. Brown trout have been much more successful since they have the ability to regulate a phenomenal amount of different environmental circumstances than do the more highly-specialized anadromous Atlantic salmon, which have a much more distinct and refined lifestyle and are thus less favorable to a broader adaptation.

## *Salmo*'s Appearance: A Morphology of Beauty by Design

When we admire the delicate and often savage beauty the animal world bestows on us, our curiosity often leads us to the truly unique attributes of their initial procreation and birth that were fine tuned for survival. Both brown trout Atlantic salmon are freshwater spawners, either in

▲ Browns and Atlantic salmon develop a similar appearance when they migrate to seas and large rivers in their ever-adapting search for food chain dominance. Credit: Jessica DeLorenzo

a potomadromous lifestyle (freshwater lake to river), or anadromous lifestyle (maritime to river). As we discussed earlier, some *Salmo* never leave the lake environment, which is usually quite rare, and caused by the absence of suitable riverine spawning applications.

They spawn after a long period of feeding throughout the spring and summer. As light levels and water temperatures affect the pineal glands and endocrine system, they migrate for spawning in the fall and winter. This all depends on the extremes of their climactic range; the influences of global climate change is now taking on a more specialized role and behavioral modifier, and that in turn is transforming the way anglers plan for migratory timing. Luckily *Salmo* are more ahead of the adaptation curve than mankind will ever adjust to, and are already showing variations in their life survival direction. What is so beautiful about the *Salmo* is that they can spawn and grow to very large sizes with multi-year class development stages, which is so opportune for population recycling, longevity, and sporting opportunities for the angler.

The Atlantic salmon is in direct contrast to the Pacific salmonids, which die after spawning. Pacific salmon also have very fine-tuned dietary requirements that often can be the death knell for their existence, in comparison to the adaptability of Atlantic salmon and brown trout. We'll discuss this more as we open up the chapters on the Great Lakes and how the exotic invaders of quagga and zebra mussels are devastating the plankton populations, which are inversely impacting alewife predator-prey baitfish relationships.

The blood bond of the rivers draws the brown trout and Atlantic salmon to seek swift, flowing, crystal-clear, gravel-laden waters. Here they search for the perfect depth, dissolved oxygen, and spawning gravel to dig spawning redds as hydrological incubators. Brown trout and Atlantic salmon have an innate sense for detecting the ideal siltation substratum, metabolic waste filtering, and life-sustaining oxygen for their river incubators. When cohabitating rivers, as is often the case with the Atlantic and Baltic seaboard, brown trout will often spawn earlier

in the fall than the later spawning salmon. A good rule is October and November for the browns, November and December for Atlantics. Certain species of brown trout, as the giant lake dwellers of the *Seeforellen* strain coming from the German Alpine range, and others with very long river migrations, have been known to spawn well into January and February.

Once hatched in the late winter or spring, the sac fry will live off the embryos and eventually begin feeding on minute riverine invertebrates such as midges and plankton, until they are eventually large enough to eat mayflies, other insects, and smaller prey.

The bond of the river again gives both brown trout and Atlantic salmon nearly identical natal upbringing scenarios, since they will share and inhabit similar river and stream ecologies that have identical food sources and will require the necessary predator adaptations to grow. This is a fine-tuned life survival force that resident brown trout modify and perfect. Keep in mind Atlantic salmon parr and yearlings can stay in the river system for up to five

▲ Although at first glance they may seem identical, juvenile Atlantic salmon (top) and wild brown trout (bottom) have distinctive characteristics. Credit: Fran Verdoliva-Nydec

▲ A magnificent Lakselfan Norwegian *salar*, caught by Arni Baldurson. Credit: Arni Baldurson-Lax-A

years, as documented in many extremely northern nursery waters such as Labrador and Kola, Russia. Here they act and look just like resident brown trout and are often misidentified as such. Their behavior is also identical in the predatory mode. But the strong pectoral fins of Atlantic salmon allow them to stay in very quick rapids and riffles usually shunned by the brown trout, which favor more placid waters.

What is unique in the salmonid world is the tendency in *Salmo* homing behavior to return to natal areas for spawning. Some resident brown trout might only have to go several bends up or down the river to find suitable spawning habitats, while others will travel long distances through valleys and rivers until they find optimal environments in small, gravelly, well-oxygenated brooks. Atlantic salmon demonstrate the most extreme homing tendencies, especially when it comes to long migrations to the ocean and seas, and especially on long river systems. Atlantic salmon used to travel over one thousand miles to breed in the upper water tributaries of the Loire, Rhine, and Rhone River valleys in Europe.

Migratory ocean/sea brown trout typically live near the coastal waters and usually do not migrate long distances to spawn in short-distance ocean estuary/river environments. In Scandinavia or the Northern European Baltic, they spawn very close to large bodies of water as low as 150 feet above sea level.

## The Magical Spawning Dance

The brown trout and Atlantic salmon spawning process is truly a magnificent ritual of nature. The female is extremely focused in her search for the perfect combination of gravel and flow to give her offspring the ideal conditions for their survival. I often spend much time watching the female. Once she is in the general vicinity, which in the wild can be as close to several hundred yards where she was originally hatched, she will usually dig several gravel areas before settling on the final redd. As she digs it perhaps a foot deep, a territorial dominant male that has already usually been watching and guarding the area chases away smaller fish who are eager to get into the spawning frenzy.

Once fully ready, she squats to release the eggs. The male quickly comes in, quivers next to her body with his kype jaw mouth completely open, and releases sperm to the eggs, which glue themselves to the bottom. It is the magical dance that I've recorded on video and is seriously a magnificent sight to watch. Immediately after this natural ecstasy, the female moves above the redd and digs more gravel to cover the eggs, being very careful not to take gravel too large that will suffocate and smother the future progeny. One large alpha male can move from female to female and service them to ensure prime alpha genetic domination in the gene pool.

Once spawning is complete, both male and female will leave the spawning grounds to quickly feed and put on the lost weight that the hardship of spawning has placed on their physiology. Note that Atlantic salmon and brown trout in the north Atlantic and Baltic rivers, and in the Canadian Maritimes of Québec and Labrador, can literally go twelve months without feeding during a long anadromous migration.

Once the alevins and fry hatch and start feeding on small midges and plankton, they start forming parr marks, which will stay with them between one and four years under riverine lifestyle. As I witnessed from my Polish tree house as a boy, where both anadromous Atlantic salmon and resident brown trout existed, they separated themselves almost perfectly by the protocol of nature. Each preferred different flows and feeding/holding profiles, which I have termed Predator Foraging/Holding Profiles (PFHP), which will help us understand their behavior later in the book.

If the browns and Atlantics are migratory, the parr stage leads into the smolting process, which usually takes place in the spring/summer of their final year of riverine life. Probably triggered by the pineal gland and melatonin biological clock system as daylight hours grow longer, their coloration goes from parr marks to beautiful spotting and red dots to a silvery-sided attire with dark gray backs to camouflage them once they reach large bodies of ocean seas or lakes. Spring usually brings storms, slow runoff, and higher water flows, which also aids downstream migration.

Atlantic salmon spend anywhere from one to four years at sea before returning to their natal rivers. Migratory sea-run brown trout often come back the first year or in the same year that they leave the river, since they spend much time in near-shore feeding grounds along the cold drop-off thermoclines. The Atlantic salmon travel thousands of miles to either Greenland or the Faroe Islands, depending on their rivers of origin. North American and Icelandic populations head to the rich pelagic baitfish feeding grounds off Greenland, whereas the Europe's population salmon end up going to the Faroe Islands.

## The Visual *Salmo*: Beauty Is Skin Deep

A very big part of the *Salmo* mystique lies in their diverse beauty. If you take a stunning brown trout from a specific river system and measured all their spotting, you will see that number varies considerably from one organism to another. Here we have a gene that can give that trout many spots smaller in size, whereas another allele can give it fewer spots but larger ones. Specific strains often have a carryover phenotypic general look.

On my home rivers here in Michigan are two strains: the Gilchrist and Wild Rose, which are uniquely different. The Gilchrest is a recent feral strain that has its origin from the original Northville federal hatchery that introduced the German brown trout *Bachforellen* to the Western Hemisphere. It had a predominant small spotting, red dot, white circle spotting formation, with a high degree of adult parr mark sequences.

On the other hand, the Wild Rose domesticated strain has larger spotting with marble and blotchy forms, which conveys a more leopard-like appearance.

Both are uniquely gorgeous in their own right. But as we come to learn and admire more about *Salmo*, these characteristics give us a more complete picture of how these phenotypic variables mutated to design the artistic palette of each beautiful brown trout and Atlantic salmon.

Brown trout and Atlantic salmon in the riverine environment from alevin to the parr state can look almost

▲ The freshwater new horizon for *Salmo salar*—Michigan's Great Lakes frontier and glacial lakes (left), and Torch Lake *salar* (right). Credit: Author

▲ A perfect *trutta* specimen from my Michigan home waters of the Muskegon River. Credit: Author

or red blotches in clusters, can be almost identical in both the browns and Atlantics. The eyes are also quite similar, being dark with big gold rim. But looking closely at Atlantic salmon, you will notice that they their eyes have a tinge of ultramarine blue, and that their mouths are shorter. The dark spots of the opercula, or gill cover/cheek, which are very prominent, tends to be more conspicuous and darker in Atlantic salmon than the browns.

A very surefire way of identifying and differentiating the two is by looking at the posterior fins in riverine parr and young adults. The caudal fin or tail of the Atlantic salmon is quite focused in a lobular pointed position. Its anal fin often lacks the white barred undertone that brown trout exhibit. Brown trout adipose fins usually have a rim of deep red, which the Atlantics almost always lack. In fully-mature adults, the salmon tail fin is slimmer and more concave in design versus the more triangular and larger tale of the browns. Also the browns will exhibit more spotting further toward the belly past the lateral line than most Atlantic salmon.

What is perhaps most striking and awe inspiring of large male *Salmo* is the prehistoric appearance of their gigantic kypes. This feature perhaps draws more attention than even the beautiful color collage of their bodies. These kypes can be so extremely pronounced that they often pierce the upper roof of the mouth during development. In the heads and kypes of brown trout, there'll be darker spotting, versus the more red blotched spotting found in salmon. Both mouths are very white and easily distinguished, especially when they are in water and open their mouth to breathe or yawn. This "yawning" is often humorously described as the salmon or trout being bored to tears by the angler's offerings, which are futile and bring no response. Males of both species use their kypes to latch on to competitors and fight for dominance during the spawn, much as stags do with their antlers. I have often seen two males in such a heated lockjaw battle that they were unable to disconnect for very long periods of time.

identical. It is perhaps in this reason that when most states and countries throughout the world set fishing seasons for *Salmo,* they always coincide together since the angler has such a great propensity to label the two together even under very selective criteria. It often takes a trained biologist to separate the two. Anadromous and potomadromous specimens with their silver blue sheen on the sides and sparse, irregular, and marbled X spottings can even be more confusing. In the two states I know best—my current home of Michigan and native New York State—the brown trout season usually closes on September 30. You will find Atlantic salmon usually under the same closure due to the fact that both of them spawn from October to January.

Let's look at some simple ways of identifying the two species from a layman's perspective. From a broadside view the dark spotting in red dots with white circles,

## Civilization's First Founding Fish

When considering *Salmo* from the romantic, nostalgic, and scientific perspectives, it can easily be said that in

▲ Brown trout or Atlantic salmon? You be the judge! Credit: Arni Baldurson-Lax-A

our shared twelve-million-year evolutionary history, they are truly modern civilization's "first founding fish." They have survived tumultuous journeys throughout the Earth's cataclysmic climactic upheavals, they enticed the dawn of primal man with their beauty and nourishment, and they survived modern civilization's industrial warfare on their habitats. They did so by adjusting, migrating, assimilating, and adapting.

As climate change, urbanization of once-wild lands and rivers, and commercial and recreational fishing pressure continue to grow, we must adopt a very conservative management agenda for *Salmo,* as proposed by organizations like The Atlantic Salmon Federation, North Atlantic Conservancy, Trout Unlimited, the Federation of Fly Fishers, and other particular watershed councils. As Bror and Nina Jonsson wrote in *The Ecology of Atlantic Salmon and Brown Trout,*

Because of all the environmental problems and human-induced mortality problems, the management of Atlantic salmon and brown trout is demanding.

New rules and regulations as well as enhancement methods have been implemented in various countries during recent years but many populations are still threatened and even exterminated, especially in the southern part of their range. The *Salmo* populations in several large rivers such as the River Rhine, one of the world's major natural Atlantic salmon producers, are extinct. There is a need to implement conservative catch quotas and adaptive management on a population level based on real-time monitoring instead of past abundance estimates A new trend in the management of wild populations is the "precautionary principle," which states that in case of uncertainty, one should exercise caution in favor of conservation.

## *Salmo* Evolutionary Real Time: The Rivers and Seas of Constant Change

Since their introduction around the world, *Salmo* has explored and conquered new niches left vacant by less-hearty chars, as we have seen during the decline of the

▲ The magnificent topography of Salmo Meccas of Iceland and Norway. Credit: Arni Baldurson-Lax-A photo

native Brook trout of North America and the onslaught of the European *Salmo* invasion.

As global climate change is very much real, will this affect *Salmo* as the earth's temperatures and waters warm? *Salmo* has survived the past fifty million years in more volatile and tumultuous climactic changes than we can ever imagine in our short human existence. Without a doubt, if there was one limiting factor for *Salmo* it would have to be water temperature, since they have and will always be a cold water species. But the Salmo's adaptability to marginal warmer waters, pushing and challenging the edge of their sustainability, is something that continues to marvel scientists and fishermen alike, as their uncanny ability to sense ecosystem changes and forming migrating adaptions to refuge areas is perhaps one of their continual strengths as a species and organism. The oxygen content of their

water and surroundings is also a constant barometer for their existence. Thus *Salmo* learn to adapt to ecologies in the harshest environmental areas of the river system—from fast cascading rapids to long, stagnant, slow waters.

As ocean temperatures continue to have volatile fluctuations in temperature, and rivers experience extreme reversals in flows through droughts and flooding, natural, and human-induced conditions will challenge *Salmo*. Since their introduction to the Americas, Australia, New Zealand, and Africa, more and more populations have formed unique adaptive measures to cope with man's intrusion and the volatility of their habitats.

As the future unfolds, they will now enter into a new age of being the canary in the coal mine that will always help gauge the health and habitability of the amazing planet Earth.

▲ Primordial rivers flowed through rocky morainal mountains and cliffs where stone age man lived, and here early man found *Salmo* teeming in their waters.
Credit: Aaron Jasper

# 3. *Salmo* History: The Journey Begins

The northern Asturias region along the coast of Spain, or "Green Spain," is perhaps one of the most beautiful and most underrated attractions in Europe. Here the magnificent Cantabrian Mountains in the Picos de Europa National Park ascend almost 9,000 feet, with green limestone rock formations and gentle rolling hills of dense green forests that have the makings of a storybook wonderland. The mild summers and snow from October through May helps create the ideal *Salmo* temperate climate. Looking down along the Atlantic coastline, you encounter magnificent sandy beaches and fishing villages reminiscent of Gaspé Québec and the Canadian Maritimes. Here the highly prized turbot and tuna, along with shellfish like lobsters, clams, and oysters are a seafood lover's dream come true. The delicious grilled or pickled herring and eels are a local delicacy that I learned to love since my time on the Pomeranian Baltic coast as a boy in Poland.

But our focus and journey to crack the first *Salmo* code lies along the stunning limestone cliffs and gorges along the pristine, cold, azure-colored waters of the Cares River. If there is a perfectly-designed ecological niche for brown trout and Atlantic salmon to evolve and exist, it would be this hallowed region. It probably was here that the early Asturias cave dwellers had a perfect vantage point to hunt and stalk the crystal-clear waters for brown trout and salmon that still occupy these magnificent rivers today. Trout and salmon are still king here, and each year the first salmon of the season, the *Campanua,* is an annual tradition dating back centuries with prize money and media attention.

The paleolithic Neanderthals used their tools for hunting and warfare here, and developed angling arts by creating fishhooks from island mollusk bones and nets woven together from twine and tree branches. Hunters and gatherers on foraging expeditions today still use the primitive technique of trapping fish by hand in low-water pools and riffles. At around this time, prehistoric cave art as we know it took place. I could just picture a tribal family, after feasting on a big haul of animals or fish, lying around the fire at night and dreaming about their existence, their future, and surroundings, that manifested into artistic forms of animals and fish that sustained them as paintings and engravings on the stone walls.

As the Neanderthal tribal colonies in Asturia were honing their tactics and fishing/gathering skills for *Salmo,* similar pursuits were taking place along the Dordogne River Valley and the fascinating Perigord region of French Aquitania. In the early fall of 1940, Marcel Ravidat, an eighteen-year-old Frenchman, stumbled on a series of caves that had tremendous archaeological impact. Here he and his friends found deep shafts with fascinating cave drawings of animals, fish, and early hunting adventures. One of the most famous depictions, "The Hall of the Bulls," featured all the primal bovines, horses, stag, and bison. The pack of black animals were the now-extinct aurochs, having massive curved horns like the African Watusi bull. Curiously, since aurochs were the Teutons' ur-cattle, Nazi Luftwaffe Reichsminister and "master huntsman" Hermann Göring pursued a scientific program for genetic recreation of the beasts in eastern Poland.

Also in the cave was "L'Abri du Poisson."—a giant drawing of an Atlantic salmon or sea-run brown trout. It is natural that this important fish should be commemorated in this way, as primal man's existence depended on their consistent availability. In primal depictions they hunted the migrating Atlantic salmon with spears and corralled them into shallow gravel backwater areas where they would beat them with clubs. To hunt the more elusive *Salmo trutta* rivers, they built fine-woven net creels and meshes of twigs and twine, and placed them near the wooded structure that the elusive and reclusive brown trout favored.

Across the Atlantic Ocean, as the glaciers began receding thirteen thousand years ago and modern river valleys took shape, Native Americans were learning their own appreciation for the amazing *Salmo salar.* The Mi'Kmaq (Micmac) Indians were strong-bonded hunter-gathering clans that took advantage of the vast eastern seaboard mountain rivers and ocean hunting grounds that were rich in fish and game, including moose, elk, and deer, vast schools of cod, mackerel, and sole, as well as shellfish such as oysters, mussels, and lobster. Here they perfected the spearheads or Clovis points of modern spear weaponry. These spears couldn't have come in handier for the river hunting for Atlantic salmon that were extremely abundant.

It is here the natives became masters of dry curing, pickling, grilling, and preserving the salmon in every way possible. Cartilage, bones, and mollusk remains served as jewelry and were useful to make fish hooks. Doubtless a master fisher in each clan attained and taught the wisdom to time the runs to perfection, and coordinated the stalking of the waterfalls chokepoints so that the community would have food through the harsh glacial winters. One of the opportune things about the fall spawning of Atlantic salmon and brown trout was that they were a

▲ The acrobatic salmon seen here on a Scottish river, received their name *salar* from the Latin for leaper. Credit: Laurie Campbell

high-fat subsistence food with sufficient protein necessary to survive cold weather extremes. Their autumn abundance couldn't have happened at a better time for early Americans.

## The Roman Invasion: The First Fly

Our first fly fishing writer and historian was an interesting man named Claudius Aelianus. Traveling with Legio V–Macedonia, a sort of Seal Team 6 of the ancient world, he documented the conflicts of the time, his transcendental thoughts, and his understanding of the natural order of things. His first epic work was *De Natura Animalium*, where he took observations of animal behavior as allegories about human behavior. His other masterful escapades were recoded in *Varia Historia*. Here his incredible fascination with local customs, folklore, and mythology, particularly with the Greek culture he venerated, set the stage for the first accounts of the local brown trout fly fisherman. Claudius, being highly schooled and trained in the romantic arts, spoke the local dialects of the region and could communicate with the locals.

Macedonia and the Balkans are loaded with amazing chalk stream spring creeks full of wild and large brown trout. These rivers are home to some unique strains of brown trout—particularly the beautiful and cunning *Salmo macedonicus*, the Macedonian brown trout. On his travels and observations of wildlife along the trout-rich Astraeus River, he documented the first selective trout encounters by the local Macedonian fishermen:

> They fastened red wool round a hook, and fit on to the wool two feathers which grow under a cock's wattles, in which and color are like wax. Their rod is 6 feet long, and their line is the same length. Then they throw their snare, and the fish, attracted and maddened by the color, comes straight at it, thinking from the pretty sight to gain a dainty mouthful; when, however, it opens its jaws, is caught by the hook, and enjoys a bitter repast, a captive.

This is the first known documentation of the act of catching a fish on a fly. Aelianus seemed to be writing in the autumn, which is, as we know, the brown trout's prespawning period. Sexual phenotypic maturity and optic nerve color preference go hand-in-hand. Physical features like kypes and deep red/orange colors predominate in spawning as an elicitor of aggression and arousal. So what

▲ The "ground zero Macedonian Red Fly," tied by master tier Jim Haswell. Credit: John Miller

a more perfect fly to entice the aggressive/active spawning mode of a territorial brown trout than a red fly, where chance and selectivity come into a perfect bond simply by coincidence.

▲ A typical Dinaric Alps/Macedonian brown trout stream. Credit: Larry Halyk

## Woman Power and the *Salmo*-Driven Dame

Dame Juliana Berners wrote the first book about fly fishing, the *Treatise of Fysshynge with an Angle,* in 1495 as part of the Book of St. Albans, a set of eight books dealing with hawks, hunting, and heralding. She is the first to describe leaders made from horsehair and how to dye them in various hues, from green, to brown, to yellow, depending on the season and the condition of the water. Juliana also described the effectiveness of stealth presentations to the elusive brown trout and Atlantic salmon. Her classroom was the placid spring creek–style waters of the pastoral Hampshire, England, which demanded amazing attention to stealth and detail. The Atlantic salmon in these waters were even more selective due to the visibility in these clear, cool waters.

Juliana's very detailed coloring of horsehair by season shows her experience with the selective nature of *Salmo*. She also learned to discern *Salmo* species-specific behaviors, and her theories still apply today.

The salmon is not bite on the bottom, but at the float. You may sometimes take him, but it happens very seldom, and with an artificial fly when he is leaping, in the same way as you take trout or grayling . . .

We shall speak next of the trout (*trutta*), because he is a very dainty fish and also a very greedy biter. He is in season from March to Michaelmas. He is found on clean gravel bottom and a running stream. You may angle for him at all times with a running or lying round line: except in leaping time, when you use an artificial fly.

Berners clearly understood the difference between nymphing (ground line) and dry fly opportunities during a hatch.

When Izaak Walton came out with *The Compleat Angler* in 1653, fishing with fly and bait was becoming a very technical art form again. Walton, a self-proclaimed expert on bait fishing, knew little about the fly, but had a good appreciation for its complexity, stating that "angling may be said so like the mathematics that it can never be fully learned." Through the eighteenth and nineteenth centuries, fly fishing gained in popularity throughout England and Scotland. W. C. Stewart, who wrote *The Practical Angler* in 1857, developed the art of the wet fly swing for brown trout in Scottish Lochs with extremely clear lake waters and selective fish.

## The British Love Bestowed: Manifest *Salmo* Destiny

The British army officer was an elite representative of all things fine in life at the time. Usually drawn from the aristocracy, they possessed a good amount of education and refined social skills, and obsessed about "gentlemanly sports" requiring exclusive access to controlled estates, including fishing, bird hunting, horseback riding, and falconry. In their finely-pressed breeches, leather Wellington boots, tweed and Tattersall vests and cravats, they used cane and whittled rods with horsehair leaders and beautifully tied wet flies dating back to the era of Dame Juliana to probe the rivers and streams of Britain and its far-flung empire in search of brown trout and Atlantic salmon. No matter where the manifest destiny of the British Empire took them they were passionately lovesick to wet a line on waters like they did on their hallowed Hampshire chalk streams and Scottish estuaries.

▲ With typical British persistence, colonial transplants transported their beloved *Salmo* quarry to all parts of the world. Australia's temperate regions such as Tasmania have a climate similar the British Isles, and thus was the perfect choice for colonization. Credit: Dave Jensen

Luckily for them, they found their beloved Atlantic salmon to already be indigenous from the Canadian Maritimes to the New England Coastline Rivers and lakes, to Lake Ontario. Though British fly-fishing technology which was still quite primitive when compared to today, they fished for them ardently with the early prototypes of rod, reel, and fly. Early officers sportsmen like Sir William Johnson and Joseph Banks were the first known writers and proponents of the art of the fly, primarily fishing for salmon in Québec and upstate New York regions, where the Salmon River of New York had wild indigenous populations, while the Saranac River featured landlocked salmon.

Perhaps the most detailed of these early fly-fishing writers was an American Revolutionary war officer named George Gibson. His family's birthplace and origin takes us back to the Cumberland Valley and mountain tops of Perry County. Here in Appalachian Pennsylvania's God's country is where my good friend and passionate *Salmo* theorist and guide Eric Richard showed me the original Gibson stone Millhouse dwelling along Sherman's Creek Perry Furnace. Gibson's father and relatives were all part of the French-and-Indian and Revolutionary War era.

These types of ideal valley waterway systems with icy tributaries are characteristic of *Salmo trutta* territory throughout its indigenous domain. Sherman's Creek, at first investigation, is not the prime blue-ribbon trout water of the nearby Cumberland Valley Limestone spring creeks. Laymen and scientists alike often misinterpret marginal waters. It is a large valley river system with tiny capillaries of ice cold springs and densely-wooded habitat that allow migratory *trutta* to perform their amazing feats of adaptation, assimilation, and migration in correspondence to environmental factors, water temperatures, food availability, and procreation. Here George Gibson emerged as the true first known documented "paid" fly angling journalist, and split his time between the mountain Freestone Rivers and the Cumberland Valley limestone spring creeks. George made incredible observations of trout feeding behavior on hatches, scuds, and nymphs, as well as the complexities pertaining to the seasonal aspects of angling.

In the noble order of the *Salmo* colonization legacy, distant lands were on their way to becoming *trutta* empires. Australia received shipments of both brown trout and Atlantic salmon beginning in 1852. But the hallowed chalk stream revolution went full steam aboard the clipper *Norfolk* when it left Falmouth in 1864, bound for the land down under. The crew rigged an ice house to keep

▲ The Sherman's creek *Salmo* thinker and guide Eric Richard explores his coveted waters. They are the classical ecological models of marginal/micro-regional perfection desired by the elusive and assimilating brown trout in its pursuit for evasiveness from civilization. Credit: Matthew Supinski

approximately one hundred thousand salmon eggs viable. Salmon were of prime colonization importance not only for their sporting appeal, but as a gourmet delicacy. But little did they know of *Salmo salar*'s requirements for nursery river habitats; the fine-tuned ecological factors that were required between the natal rivers in the ocean environments were much more complex than just having a body of salt water attached to a freshwater river.

The British fly fishermen who pursued brown trout in the Hampshire Rivers persuaded the British settlement to emphasize brown trout. Celebrity anglers such as Francis Francis, Frank Buckland, and Lord Delamere added fifteen hundred Itchen River brown trout eggs to the Australian shipment. Only several hundred trout survived the journey, but hatcheries sprang up along Australian rivers like the Plenty River and others in the region until a wild breeding source eventually occurred in the Tasmanian streams. Tasmania soon began to grow trophy brown trout up to forty pounds.

The next colonization took place on New Zealand's South Island. Here the Maturi and a handful of other

▲ *Fly Fisherman* magazine chief editor Ross Purnell with a gorgeous New Zealand Brown. Credit: Ross Purnell

rivers soon became epic trout fishing destinations and yielding leviathan trout. As the British started to conquer the African continent they discovered tiny hidden jewels of rivers high in the mountainous temperate climates. Lord Delamere Major Grogan envisioned settlers' requirements in these new conquests, and their mandate was to "get the settlers in the farming fields and the trout in the rivers." The vast Cape province in South Africa received the first shipments in 1875 on the Umgeni and Mooi Rivers.

But getting trout to these rare and exotic places was no easy ordeal. At fifteen thousand feet above sea level the two thousand kilometers of pristine, icy rivers emanating in the equatorial Aberdere range in Kenya were void of fish. The invincible Major Grogan funded an expedition to ship eggs from the European and Loch Laven strains almost 7,400 miles through the Red Sea, over rail, and via pack horses to reach the mountains.

Colin Fletcher was a remarkable romantic adventuring naturalist, mountaineer, and fly fishermen of Welsh origin. He moved to open a hotel with his wife in the mountains of Kenya, where the Fletchers and their guests could go mountain climbing, hiking, foraging, and investigating the local peoples. Typical of many Brits besotted with the brown trout mystique, Colin Fletcher once reflected on Kenya's brown trout in this touching way:

> Should some evil chance restrict all my fishing to one place . . . I'd pick a certain small brown trout stream in the Kenya Highlands. The fish are small; they average perhaps a half a pound. But every inch of that stream is different, every inch is fly water. And each of those little trout is an individual that has to be selected. Stalked and overcome . . . to me, it typifies brown trout fishing at its best.

To me and the many *Salmo* lovers throughout the world, Fletcher's words sum up our passion and love for the gorgeous and cunning *trutta*, which becomes a lifelong journey to understand their enigmatic code, a task that is forever a joy and honor to decipher. As the British Empire spread to India and the stunning and majestic snow-capped Himalayas, this mountainous nirvana with its glacially-cut valleys and ice-cold rivers was the next stage of a perfect ecology tailor-made for the brown trout. The western side of the mountain range in the Afghanistan/ Pakistan Hindu Kush region was the magnificent wild utopia of the other side of the Himalayas.

## Kashmir

If there ever was a perfect utopia for the advancing British Empire to spread its beloved *Salmo trutta*, the stunning rivers of the Kashmir valley is the ideal place. It is a breathtaking region of snowcapped mountains that look

▲ The Kasmiri Pandits of the valley belong to the Shaiva sect of Hindus. The Himalayan Sherpas are the ideal guides to have when traversing the many rivers and streams of the valleys. Credit: Jim Klug-Yellow Dog

very much like a cross between the Rockies and the Alps. The carpeted deciduous and pine forests reveal aqua-blue clear-flowing rivers that cascade through rocky moraine and gorgeous pools. Along the riverbanks are Tibetan gazelle and musk deer, ibex, Kashmir stag, and the Snow leopards and brown bears that hunt them. The water temperatures are ideal for brown trout.

The British instituted a traditional beat system and river-keeper to manage the rivers. It was also advantageous for the British officers in those early days that the guides and Ghillies were vegetarian Hindus who did not compete for the gamefish.

A very good fishing friend of mine during my Georgetown days was a brilliant atomic energy scientist and fanatical fly fisher of Indian descent named Ashokla Law. His father, who was in the British Army, learned the fly fishing tradition as part of the mandatory officer camaraderie and gentlemanly pursuits. When Ash Law visited Kashmir, he told me of the signs that were often placed along the side of the streams by Shaiva Hindus stating: It Is Against the Law of Brahma and Shiva to Eat the Fish of the Rivers. In a perfect world of catch-and-release fly fishing how good does it get to have people that surround the rivers unable to poach or pillage the wild populations of brown trout?

Back in the day of colonization and exploration it was very popular for aristocrats to exchange exotic animal species. Nobility who hunted the wilds and fished the rivers were often fond of other wildlife, and *Salmo* was always viewed as a fish of the aristocracy. At the turn of the nineteenth to the twentieth centuries, Herbrand Russel, the eleventh Duke of Bedford, a fly fishing fanatic who honed his skills on the chalk streams of Hampshire, gave the maharajah of Kashmiri a shipment of brown trout eggs in order to secure specimens of the famous Kashmir stags for transport back the United Kingdom, where they could possibly prosper in the northern highlands. The initial shipment did not take hold, but subsequent ones did, eventually developing the Kashmiri brown trout dynasty that the British have come to love. Kashmir is truly a special experience where one can admire the amazing wilderness cuisine of honorable people as you pursue their unique rivers of *Salmo* gold.

## The Germans are Coming: The Western Hemisphere Invasion

The Black Forest of Germany, the Schwartzwald, and its intersection with northern Bavaria of the Franconian Jura, is an enchanted pastoral landscape of romantic medieval charm. Along these magnificent limestone valleys and bluffs near Streitberg, not far from Bamberg, the rolling farmscape with its Holstein cows and sheep intermingled with the beautiful dense forests of spruce, pines, and birches give this land a Hansel and Gretel appeal. The beautiful A-frame wooden Bavarian homes of clay tile and thatched roofs still embody the spirit of this amazing land once known for its clock making and glassblowing. The limestone hills shroud old castles like the Neideck Fortress tower, once a lookout for the knights of the Teutonic warriors.

The limestone grist mills are sort of the Holy Grail once you find them, as they are always built near the springs that emanate from the hillside and limestone outcroppings, and usually connect the flowing river with the spring-fed Mill Pond. Watercress mill ponds are chock full of scuds and sow bugs and visons of them take me back to the Big Spring "ditch mill pond" in Pennsylvania in the 1940s, when an angler named Don Martin took what was then the Pennsylvania state record of sixteen pounds. In these cold Black Forest waters you'll usually find our amazing German brown trout—*Bachforelle*—with beautiful red spots and white circles sipping the *Simulium* midges or mayflies as the buggies and carts of the farmers clop down the road taking their produce, cabbage, asparagus, potatoes, and cucumbers to the marketplace. The grist mills also served as temperate storage provisionary pantries where fresh-made Fränkische Würsten sausages hung to dry and smoke.

Since the limestone spring mills moderate the temperature in summer or winter, these are also great places to ferment the beer in the barrels and store the spirits and wines. This region is a mecca for the microbrew connoisseur, as it was a precursor to our craft beer society of today. The world's highest concentration of microbreweries exists here, as literally every village has its own particular style and flavor. What a magnificent way to satisfy the hungry appetites of hunters and fishermen than to have hardy beers along with gastro-pub sausage delicacies on a country excursion. The Black Forest was the land of the traditional German sporting gentleman. In the River's limestone springs and brooks, between Forcheim and Nuremberg laid some of the finest hunting grounds. This is the land of the original "German brown trout" that was imported to the western hemisphere.

The amazingly-talented architect and fly-fishing writer Ernest Schwiebert, whom we will discuss later throughout the book, was the epitome of the modern *National Geographic*/Condé Nast connoisseur traveler. His architectural occupation and passion for world traveling brought him to come to this wonderful land, which he wrote about so eloquently in his masterpiece, *Nymphs*.

But perhaps the most notable writings on the brown trout of this area came from Norm Zeigler, a passionate fly fisherman and outdoor columnist for the *New York Times,* who divided his passion between his Montana trout and his Florida saltwater love affair. In his amazing book, *Rivers of Shadow, Rivers of Sun*, he wrote of this mystical Franconian area of the northern Bavaria/Black Forest region and its delightful brown trout rivers and streams. In Ziegler's writings you could taste, smell, and feel the romantic qualities of this enchanted land.

▲ The quintessential Black Forest mill and brown trout stream. Credit: Hermann Schmider

It is perhaps in the limestone valley of the River Wiesent that some of the Ice Age *Salmo* ideally made the first inaugural appearance. It is likely that the first genotypic stock that came to America originated in the tiny limestone chalk stream capillaries of this Regnitz River Valley. Zeigler eloquently describes the origin of this wonderful prototypical genesis for *Salmo* in his book:

> The central geological feature of the region is the Franconian Jura, the massive limestone formation that underlies much of northern Bavaria. Formed beneath ancient seas more than 150 million years ago, it provides a soft and porous substratum for the springs that feed the rivers.
>
> Over the eons, the flowing rivers scoured out some twenty valleys here and there adorning them with these fantastic rock scapes of towering cliffs, stalactite caves and giant dolomite towers that rise above the valley walls. The most dramatic landscape is the valley of the Wiesent River.

When we speak of brown trout in America, as a matter of fact throughout the world, "the German trout" is often the first connotation that people have. I'll never forget a time years ago, while pursuing the wonderful limestone spring creeks of the Driftless area of Wisconsin with a good doctor friend of mine who owned a beautiful summer retreat there, when I encountered a band of Amish boys fishing in the local Baraboo Creek. As I approached them and asked them how their luck was one replied "no luck today English sir,"—(many Amish call Americans "English")—"but my brother got a big German when the waters were higher and muddier in April. We know they are here, but they are very tricky to catch. Sometimes when we are coming back from haying or plowing the fields late at night we heard loud noises in the creek—we think that's when the big Germans feed."

Our German invasion was another product of diplomatic friendships in 1890 between America's first ardent pisciculturist Fred Mather, and the president of the German Fisheries Society, Baron Lucius von Behr. Berlin in 1890 was a bustling metropolis, as the tram and rail service boomed and the Hohenzollerns unveiled the new Reichstag. That year the international fisheries exposition occurred in Berlin, bringing Mather and Von Behr together. Von Behr insisted that Mather come and experience firsthand the beautiful northern Bavarian brown trout on a fishing expedition. Mather, a true piscatorial

▲ Mather was overwhelmed with joy by these stunning brown trout, as seen here from a Michigan spring creek, which still has the original German genetics. Early documents revealed that he would spend hours and days looking over the eyed-up eggs as if they were the lost Holy Grail. Credit: Author

romantic, fell immediately in love with the German brown trout's sporting qualities, in addition to its colorful beauty.

Mather started his fishing aquaculture near Honeoye Falls in New York by building hatcheries to raise grayling, sea bass, and shad. He was also an inventor of equipment for aquaculture: trays to store eggs, as well as ice boxes that allowed the transportation of fish to distant places. Throughout his visit to Germany, Mather was also

▲ The Rochester/ Caledonia, New York Spring Creek hatchery and the rivers of western New York, where the German brown found a new destiny. Credit: Andrew Steele Nisbet

contemplating the dismal future that the brook trout of America since the industrial revolution, where acid runoff from foresting and coal mining pollution, along with tannery mills, was decimating rivers. Although much of the industrial revolution had already swept a good part of Germany, the brown trout seemed to be quite tolerant of civilization's encroachment. They could survive higher water temperatures in the low-lying valley streams and had elusive tendencies, all qualities the American Brook trout did not have.

The new invasion began in February of 1883. Mather was then appointed an administrative position at the New York fish commission's Cold Spring Harbor Station, which was then nearing completion, where he raised brook trout and experimented with coasters, lobster, and other shellfish. As von Behr promised, on that cold spring day, Mather received the first shipment of brown trout eggs from Germany and the new age of trout fishing in America began. He prudently divided the shipment to avoid any mishaps that would lead to the loss of the entire stock, such as disease or a loss of electricity, refrigeration, or water supply. The New York State fish hatchery at Caledonia near Rochester, New York and the US fish commission hatchery in Northville, Michigan received the first shipments.

The first fish I ever caught with a fly rod in my home state of New York was a brown trout. My Polish dad and I would take weekend fly-fishing jaunts to the brown trout streams in the southern tier of western New York—creeks and rivers like the Cattaraugus, Wiscoy, and East Coy, were our favorites. We would also ride out to the start of the Finger Lakes near Rochester, Oatka Creek, and Caledonia's Spring Creek for their extremely beautiful brown trout. Little did I know that Mather's program planted North America's first German brown trout in these places.

## Michigan's Legacy Begins

My *Salmo* journey came full circle like an enchanting fairytale once I arrived in Michigan. I came there to advance and then eventually leave my lucrative corporate hotel career, and begin to live the dream—or curse, as may it be on any given day—of being an illustrious pauper, fly fishing guide, lodge owner, and writer, trying to follow a romantic dream in the shadows of Schwiebert, Hemingway, and my old mentor Vince Marinaro. Though I was aware of being in hallowed trout territory, little did I realize the very first planting of a brown trout in the western new world Americas took place in the creeks and rivers down the road from the Lodge that I was soon to build and operate. The 1880s were an exciting time in the Detroit lower "thumb" area of Michigan, at the beginning of the area's industrial revolution. Iron ore foundries were prospering all over Metropolitan Detroit, bringing in immigrants from all over the world as skilled laborers. The Grand Trunk Railroad expedited passenger and freight service to Chicago. Lumbering operations in the western part of the state proliferated along the rivers and brooks, waters that were soon to become homes for the German invading brown trout. During that time, the first US federal fish hatchery along the springs of Northville, Michigan would bring a new age of progressive fish aquaculture to the mitten state.

▲ Trains and brakemen ladling oxygen in the canisters brought the German invasion to the waters of the Pere Marquette and its local spring creeks. Credit: Kurt Kale (top); Author (bottom)

The Clark family started the private hatchery and when the father passed away it was bestowed upon Frank Clark. It eventually was leased and sold to the US government. Many a night Frank and the federal scientists sat around drinking fine ales after a long day, talking about rumors of how the trout streams of the Western Huron Manistee forests were being destroyed by the greedy lumber barons through clear-cutting vast swathes of the area.

When the shipment of brown trout came from Cold Spring, New York they looked at it as a blessing in disguise that might heal the future of trout in Michigan and elsewhere in the Americas. Once the eggs turned into fingerlings, it was time to get to work and spread the new immigrants into the western waters whose wild trout populations were suffering. They loaded the beautiful parr-marked fry into milk canisters, which then went by the horse and buggy to the US Fish commission train car on the Grand Trunk Railroad, bound for Grand Rapids. Their eventual destination, the stunning spring-fed streams of the Huron-Manistee Forest, would be similar to the sandy-soiled, birch- and pine-lined forests of Europe.

In my many interviews with locals, and from historical DNR documentation, I pieced together some not-so-familiar historical possibilities. Once the conductor of the train drove over the large Muskegon River in Newaygo, where I now live, the biologists on the fish car instructed the conductor to stop at any "spring creek looking waters". They would run and take water temperatures looking for cold springs and dump several canisters of the new German transplants off the bridge. Thus the Bigelow Creek, the White River (a stone's throw from my lodge), the Pere Marquette, and the Baldwin Creek tributary all received the first transplants. The railroad bridge near Baldwin Creek was the last and closest to town, and thus received credit from the press as being the first stocking, but the inaugural event actually took place along a series of creeks. Soon they were planted on one of the world's most iconic and famous brown trout spring creeks, the legendary Au Sable River, home to the origins of Trout Unlimited.

Michigan's sand and gravel, and wooded spring creeks couldn't have been more perfect for the *Salmo trutta*. Its ice-cold waters run on the alkaline side, fostering amazing mayfly hatches and vertebrate prey. Today, living in this magnificent Huron-Manistee national Forest is a lifestyle of brown trout worship that forever reminds us of its historical past. These magnificent cool-flowing rivers harbor incredible wild populations and evolved unique populations.

At nighttime I still hear the Pere Marquette Railroad make its trip from Grand Rapids to Traverse City on the railroad tracks down the road from our Lodge in the national Forest. Back in February 1883, the ice cold little

▲ Folklore has it that it is here, on Bigelow spring creek, down the road from my lodge, that the first milk canister of the German brown invasion arrived. Credit: Matthew Supsinski

creek down the road, the Bigelow, most likely received several canisters of the small fingerlings, as did other tributaries of the White River and the South Branch of the Pere Marquette that I visit regularly today. Their progeny all bear those striking golden butter bellies with beautiful red spots and white dots and gorgeous array of brown spots and blueish parr marks—some almost leopard-like in spotting—that are so distinctive among Von Behr's brown trout of the Schwartzwald.

In the years to follow, Derbyshire and Scotland soon got in on the act with their stunning Loch Leven strain. Here was a big water lake or loch *trutta* that had more silvery coloration, larger and less spotting, and were known to be great migratory fish. Over the years the two strains spread throughout the East Coast and North America, both on the state and federal level. Both in the wild and in the hatcheries the two strains intermixed their genetics, leading to the great diversity of the American brown trout today.

By the early 1900s, the brown trout had taken hold in almost forty US states and Canadian provinces. The perfect wild frontiers of the rivers of the Rocky Mountains, Montana, Wyoming, and Colorado became ideal new frontiers for the elusive *trutta*. With their cunning ability to adapt, they took hold in every stream and postured

themselves as the alpha fish in every pool and riffle in every tributary or main river. However, American fly anglers who love their brook trout and grayling did not appreciate the newcomers, since they competed heavily and eventually pushed the brookies higher up into the river systems' cold-flowing capillaries.

But as we will examine in detail in the next chapter, they each sought different conditions more suited to their likes and dislikes. The brook trout are fonder of small ice-cold tributaries and headwaters in higher elevation streams and rivulets. The introspective and secluded brown trout seek the bigger river systems with more cover, more fertility in the marginal water temperatures, and more of a mix of prey. What was to follow was an interesting cultural and socialization process beginning with extreme resistance that ultimately led to their widespread acceptance today.

Keep in mind that the 1890s trout bum was predominantly a kill fisherman. Though the art and science was slowly developing, the hallmark of an angler's skill at that time amounted to a wicker creel lined with ferns and beautiful gutted brook trout. This new European immigrant was not so quick to succumb to the turn-of-the-century trout bum's tactics, much to their dismay. Their tendency to eat smaller brook trout led to a reputation

▲ A beautiful German "Bach Forelle" from Michigan's Pere Marquette. Credit: Rich Felber

as "cannibal Germans," and comparisons with less-tasty fish—"they taste of poor quality and nothing more than a spotted carp."

Since Michigan and New York were the first to stock brown trout, they came under heat from anglers who loved their native brook trout and grayling. The Michigan DNR, known then as the conservation commission, stated in 1897 that "experience and experiment has convinced us that the brown trout is inferior in every aspect to the brook trout or rainbow." Keep in mind that the California Rainbow trout experiment took place in 1876 and was already heavily vested in all the Michigan Rivers that ran to the Great Lakes, such as the AuSable, Manistee, Pere Marquette, and Platte. The migratory steelhead rainbows most likely got along much better with the brook trout since they simply spent a majority of their feeding time in the big lake systems and only returned for spring spawning, whereas the brook trout tended toward small waters.

As Mather got more involved with the different taxonomic varieties and brown trout coming into America from Europe, he saw great diversity of the super modified creature that had adapted abilities beyond the native chars. Mather was as strong proponent of Darwinism and saw its prevailing influences in his aquaculture experiments. According to a press release, Mather said the following concerning his beloved brown trout:

Some anglers have objected to the introduction of brown trout streams because they grow too fast and

might eventually kill our native fish. To this I say "let them do it if they can and the fittest will survive." . . . A trout is a cannibal when he gets to be three years old. Whether he is native or an adopted citizen is only a question of which fish matures in the shortest time for the angler.

Mather's comments were realistic, since brook trout can be the most ferocious cannibals of all, and every angler knows that a salted minnow or a white zonker or streamer will slay adult brook trout.

## The Invasion Spreads to the Ends of the World

The new era of aquaculture in nineteenth-century hatcheries formed fishery societies whose dialogues and note-sharing served the brown trout's dissemination. Elsewhere in the western hemisphere, Patagonia features climates and ecology similar to Montana, where the brown trout became king very quickly. In Tierra del Fuego at the tip of the world the migrating and anadromous capacity of the brown trout quickly took advantage of the tremendous pelagic baitfish, crustacean, and squid prey off the Straits of Magellan and Strait of La Marie, which link the Atlantic and Pacific currents.

New York's famous Caledonia fish hatchery, where Seth Green mastered the art of raising the temperamental *Salmo,* was the launching point for transporting lots of brown trout eggs in the Canadian Maritimes of Newfoundland, New Brunswick, and Québec. By the

▲ With all the channel and inlets teeming with food, and brown trout's fondness for staying close to their rivers of origin—primarily the Rio Grande and Rio Gallegos—a large sea-run brown trout Empire took hold and is still today on the bucket list for all *Salmo* fisherman. Credit: Jessica Delorenzo

1920s the western provinces of Canada established brown trout populations, creating perhaps one of the greatest fisheries to exist North America today. The Bow River in Alberta was a perfect environment for a large valley river system with tributaries and vast pools of tranquil water mixed in with rapids.

Perhaps one of the greatest brown trout transplantation Cinderella stories took place in the Patagonian Mountains and valleys of Chile and Argentina. It is the land of the famous gauchos that roam the windy mountain valleys as nomadic herders at the ends of the earth. These rugged sheep- and cattle-herding cowboys live the dream with some of the finest cattle, lamb, venison, and wild boar cuisine in the world, featuring the European traditions of curing meats, charcuterie, and pâtés, along with dishes from indigenous vegetables. Near the coastal areas shellfish and sea bass coupled with the outstanding wineries can make for an unbeliev-able fishing and culinary experience.

But what was so special about the lakes and rivers of Patagonia, aside from their natural beauty, was that the waters truly lacked an alpha predator. The indigenous *Perca trucha*, similar to smallmouth bass and perch popu-lated the rivers, along with an array of sculpin-like fish.

These were ideal prey items for the highly carnivorous brown trout that take full advantage as they infiltrated the region.

▲ Here with this Patagonia beauty by Josh Miller, now the stage is set practically throughout the world for the brown trout and Atlantic salmon to be the most widely-distributed fish species. As with all immigrants to a new world, the road to appreciation, relevance, and assimilation often has had its trials and tribulations. Credit: Josh Miller

# The Foundation of *Salmo*'s Technical Renaissance and the British Schism:
## Halford vs G. E. M. Skues

▲ The stunning and pastoral River Test in Hampshire, England. Credit: Ken Takata

There is no disputing Salmo's fond infatuation for the surface. The "dry fly only" angler, armed with cane rod and the historical Adams dry or Quill Gordon, can be considered this stoic type of *Salmo* connoisseur. Thus the first purist school of snobbery in the late 1880s emerged with the fury of the Protestant Reformation.

Enter Frederick M. Halford and G. E. M. Skues. As with all things British, "proper" has by far the most importance when considering anything from cricket to drinking Scotch whiskey. Hence the art of fly fishing is perfectly right for this type of exclusivity. There in its prime selectivity laboratory were the dainty English chalk streams (spring creeks) of the hallowed Hampshire countryside, where the Rivers Test and Itchen flowed through the pastoral farms and villages. Since the writings of Stewart described the wet fly swing tactic for the dark and tannic waters of Scotland, the crystal clear chalk streams offered the study of trout feeding on mayflies and sedges unlike any other fisheries at that time. Sight fishing for trout on spring creeks reveals the essence of the trout through its acceptance or refusal of the fly.

Halford introduced the upstream dry-fly approach in his work *Floating Flies and How to Dress Them* (1886), followed by *Dry Fly Fishing in Theory and Practice*. What started as a progressive approach to sight fishing for trout geared toward surface-oriented chalk stream situations, became an absolutist ideological dogma that "only the fine gentlemen will and must fish in this precise upstream dry fly manner."

If Halford was "Catholic" in his new fly angling religion, G. E. M. Skues was fly fishing's Martin Luther. Born in Newfoundland in 1858 and later transported back to Aberdeen, Skues was an extremely brilliant thinker, writer, and solicitor, who was part of a prestigious law firm where he practiced until retiring at the age of eighty-one. He applied his considerable analytical observations from the minute to the grandiose to his fly fishing. Skues has written more words about selectivity and trout than any man that ever graced the planet; he was the Mozart of fly fishing. While Halford drew the line in the sand with the dry fly, Skues did the same with the nymph. Although Skues agreed with Halford that the dry fly was very effective at

▲ Halford fishing his beloved dry "Danica" mayfly. Credit: Catskill Fly Fishing Museum

certain times, for sheer efficiency of catching trout on the fly nothing could beat the virtues of an experienced chalk stream sight nympher.

## The Catskills

Growing up in the Southern tier foothills of the New York Allegheny Mountains, I plied the small freestone and spring fed creeks and rivers of this rolling valley pastoral countryside for wild populations of brown trout, rainbows, and headwater brook trout. In this landscape dotted with Amish farms, Indian reservations, scenic valleys, grape orchards, and state forests I learned about mayflies, caddis, and stoneflies and how to fish them. Despite having great streams on our western side of the Empire state, every spring my dad and I would take the big scenic six-hour drive to fish the hallowed waters of the Catskill Mountains. The scenic drive along the Route 17 expressway was all eye candy as we drove through the glacially cut valleys of other trout streams and the Finger Lakes freshwater mecca district that was carved out two million years ago. Those who think New York is just the "big apple" and don't really know the beauty and riches of its stunning mountains, glacial lakes, and rivers, should take

this drive. The wineries and Niagara scenic wonder are an amazing sight. Cayuga Lake is over four hundred feet deep and at one time the eastern Finger Lakes connected to Lake Ontario where Atlantic salmon were indigenous. Today they are a brown trout and Atlantic salmon wonderland, along with wild migratory rainbows that run the creek tributaries in the spring.

It was on a Memorial Day weekend at the end of May as the smell of the enchanted forested Catskills were peaking in their fresh, deep forest green, as the first spring wild flowers of trilliums, violets, and Dutchman's Britches adorned the ravine along the river. The Beaverkill River was the king and mecca of all the Catskill brown trout gems at the time and it is here I got my first truly large brown trout, a gorgeous red and brown marble-spotted monster of eighteen inches. It had a short kype and was the most beautiful creature I'd ever laid eyes on. It happened downstream from the Junction confluence on a pool now known as Hendrickson's. It was a cool afternoon and as soon as the sun peeked through the clouds, a nice hatch of Grey Fox *Stenonema* brought every trout up in the pool in an aggressive and very active way. They slashed at the emerging adults and watched the floating duns for a good time before feeling comfortable enough to accept them. My dad and I were still familiarizing ourselves with the peculiarities of Catskills fishing by spending time on the water. However, on that day even a poorly-presented fly did the trick. After botching up the net job several times my prey was in my hands. I screamed for my dad to get his vintage Leica M3 German SLR camera to commemorate this achievement, and I still dream about releasing that fish.

Each night at the campfire by Wagon Tracks, my father's seemingly inexhaustible stories about his journey from war-torn Europe to the new world captivated me. We always went further up the Beaverkill by the wonderful Lew Beach wooden covered bridges and managed to catch a few brook trout. We wrapped them in bacon for dinner with hot potatoes cooked in the tinfoil in the coals. In the Catskills, my dad, who was a lover of history and nostalgia, always alluded that these hallowed waters were the birthplace of American fly fishing.

A trip to watch the Dettes tie flies was always in the mix as we spent hour after hour, rain, flood, or snow, trying to catch a Catskill brown trout. The legend of the giant "Beamoc" brown trout with two heads due to being confused on which River to swim up—the Beaverkill or Willowemoc—became a preoccupation. That mythical creature was very real in my childhood streamside daydreaming, and I always dreamed it would be possible to catch this beast on my next fly presentation. That day my eighteen-inch brownie became my "Beamoc."

▲ The names of Gordon and Hewitt and an appreciation for the Catskill brown trout legacy and its stunning rivers came to me early, bestowed from my very traditional and historical minded Polish father, who was still struggling with the English language. Credit: Author

## The Thinking *Salmo* Angler Emerges for the Brown Trout Litmus Test

The beauty and magic of New York's Catskill region is home to thousands of miles of charming freestone and tailwater rivers with abundant trout. Here around the turn of the century, the railroads built train transportation to bring leisure-seeking city dwellers to the cool mountain retreats. Wealthy New Yorkers soon discovered the Catskills' charm and angling opportunities. They learned to fish the Catskills while sporting the finest clothing, in what was becoming an important social venue; it was the chic thing to do. In all the hoopla about fly fishing in the magazines of the time, many were laying down an eclectic snob culture of theoretical fly fishing.

These magical mountains of gentle, sloping, broad vistas are reminiscent of *Rip Van Winkle* and the *Legend of Sleepy Hollow*. Predominately settled by the Dutch coming up from the Hudson Valley, each river has the name *-kill*, or "river" in Dutch. A large number of cold water springs and creeks form to make large freestone rivers, cascading down the mountain valleys. These rivers are alive with mayflies and other aquatic life, wildlife of all kinds, and most importantly, trout. The indigenous brook trout were the main target, and plenty of anglers scoffed at the newly-introduced German brown trout because the usurper refused their crudely tied flies. Once the anglers had surmounted the learning curve required to catch them, the brown soon became the favored species, and the evolution of the Catskill dry fly was critical to the growing admiration of the brown trout.

As the new Catskill rivers were being described as the "best places for trout fishing" in the world, private Wall Street and company moguls bought up private stretches of rivers and turned them into elite private clubs and spas for the wealthy. It was, however, the less-well-heeled anglers who developed the Catskill Bible for fly fishing in these hallowed American waters. One must for the most part keep in mind that the Catskill rivers were drastically different from the chalk streams and spring creeks of Hampshire, the fly fishing standard of the time. Catskill trout rivers are mainly fast, cascading, boulder-strewn rivers with great fluctuations in flows, as opposed to the gentle spring creeks of consistent flow and temperature of Hampshire. This was a crucial ingredient of historical significance in the development of the selective presentation that would evolve here and influence the way we fish everywhere today. In the glory days of brook trout fishing, anglers would cast three wet flies on the leader and fill their creels with plenty of tasty brook trout in a day for a lodge meal. "Fish hogs" and killing was widespread throughout the angling fraternity. The famous writer and angler Sparse Gray Hackle once wrote that the fish-killing atrocities were rampant, and in an 1889 issue of *The American Angler* Magazine described the phenomenon:

> The two largest catches truthfully reported this season were made a day or two ago and the upper waters of the Neversink River by three young men of Liberty, who do not claim to be experts. In one day's fishing, Charles Humphrey and James Theobald took 470 trout, weighing altogether more than 40 pounds. F. M. Lamoreaux, fishing alone for nine hours, 478 trout, weighing altogether 33 pounds. Catches of 10 to 15 pounds weights are matters of everyday occurrence.

With this maddening pace of wanton killing, it was no wonder that the brook trout disappeared from the main stems of Catskill rivers. By the 1890s, the brook trout, due to angler devastation and the tanneries and acid factories polluting the rivers, were all but gone except for the small, remote cold water mountain brooks and tributaries.

In 1886, Aden Brook, a tributary to the Neversink

▲ An evening hatch on the historic Neversink. Credit: Matthew Supinski

River, received the first planting of German brown trout. Everything in fly angling in the Catskills was soon to change in a big way. *Salmo trutta* was not about to be pushed around and hung by the hundreds on the trophy polls in front of exclusive lodges like naïve dead brook char. Millions of years of evolutionary survival taught them well, and thus, innately wary and elusive, they soon commanded the newly conquered waters.

Soon after the transplants took hold in North America, the old European order of aristocracy, imperialism, and industrial decadence aligned itself into the self-destructive conditions leading to the First World War. After the hostilities began, British and American propagandists were successful in turning sentiment against anything and everything German. Coupled with the fact it was a displacing the well-loved and beautiful brook trout, our brown trout friend came under the same scrutiny and hatred in the press and society.

## Theodore Gordon: America's First Brown Trout Evangelist

When the brown trout made its first Catskill debut, needless to say it was scorned for its shyness, stubborn demeanor, and inability to "fill basket creels to the brim."

The thinking, theoretical fly angler was ready to make his debut. The time was ripe with throngs of anglers who were ready for a sermon and a solution, and Theodore Gordon stepped in to the role as the first father of the American selective brown trout angler.

In his 1987 masterpiece, *American Fly Fishing: A History*, Paul Scullery wrote of Gordon's significance, but as part myth and fallacy. Since there were so many new fly fishers looking for advice and direction, Gordon became a cultural necessity of being—just as many religious icons have appeared throughout the ages. Schullery writes:

Theodore Gordon has become the central figure in the history of American fly fishing. For all the wonderful things that have been written about the other "giants" such as Thaddeus Norris, Lee Wulff, Ray Bergman, and so on, it is from Gordon that the modern tradition is most often said to flow. He has been glorified more with each passing generation, until within the past ten years he has been given credit for, among other things, the invention of the streamer, the original study of angling entomology in America, introducing the dry fly to America, introducing the nymph to America, originating an American-style dry fly tying, originating the American approach to imitation, and being, finally, "the father of modern American angling." Such a figure, so enshrouded in the love and legend of a sport, will not be lightly tampered with.

Schullery's description is from a unique perspective and somewhat of a "niche creation" point of view. Fly fishing lore and history is replete with hermits and socially-challenged people, just as with artists, musicians, and great theological and scientific theorists. Occasionally brilliant minds can be associated with extreme gregarious behavior, but that is rarely the case with geniuses, and Gordon's accomplishments and habits seem to reflect this tendency. A trout bum's preoccupations with the massive complexity of fly fishing sometimes do not allow for social contact, marriage, family, and "hanging out with the boys." It's amazing how some of the trout bums that I know have let their passions take over their entire lives, and I imagine that the reclusive Theodore Gordon was similarly disposed. If there ever were a dogma or mission statement for selectivity and its fusion with *trutta*, Gordon summed it up as follows:

It is the constant—or inconstant—change, the infinite variety in fly fishing that binds us fast. It is impossible

▲ Gordon was on a mission to set the theoretical model of brown trout selectivity for the new Catskill fishery, now dominated by the epicurean and finicky selectors of the fly—*Salmo trutta*. Credit: Catskill Fly Fishing Museum

to grow weary of the sport that is never the same on any two days in the year. I am fond of all sorts of fishing, in fresh or salt water, in the interior of the country, or on the coast, but trout angling takes a grip upon the imagination. It is more of a mental recreation and other methods. There's always something in question, something to discuss.

As Schullery goes on to mention, although his significance far outweighs his actual contributions to the world of *trutta* selectivity and the hatch matching connection, he made many valid points. I quote Schullery again in the following passages about Gordon:

He did not write an angler's entomology, but he tirelessly preached its importance. He never stopped telling his readers to look at the insect and learn its ways, then imitate it. But he did occasionally mention some specific emergence he had witnessed, or attempted to imitate, usually telling the readers that it was a caddis, or a mayfly, or whatever, and giving the times, dates, and locations. It would be worth the time for some enterprising Catskill angler to extract this information from the entire twenty-five years of articles and unpublished letters and see what kind of "hatch chart" it would turn into. Then it would be worth that same angler's trouble to go on and compare those flies that Gordon observed and recorded with the color portraits of the flies and Louis Rhead's book *American Trout Stream Insects* and see how the two of them line up. Rhead also gave emergence dates, and perhaps between the two of them they may have given us a valuable resource that could then be compared with various modern works on the same subject. Even after this exercise, the best we can say for Gordon as an entomologist is that he tried his best to encourage others to care about the subject.

Schullery again discredits more speculation and claims by ardent Gordon admirers with the following passage:

Gordon did not introduce the dry fly to America. Even the Quill Gordon, for its wood-duck wing, is a nearly direct copy in the materials of a Halford pattern. So the question becomes how he transformed the British patterns.

So given all of the "Gordon didn't-do's," Schullery describes Gordon's important contributions:

Gordon soon found that the daintily-tied dry flies of Halford did not hold up to the new Catskill's rugged, more volatile cascading waters of its freestone

River. This was a totally different environment from the Hampshire chalk stream. So he started adding stiffer features and hackle, along with more appropriate natural dry fly form and how the fly rolled on the surface. Where Gordon was most significant in his contribution was definitely in the design and analysis of how flies look to the trout, thus breaking away from the British entomological imitations of gaudiness and uncrackable nature for the new colonies' purpose. He did what Swisher and Richards in *Selective Trout* did for modern-day fly design with the no-hackle wing dry. That is to give a realistic look, unlike the scene before in the British school.

Keep in mind, the brown trout's extreme wariness and finicky nature was the underwriter of all this thinking man's new approach to trout in the Catskills. Gaudy English wets were not doing the trick on the slow Catskill pool eddies, as *trutta* scoffed at the traditional flies. *Trutta* was the subliminal if not direct instigator of all the fuss about

attention to form and detail, in my opinion. The use of the divided wood-duck wing and stiffer sparse tackles started with Gordon and was later perfected along the banks of the Beaverkill River by the Dettes and Darbees of Roscoe, NY. Gordon can be seen as a messiah to the developing theoretical schools of Halford and Skues who put them in full focus in the New World.

Gordon's clean, innovative, and Spartan fly design couldn't have appeared with better timing. The gaudy English wet and dry flies purveyed to the general angling public at that time were becoming less effective. The brook trout were slowly diminishing and being replaced by the highly selective new brown trout from Germany. The brown trout's penchant to be very surface oriented coincided with Gordon sparse fly designs and focus. Though he did not disdain nymphs or wets, the dry fly, by its coincidental effectiveness on the new Catskill fisheries, quickly attained acceptance.

Another aspect affecting brown trout selectivity is one that I believe many historians do not take into sufficient

▲ Gordon's attention to detail (tying his wings slightly backward to imitate a mayfly dun silhouette), and the sparse clean qualities of his designs like the Quill Gordon, set the mold for the others he showed how to tie, such as Rube Cross, Roy Steenrod, Herman Christenson, and others. Credit: Stacy Niedzwiecki

account: Whole river ecosystems were changing drastically. Mill dams and pollution, greater development, surface run-off, and the sewage generated by all the fishing/spa resorts/lodges started to make profound changes to the once-pristine primordial Catskills. Nutrient enhancement of the rivers actually rose, which eventually is a good thing for aquatic benthic invertebrates such as mayflies, stoneflies, and caddis. Thus, hatches and hatch imitating was becoming a Catskill fly fishing tradition that Gordon's dry fly addressed.

But it is once again the circumstantial role of the brown trout in its quest for ideal habitat that brought Gordon's dry fly revolution into full swing. Casting gaudy wet flies in cold, oxygenated upper headwaters for non-selective brook trout was not common practice anymore. Brown trout love the slower, long, flat eddy pools of the larger Catskill rivers. They tolerated warmer water temperatures—actually preferring something a little above 60 degrees Fahrenheit—thus giving the Catskill angler the experience of wading and casting into large flat eddy pools for selective, extremely wary trout on a consistent basis for the first time in its history. Gordon's applications were perfectly suited. However,

anglers required a more advanced entomological model to refine these applications.

In the end analysis, I believe timing and coincidence were perfectly suited for Gordon to emerge as a modern icon of selective trout fishing stemming from the *Salmo trutta* invasion, even though his theoretical contributions were nowhere near as observant and thought-provoking as Skues or Sawyer. Just as many have disputed the admirable qualities of our first president George Washington, he was the right man at the right time, and in his own way Theodore Gordon is likewise the first founding president of the American selective fly fishing movement.

## The Modern Entomologist Emerges

Louis Rhead came to the United States in 1883 as an illustrator and artist of books. Rhead spent many hours along the Catskill Rivers and was the first serious sketcher of mayflies, stoneflies, caddis, and other insects as a sort of entomological John Audubon. His book *American Trout Stream Insects* (1916) was the first concise treatise of entomology that New World would embrace. He experimented with reverse downstream flies, adding cork bodies

▲ A magnificent Catskill *trutta*. Credit: John Miller.

to stoneflies, and other very unorthodox approaches. Rhead was considered by many a snake-oil salesman of trout flies who failed to knowledge the establishment and achievements of the British/Catskill dry fly as a proven and favorite fly presentation.

In 1935 released *A Book of Trout,* which came to be described as "the most important work in American fly fishing presentation," and "the best book a fly Fisher will ever see." The work was as significant as the contributions from Swisher/Richards and Caucci/Nastasi, using many entomological academics for references, and concentrated on the mayflies of the Catskills. Though his contributions about caddis was weak, he suggested that all anglers should become amateur entomologists, and showed how to collect insects and study trout rises.

At the same time, Jennings's contemporary Frank Sawyer was doing the same work and coming to similar conclusions so on his own beloved River Avon with its cheeky wild brown trout. Jennings's and Sawyer's entomological endeavors are almost identical in their approach. Generally Jennings's work was much more scientific than Sawyer's

streamside speculating and observations, and detailed the emergence of the mayflies of the Catskills in a fashion like no other, providing specific hatch-matching patterns such as the March Brown, Grey Fox, Hendrickson, and others. It quickly became a Bible of American anglers, distinct from the previous arrogant British theoretical models that had limited applications in American trout waters.

## The American River Steward: Edmund Ringwood Hewitt

E. R. Hewitt was the true "Renaissance man" of the emerging selective Catskill brown trout school, having the highest attributes of the empirical and well-versed trout angler. His contributions are very often overlooked in light of the previous names I've mentioned. Hewitt did it all. Hewitt was the well-schooled and blue-blooded son of a wealthy steel mogul. He was versed in all the disciplines and applied his analytical mind towards all things trout, salmon, and fly fishing. He wrote several books, *Telling on the Trout* (1926) being his most analytical work of trout behavior. He was also fascinated by Atlantic salmon and

▲ These Hewitt patterns are particularly effective to catch the curiosity of wild browns when skittered along the surface, mimicking the stoneflies and caddisflies common along the Neversink's vast boulder-strewn waters. Credit: Jim Haswell

wrote *Secrets of a Salmon* (1922) and *A Trout and Salmon Fisherman for 75 Years* (1948).

Hewitt was a master fly tier who broke some of the newly created entomological trends of exact hatch matching inspired by Jennings. His approach to fly design and construction was very similar to Sawyer in that he preferred simplicity and function over exact representation. Hewitt's minimalist approach was refreshing to the everyday anglers as they tried to grasp the higher entomological concepts laid out by Jennings. Hewitt's *Handbook of Fly Fishing* (1933) detailed five winged flies and five hackle flies in a variety of sizes, and stated confidently that these were all the flies a trout angler would ever need. This is very similar to Frank Sawyer's handful of deadly nymphs. Hewitt was the first to emphasize presentation versus exact duplication, "as a new emerging school of thought," and the famous Catskill trout fisherman Ed van Putt was noted for just fishing the Adams dry fly, in contravention of the complex Delaware hatch-matching school. He carried them in all sizes and seemed to have as much success as when using more precise duplications.

Hewitt used only one style of nymph, the hardback brown nymph. He claimed he could wipe out whole trout streams with this pattern. As with Frank Sawyer's Pheasant Tail, Grey Goose, and Killer Bug, Hewitt's approach to midges, crustacea, and streamers was similarly limited and simple. I have often viewed minimalism as a copout to avoid learning the deeper scientific world of entomology and trout behavior. However, as Sawyer mentions, the brown trout and salmon will always be the ultimate judge of whether the fly is of significance.

As we all know, the beat-up and ratty-looking flies usually catch fish. Hewett realized the importance of the motion and impression a fly gives on the surface of the water. Exact identification was not always possible on his beloved Neversink River, with its cold, fast-flowing waters, frequent riffles, and boulder-strewn runs, and Hewitt found that impressionistic, gaudy patterns often had a higher degree of success than the more daintily-tied mayfly duns. Two of Hewitt's highly effective patterns are still in common use today to fool fussy trout—the Neversink Skater and Brown Bivisible. The Skater is a waking fly said to imitate butterflies, which Hewitt saw the trout jumping for in broad daylight. The Bivisble is a heavily-hackled dry that skitters and wakes the surface.

As with Sawyer, Hewitt was a fish culturist, stream engineer, and one of the country's leading stream improvement experts, which brought him worldwide critical acclaim. He imported Atlantic salmon from Norway and Scotland and raised them in his Neversink laboratory, stocking them in the river itself. Today, the 2700 acres of Hewitt's flooded estate that created the Neversink Reservoir, receives landlocked Atlantic salmon.

## The Dark Ages

With the selective brown trout appreciation in full bloom, the rumble of the Second World War was rearing its ugly head. Private fly fishing clubs sprang up on prime trout and salmon waters all over the United States and Canada. Spring creeks from Long Island to the Castalia Club in Ohio charged steep fees to fish their well-manicured trout-stocked waters. Public trout waters were actually diminishing due to large corporations buying up huge tracts of land for their wealthy clients. Guides and River keepers were the holders of the eclectic trout knowledge, since they were meager locals that took rich people fishing. In today's economy it's amazing how little things have changed for the modern guide, having personal experience with this scenario.

Makers of fine fishing tackle like Charles Orvis and the bamboo rod geniuses of Garrison Payne, and a host of others were demanding high prices for their outstanding quality—and rightly so, since they were the first craft pioneers. Besides the writings of LaBranche, Jennings, and Hewitt, another notable trout contribution prior to the Great War was Ray Bergman's *Trout* (1938), which soon became a fly-fishing Bible. He was the first to write about using a bushy dry fly as "an indicator when fishing the nymph upstream and dead drifting"—a practice commonly used today. He also was very articulate when describing the trout rise forms: dimple, slash, bulge, landing, refusal, and "double-ender." All in all, Bergman gave anglers much to learn from, and discussed stream ethics and proper sporting behavior as it pertained to the increasingly crowded East Coast waters.

His analysis of the slow, contemplative analytical approach is still relevant, especially on heavily-fished catch-and-release brown trout fisheries:

Study the water before fishing it. Select the most advantageous spot to fish from. Remember that the obvious places in the hard-fished streams are less likely to produce than the tough spots that no one fishes. If you are fishing places you do not know and fail to take a fish, don't leave it until you examine it carefully. It is possible that you didn't fish the right spot or from the right position. A careful investigation is quite likely to reveal the reason you failed. Use the longest leader you can handle. Usually you can handle one much longer than you can imagine. Fish slowly and thoroughly. Haste never paid dividends. Don't worry about the fellow ahead of you. If you start racing to get ahead of him, he'll probably try to beat you, and from then on will become nothing but a footrace instead of a contemplative inspiring recreation. If you like a certain section it may pay you to wait if someone else is fishing it. Wait until he goes, then wait some more and do some observing.

After World War II, the revitalization of the US economy, the great automobile explosion, and the suburban American dream created a sort of consumer hysteria. McDonald's hamburgers, TV dinners, vacations, and leisure spending hit new heights in the lifestyle of an everyday American. Now homes were filled with televisions, radios, record players, and toasters. Unfortunately for the theoretical and empirical fly angling school of the previous decades, Americans became infatuated with "bigger, faster, more" in an atmosphere of ease and grandiosity. Spin fishing was the "cool" way to go, getting dozens of fish with little discipline or effort.

State and federal hatcheries were producing "super-genetically engineered trout," like golden trout, tiger trout, and splake. If nature was broken and producing less, man could fix it better! The victorious Americans were on the fast track to destroying the tradition and legacy laid out in fly fishing for the past several centuries. If it were not for the old tried-and-true cane rod purists still fishing classic Catskill-style flies on waters from New York to California, the eloquent sport of fly fishing would have fallen by the wayside. These old-timers carried on the hallowed traditions with their prestigious fly fishing clubs and private lectures, in a manner much like the monks of the dark ages, by preserving books, Bibles, and scientific thought.

## The Pennsylvania Brown Trout Think Tank Emerges

Pennsylvania's Cumberland Valley is very special for me—I doubt that any other place has had a more profound impact on my thought process, emotions, and the quest for fussy trout than these magical spring creeks. I first read about the world-famous Letort Spring Run and Falling Springs in an article written in the 1970s by the fly fishing deans of its Valley documenting the huge selective wild brown and rainbow trout and the "Caenis/Trico" hatches they ate. Being in the international hotel business, I received a position as a food and beverage director at the Sheraton Washington hotel in 1982, and I lived a quick hour and a half from the legendary Falling Spring Run. I always tried to take jobs that were near good trout streams. I was shaking with awe on the first day I saw these gentle little limestone jewels. They were God's perfect creation for selective trout and I was blessed just to feast my eyes on them for the first time. Though many have tried to describe the natural and subtle beauty of these delicate limestoners, Ernest Schwiebert perhaps captured it best in his work *Nymphs* (1973):

> It is a pastoral landscape of prosperous farms, their cornfields and rich pastures lie sheltered between the folded tree-covered ridges of the Appalachians. It is a countryside of well-filled granaries in silos. Herds of black-and-white dairy cattle graze lazily in the

meadows and stare at fishermen from the sheltering buttonwoods. The whitewash fences and those tailored fields are as immaculate as the clapboard farm houses themselves. The barns are painted bright red, their cantilevered hay-wagon floors sheltering the cattle stalls toward the south. The builders mixed this primitive functionalism and climatology with witchcraft too, covering their bets both ways, with hex signs to protect the farm and its livestock and its inhabitants from evil spirits. The foundations and gable ends of the barns are examples of the magnificent amber-colored masonry work typical of the Pennsylvania Dutch.

Its trout streams are unusual too. Many emerge full-blown from limestone fissures that release the flow of vast underground caverns. Their currents are so rich with lime salts that the fertility rivals the storied chalk streams of Europe—Rivers like the Risle and Andelle in France, and the still more famous Rivers Itchen and Test in the chalk downs of southern Britain.

The limestone springs are remarkable for their volume and clarity, surrendering thousands of gallons per minute into these gentle little meadow rivers. The result is a habitat rich in fly life, currents that remain ice-free, and water temperatures so constant that the fish feed and grow steadily throughout the winter.

The Cumberland Valley will always be about memories for me. When I was in the hotel business and my soon-to-be wife, Laurie, was a lobbyist on Capitol Hill, we needed a place to escape and relish in a secret world that time seemed to have forgotten. We would scramble out of work on Fridays to avoid the rush-hour Beltway traffic and head north to have happy hour Bloody Marys on a blanket along the famous Falling Spring Run. Some years later we got married at the Allenberry resort along the historic

▲ The hallowed Letort Spring Run at Bonnybrook. Credit: Author

▲ Church typical of limestone country in the Driftless of Wisconsin. Credit: Author

Yellow Breeches Creek. Most of my friends showed up to the wedding in waders, as they stayed out late fishing the famous "white fly" *Ephoron* Hatch.

Whether it was convincing a wise old brown trout to take my sculpin on the Letort, or figuring out the feeding rhythm of the fussy Yellow Breeches *Trico*-sipping browns, every aspect of the limestone spring creek process was a major inroad to understanding extremely selective wild trout—especially the most difficult and wickedly fussy browns.

Pennsylvania's limestone legends—Vince Marinaro, Charlie Fox, Ed Koch, Ed Shenk, George Harvey, and Joe Humphries—all took the sport I am writing about to new levels in pursuit of leviathan brown trout. A new Renaissance era emerged with these humble Pennsylvania limestone legends of the mid-1900s from the dark ages of World War II. It is uncanny how spring creeks and chalk streams cast a spell on those who pursue fish. As we will see in the tactics chapter to come, the "Letort regulars" contributed much to the understanding of the persnickety foraging by browns, especially minutiae and terrestrials, along with the big meat of the sculpins.

## Browns Go to Big Sky: The Rugged *Trutta*

Though it is the home to indigenous Rainbows and Cutthroats, it wasn't long before Montanans realized how special *Salmo trutta* really were. In a statement by the Montana Fish and Game Department about their new exotic trout, they said the following: "The brown trout is a good fish but the average angler is not skilled enough to catch it."

Since the selective trout renaissance is primarily an East Coast and Michigan phenomenon, the amazing ice-cold wild trout waters of Montana, with its freestoners, tail waters, and spring creeks was like a new frontier fly-fishing gold rush. Big Sky Country was ready for the empirical fly revolution, as Montana was to become a utopia for the brown trout aficionado. No other state in the union placed more emphasis on trout fishing for its economy and existence than this new vast mecca.

In the 1970s renaissance era of historic books, Charles Brooks became its first Montana master. Brooks embodied the empirical technician, observer of trout stream ecology, avid big brown trout hunter, and all-around "complete angler." In the same league as with Marinaro, Wulff, and a short list of others, Brooks was if anything undervalued.

In *The Trout and the Stream*, Brooks wrote in the Skues/Waller Hills–style to describe trout rivers. He looked at every ecological component of the trout stream, presenting the conditions of volatility of the river that influence the selectivity of the trout that live there. Brooks bucked the contemporary craze of exact hatch matching, to focus on the trout hunter's big picture by using the approach that a naturalist views chaos and stability of riverine ecosystem forces and its hydrodynamics, which in turn affect what trout eat and the degree of selectivity they exhibit.

It is clear that Brooks was a naturalist from the get-go. In his books, *Larger Trout for the Western Fly Fisherman* and *Nymph Fishing for Larger Trout*, Brooks became very Skues-like, with extreme emphasis on nymphing the large boulder-strewn rivers of his beloved Madison for its hunkered-down browns. He developed the dead drift "pot-shooting" method to get down into the fast, oxygenated waters where the large *Pteronarcys* stone flies love to reside. His creation of the Brooks Stonefly is one of the best large patterns used for trophy brown trout all over the world. After researching the stonefly, his thoughts on the subject could perhaps be best summarized by the following passage:

> My feeling is that nymphs form the "meat-and-potatoes" of the trout's diet, and that adult aquatics, terrestrials, and other foods are like caviar—welcome, but not too regular a component. So I spend most of my research time studying nymphs and most of my

▲ Brooks's most important contribution to deep-feeding brown trout was tying stonefly nymphs by "in the round," so the trout could see the legs at all angles," he stated. In his book *The Living River*, Brooks poured his heart out about his beloved Madison River, its stonefly hatches, and its trophy brown trout. Credit: Mike Tsukamoto (photo); Ken Morrish (fly)

fishing time using artificials to imitate them. I know I will catch more fish the more I know about the nymphs they feed on. The nymphs simply drift along about mid water at the same speed as the current. Fish station themselves along the line of drift and feed continuously as long as the conditions last. The fish will move slightly right, left, up, or down to intercept food drifting in but he will not move far; he is in a feeding groove and will remain there until the drift of food has ceased.

Around the same time Brooks was writing his collection of books on fishing the West, Al Troth arrived on the Madison and was a pioneer in shaping the new western trout selectivity school, with the brown trout being a key component. Troth was a master fly tier and guide and created one of the deadliest flies of all time—the Elk Hair Caddis. His Troth's Terrible Stone, Salmon Fly, and Gulper Special are still standard patterns today.

Many great names contributed to the new Western school of fly fishing. The great Bud Lilly of West Yellowstone fame paved the way for fly-fishing only catch-and-release waters. Don Martinez developed the famous wooly worm. Dan Bailey adapted his Catskill fly-tying roots to the Montana fisheries with his woven Moss-back nymph creations. Big attractor flies were a new rage, forming a new schism away from the minimalist and natural school of the East Coast and Michigan. It was big sky country: big rivers, big trout, and big flies. What more could a true American cowboy want?

Today, more transplants live the Montana dream, embodied by former Michigan guide, Kelly Galloup, who is now a modern-day dean of the Madison River legacy, whom we will feature more of as the book progresses.

### *Salar*'s Aristocratic Lineage

For approximately sixteen thousand years or more, leaping silver salmonids have mesmerized mankind. The rivers of ancient Gaul, an area that in total includes France, Germany, Switzerland etc., was teeming with Atlantic

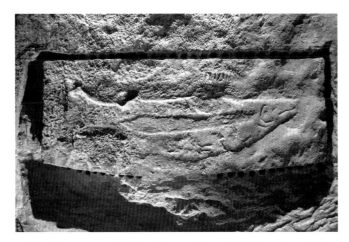

▲ The *Salmo* cave art at Abri Du Poisson and Asturia in Spain, sculpted with bones and animal antlers. Credit: French Ministry of Culture

salmon that came up the Rhine, Rhone, and Danube, and hundreds of other rivers along the Atlantic and Baltic seas, to the Canadian Maritimes, New England, and Lake Ontario. Stone Age man eventually drew cave art of animals including their worshiped *Salmo*. As they conquered the areas along the river valleys, Roman legions were astonished by these outstanding "leaping fish" that hurdled up rapids and falls.

The fact that Atlantic salmon don't eat upon their arrival in the rivers from the oceans presents a "unique cerebral conundrum" to the fly angler in pursuit. *Salar*, being dubbed "the fish of ten thousand casts," are highly aloof, reclusive, and sometimes downright impossible to catch. Although *Salar* can live as long as twelve months on stored body fat without eating, they love to play and take the fly, much like a cat playing with its food. The great Atlantic salmon icon, Lee Wulff, put it best: "Why does the salmon rise [to the fly]? Why does a small boy cross the street to kick a tin can?"

It is extremely challenging to write of Salmon and Steelhead from any absolutist standpoint. This stems from the fact that any given time it can change from one selectivity phase to the next—aggressive, active-passive, to dormant—in a heartbeat. Col. Robert Venables observed that "the salmon takeith the artificial fly very well," but, he also noted the importance of color stimulation: "use the most gaudy and Orient colors you can choose."

Two British authors in the early 1770s developed the first two modern Atlantic salmon flies. James Chetham mentions the "horse leech, Peacock fly, and dragonfly," is extremely effective. The "piquing" of the salmon's interest and sensitivity to size and color, which is much apparent to the early angler, was a result of sexually aggressive, territorial marking behavior of spawning salmon. Charles Bouulher wrote in 1774: "For salmon flies, in general, are made just as a painter pleases. Salmon being fond of anything that is gaudy . . ."

As we will probe more deeply in the Atlantic salmon chapters to follow, George M. Kelson wrote the first true authoritative look on salmon fishing, *The Salmon Fly* (1895). He became the "high priest of salmon fishing" just as Skues/Sawyer etched their names in glory for trout fishing. In Joseph Bates's masterpiece *Fishing Atlantic Salmon* (1996), he spoke highly of Kelson as the modern-day prophet of salmon and its flies:

> Kelson believed that salmon most evidently took moths or butterflies, and the gaudy patterns of his era reflected this. Famous ones, still in use, include the Thunder and Lightning, Green Highlander, Black Dose, and the blue, silver, black, white, red, and Helmsdale Doctors. He was one of the first writers to give detailed instructions and to offer a system for tying salmon flies.

The aristocratic Victorian era saw a surge in Atlantic salmon angling—it was the chic thing to do. Most salmon rivers in the UK and Europe were owned by landed gentry on estates of palatial grandeur.

As British soldiers and merchants often visited and traded in the Orient, they brought back exotic feathers for us from animals and birds—perfect to tie the gaudy and highly-colorful Atlantic salmon flies. Fly patterns became complex and categorized as either patterns that "caught fish," or as fanciful decorative flies.

Unfortunately, from a cerebral thinking man's aspect, all or most that was written about the anadromous salmon experience was about fly design, with little to do about the actual Atlantic salmon's behavior, effective fly presentation, or the crux of the migratory challenge. That all changed with Lee Wulff and his groundbreaking views on *Salmo salar*, as we will see in the chapters to follow.

▲ The Atlantic salmon fly art of Linda Bachand. Credit: Linda Bachand

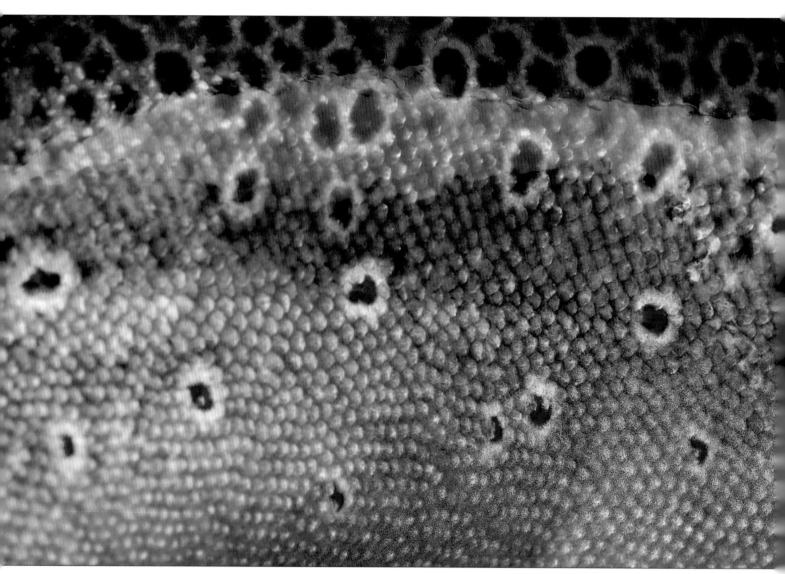

▲ The classic deep European forested spring creek morphology of red spots/white circles. Credit: Jim Klug, Yellow Dog Photo

# 4. *Salmo* Fusion: Cracking the Enigmatic Code

*T*hough millions of people have fished or admired brown trout and Atlantic salmon for millennia, it is amazing to me to know how few people know how closely they are connected to each other. When I present the two species' genetic and phenotypic parallelism to many knowledgeable anglers, chefs, and artistic aficionados, they are amazed in hindsight. In this chapter I will discuss the many uncanny behavioral cues, quirks, and similarities between the two species.

From an evolutionary standpoint, it is still unclear whether *Salmo* originated in the ocean and was anadromous—migrating back and forth between the seas and the rivers—or was river-born and eventually found passage to the ocean. But one unifying factor was the adherence to the genetic blood bond of the rivers that they love so deeply. I often look at the amazing leaping ability of the anadromous salmon and sea browns to negotiate any river obstacle like some giant falls as a "leap of joy" to be back home in the river. Another commonality are their survival adaptive strategies, as described by the Jonssons' *The Ecology of Atlantic Salmon and Brown Trout*:

> What is clearly known is that *Salmo*—both Atlantics and brown trout—survived glaciated periods through the millions of years by using habitat refuges south of the glaciated areas in the north and then eventually emerging and redistributing themselves by inhabiting and colonizing the northern rivers that became

available and hospitable during the interglacial periods.

Couple these unifying factors with the fact that they look almost identical at the parr juvenile and spawning adult phases, and you start to see how closely the species resemble each other. The anadromous sea stage, where the sea-run Atlantics or browns don the silvery gray hunting attire with marbled black spots, versus the more golden orange belly and red spotting of the river adults, is perhaps the only time you can get confused with differentiation.

The great *Salmo* legend Lee Wulff once said, "brown trout are the poor man's Atlantic salmon," referring to how difficult and finicky both species can be at any given time during the fly fishing experience. Much of what I wrote about in my book *Selectivity* (Stackpole) was born out their often-obstinate refusal to bite. Friedrich Nietzsche once said that "only through experiences of trial and suffering can the soul be strengthened," and this is no more true than when fishing for the finicky *Salmo* species. Trials and tribulations strengthen a selective *Salmo* fly fisher's soul more than conquest and elation; perhaps no other gamefish in the world has wreaked such havoc on the pursuer than *Salmo*.

## Mental Preparation for Understanding *Salmo*

As a year-round brown trout and Atlantic salmon guide, I am often asked the question "who makes for the ultimate

▲ Often misreading or over-interpreting "the bite," like misreading hatches, wrong fly pattern selection, and technical applications gone astray, can be a *Salmo* angler's downfall. Here the angler chose correctly. Credit: Albert Pesendorfer

guided client: A beginner or expert?" Obviously, having a client with a good casting efficiency is paramount to success, much like a coach training an ice hockey team that knows how to skate. But once this basic skill is established, the next most important attribute is to have an open mind and be willing to "think outside the box." Many anglers fail to realize this, which is the crux of my selectivity theories. Often the angler that has enough knowledge to be dangerous is the one that suffers from nearsighted tactical judgment.

*Salmo* selectivity issues creep into the lives of the average fly angler on occasion. It might happen a couple of times a year during complex hatches or when conditions change dramatically, causing browns or Atlantics to be fussy. To guides and anglers that are on the water close to three hundred days a year for decades, selectivity has made angling situations difficult, whether we liked it or not. We eventually learn to come up with ways to cope with the "if not A, then B, or C" in proven theoretical logical deduction. But quite often stupid dumb luck, a ridiculous presentation by less skilled angler, or a fly pattern that makes no sense reveals a hint to the solution. "Eating humble pie" and paying your dues as a fly angler, will bring you more satisfaction and eventual conquest than everyday ease. In such a way we should approach every *Salmo* refusal to a fly, skunked days, and "WTF!" moments by appreciating the frustration that leads to the much sweeter spoils of the conquest by finding the solution.

The Bible states that "men will have dominance over all the animals of the earth." I don't think brown trout and Atlantic salmon were included in this statement. If the almighty creator is a Troutsman, He will be seen scratching His head and looking into the fly box on Cairn's Pool of the Beaverkill River when trout were having a Midging fiesta as they cruise the surface ignoring excellent fly imitations, only to sip the perfect size #28 natural. I truly believe the creator designed *Salmo* to show mankind humility in its reverence for the natural world.

## Synthesizing *Salmo* Traits: The Surface Vision Infatuation

Having chased Atlantic salmon and brown trout for almost fifty years, and guiding for them year-round for over twenty-five, I have observed a series of extremely strong unifying *Salmo* factors, beyond their phenotypic appearance and genetic evolution. One very common denominator that unifies brown trout and Atlantic salmon is their orientation to surface foods.

My first experience of the surface rising factor was as a boy in my tree house on a large pool of the Wieprza River off the Baltic. The pool was a perfect laboratory for all three *Salmo* species—resident brown trout, sea trout, and Atlantic salmon occupied it at any given point in time.

▲ Poland's Wieprza River, my boyhood treehouse laboratory. Credit: Rafal Bartels

What struck me the most was no matter how deep the fish were in their current lie, they were extremely aware of everything going on the surface. The slightest wind ripple upon a calm pool seemed to change their position and alarm them. The shadow or visual cue of a bird of prey flying above like a heron, tern, or seagull would cause a nervous scurrying reshuffle of the fish according to the pool's unwritten spatial pecking order.

But perhaps what was most interesting, and affirmed later on in life, was the rising to the tiniest floating leaf, mayfly, or even a miniscule piece of twig that would often bring the Atlantics and browns up, almost with their nose practically touching it in the meniscus in a playful, nonpredatory way. This common occurrence is a testament to *Salmo*'s highly-refined binocular and peripheral vision. It also demonstrates how they focus on food in the main river system, with its nymphs and other aquatic vertebrate, while at the same time paying attention to anything on the surface, whether it is prey, foe, or a leaf.

This observation gained new meaning for me in 2007 when fishing the Mrs. Guest beat pool along the lower Grand Cascapédia River. I was with the famous Mic Mac guide Quinten, who really knew a tremendous amount about his indigenous salmon's behavior. With low water predominating at that time, we were watching a pod of very large salmon in a holding incubator pool—some over thirty pounds—finning in a perfect spatial unison school formation. It was September and a few leaves were already falling and turning color. One very large male Atlantic would come to the surface and inspect a very small orange and green leaf in the vertical complex rise formation as if he were ready to engulf it. This went on all day and continued by inspecting and refusing my green-and-orange tagged bomber dry fly. My heart wound up in my throat on several occasions as the large behemoth was just about ready to put its mouth over it, yet it stubbornly held back at the last second.

The surface arousal of brown trout and Atlantic salmon often leave us with smiting refusals coupled with a nonchalant "don't care" demeanor. Even during a good mayfly hatch this arrogant and indifferent rise form is very common among brown trout, even to perfectly-placed and drifted dry-fly presentations, and even to the most ideal natural insects. What is truly amazing is the depth and field of vision that both fish have, as well as their innate fine-tuned selectiveness.

## Psycho Fish: It "Wants What It Can't Have"

The Native American and Canadian Indian have always worshiped nature and its powerful icons by usually adoring them as godlike or spiritual in status. No matter where I traveled—from the St. Mary's River on the Ontario/ Michigan border, to the New England states and the Canadian Maritimes where both ocean migrating and landlocked Atlantic salmon exist—the unpredictable and enigmatic nature of *Salmo* has always perplexed man since the dawn of their interaction.

Both the Chippewa Indians and the Mic Macs of the Canadian Appalachian range have unique descriptions for *salar*. The Chippewas of the St. Mary's River call them "psycho fish." In the native Mic Mac dialect, *elue'wiet taqawan* often referred to crazy grilse salmon that behaved bizarre and oddly when interacting with a larger school of fish. The novel or abnormal reactions to the fly or a presentation that can totally change a *Salmo*'s demeanor and behavior, as we will see later in chapters on more specific presentations.

▲ Often the most bizarre fly and the most unconventional presentation will elicit a strike or strong interest from both brown trout and Atlantic salmon.
Credit: Arni Baldurson-Lax-A

## The "Don't Let It Get Away" Syndrome

Piggybacking on the above theme, *Salmo* is preoccupied by the movement of prey that is fleeing or escaping. The streamer hunter is very familiar with this behavior, which we will explore fully in the aggressor chapter. The classic Atlantic salmon wet fly swing is perhaps the best elicitor of this response. Also, the classic soft hackle fly technique, born on the English chalk streams and later refined in the early history of New York and Pennsylvania's brown trout waters, elicits this innate *Salmo* behavior.

To condense the response for practical purposes, it begins with a down-and-across broadside swinging motion of the fly, and the strike response being the most powerful in the critical phase between the broadsided swinging into the upward, upstream movement. It is an elicited response that resident brown trout, landlocked and ocean-running Atlantic salmon, and sea-run browns all demonstrate with a vengeance. What is truly remarkable is the degree of distance a fly can have from the *Salmo* predator subject to be noticed, and how their extreme sensitivity to movement and vibration and other visual cues plays a very powerful role.

The chasing predation response of brown trout and Atlantic salmon is very constant between the two whether they are resident or anadromous models. Here one must consider how the wild populations of both fish imprints to food forms and this prey movement at a very early juvenile state. This is contradictory to complacent hatchery fish due to the fact that their food is tossed to them.

The ability of the trout and salmon to store and maximize its potential for life survival in the form of energy is a very powerful behavioral modifier of what is prey and whether to chase it or not. Thus the perfection of wild foraging by brown trout or Atlantic salmon cannot be usually matched by hatchery mutant genetics. But given the nature of the genotypic evolution of both, eventually their predator profiles can be refined over time. By using stocked wild strains in a put, grow, and take situation, which is becoming more of an overlying fisheries management theme for much of the world's *Salmo* populations, has great implications to create wild, or near-wild behaving populations. Bror and Nina Jonsson touch on the bioenergetics of *Salmo* which they describe as:

$$P = C - (F + U) - R$$

P represents growth or surplus energy, which translates to dominance and survival of the fittest. C is the energy

▲ Master Roman Moser probes a European *Bachforelle*. Credit: Albert Pesendorfer

consumed, R is metabolic loss cost, and F and U constitute excrement and excretion, respectively. This model superimposes on the mass, length, and scale sample models that are used to determine very fit and growing *Salmo* populations, since much of a *Salmo*'s life is preoccupied with feeding and procreative spawning.

Thermal water extremes also have extreme effects on energy, and thus preferred ranges maximize growth and food consumption. Brown trout and even Atlantic salmon can tolerate higher water temperatures and have stronger energy levels, which in turn fosters a greater habitat diversity and adaptation to new environments. Adaptation has come very easily for brown trout, whereas other trout species' growth can be impacted by current flows and volatile hydrodynamic conditions. But it is the tremendous ability for brown trout and Atlantic salmon juveniles to use the rivers' hydrodynamics and current shielding by rocks, ledges, and other stream flow deflectors to cushion energy loss through exertion, due to *Salmo*'s preferred niche habitat preferences of jagged rocky substrata.

The importance of wild fish cannot be emphasized enough, as Sundstrom et al (2004) showed in their studies of how wild brown trout grew. The wild trout were more willing to attack novel objects at a sooner age than hatchery fish, which gave the wild trout an elevated dominance status in the pecking order of stream life.

The fact that *Salmo* has been interwoven for millennia between migratory strains of low-lying sea/ocean and rivers, to resident strains of often higher altitudes and diverse ecosystems, gives them the genotypic behavioral programming array of niche adjustments and diverse predator foraging profile (PFP) diversity that many other fish do not have. This diversity transcends into predation preferences along with different comfort levels of habitat, based on their unique realized/occupied niches to diverse ecosystem qualities around the world where they are now found.

## Just When You Thought You Understood *Salmo*

Ask any brown trout or Atlantic salmon angler and you will find periods of phenomenal fishing, periods of angling drought, and periods of extreme volatility. There is no question that ecosystem changes play a large role in these whimsical occurrences. Habitat variables trigger the highly-tuned survival instincts that have refined over the millennia. Often, they "go off the grid" to forage undetected. When pressured again and again through angling or unfavorable natural conditions, they will wildly change selectivity phases.

Brown trout and Atlantic salmon populations are quick to adjust, especially in high-pressure catch-and-release environments. Therefore, one cannot be surprised that the fish does not respond like trained rainbow trout from a hatchery for a pellet or bread fly. I have experienced waters where brown trout have gone to extreme carnivorous

▲ In my book *Selectivity* I detailed individual predator personalities of brown trout and Atlantic salmon and how they varied from fish to fish, river to river, and as a function of habitat and food, as here on this New York southern tier brown. Credit: Nicholas Sagnibene.

night feeding activity, or have gone to feeding on minutiae so small that you cannot tie an effective imitation. Here on my home waters of the Muskegon River during the summer, the big browns will feed on microscopic daphnia and zooplankton below the tailwater dams by the billions, like a whale filter-feeding krill, which make the fish almost impossible to catch at times. This highly-specialized feeding can instantly switch to extreme carnivorous-style forager feeding, or selectively pick out every detail of a fly or flaw in your nymph or dry presentation.

I am often amused by Robert Mansel, a very good friend and local brown trout bum of extreme tactical proficiency, who fishes for browns almost every day and has great fluctuations of luck. He tends to crush the resident fish by the dozens one day and then goes back to the same spot the next day and can't buy a fish hook-up to save his life. Migration from feeding lies and selective refusals, even to naturals, does take place, especially when *Salmo* learn a catch-and-release lesson quickly. Whether it was the Atlantic salmon I hooked as a little boy with the Green Highlander that took months for the hook to dissolve out its mouth, or a large brown trout that was caught on a double *trico* pattern spinner on Silver Creek in Idaho who subsequently learned to avoid *trico* spinners, habituation

and assimilation are part of the states of a *Salmo*'s constantly changing adaptation code.

Thus, *Salmo* are the poster children for selectivity's whimsical phase changes that is so critical for *Salmo* angling success. The adage "can't catch a fish with your line out of the water," or "can't catch a trout sitting home on the couch," brings to mind an adventure in persistence and timing I had on the Big Hole, perhaps one of Montana's most beautiful rivers. Snowcapped mountains mixed with jagged and odd-shaped rocky hills and canyons give its topography a moonlike appearance. It has arid looking tundra-like qualities, with mountain goats grazing along its conifer hillsides, as it meanders for 150 miles before meeting the Ruby and Beaverhead to form the Jefferson River. Above Wise River, it holds brook trout and grayling like a classic freestone river. From Divide down to Melrose, it is a fast-moving, cold-water sleigh ride by inflatable pontoon boat through some of the most spectacular-looking trout water your eyes will ever lay sight on. With four thousand trout per mile—the bulk of them in the 14- to 25-inch class—makes this a superb freestone wild trout fishery.

After a long spring and early summer of packing on the pounds during the prolific hatch of giant salmon flies, the Big Hole's wild browns tend to be a little fussier toward

▲ The bold and brawling brown trout utopia of the magnificent Big Hole, Montana. Credit: Craig Fellin

tiny blue-winged-olives and small caddis in late summer. This fast, cold, tumbling water doesn't hold the mayflies like other lower elevation systems, due to its violent rushing gradients. I had two days in August to float with Wise River Outfitters back in the late 1980s. Back then, it was tough to find a beer and a burger at a diner after 7:00 pm.

"Fishing has been tough," the outfitter said when I called. "No one has been catching anything with the really bad drought we have been having. We even stopped fishing for a long time. You still want to go?"

"Hell, I'm booked, I'm here, and I'm going!" I said. "The good news is we've got some really nasty weather coming—thunderstorms and a cold front—maybe the fishing will change!"

"I doubt it," said the guide, as he snacked on a bag of potato chips in his little guide cabin. In my entire lifetime of hiring guides, I've never had someone try to talk me out of going out on the river and giving them some money to do so. I must applaud this dude's honesty though.

We started off adrift at Divide. It was cold, rainy, nasty, and perfect. When we got to the put-in landing, I picked a few large *Pteronarcys* black stonefly shucks off the rocks with a smile as we slipped the floatable in the river. I showed the guide and said, "These bugs are incredible predictors and indicators of a huge barometric pressure changes in storm conditions; this has to be a good sign for water!" I told him.

"I gave up floating parachute Adams dries. They normally work but haven't for a month now," he said. It was going to be a long and hellish boat ride if fishing sucked. I took a swig of Scotch out of the flask, bundled up the raincoat and blessed myself like a good Catholic boy as we went through the first whitewater Canyon.

▲ A wild Big Hole *trutta*: Total perfection! Credit: Craig Fellin

"What are we going to throw?" I asked Darrell.

"Hell, I don't know, your guess is as good as mine." He spit tobacco chew and phlegm between mumbles. Then he had a stroke of genius. "Why don't we slap black and olive buggers against the banks?"

Amen . . . let's do it! I had a pretty stiff ten-foot, 6-weight rod that seemed perfect for the job, armed with 0X Tippet. After the fifth or sixth cast tight to the bank, the "stupid brown" gods showed up—Amen!

"What the f—?" I had a huge brown trout attack that fly and miss it. The next cast, twenty feet down, I hit pay dirt—an awesome twenty-three-inch brown that inhaled the fly. I kept casting, and caught another nineteen-inch brown. Then another twenty-one-inch brown—then another—and another! My guide was speechless for a while, then said, "I've never seen anything like this! This is just stupid!"

By the time we got to Melrose I quit fishing—my arm was literally sore. I've never seen selective brown trout become so aggressive in my life. Darrell was beside himself and smelled a very big tip, which he got. He made the brain-trust choice of fishing a common black-and-olive woolly bugger, I thought. Why not? He deserves the credit. With all that action, we never did have our gourmet streamside lunch of bologna sandwiches and Mountain Dew. What a shame.

In all hindsight, everything we did that day made sense. When we put the pontoon inflatable in at the boat landing I noticed all the large black stonefly shucks along the bank and rocks. The pounding rain of the big cold front finally broke the passive/dormant phase of the trout, as relief came in both cooler water and a massive stonefly hatch on the shoreline boulders, which these fish haven't seen since early July. The big, selective browns lost their minds and went on the hunt in the shallows looking for large *Pteronarcys* to compensate for all the stressful weeks they'd lived in the dormant phase. The last tally was seventeen brown trout landed in the sixteen- to twenty-five-inch range.

Craig Fellin of Big Hole Lodge sums up Big Hole *trutta*: "Browns are hunters; therefore, their feeding lies will take them anywhere they will find prey. They are often on the fringes in the shallows and shin-deep water, where only a perfect cast will fool them."

In closing, I never had a day like that ever again—or probably ever will. If you show up with a positive attitude, sometimes you hit the jackpot! As part of the brown trout selectivity process, the decision to show up and stay the course is a critical element, also with a changing weather system as a bonus.

▲ Credit: Torrey Collins

# 5. *Salmo Trutta*: The Master of Adaptation

To the dry fly fishermen, the brown trout is the wariest, wiliest, most fascinating, challenging, respected, and best-loved trout of all!
—Cecil E. Heacox,
*The Complete Brown Trout* (1974)

Everybody is in love with brown trout. As a guide, the sheer mention of a trophy, hogg, donkey brownie will light up customers' eyes. Everyone has their personal benchmark for their best-sized brown trout and yearns for a true leviathan. From the early writings of the English chalk stream school, to the New World mecca of the hallowed Catskill waters, to the *trutta* frontier of Montana, the brown trout is the discriminating fly fisher's *sine qua non*.

Let's look at why a brown trout is such a hyper selective creature. As with all adaptable creatures, the brown trout has been around humans for longer than civilization itself. Like dogs, it has learned to be around mankind's intrusions and has the uncanny ability to survive. Brown trout have tremendous vision capabilities in both low and high light. It is said to be negatively phototropic in that it shuns light more than others salmonid species. Thus it is very fond of cover for its holding lies in rivers and streams. Logs, boulders, bridges, deep pools, mill dams, undercuts banks—anywhere cover and security can be found—are big brown trout magnets. Lowering light levels bring out brown trout to feed—regardless if there is a hatch or not. It is no wonder that most brown trout are caught in the evenings and through the night with mouse patterns, big streamers, *Hexagenia* mayflies, and large stoneflies. As a guide, I can surely tell you on my home Michigan waters, where a good even ratio of browns to rainbows exist, the sunny days always produce more rainbows, and the cloudy or rainy days produce browns. You see the same on the big Delaware, Missouri, and other tailwaters throughout the country.

## The Eye of a *Trutta*

Were the trout so infatuated with their food that they did not care about me during the rise, or was it that, with their eyes concentrated on the nymphs and duns coming down to them, they could not see me without a special effort, or without some special cause attracting attention? If one supposed that for some reasons of self-protection, or for some other sound natural cause, the eye of the trout had a wide range of focus, so that he could see—even behind him—to quite a distance out of water when not intent on his food, and that when food was toward that focus shortened to a few—perhaps a very few—inches to deal with the business in hand, would not explain his comparative unconsciousness of the angler's presence far better than the supposition that appetite was so strong upon him as, without diminishing the acuteness of his vision, to cast out fear? It is worth thinking about.
—G. E. M. Skues, *The Way of a Trout with a Fly*

I'm quite sure that the brown trout was fully aware of Skues's pursuits, but was undaunted in light of the feeding opportunities. Anglers and scientists have studied what, how, and when a brown trout sees for the past two centuries. It wasn't until the modern works of Marinaro and the English duo of Goddard and Clarke, that we really had a clearer grasp from a fly angler's standpoint on what, and perhaps more importantly when, a trout sees what it does. By applying the principles of refraction—the bending of light rays as it passes through one medium of optical density (air) to another optical density mode (water)—which provides vision difficulties at low angles and distorted double imaging, we can now have an understanding of salmonids' optic perceptions.

The first true entomological scientist to come along as a fisherman and formulate the vision principle was Alfred Ronalds. He speculated that "brown trout could see around corners" due to the bending of light rays in refraction. He dealt mainly with how a fish perceives its predation—the angler—and vice a versa. Marinaro delved deep into underwater world of what the trout sees and if any single greatest contribution of his would be cited at the top of the list, this would be it.

His "Felix"—the brown trout images in his masterpiece, *In the Ring of the Rise*—made the complex vision easy to understand. "The inverted pyramid" was the trout's window—his eye at the downward-pointed pyramidal window. Simply put, the deeper the trout would lie, the wider and broader the window. As it approaches the surface, the window becomes narrower and more focused. Through "slant boxes" with a built-in mirror, he was able to see how a fly on the surface came into the trout window. Most flies and naturals looked like white spikes in the film; the natural had the effect from its legs, while hackle fibers on dry flies gave the same effect.

As the fly approached the trout's window, the first

▲ An angler would give his or her eyeteeth to know what it is like to see the world through a trout's eyes. Credit: Dave Jensen

obvious ascertainable fly parts were the tall wings of a dry fly or a mayfly adult. At the 10 degree angle, the silhouette of the fly became more apparent, as refraction allowed the trout to see "around corners." It was not until the fly would reach the main window that its details, body, hackle, and wings all became perfectly clear.

Since that is what a brown trout sees as it approaches from a downstream position, many anglers and theoretical observers today still feel that color is not important. But to the selective brown trout, that is absolute hogwash. We have at least a half-dozen shades of Blue-Winged-Olives and Sulpher dubbing because each degree of color intensity matches specific mayfly species, thanks to the complex scenario of light rays and their interaction. Today it is now known that UV light rays play a very significant role in brown trout vision, and it is no coincidence that more and more fly-tying materials are incorporating UV illumination into their designs and materials. In the words of Mike Depew, a fisheries biologist:

Human eyes have three types of color receptors. Specialized cones responding to light frequencies of 565 nanometers allow us to see reds. Other cones set for 535 let us see greens, and blues are detected at 440 nanometers.

Trout have four color receptors. They see the reds, greens and blues seen by humans but with some differences—what an angler sees as a dark red lure is perceived as bright red by the trout. But with the fourth set of color receptors, trout can sometimes detect ultra-violet frequencies as low as 355 nanometers, below the spectrum visible to humans.

Those ultra-violet cones are only active when the trout is young and during spawning runs. Science doesn't quite understand that. Maybe it helps them track really small prey when they're young, up to about two years old. It reappears when trout mature. It's unclear if that occurs [throughout the trout family].

Another pioneer in trout vison and UV light, Reed Curry, in his epic treatise, *The New Scientific Angling: Trout and Ultraviolet Vision* writes:

Clearly, trout possess all the mechanisms for vision in the near-ultraviolet wavelengths. Some might say "We don't know that trout *use* their UV vision in predation." However, a 2013 study done with three-spined sticklebacks, which have natural UV-reflective patterns, and yearling brown trout showed that "The presence of UV wavelengths did affect the prey choice behavior of brown trout, sticklebacks inside the UV-transmitting chamber were significantly more often attacked first than those enclosed in the UV-blocking chamber." In other words, the trout chose their prey based upon the UV-reflectivity. To trout, UV is just another color. Once the neural pathways are in place from fry-hood,

▲ A *Lithrobrancha recurvata* breaking the meniscus to hatch the classic red hex mayfly. Credit: John Miller

there is no option but to see all the "colors" the cones and rods provide. So, if trout use color at all in predation, they inevitably use the UV color as well.

Sensitivity to ultraviolet light may be useful for all of these purposes, but of course how it helps trout locate their food is what anglers are really interested in. The beta-band allows trout to see ultraviolet and see it especially well in the evening and early morning (when short wavelengths are more prevalent) as well as at night when rod cells take over the visual job.

Vince Marinaro's aquarium images encourage anglers to become more science-oriented, since scientists tend to make some of the best observations. In his tanks looking from below, aquatic insects and their imitations revealed that when a mayfly spinner is "in the film," its body and color are fully exposed. The flies that rode very high in the surface like palmered skaters or hackled Catskill-style dries only showed a few surface piercings of the feet or hackle barbules.

Since brown trout evolved on chalk streams, spring creeks, and placid free stone pools, their visual abilities adapted to the insects on these waters, usually riding "flushed" in the film, giving it its true color. If the trout's

inquiries to whether the fly is fake or real starts at the refractive angles upstream, and yet too early outside its window, the wings on the dry are first to come into the mirror's focus. So it makes sense to make sure your fly's wings are the perfect color and silhouette. As the body of the fly floats flushed in the ultimate trout window, the body segmentations and color can be easily perceived.

We have spoken much about color, but one overlooked part of the fly is body segmentation. Could this be why caddis pupae and emergers are so carefully examined by the trout, and why they have found a vogue new importance in selective trout fishing? I believe so.

## Extrasensory Perceptions

And what of the experienced fish—the fish that has seen it all before: that is not content to commit its soul to a starburst of hackle points on the surface film. For this fish, we believe that everything has to be right, including body color.

—Goddard and Clarke, *The Trout and the Fly*

The enigmatic code of a wild brownie, or even a stocked one that had at least a few months or a year to acclimate to its environmental demands, is uncannily perceptive.

Extrasensory perception—ESP or Esper, also called the sixth sense—includes information not gained through the recognized physical senses, but sensed with the mind. This "sixth sense" is a paranormal psychology term that this author should probably not be attributing to a "pea-brained fish," and many have said my observations are often over-zealous, which I am not too proud to admit. A former editor once said that I definitely tend toward an insatiable romantic anthropomorphism with my piscatorial subjects. Nevertheless, the uncanny ability for the brown trout to display a seemingly sixth sense of awareness and stay one step ahead of the angler continues to baffle the trout bums who pursue them.

Skues, Marinaro, Frank Sawyer, and many more have often concentrated on salmonids' visual abilities and the ability to discern objects and target their prey, which is very important aspect of the brown trout hunting game. But very little discussion addresses their ultimate survival mechanism—the lateral line.

Brown trout and Atlantic salmon have a highly-developed sonar-like chamber that makes up for what they lack in auditory organs. This organ, which leads directly to the nerve trunk of the brain, is perfectly able to detect the tiniest low-frequency vibration or variation in water stability. This amazing adaptation may very well be what I speculate to be the trout's sixth-sense organ. The ability to detect another swimming object or fish, whether predator or prey or schoolmate, and to discern how vibrations pass between rocks the shoreline and current flow, is an amazing way to proceed without actually seeing, especially for nocturnal feeders such as brown trout.

The brown trout is finely attuned to its habitat, and through the lateral line it can detect changes in thermal conditions, dropping river flows, etc., which will necessitate rapid evacuation or infiltration of new habitat water systems if the trout is to survive. Since its Ice Age glaciation period evolution, this lateral line became fine-tuned to the vast aquatic discrepancies from global heating to ice ages on a frequent basis.

An aspect of brown trout physiology that is particularly interesting is that as the water temperature warms up, the trout's feeding will increase until the temperature reaches a lethal zone, whereupon the trout becomes dormant and migrates to cool water thermal refuges, often a considerable distance away. This uncanny evolutionary adaptation

▲ Much of what is attributed to brown trout as being very elusive and extremely fussy in nature can be directly linked to the fact that most anglers pursue them like a bull in a china shop. A slow, steady approach, as demonstrated here by Trow and Cramer on Mossy Spring Creek, Virginia, in a very stealthy fashion, is perhaps the most important tactic a brown trout angler can employ. Credit: Matthew Supinski

allows the fish to gain as much weight as possible before going into a lockdown survival mode. This is perhaps one of the main reasons why large brown trout are so successful in pursuing and conquering mediocre and marginal trout habitats that are inhospitable to other species of coldwater trout.

## The Verve to Exist

From the moment of a brown trout's existence as a sac-fry, newly born and struggling out of its gravel cradle, it is programmed for the rest of its existence. Its senses, genetics, past experiences, carried on through behavioral DNA coded signals and evolutionary mutations, which are forever ongoing, inform the amount of "fussiness," depending on its nurturing or volatile feral surroundings. Evolutionary modifications on behavior and physiology are probably occurring at a more intense and alarming rate than ever before in brown trout and Atlantic salmon's existence, due to the instability of global climate change and civilization's encroachment on habitat. Floods, droughts, heat waves, severe anchor ice in winters, changing dramatically in short durational real time, is very damaging to the survival of a delicate cold water species unique to a particular river or ecosystems.

## Habitat

> The limits of sensory evolution in fish are defined very largely by their habitat. Water is physically supportive, carries some kinds of odor well, and is kind to sound—letting it travel several times faster than air will allow, but it inhibits other more personal kinds of communication.
>
> —Lyell Watson

Lyell Watson was a very famous South African scientist who studied nature by focusing on the unknown dimension of the human and animal world that cannot reasonably be explained or seen. If Lyell were a trout fisherman he most surely would have chased the wily brown trout, since it harbors so many interesting "sixth sense" attributes. As the old saying goes, "you are what you eat" and "you are what you wear." To the brown trout, its habitat choice preference and dominance reflects those colloquialisms perfectly.

The blood bond of the rivers that all *Salmo* have, whether it be Atlantic salmon, sea trout, or resident browns, all revolves around the details of the riverine or lake structure the brown trout choose to call home. The variables that incorporate the ideal home environment for brown trout depend upon a tight interaction of habitat features that can vary drastically from river to river but still have the same blend of significant desirable attributes.

## Niche Fusion

The Jonsson's were big on niche templates to describe the adaptable and assimilating *Salmo*. The "niche" system is a triad of four types, with water flow, velocity, oxygen, and temperature (Hutchinson, Jenkins, Bachman, Fausch, Giller). Spatial niches are the substrate and structure. Feeding niches are ones occupied for such—it is often difficult to separate spatial and feeding since they overlap. Fish use thermal niches to regulate prime water temps and oxygen content during regime fluctuations and metabolic balance alarms. And finally, trout use realized niches for shelter. If you have a fusion of the four niches you have the prime alpha lies that leviathan brown trout and Atlantic salmon seek and protect. Shelter, substrate composition and structure, current flow, and depth are the main variables in ecosystems where you find *trutta*.

## The Holy Grail of *Trutta* Territory

The study of riverine substrate is a function of how water and time etched prime *Salmo* habitat. Brown trout are extremely fond of gravel, midsize rocks, and larger boulders that provide bioenergetics conservation, shelter, ambush feeding advantages, and shade for these dark-loving photophobes. The strong attraction to these rocky

▲ Cow pasture spring creeks and finicky brown trout are synonymous, whether here on Spring Coulee in Wisconsin, or on the Wiscoy in New York. Credit: Matthew Supinski

places was revealed to me at a young age by coincidental encounters.

As a boy my dad took me fly fishing on the wonderful rolling hills and valleys of New York's southern Alleghenies. Wyoming County was a true gem. It was a pastoral landscape of rolling hills, cattle, sheep pastures, and the most fertile farms, often with an Amish influence. On our weekend outings we often camped by the stream and had fire pit grills. We purchased from a local farmer some of his Angus beef and some of the sweetest new potatoes I ever tasted. We wrapped them in tinfoil, threw them in the coals, and ate them with wild chives, garlic, and butter. With the grilled steaks, my dad would always find some wild mushrooms and sauté them in a pan with sherry—it was a meat-and-potatoes man's ultimate meal.

It was absolute paradise for two guys camping under the stars by a trout stream. My dad shared war stories about his time as a Polish partisan, and how they sent many Nazis to meet their maker. I was always entitled to a beer no matter what age I was. Life could get no better. Those are magical moments that are never forgotten.

Wyoming County had glacially-cut swift-flowing river gorges and small, gentle freestone streams emanating from spring creeks. Our favorites were the spring-fed East Coy and Wiscoy Creeks. This was serious cow country. Every adventure I seemed to have involved a run-in with a big ornery bull and a panicked sprint back to my dad, who always assured me that the cow wouldn't hurt me. I didn't believe dad when I once saw an angler get hit hard in the ass by a bull as he tried running to the other side of the creek.

East Coy was heavily stocked with yearling brown trout, which quickly started to act quite wild once the series of hatches began. Wiscoy was a totally wild catch-and-release brown fishery. Since the stream had a good combination of gravel, sand, and rocky pools, the trout were spread out throughout the river system. The boyish lure of adventure on private and posted waters would often get the best of me.

Upstream from the bridge in Hermitage was old lady Wolcott's posted property that looked just so fishy and irresistible. I would often break away from my dad and sneak into the property to catch its big aggressive fish. Only when a local sheriff asked my dad if he seen a boy of my description—scrawny Polish kid with blonde hair—did my dad realize that I was a full-blown trout-poaching trespasser.

▲ Beware of bulls in the heat of passion when fishing in cow country. Credit: Matthew Supinski

▲ Andrew Steele Nisbet with a perfect Wiscoy *trutta*. Andrew is the modern master of these western New York waters along with Nicholas Sagnibene. Credit: Andrew Steele Nisbet

Old Lady Wolcott's was a piece of *trutta* habitat perfection. It had a spring creek branch tributary coming into a deep rocky pool of gravel and boulders of all sizes, with a huge undercut bank that was the perfect leviathan brown trout condo. I had never seen such good-looking trout water throughout the entire river system. I once mustered up the courage to ask her for permission, but she looked like an old witch and scared the hell out of me when she came to the door wielding a big rake. Needless to say I ran like hell.

It was here at "the old witch pool," as I called it, that I had my first encounter with a giant brown trout on a Grey Fox Hatch. It ate my fly and broke me off due to my inability to understand how to fight big trout on light tippets—and also my poorly-tied knots. It was here on Wolcott's pool that the largest and most beautiful brown trout lived in a perfect *trutta* wonderland, where both wild and holdover stocked beasts, due to perfect union of substrate structure interacting with cold springs and diverse foraging areas, gave them the ideal "fusion niche." The newly-stocked brown trout quickly gravitated to this area as if they knew they would be protected by Mrs. Wolcott's posted signs. Anytime I found this perfect structure habitat throughout

rivers I was soon to fish, I would find the wily leviathan brown trout in command of its domain.

Besides Rocky morainal substrate, undercut eroded banks are big brown trout bunkers. These can combine nicely to add depth, even in shallow areas. Drop off shelves in the river bottom, combining with back eddies, forming with undercut bunkers from the rotational spin of the river's flow, tend to trap the biological drift into an ultimate brown trout smorgasbord. If wooded debris ties in with these niches, one complements the other and usually identifies the primary alpha dominant holding lies notorious for big brown trout.

Depth, though highly prized for concealment, cannot be too great, since usually depth allows less light, which is necessary for the lowest levels of the food chain, which translates to less trout food. But depth does often act as a thermal refuge area along with concealment and security in summer warmer months. Depth, especially when combined with high banks, is usually an indicator of underground springs entering the pool. Whenever water carves through steep rocky morainal areas, springs are exposed. On my home waters of Muskegon River in Michigan, if you find a high banks, you'll find the springs and thus larger trout.

As for flow, brown trout exhibit tremendous adaptive diversity throughout the world. This ability allows them to occupy fast flowing brooks and rivers at the highest elevations and extremely cold temperatures, down to the warmest and most marginal sections of low-lying valley rivers. Though they are niche dominators, their overall preference is for lazy, meandering rivers with higher oxygen contents and greater food source diversity. Thus flow does not always determine where trout will be, but you can always rest assured that if given the choice they will favor slower, deeper water, which is often found on the more stable, relaxed spring creeks and tailwaters that they love.

Biotic structure such as alkaline-loving shoreline vegetation like duckwort, and mid-stream weed beds such as watercress, elodea, and chara in spring creeks and tailwaters, often have perfect holding seclusion in the root channel systems that develops undercut fish hides like a tree canopy.

Manmade abiotic structures such as bridges, train trestle remnants, concrete foundations, etc. will almost surely attract a dominant *trutta*. I am forever a lover of bridges, cow stiles, waking grates, concrete and steel flow conduits, old mills, and wooden tractor bridges, because they are all magnets for large *trutta*. Bridges are the ultimate alpha big brown trout shelters. They provide the ultimate shade concealment, temperature refuge, and gather a host of food items, from mayflies, stoneflies, and caddis crawling up on their walls, to field mice running under their rafters. Water erosion against the bridge abutments usually features deep undercut banks, which are the ultimate leviathan brown niches for holding and hunting. Since the bigger browns become very carnivorous as they grow older, bridges are also familiar state and federal and provincial hatchery truck/young trout releasing points. The larger brown trout will gravitate toward bridges as water temperatures warm in the spring and cool in the fall, as if they know that hatchery trucks—Meals on Wheels as I like to call them—are on their way to deliver 8-inch hatchery fish. Another very important point on stocked, put-and-grow streams: Fall and winter will see large browns migrate to their youthful natal imprinting point of release at bridges as a spawning honing instinct, which explains their concentrations there in colder temperatures.

## Take Your Thermometer

The *trutta*'s incredible adaptability allows it to spread to more waters and watershed ecosystems than its cousins the brook and rainbow trout. Enduring water up to 80 degrees (26 degrees C)—functioning metabolically and feeding in the low 70 degrees F (21 degrees C) range, it

▲ The iconic "Three Dollar Bridge" on the Madison River, Montana. All bridges and small dams are abiotic *trutta* magnets. Credit: Mike Tsukamoto

prefers slower moving waters, which is probably 70 percent of all the trout streams and rivers with lower gradient sections; thus establishing itself in sections of rivers that are non-designated trout waters.

The brown's extreme curiosity and urge to venture into somewhat undesirable ecosystem niches make it kind of a "junkyard dog" of the trout world. Some of the best trophy brown trout waters of major rivers are near sewage treatment plants, heavily-polluted hatchery effluents, suburban artesian wells, waste discharges, and inner-city environments.

On Michigan's Au Sable River and Vermont's Battenkill, some of their halcyon days in the prime fishing decades, when anglers caught monster browns on a regular basis, sewage treatment plants were pouring unfiltered human waste into the river systems in unacceptable amounts, as compared to modern EPA standards. After the massive hatchery on the Big Spring Run of Pennsylvania ceased operation, and stopped dumping fish fecal matter, its upper stretches have become almost devoid of trout. Here, monster browns were feeding ditch pigs and ate "honey

bugs"—hatchery sewage loaded with midge larvae—which the brown trout relished and fly fishers imitated with cream chenille.

It is a fact that the food fertility of rivers and streams, especially when ultra-rich, have some invasive source that contributes to its nutrient load. It is usually overloading organic pollution or mild chemical pollution. Agricultural livestock grazing can contribute organic nutrient loads. The food chain takes a kick into overdrive when nutrients are infused into the system.

My late mentor and friend Vince Marinaro once said, "The best thing that can happen to a limestone Spring Creek is for a cow to take a dump in it!" Unfortunately the downside of riparian grazing is habitat destruction, bank degradation, and siltation. Since spring creeks emanating out of the ground are almost devoid of nutrients and oxygen, they are quite sterile. It's funny how the best fishing for large brown trout on spring creeks took place when riparian grazing damage was at its peak—Skelly's old meadow on Falling Springs Run in Chambersburg, Pennsylvania, is one such place. Here, not only did livestock roam freely,

▲ The most lethal tight-line lady nymph mistress, Nanda Sanise from Connecticut. Credit: Torrey Collins

but it was also below a small private trout hatchery, where its effluent of fecal matter contributed to the nutrient mix.

The brown trout is a highly specialized, nomadic, wild, untamed beast, whose skills have been honed for survival. It is a phantom that appears in long-lost fisheries thought to be void of trout. When Michigan decided to use wild brown trout strains from Gilchrist Creek and Sturgeon River for their hatchery and stocking programs, they found that the fish did not like being raised in the hatchery raceways. They shunned light, had to be covered, did not eat very well, and were just stubborn, like newly-captured wild cougars in a cage. When stocked as six-inch fingerlings in their new river homes, they disappeared, only to come out of hiding as fat, beautiful, wild-looking twelve- to fourteen-inch trout, ready to behave like apex predators. Today the brown, rainbow, and brook trout cohabit watersheds. Biologists must keep an eye on the extremely dominant and aggressive Brown so it does not overpower the balance, but as we will see in the last chapter, this may be inevitable in the laws of survival and evolution.

## The *Trutta* Trophic Conection

The habitat we discussed fuses with individual quirks of *trutta* behavior and biotic riverine ecosystem richness to define the rivers and lakes that *trutta* occupy. Tropism is the tendency "to be involuntarily drawn toward or away from a stimulus." *Trophic* pertains to nutrients in an ecosystem. There are peculiar individual quirks that brown trout tend to exhibit over a wide range around the world. There is no question that brown trout avoid light. If you look at the catch rates on rivers where brown and rainbow populations are roughly equal, there is no question that the cloudy rainy days often produce the best brown trout conditions.

Also, nocturnal feeding has been a long-established tradition since Jim Bashline wrote about the first angling fraternal/nocturnal order—night fishing for trout in the Allegheny Mountains. Now fishing *Pteronarcys* stoneflies, giant *Hexagenia* mayflies and mouse patterns are an increasingly popular tactic when targeting large, photosensitive, leviathan brownies.

Tactile tropism is also another very broad range attribute. Brown trout do not like to touch objects and are free-swimming creatures. They never rest on the bottom or touch obstructions, even though they hide underneath them or practically touch them.

As for temperature regimes, being cold-blooded creatures they must have a certain cold-water range dealing

▲ Dystrophic rivers can also be nutrient rich, but usually slightly acidic and less fertile because of influences outside the nutrient load of its rivers. Usually they emanate from heavily forested regions/peat bog systems that pump organic hummic acids into the system, thus run more peat/tea stained in color, like we have in Michigan and on the Dartmouth here in Québec. Credit: Matthew Supinski

from freezing to the low seventies with a preference for the mid-fifties to mid-sixties. Oxygen is a must for all fish but particularly *trutta*, which like high dissolved oxygen levels, even if they align with warmer water temperatures. This holds completely opposite for the brook trout char, which must have much colder water that is often less rich in food and oxygen, especially if it is an ice-cold underground aquifer-enriched system.

From an evolutionary and genetic viewpoint of the *Salmo* strains, each river, lake, waterway, etc. is different, but are united by ecosystem regions; that is to say, when they are in the same valley or mountain range. Trophic concepts classify the nutrient richness and productivity, which is vital for a river's ecosystem to produce unique character and life. Its character dictates how the biological food chain and its prey and predator relationships will behave on a daily basis. For instance, are the fish more surface or sub-surface oriented? Do they take larger streamers or are they focused on minutiae? Here we enter into the classification system of organizing rivers, and for all practical purposes there are three types: eutrophic, oligotrophic, and dystrophic rivers.

Oligotrophic systems are poor in nutrients and feature low-productivity food chains overall. They mainly emanate from rock and calcium carbonate headwaters, from deep subterranean caverns that are often devoid of oxygen. They usually have little organic matter until they become exposed to sunlight and wide-open spaces. If these systems were what was left after the glaciation periods ended and the brown trout infiltrated various river systems, they have adapted well to these cold sterile environments by having slender, smaller, silvery bodies. With fewer growth demands for dominance, they adapted to spawn at very small sizes. If these waterways contain aquatic insects and crustaceans, the fish will adopt bright coloration of the *Fario* European brown trout, with the red spotting and the golden orange profile.

Eutrophic rivers are the complete opposite. They are very rich in nutrients such as plankton, benthic invertebrates, etc., and tend to be more alkaline on the pH scale. These waters can often turn into marginal waters that warm up. However, large brown trout tend to thrive in these environments due to the vast array of food opportunities and their quick nomadic migratory ability.

## Ultimate *Trutta* Fusion Rivers

The key is to find rivers that have a combination of all these three factors. These rivers/streams are called "Ultimate Fusion Ecosystems." In this three-trophic utopia, you have the ideal brown trout and Atlantic salmon systems. Oligotrophic waters are very pure, cold, and clean, with ample spawning gravel, high reproductive success, and dense trout populations. Eutrophic waters have the nutrient load for a healthy diversity of aquatic insects and crustacea, along with baitfish and plankton. Dystrophic waters have the tinted stain often conducive for gregarious trout feeding and cloaking behavior, along with certain food forms like stoneflies, which prefer the acidity. Dystrophic rivers also have much wooded debris like sweepers, stumps, and log jams, which are ideal cover for lunker alpha brown trout, and harbor multi-year class brown trout populations. One highly-attributed tropism that is directly related to these dystrophic waters is the preference for cover of the wooded debris, which will satisfy the dominance and territorial aggression of adult brown trout spawners necessary to maintain high trout populations.

Thus when we find a unique balance of these factors, you'll find world-class salmonid rivers. The Big Laxa River in Iceland is an ideal "fusion" river that is a brown trout and Atlantic salmon haven. It displays the characteristics of freestone, spring creek, and tailwater with extreme fertility levels in the vast array of aquatic vertebrate and invertebrate. Other brown trout "fusion" areas are the Pere Marquette River in Michigan, Penns Creek in Pennsylvania, the Madison River in Montana, the White River in Arkansas, and the South Holston in Tennessee.

▲ Credit: Albert Pesendorfer

# 6 Food and Mimicry: *Salmo* Predator/Prey Relationships

A trout does not eat in the manner of humans or even as animals do. Humans have worked out a very satisfactory way of eating. We sit in a comfortable chair before a solidly positioned table on which are displayed, within easy reach, all the food that we may need for a full meal, and we do not need to spend much time at our eating. It is usually a very relaxing and pleasant affair. We do not go rushing about the dining room for endless hours, plucking a little bite here and there, tasting some, inspecting some, eating some; sometimes spitting out some that we do not like.

A trout does all this and more. He is forever sorting out things, constantly bringing all possible food under close scrutiny; and questions every bite that he gets. His dinner table is always in motion, sometimes very fast, and heaving violently. The bits of food coming his way are moving just as fast as the table. Then there is the endless exertion to hold his place at the table. He is not allowed to remain there but must move his entire body, sometimes a distance of many feet, to obtain something from the moving table. And always there is that reoccurring crisis of inspection and decision-making. All this is usually concluded by an amazing skill displayed in the active interception, gracefully executed with consummate ease and precision.

—Vincent Marinaro, *In the Ring of the Rise* (1976)

The brown trout is perhaps by far the most complex feeding machine or "kill artist" predator, as Vince Marinaro described it. They are a highly-evolved species with divergent predatorial urges that range from the gargantuan—small snakes, mice, and ducklings—to mayflies, aquatic insects, and minutiae such as midges. Brown trout can switch between all of these prey items in a single twenty-four-hour period.

Most aquatic animals and fish are creatures of habit and specialization in regard to their diets. Whales for instance sift large tons of krill in such a highly specialized way that it must be an evolutionary adaptation. Brown trout and bears have a lot in common; they will practically eat anything that doesn't eat them and do not discriminate their preferences but take advantage of the availability and abundance of their prey in seasonal and migratory habitat exploration.

In *Ecology of Atlantic Salmon and Brown Trout*, the Jonssons describe *trutta* as a "sit-and-wait" predator. By taking up dominant alpha lies in the appropriate habitat and tropism/trophic coordinates to their liking, the stream flow and biotic fertility in combination with their migrating ability allows them to be such connoisseurs of just about anything that could be biologically identified as food. One extreme behavior quality among brown trout that is well known to many brown trout fly fishermen, is that their fussy behavior can also result in refusals, regardless of how lifelike the fly may be or how well an angler presents it. Anglers have also experienced instances when brown trout instantly switch to feeding on a novel food item after the angler has finally determined what they were previously eating. The brown trout's curiosity and a fondness for the novel and bizarre can drive a brown trout fisherman to distraction in the constantly-changing practice of creating, redesigning, and enhancing new fly patterns that will hopefully turn the trick. No other fish inspires as much attention to detail in an angling arsenal.

## King of the Niche: Predator Foraging Profiles

If you release a large wild brown trout into a new river system that exhibits complex habitat fusion, the fish will move and migrate until it finds the ideal dominant lie that will fuel its predator preferences. Hence brown trout will take preferred feeding stations close to shelter, but also in open, fast-flowing water where the abundance of food is greater and diverse. Water clarity and viscosity has a huge effect on territorial dominance. More colored water has less visibility and allows greater fish densities with less territorial aggression. In clearer water, brown trout sense greater competition and require greater spatial separation to feel secure and dominant.

When one thinks of brown trout and Atlantic salmon, the surface feeding tendency is always emphasized. Studies conducted in Iceland, Europe, and North America suggest that this initial preference begins when small parr and fry feed heavily on black fly larvae and *Chironomid* midges. This high degree of imprinting to minutiae at a very early age translates into natal imprinting mimicry feeding at a later adulthood stage, since often parr and young of migratory fish will remain in the rivers up to four years.

Under my observations and that of scientists that have studied *Salmo* in depth, brown trout have distinct predator/prey feeding styles. The "sit-and-wait" predation detailed by the Jonssons prevails most of the time, since dominance and claim to spatial prime holding and feeding niches are highly guarded. I think that in addition to this,

▲ A curious Delaware River wild brown on the ascent. Credit: John Miller

they "roam-pick/eat-hide." These two styles will define the predator foraging profiles of a given trout's daily and lifetime foraging regime. The sit-and-wait profile is common with carnivorous attacks on baitfish, other smaller trout, crayfish, and smaller animals. In the carnivorous attacks, leviathan browns often use concealment structure or interception points for ambushing prey and it is likened to a moray eel hiding under coral and ready to pounce on its victims. It also holds true when a brown aligns itself with a perfect "bubble line," that is carrying a full-blown hatch of mayflies to it.

In a trout's "roam-pick/eat-hide" mode, the browns are more apt to take advantage of a greater diversity of prey and willing to cover territory to do so. This style is usually a result of a lack of food or of a moving food supply, like the progression of a mayfly hatch from lower river systems to the upper reaches. Or it may result from dropping water levels and increasing temperatures. In this "cruising and foraging" style, they can intercept a mayfly, stonefly, or caddis hatch near gravel riffles, drop down over weed beds of watercress and elodea and gulp crustacea, or sit positioned close to shore looking for *Chironomid* midges, and black flies, or tiny *trico* mayflies, eventually hiding to ambush a smaller sculpin or naïve trout parr as it feeds carelessly.

Brown trout predator foraging profiles (PFP) are often difficult to pinpoint since they change them so quickly. A brown trout focused on the bottom will definitely be targeting nymphs or larvae. One that is suspended in mid-depths will usually be targeting ascending emerging mayflies or caddis pupae and the occasional adult surface insect or cripple for an easy meal. Concealment brown trout obviously have larger prey on their minds, but those associated with cruising shallows and shorelines especially at nighttime will find a greater diversity of larger prey, since baitfish, small fry, and trout and salmon parr will inhabit these areas. The darkness of night conceals their presence and motions.

As for feeding and the predator/prey relationship, brown trout spend probably more time in the selective phase than most trout as a result of extreme caution. Only during intense hatches or influxes of carnivorous offerings, such as baitfish, cicadas, and abnormally large food item opportunities, will it become more careless and aggressive on the hunt, which triggers aggressive/active behavior.

## Aquatic Entomology

> The brown trout affinity for a natural floating fly—almost always a mayfly—makes dry fly angling the most fascinating, most satisfying of the trout fishing opportunities. Those anglers who have been held on the romance of the brown trout–dry fly marriage, there are few pursuits in life equal to the witchery of watching a well-directed dry fly to its appointed task. If these thoughts strike no responsive chords then no amount explaining will explain them. It is akin to a wine sophisticate trying to explain the subtle distinctions between a burgundy and the Bordeaux to a confirmed Dr. Pepper drinker!
>
> —Cecil Heacox, *The Complete Brown Trout*

Entire books have been written about each entomological peculiarity and vertebrate prey genres, so for me to get all and every specific detail would be impossible to undertake in this overall perspective. What I will attempt to do is present the *Salmo*-specific predator/prey specifics, which relates directly to my subject matter.

As a dry-fly aficionado myself, Heacox's words ring true. Heacox, a highly-trained ichthyologist from Cornell who worked for the New York State Department of Environmental Conservation, stated that mayflies make up 80 percent of the brown trout's diet. This may be true of the mayfly-rich freestone streams and tailwaters of New York. But the brown trout's adaptation allows it to adjust to the most highly substantial food forms present. The vegetation in old Big Spring in Pennsylvania was loaded with *Mancasellus* sow bugs, and comprised approximately 95 percent of the trout diet. Similar heavy feeding to one form occurs when heavy caddis fly hatches on Montana's Missouri River and Michigan's Muskegon take place.

Aquatic and terrestrial invertebrates and vertebrates form complex prey mimicry interactions between the angler and the brown trout. *Trutta* pursuers must study bug Latin, zooplankton, crustacea, bottom-scraping stoneflies, and "chicken-slinging meat" streamers. The late great Carl Richards of *Selective Trout* fame, friend and occasional fly fishing partner here on my Muskegon River in Michigan, wrote an excellent book entitled *Prey* (1997), which sums up the micro and macrocosm predatory world of hunting or being hunted. Just as a giant black hole sucks up and feeds on celestial objects around it, so in the aquatic world a *Mysis* shrimp perpetually hunts for *Daphnia* plankton. It's an ecosystem tightly connected by biochemistry as prey and predator interact in the ongoing cosmic food chain.

## Entomological Hard Drive: The Mayfly Mystique

Perhaps the single most important prey to start the Nexus food chain are the entomological elements of mayflies, stoneflies, caddis, and *chironomids*—all essential for starting juvenile and sustaining adult life in the *Salmo* world, as the combination of light and water richness fuses with the initial zooplankton and phytoplankton. These initial

▲ The mayfly is the trout's manna from heaven, here the green drake or Danica in Europe. Credit: Andrew Steele Nisbet

building block elements, along with vegetation and decaying detritus, nourish aquatic insects and baitfish as well as young *Salmo* fry and parr until they leave for the large oceans and seas, or remain as permanent *trutta* residents.

*Ephemerides*—"lasting but a day" from the Greek—shows the perfection of function through design that nature gives to all its creatures, and is a subject of passion to those who choose to fish with a dry fly. Exclusive dry fly anglers sometimes have the trappings of the British school of 1880s snobbery, and are often called purists or snobs. Thus armed with a cane rod and the historical Adams or Quill Gordon dry, they can be considered a type of stoic *Salmo* connoisseur.

As with all things British, "proper" has by far the most importance when considering anything, from cricket to drinking Scotch whiskey, and fly fishing is no exception. Frederick M. Halford and G. E. M. Skues had as their theoretical laboratories the dainty English chalk streams of Hampshire countryside. Just as Stewart vaulted the wet fly swing to the dark and tannic waters of Scotland, the crystal-clear chalk streams of the Rivers Test and Itchen permitted the close observation of brown trout as they fed on mayflies. In their "proper gentleman" tactical tug-of-war, Halford condoned dry fly adults, whereas G. E. M. Skues was a proponent of the emerging nymph. Each focused on a different aspect of the mayfly hatch; at the right time, each approach can be extremely effective.

The arrival of the German brown trout to America in the Catskill Mountains gave extreme precedent to the mayfly as the primary choice of *trutta*. The brown trout, in a perfect ecological environment like English trout stream, proceeds about his daily feeding with ease, scrutiny, and a comfortable wariness. A spring creek's ecosystem allows a food supply in ample number and diversity, every day of the year, allowing the persnickety *trutta* to play with its food. The mayfly held a strong influence both on the brown trout and the early pioneers of fly fishing such as mayfly disciples Theodore Gordon, George La Branche, and Preston Jennings.

## The Modern Mayfly Bibles: *Selective Trout* and *Hatches*

As for Theodore Gordon and the mayfly—the Catskill-anointed dean of fly fishing did not write an angler's entomology, but he tirelessly preached its importance. He never stopped telling his readers to look at the insect and learn its ways, then imitate it.

—Paul Schullery, *American Fly Fishing: A History*

The discriminating tastes of *trutta* must directly be credited for inspiring these two masterpieces. Richards and Swisher had the massively rich mayfly waters of the Rogue and Au Sable in Michigan, as Caucci and Nastasi had the Catskill

mayfly freestones and tailwaters to the east. Sprinkle in Schwiebert's *Matching the Hatch* and *Nymphs*, and Art Flick's wonderful *Streamside Guide*, and you begin to crack the enigmatic *trutta* mayfly code to these meaty delectable morsels.

I was bagging groceries at a supermarket as a young teen growing up in upstate New York when I first saw *Selective Trout*. A guy and his wife in a big new orange 1972 Chevy Suburban truck would pull up every Thursday night. He would sit in the truck reading while his wife was grocery shopping. I noticed the Trout Unlimited bumper, and thought to strike up a conversation so that I could pick his brain. Since I was on the hunt for every book and every article on fly fishing, I was astonished to see what he was reading. As I loaded his wife's groceries into the hatchback, I would always swing around to the driver side where he would give me a dollar tip. This time I saw *the* book.

"What are you reading, sir?" I asked.

"It's called *Selective Trout* by two guys from Michigan. It's really fascinating stuff. The fly patterns are incredible!"

"Wow, where can I get a copy?"

"Well, since I'm the president of Western New York Trout Unlimited, our chapter got it directly from the publisher."

"Damn—have to have that book," I mumbled. Being an avid fly tier and a fifteen-year-old know-it-all, the only place I could get the latest book was at the library—I couldn't afford to buy one at the only fly shop in Buffalo.

So what seemed like almost every day, I drove my Schwinn bicycle to ask the librarian, "Did you get that new trout book in yet?"

"No, it's on the way!"

Finally, it showed up. I felt like a Roman warrior savoring the spoils of victory as I laid my hands on this new Bible. As I signed it out and ran out of the library, I felt like I made my first car purchase. The images and sketches were amazing, the fly designs impeccable. Swisher and Richards were my new gods! I read it every waking moment between school, fishing, sports, and bagging groceries. I started tying some of the new duck wing fly designs and they fooled even the wisest wild brown trout on my beloved Wiscoy Creek. I was now the new king of all troutsmen!

I used the book so much, the pages start to fall out, thus I taped them to stop damaging my new manifesto. The cover was starting to tear and eventually fell off. I ignored the return notices and eventually became scared to death to return it. Finally my mother got a hold of a delinquent return notice and cornered me into a come-to-Jesus moment.

"Mathias! *Wo ist das buch?*" It sounded like the Gestapo had just discovered my sins.

"I don't know, I lost it!" She immediately paraded me

▲ The classical literature of the Golden Era of fly fishing. Credit: Matthew Supinski

down to the library like a war criminal and made me pay the meager five dollars—my life's savings—for the lost book charge. I apologized profusely and was grounded from playing outside.

To this day it is one of my shameful highlights of my earthly existence. The book was so powerful and addicting, I could not part with its insight. Being a diehard Catholic, I went to confession and told him about my sin. "Forgive me father for I have sinned. I stole a book on trout fishing and I have an addiction." Father Stanley, surprisingly to me, was also was a troutsman—and had my same affliction.

When Doug Swisher, an engineer, and Carl Richards, a dentist—both from Rockford, Michigan collaborated on this epic work in 1971 they knew they had something special. They subtitled the book, *A Dramatically New and Scientific Approach to Trout Fishing on Eastern and Western Rivers*. Anglers far and wide quickly heralded it as a revolutionary addition to the canon. Dan Bailey of Livingston Montana fame said that *"Selective Trout*, will be the most important contribution to fly fishing which has appeared in many a year."

Starting right off in Chapter 1, Swisher and Richards make the premise for the work and the crux of what is now my book:

The selectivity of trout has always been the most difficult and challenging of the numerous problems that confront the fly fisherman. Now and in the future, with fishing pressure increasing at a tremendous rate, the problem will become even more acute. The growing popularity of fly fishing, combined with the activities of the great dam builders, will continue to increase this pressure in the coming years. Each season we find more and more fishermen wading our favorite pools, and paralleling this trend, we find our friend the trout becoming more and more selective. With the advent of special fishing regulations and an increase in the number of no-kill areas, trout that are caught more than once become even more selective and leader shy.

Swisher and Richards realized that hard-fished Michigan and Montana favorites such as the AuSable, Pere Marquette, Muskegon, and Rogue in Michigan (rivers that I frequent and guide on today), the trout were becoming more and more selective and fussy, especially brown trout. The old Catskill patterns that seemed to work so well for decades were falling out of favor and success. These Michigan Rivers are entirely spring-fed, and gentle rivers

▲ The magnificent spring-fed Au Sable of Michigan: hallowed *trutta* laboratory for Swisher and Richards. Credit: Josh Greenberg (left); Jeff Turner (right)

or long, slow-moving tail waters like the Muskegon and Manistee produced ultra-selective fish during the caddis hatches. Combine the added new pressure of the affluent postwar leisure-seeking fly angler, and these highly-analytical and scientifically-grounded new authors presented their findings with perfect timing. The "presentation versus imitation" schools now forming throughout the world of fly fishing resembled the previous Halford dry fly versus Skues nymph debate.

Some argue presentation is 80 percent—fly choice is 20 percent—of the reason for success. Others like myself say it is highly situational and depends on the body of water, the species, and the prey fertility of the ecosystem. The entomologically-minded Swisher and Richards had no doubt about their priorities:

For us, having the right fly for a given hatch is 100 percent more effective and much more satisfying than fumbling along with something "fairly close." The right fly is the one that resembles the natural so closely that the fish seem to prefer it over the real thing. A good imitation can mean the difference between thirty fish and no fish on a given day. Many of the old standard patterns just do not work well during the selective situations. If the fish move for them at all, they drift up, take a long leisurely look, and then turn disdainfully away. But before even a realistic imitation will raise a trout, is necessary to know which fly the fish are feeding on. The Au Sable River in Michigan and other even-flowing rivers like it all over the country have many different species of aquatic insects hatching every day of the season. These rich rivers have a high lime/PH content that results in tremendous hatches; often two or three different species will be on the water at the same time.

Carl Richards's amazing insect aquarium laboratory macrophotography allowed him to delve into the underwater world of entomology unlike any other empirical fly angler that came before him and see the underwater world like his beloved browns. Using high-powered microscopes and photographic bellows in aquariums loaded with nymphs, they gave anglers a glimpse of what the brown trout sees. They analyzed their "No-Hackle" duck quill mayfly dry flies, para-duns, and emergers for countless hours in aquariums. Their articulated wiggle nymphs and sparsely-tied Sulpher and Hendrickson nymphs enhanced the slender, realistic designs pioneered by Frank Sawyer. In a stroke of genius they laid out fly charts of specific species and corresponding designs for all the mayfly, stonefly, and caddis groups.

But as perfect as their "No-Hackle" models were, there were some problems and issues with their concepts for many waters. The "No-Hackle" minimalism worked great for the gentle spring creek waters of the Au Sable where Richards crafted his work, but they were not as well-received in the fast, sweeping, frothy, boulder-strewn rivers of the East Coast or high country in Montana. The flies did not always ride high and true to form and shape. They were delicate and fell apart after one or two fish.

When I moved to Michigan back in the early 1990s, Carl Richards was a legend of the highest stature. Along with Doug Swisher, the two put up several more groundbreaking books like *Emergers*, which focused on the very misunderstood phase of the nymph to adult transformation. Their close-up time-lapse views of caddis pupae emerging underwater and wiggling *Hexagenia* nymphs were truly cutting edge. The highly scientific and clinical approach had extreme validity and shattered many myths about how nymphs and pupae ascended to the surface.

## Caucci and Nastassi: The Catskill Mayfly Renaissance

Theodore Gordon was perhaps the first mayfly designer to pick up on a *trutta*'s impeccable appetite and affliction for detail in its fly design choices. So on the foundation that Gordon and the founding Catskill gang of the modern-thinking fly designer came the Caucci and Nastasi pinnacle of Mayfly treatises.

New York City used the newly-constructed Catskill reservoir system for its freshwater supply. When the Cannonsville and Pepacton reservoirs were constructed in the 1950s, which blocked the West and East branches of the world-famous Delaware River, little did anyone know its implications for creating one of the greatest wild brown trout meccas is history. Here we have these two huge impoundments containing roughly three hundred billion gallons of icy water up to two hundred feet. Prior to these man-made creations the upper Delaware watershed was primarily warm water rivers with trout in their headwaters and bass and shad in their lower reaches. The "Big D," as Delaware is called, always had many fishing opportunities all the way to its New Jersey border. They stocked it with Atlantic salmon back in the late 1800s and today have runs of shad and eels. Also, every type of warm water fish is found. This quickly changed in a radical way. The West, East, and Main Delaware had ideal temperatures and habitat for supporting wild brown trout almost overnight. Actually, they were almost too cold and perfect!

So with the native brook trout and newly transplanted German browns in the upper watersheds established, along with a fantastic new California rainbow trout strain, the last pieces of the newly-transformed river puzzle was about to be unleashed by nature—mayflies! With the cold, stable spring creek–like flows, harboring tons of vegetation, gravel, boulders, and silt, mayfly life exploded by the early 1970s. Every species and family of *ephemerella* blossomed at an incredible rate. Soon wild brown trout populations were becoming dominant in the main stem of the River, along with its 1880s rainbow transplants who were already very wild and selective mayfly takers. Over a dozen types of mayflies from Blue-Winged Olives and Sulphers, anywhere from size 10 to 26, was a common sight on the Delaware. Anglers soon found the old Catskill-style dries to be less effective. The appearance of the book *Hatches* by Al Caucci and Bob Nastasi couldn't have appeared at a more critical and appropriate time.

Al Caucci and Bob Nastasi were two very different personalities. Caucci, a mechanical engineer, was scientific,

▲ The wild brown utopia of the Catskills' Delaware. Credit: John Miller

and bug-minded. Nastasi, a graphic artist in advertising, had an eye for detail. Soon afer the release of *Hatches*, fly anglers along the Delaware started to drop Latin buzzwords like, *iso's*, *steno's*, *lata's*, and *pseudo's*. Almost overnight, anglers invested into the Latin concept with confidence and no longer referred to a hatch as "those little green thingies."

But no fly fishing book can hold an audience with just scientific facts. There has to be a solid recognition to fly fishing techniques for it to be interesting—and this book provided that link with the Compara-Dun flies. The Compara-Dun dry fly concept, with durable and buoyant wings of deer hair, proved so much more practical than the delicate Swisher/Richards feather- or quill-winged flies, that they quickly captured the loyalty of many trout anglers. Caucci and Nastasi soon capitalized on their moment by selling their "Compara-Brand"—Lebron James style. Insect hatch charts, Compara-Dun materials, dubbing, coastal deer hair for adults and their Compara-Emerger, as well as their guide service and Delaware River Club Lodge made them marketing masters and helped thousands of fly anglers delve deeper into the world of selective trout fishing driven by Delaware's fussy browns.

## Keeping Aquatic Insect Prey in Perspective

For anglers, bug Latin can be controversial. As we have seen with the early Catskill angling, where the rocky gravel substrata of its rivers generated massive numbers of mayflies, the first authors who wrote the annals of entomological hatch-matching, such as La Branche, Rhead, Jennings, Gordon, and Hewitt, showed a profound fondness for mayflies. There is no question with the relationship that mayflies have with *Salmo*—brown trout, Atlantic salmon, and landlocked salmon—since the East Coast and Michigan waters were their initial domains. Michigan can be saturated with mayfly hatches of overabundance to the point where it is often difficult to fish during hatches, due to the sheer numbers of mayflies from the very large *Hexagenia*, to the micro *Pseudocleon* Blue-Winged Olives and *Tricos*.

*Salmo* will always humble the hatch-analyzing angler, as their food choices are a reflection of the unique micro-regional ecosystem adaptations to insect prey and what seems to be the most popular item on the menu in that region. Scientists studied a stream in the Spanish Pyrenees (Montori et al, 2006) for *trutta* aquatic insect preferences and discovered that the trout consistently chose *Ephemeroptera* over other aquatic insects on a consistent basis due to the rock/gravel formations of the freestone streams and dense forests, which are ideal habitat for mayflies.

In another study (Fochetti et al, 2008), the exact opposite took place on an Italian River, where there was a *negative* reaction to micro-mayflies throughout in all age classes of brown trout. Fish three years and under instead preferred *Trichopteran* caddis larvae, while fish three years and older favored larger *Pteronarcys* stonefly nymphs. So even when mayflies are abundant, trout can exhibit food preference imprinting for other species on an ecosystem-by-ecosystem basis. It is thus very important to learn the rivers that you fish on a consistent basis, take some samples from stomach pump suction tubes, constantly turn rocks over, and study the benthic ever-changing environment.

Larger stoneflies often hide under stones and logs that are very difficult to capture for smaller *trutta* and *salar*. The older your classes manage to creatively invent ways of moving rocks and twigs with their snouts and bodies to forage larger food items. These behaviors eventually become carnivorous.

Overall in the parr and riverine states, younger brown trout and Atlantic salmon often develop very similar likings for all the insect groups and macro vertebrates. One spatial separation niche that occurs in Atlantic salmon is that they will often pick up stronger stream current positions than juvenile brown trout. Thus they often see insects that can handle the stronger follows, and can become dependent on those insect types.

Is also important to note that young-of-year parr brown trout and Atlantic salmon feed in groups based on hierarchy structure, body size, and current flow tolerance, which is directly related to predation. These hierarchical predatory groups will then translate into future aggressive predation personalities that manifest in pelagic school hunting in the ocean as adults, and to brown trout territorial spawning and habitat-seeking dominance in river systems. We will see more of this learned dominance as we go into the chapter on *trutta* the aggressor, and discuss the implications for school-related feeding.

## Mayfly Manna Effortlessly

Many accomplishments had a prideful beginning; this book, however, started as a direct result of a humbling experience—an evening of angling failure in the West branch of the Delaware some year ago. The stream was as peaceful as ever, the serenity of impending nightfall only interrupted by the reverberating sounds of trout feeding gently on delicate pale evening duns. It is the memory of two big browns that rose for over an hour that caused that evening to remain so fixed in my mind. Steadily those two old-timers seized every unfolding winged adult as they barely slipped out of their nymphal cases, while they remained unmindful of my created "hatches" of artificial nymphs and dries of many sorts.

—Fred L. Arbona Jr., *Mayflies, the Angler, and the Trout*

▲ A Delaware guide's mayfly CDC arsenal. Credit: John Miller

There is no disputing the hard-wired feeding habits *Salmo* have for mayflies. Michigan aquatic entomological masters from East Lansing's Michigan State University produced masterpieces—*An Introduction to the Aquatic Insects of North America* by Merritt and Cummins, and *Mayflies of Michigan Trout Streams* by Leonard and Leonard—demonstrating *trutta*'s ferocious appetite for mayflies of all sizes. Again, their habitat preference for rock boulder/gravel definitely gives them a strong bond with this prey of choice, or perhaps coincidental convenience:

> In Michigan trout streams, the greatest number of mayfly nymphs, both in species and individuals, will be encountered in gravel riffle areas. One such riffle in the Pere Marquette River in Lake County, sampled in May of 1947, yielded nymphs of thirty-three species; and a square-foot bottom sample from a gravel area in the North Branch of the Au Sable River in Crawford county contained 1,374 nymphs; 1,277 of them *Ephemerella* invaria and subvaria.
>
> —Leonard and Leonard,
> *Mayflies of Michigan*

I have always been a big proponent of chicken-or-the-egg theories. Much of what has occurred in evolution in nature and niche specialization usually results from a series of events and circumstances that eventually shape and mold the creature as a direct result of situational repetition and being in the right place at the right time. Just as a large gluttonous human prefers to slowly meander down a very long and heavily-stocked buffet line versus picking at daintily arranged artistic tidbits on nouvelle cuisine plates, so goes it with the brown trout's love for mayflies.

For the most part mayflies are very slow swimming and emerging insects. Once on the surface they seem to spend an enormous amount of time drying their wings and struggling to break free of their nymphal shucks. Except for the fast-swimming nymphs of *Siphlonurus* and *Isonychia*, they move as slowly as a brown trout does in its predator attack speeds. Out of all the salmonids the maximum brown trout predatory strike speed is approximately 5 to 8 miles per hour. By contrast, its direct cousin the Atlantic salmon can attack at up to 32 miles an hour. These differences reflect the two species' habitats and prerequisites.

In my *Selectivity* book I analyzed situational quagmires or coincidences in relationship with how the genetic programming behavior of the trout and salmon evolved and habituated to feeding. Does a brown trout come out in the evening knowing that it will experience the evening mayfly

hatch and spinner fall, or does it come out because light levels had diminished its photophobic paranoia?

Mayfly hatches often have a short and concentrated duration in ideal hatching situations and thus pack a powerful caloric serving for the predatory brown trout, which does not like to be exposed for very long periods of time and is forever paranoid of avian predation, shadows, noises, and anything that can send it for cover. Of all the trout, *Salmo* is by far a paranoid creature and the more the angler can identify with that the more successful they will be. In *Mayflies, the Angler, and the Trout,* Arbona sheds light on this paranoia, in the context of selectivity:

Selectivity on the part of trout during concentrated hatches of certain insects is finally being accepted by anglers. However, the reasons for selection are probably more complex than just being a direct function of availability (abundance of the emerging natural) and consequential short-term conditioning. In the case of the little *Baetidae* it is just as plausible that selectivity is also the trout's best defense against anglers. Since very small artificials (hook sizes No. 18 and smaller ) are seldom used by anglers, a trout's negative experiences with artificial imitations of such sizes are rare enough for it to consider feeding on the small mayflies safe, free from the treachery of man.

## The Ephemeridae Smorgasbord

For sheer simplicity, most biologists will agree that four families or groups of mayflies form up to 90 percent of a riverine brown trout's or Atlantic salmon's diet. They can

▲ Author's Nexus Nymph Articulation. Brown trout love *Isonychia* and other meaty mayflies that are fast swimmers. Articulation is the prefect mimicry. Credit: Stacy Niedzwiecki (top); John Miller (bottom)

▲ Credit: Albert Pesendorfer

▲ Matching the mayfly adult hatch is crucial to catching selective *trutta*.
Credit: John Miller

thrive in either acidic or alkaline waters, but prefer a mix of pH ranges in the middle or towards alkalinity.

## CRAWLERS

Genus: *Ephemerella, Caenidae, Tricorythidae, Leptophlebidae, Baetiscidae*—including subgenus groups like *Drunella* etc.

**Habitat:** This group is the most diversified habitat can tolerate every type of water condition from slow to roaring rapids, due to its crawling capacity to the benthic environment. The *Ephemerella* group—such as Spring's Slatewings, Hendricksons, and large Blue-Winged Olives—is extremely vulnerable to *Salmo* because of the time it takes to emerge and eventually hatch. These important yet delicate mayfly hatches of April and May along most of the eastern and Midwestern rivers are usually the first significant mayfly emergences *Salmo* will encounter. The *Paraleptophlebia* and subvaria will usually choose the warmest part of the day—around noon till mid-afternoon—to emerge, waiting for the cold spring waters to warm up. Spinner falls will occur around dinnertime or earlier on very cold days, and as the spring gets warmer with more sunlight, spinner falls occur later.

**Notes:** These insects have very lethargic hatching times and long biological drifts for the nymphs. Browns will often take their time leisurely feeding on duns or emergers, even when adults are on the water in good numbers. In this case, fishing an emerger nymph tandem rig often works best. The females have a very pronounced orange egg sac, which many fly tiers incorporate into their adult patterns. A simple pheasant tail nymph is very effective during this hatch.

The dark rusty colors of the spinners are often difficult to detect. One common mistake most fly fisherman do on warmer days is to leave the stream too early. Their flights will gradually go towards dusk, where the bigger browns will feed, often undetected by the angler. Selective trout relish a thick, juicy spinner of the crawler family, and canny hatch-matchers are well-advised to target this spinner fall.

## Black Quills

These thick, meaty mayflies are lovers of slow, slack waters with abundant riverbank vegetation and wooded debris. They also are very sluggish when hatching and will climb onto vegetation, tree roots, or rocks to emerge. Dead-drift a nymph slowly towards the shoreline and you'll be rewarded.

The spinners look very similar to the gray drakes and are often confused for them. Michigan's rivers like the Rogue and Pere Marquette, along with the Au Sable, have excellent habitat for these mayflies, which coincide perfectly with prime brown trout holding lies next to wooded debris.

## Sulphers

Perhaps no other mayfly stirs up more attention than this group. The eastern *invaria* and *dorotheas*, and western Pale Morning Dun *infrequens*, are slow-hatching drifters, which *trutta* and small migrating salmonids target heavily. They favor medium to fast water habitats and wiggle enticingly during their ascent. As adults, their emergence is very slow, and they will also float and quiver for long distances, which *trutta* selectively notice. A twitch to your meniscus natural is often the key to a take. Selective browns are extremely particular to the varying shades of these mayflies—from greenish-yellow/deep orange/light yellow white.

▲ The well sought-after sulpher known as "Pale Wateries" by the English.
Credit: John Miller

▲ CDC sulpher emerger. Credit: Stacy Niedzwiecki

A cul-de-canard adult/emerger compara-style pattern with a brown Z-lon shuck and a pheasant tail nymph is all you'll need to fool the most selective fish. Snowshoe rabbit also makes excellent emerger wings. The spinner falls at dusk and can be extremely heavy; don't leave the river too early. On ice-cold tail waters and spring creeks, they have multiple broods, and can emerge all summer. Most freestone rivers will see a spring emergence. As for the "white curse"—*Tricos/Caenis*—big selective browns will often target double or triple spinner patterns. A very stealthy approach and careful timing of fish rise intervals is critical to success.

## CLINGERS

Genus: *Stenonema, Epeorus Heptagenia, Rhithrogenia, Cinygmula*

### Quill Gordon and March Browns

Due to their hearty size and the fact that they emerge sporadically throughout the day, these large, early-season, mottled-winged delicacies are relished by large browns throughout the East and Midwest. When they hatch they struggle strenuously to emerge in the cold surface meniscus; their vulnerability is enticing. As the adults dry their wings, they float for long distances before flight, and are easy prey in the cold water conditions of May. Their high wing profile appears to be particularly noticeable to browns, particularly in faster-flowing freestone rivers.

If you are in search of an early spring trophy brown or landlocked salmon, the Quill Gordon and March Brown hatches bring bigger fish up to the top that usually don't feed there.

### Light Cahill and Grey Fox

These beautiful and delicate-looking white and peach

mayflies are often impossible to miss, even for anglers that have a tough time seeing hatches. Their amber-colored bodies are best imitated by an articulated wiggle nymph or a bushy Hare's Ear. Browns take a affection to the peach thick bodied female spinners.

▲ Classic Cahill/Stenonema eyes. Credit: John Miller

When the adult Grey Fox hatch in the spring, as well as Cahills sporadically from spring through fall, the clumsy attempts to get off the water attract feeding trout in good numbers. As they float they flutter relentlessly; many trout only target fluttering duns, so impart twitches to your presentations. Their spinner flights can be very impressive and happen at dusk and well into the night. On large, long, flat tail waters and freestone streams like the Delaware and Beaverkill, surface dimpling occurs till midnight.

## BURROWERS

GENUS: *Ephemera, Hexagenia, Lithrobrancha, Potamanthus, Ephoron*

### Green and Brown Drakes

With gargantuan sizes compared to the other mayflies, the Green and Brown Drake with their big, fat meaty bodies and mottled wings bring up the most selective leviathan browns and migrating salmonid juveniles. On the first night of their hatch, many anglers are often confused as to why the fish are not targeting such a perfect easy prey. It may be out of sheer caution, or perhaps because the trout have been feeding on the nymphs several days prior to the adults' emergence. But once the trout start targeting adults, this hatch becomes an incredible selectivity game all unto itself. In famous Green Drake waters like Penns Creek and the Delaware tailwaters, the trout drive anglers crazy with complex and compound rises to the adult mayflies. They look for the tiniest twitch or

▲ Brown drake above and the author's new Nexus creation: The Frosty Drex.
Credit: John Miller (top); Author (bottom)

silted parts of the river where large browns love to hang out. One case in point is the Yellow Breeches in Pennsylvania and long silted pools of Catskill rivers.

These giant kings of all mayflies are a spectacle of nature. Fish of all sizes try to gorge on them during their short June–July emergence. *Hexagenia* nymphs are lovers of silt bottoms in low gradient rivers, like the Au Sable, as well as the Pere Marquette and all its spring-fed systems, where brown trout, immature steelhead, and salmon target them. Its amber-brown body is best imitated by a wiggle-articulated nymph, which brings strong violent strikes, and calls for heavy tippet material.

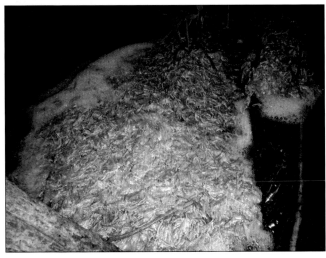

▲ The giant *Hexagenia*, king of all mayflies, and the massive "mush" of congested spinners in a backeddy that giant browns slurp all night. Credit: John Miller and Aaron Vanderwall

twitter that the adult might impart, for the trout to signal in on the real deal, versus the imitation. The Green Drake nymph—along with the Brown Drake, is best imitated by a wiggle-articulated nymph, stripped, twitched, and swung down-and-across the surface. The Coffin Fly spinner will also bring tremendous rises.

Every trout in the River will feed on these large Green and Brown Drake mayflies, so it is important to target a specific large browns, which rise less frequently but with larger air bubbles when they sip these bugs. While the Green Drake is predominantly an East coast affair, the Brown Drake has a significant Midwestern and West Coast emergence, particularly on the Au Sable of Michigan and Silver Creek in Idaho. Timing is everything with these two hatches; being there when the hatches are at peak is sometimes not the best, since there are too many naturals. The beginning of the hatch, and as the hatch wanes, usually produce the bigger, more selective fish.

### Hexagenia and Potamanthus

These mayfly hatches consistently catch the largest browns in a river system. Even many seasoned troutsmen who know their rivers well don't realize their streams have *Hexagenia* hatches, often in the lower, more marginal,

Adult patterns usually incorporate deer hair, new extended body foam imitations, white calf tails, and grizzly hackle wings. *Hexagenia* have taken over the entire Great Lakes habitat, and bring on blizzard swarms that cover city streets like Cleveland along Lake Erie with yellow snowflakes of mayflies. In the St. Mary's river emanating out of Lake Superior, giant migrating Atlantics feed on them for weeks on the surface—imagine floating a dry to a fifteen-pound *salar* that is targeting mayflies!

The *Hexagenia* has become an incredible food source for Great Lakes steelhead and brown trout into big lake environments due to their proliferation. Thus, it is a very important nymph to have.

The *Potamanthus* or Golden Drake is a July emerger on big, silty pools of freestone rivers. They are not as prolific in their hatching as the *Hexagenia* and are usually sporadic in emergence throughout the day on cold tailwaters or sporadically in the dusk on a warmer freestone river, predominantly in the Catskills. When they emerge, usually you'll see one here and there. They float for long periods of time and very few escape a large trout's inspection and palate.

## SWIMMERS

Genus: *Baetis, Pseudocloeon, Callibaetis, Centroptilum, Isonychia, Siphlonorus*

### Tiny Blue-Winged Olives

From spring creeks to tail waters and Freestone Rivers, Blue-Winged Olives are probably the most important and consistent hatches for selective rising *trutta*. Ranging in sizes from the #16–20 *Baetis*, to the tiny #26 "*Pseudos*," these mayflies are usually on the water year-round, having multi-brood potential. They are lovers of cloudy, overcast, drizzly days and hatch very slowly as the nymphs wiggle to the surface. As adults, they flow for long distances and emerge very slowly, thus making them extremely vulnerable to the trout. In big tailwaters like the Delaware and Farmington, there will be every size of Blue-Winged Olive hatching at one time, creating a complex masking hatch scenario. Trout will tend to feed on a particular size to their liking. If you are getting refusal after refusal, a hand seine net to observe what's happening on the surface of the river will give you an idea of what to present to picky fish.

*Centroptilum* is a Sulpher-colored #20 mayfly, and extremely important on Western spring creeks in late summer and fall. It is also a lover of cloudy, overcast days, and I have had spectacular fishing in the Poindexter Slough near Dillon, Montana, just as a thunderstorm was passing through on a hot summer's afternoon, when its impossible-to-catch browns went crazy for emergers.

▲ The delicate Blue-Winged Olive, or Iron Blue as it is sometimes known in Britain. Credit: John Miller

▲ The author named his lodge after the massive, six-week long, stifling thick hatches of the Gray Drake *Siphlonurus*. Credit: John Miller

Mention the word "ISO" to any dry-fly hatch-matcher, and his pupils will dilate with excitement. This big, meaty, juicy mayfly with its purple-greenish body will elicit severe attention from large browns, as it hatches from the spring through summer and into the fall on Eastern and Midwestern rivers. Its nymphs are extremely fast swimmers, and swinging an wiggle-articulated Isocaine nymph of my own creation down and across and near the surface, can bring jolting strikes. *Isonychias* will either emerge midstream or crawl up on the rocks in the bank to emerge.

Though Gray Drakes exist from the East Coast to West Coast, their heaviest emergence is in Michigan, on low-gradient silt and gravel rivers with woody debris and shoreline vegetation. The Gray Drake nymphs swim as fast as minnows, and scurry to the shoreline to crawl off and hatch. The spinner fall is the most important game. Each night from mid-May to early July, massive mating swarms hover over the riffles, only to fall en masse to hungry browns waiting in runs and pools below. The body of the spinner shrivels up and curves; tying imitations with a similar curve can often be the trick for very fussy fish.

## Stoneflies

If I had but one fly to use to entice a large "*trutta*-saurus" brown trout or even an Atlantic salmon, it would unquestionably be a large, meaty, black, and buggy-looking *Pteronarcys* stonefly nymph. With the stonefly, the *Salmo* prey/predator relationship is a perfect collaboration of preferred habitat, and large, meaty morsels of food coming into a coincidental relationship that benefits the *Salmo*. Where conditions and habitat are perfect for *Plecoptera* thriving in incredible numbers, it is usually at the expense of the mayfly nymphs, which the larger stoneflies eat.

My initial experience with "Steinfliegen" as they are known in Germany, once again goes back to my youth in the US and in Europe. It was first in western New York, as a young boy growing up on the Niagara frontier, where on the fertile spring creek waters of the Wiscoy and Oatka Creeks, and then again later as a college graduate touring Europe while doing a culinary apprenticeship, was when I experienced the full scope of the importance of stoneflies.

In the summer of 1981, I was given a culinary apprenticeship in Rome. Since my parents bought me a Eurail

▲ The magnificent stonefly. Credit: John Miller

pass, during time off, I went to nearby Austria and Poland to visit relatives I'd never met or vaguely recalled. I remember stories about Hemingway and Charles Ritz fishing the high Austrian trout rivers, where European fly masters like Roman Moser ply their trade today. The scenery itself is breathtaking.

One holiday jaunt, Aunt Ingrid met me at the train station in Salzburg. The Trans-Alpino train ride took me past the towering snowcapped Alps, the green valleys of grazing sheep and cattle, and over countless cascading bluegreen rivers that probably teemed with wild brown trout and grayling. After a great dinner of Austrian sausages, sauerkraut, breads, and pastries, I indulged in the large steins of Märzen beer and shots of schnapps. After feeling no pain my first order of business was fishing. "*Meine liebe tante*, how can I fish for trout here?" I asked. Aunt Ingrid replied that the rivers were private, and access to them too expensive for a college student, but that she knew a family with a sheep farm that ran along the Salzach River as well as other rivers. The sons were "*Fliegenfischers*." After a few calls, my uncle drove me to the estate to stay with the family and fish.

There I met Stefan and Jürgen, who were then in their mid-thirties. They had French-made Pezon-et-Michel cane rods, Hardy reels, and tied their own flies. They said they guided tourists from France, Switzerland, and Vienna during the summers. I told him I was a poor American student with a ravenous appetite for big brown trout, cute blond Austrian girls, beer, sausages, and schnapps. I could only repay them by sitting at their vice and tying some fancy upscale American flies and offered to take them steelhead fishing on my home waters of the Great Lakes if they ever come to America. We had a deal!

They told me I could not have timed my arrival better— the "Steinfliegen," were on the water. The trout and grayling were sucking them up fast, but could be really fickle. Ernest Schwiebert's *Nymphs* was my bible in high school, which took *Plecoptera* to a higher level, thus I was well familiar with *Pteronarcys*, *Isoperla*, and *Acroneria* stoneflies. I had a good selection of them in the fly box I brought with me, that I used on my southern tier of New York State trout streams. When I woke up the first of two mornings, I scoured the rocks and boulders along the shoreline of the river by my farm bunkhouse. Giant yellow brown and dark stonefly shucks were everywhere. The brothers lent me a hand-me-down bamboo rod reserved for guests, for which I was much obliged, along with some French Tortue tippet material and a few of their crude stonefly imitations.

▲ Stonefly nymphs, the Angus prime meaty delights of *Salmo*. Credit: John Miller

"No thanks on the flies—I have a few of my own!" I said, in my brash cocky American manner, and proceeded to open up my fly box. Their eyes popped wide open as they started grabbing! No worries I thought, I got plenty! Most of my patterns were Brooks-style Western Madison River patterns, along with some sofa pillow dries. Tying one on, my hands were still shaking from the previous night's indulgence of the beer and schnapps. It felt like Saturday morning at the fraternity house. "We will meet for dinner, have more Märzen beer and schnapps around five. Have fun! If you catch any nice trout, club them on the head and we will have it for dinner—or for the smoker!" Jürgen told me. "No thanks, I let them all go!" I replied. They smiled and mumbled something like "crazy American," as they drove away, leaving me to the trout stream by myself. I was in paradise!

The first thing that caught my attention was how amazing it was that the browns and grayling hunted the rocks in the shoreline for stoneflies migrating toward them, or to pounce on the occasional hatching adult. It was a dark, rainy day—the stonefly emergence was sporadic, and I was tight-lining deep in the water. Now I know why Czech/Polish nymphing is so effective there. You are dredging the bottom, often close to shore and rocky boulder situations, which are perfect hangouts for stoneflies and caddis larvae. You somewhat lead the fly in this technique with a very tight line, allowing the nymphs to slide up and down the rocks and boulders just like a natural crawling stonefly and watching a sight indicator, which back then was a little orange yarn in the leader.

The grayling were much more cooperative, with some pretty fat specimens taken. But the wild browns were a different matter. The giant golden *Acroneria* stonefly nymphs had a peculiar crawling and tumbling behavior that these freestone trout keyed in on. Due to the extreme clarity of the water, I could sit on a rock and watch them feed.

▲ Even with very swift Alpine waters, browns are selective, and Roman Moser makes the art of stonefly nymphing a challenge and a delight. Credit: Albert Pesendorfer

When I fished the nymph, I drifted it, then twitched it, and drifted it again. My first good-sized brown trout, a beautifully-colored specimen about sixteen inches, smashed the nymph pattern very hard. I could see the golden-orange belly in the deep, rocky shoot of swift water. But for every take I had, there were many flash refusals—they either missed the fly due to the sheer flow of the water, or rejected it at the last second. Most of the fish were beautiful wild browns in the twelve- to fifteen-inch range, and had magnificent red dots with white circles.

I did manage to see one very large twenty-plus-inch brown over the two days in Austrian angling nirvana. The big brown wanted nothing to do with me and gave me two major refusals to meaty stones. This guy has been educated! Here the key factor for success was the behavior of the natural and moving the stonefly the way it did as it gyrated, crawled, and bumped along the swift alpine river floor. In hindsight, I believe the flashes I saw, which I presumed to be refusals, were actually takers and that I set the hook too early and pulled the nymphs out of the fish's mouth. The moral of this story is, let the fish take your fly in swift-current waters: the flow will set the hook for you, so don't blow the deal!

## Plecoptera on the Madison

The nymphs of the big *Perla Pteronarcys* on Eastern rivers emerge sporadically for several weeks, with a hatch that is never equal to the blizzard like stonefly flights typical of early summer in the West however. Big East coast species are readily recognized and accepted by the trout, and imitations of the nymphs consistently produce large fish.

The Madison is a special case, and when the big autumn browns are running and in a taking mood, it is like a run at the tables of some elegant casino.

—Ernest Schwiebert, *Nymphs*

When I first laid eyes on the headwaters of the Madison River in the wild and rugged Yellowstone country, I was completely blown away by the most perfect-looking trout water that ever existed on this planet. In retrospect today, I could understand why Kelly Galloup, a Michigan guide, author, and lodge owner, moved there to establish his Slide Inn trout legacy. The headwaters of this rich and fertile alkaline river are born in geysers and hot springs. The *elodea, chara,* and watercress channels look like a

▲ The incredible diversity that the Madison possesses in its Alpine Lake Meadows quickly changes character as it gathers more water and stronger current into deeper holes and fast boulder structures, and the stonefly is its most productive for the angler. Credit: Mike Tsukamoto

giant spring creek you would see along the River Test in England. Its rich insect life inhabits boulder and gravel riffles that are home to some of the most magnificent stonefly populations, and it is indigenous to Western rainbows. But the evasive and aggressive brown trout now dominate and grow large in size.

The Madison's water is tricky to read at times since it can go from shallow boulder runs to deep holding lies quickly. The beauty of this water is all the detritus food the stonefly nymphs have, being the perfect boulder habitat and vegetation. The Woolly Worm, Montana nymph, and Bitch Creek nymphs are all attractive to the hefty *trutta*.

Farther to the north, the Big Hole runs cold and fast. From the gorgeous stretch down from Twin Bridges to the spring creek–like waters of the Wise River, the giant salmon fly, *Pteronarcys californica*, sends the wild browns into a frenzy. The nymphs have a deep, dark chocolate color. When the huge bugs hatch, twitching and skittering a golden salmon fly sofa pillow can be irresistible to the

browns. Initially they feed cautiously, but then become aggressive and eat with reckless abandonment.

Brown trout and Atlantic salmon both are fond of the entire spectrum of stoneflies, including the golden, yellow brown, and olive stones. The Northeast of the United States and Canada has a very unique-looking bright chartreuse green stonefly that is imitated by Atlantic salmon fishermen with Lee Wulff's needle tip designs.

On my river in Michigan, the Muskegon, and many Eastern rivers and trout streams, the early tiny black stoneflies *Taeniopteryx* and *Allocapnia* are often the first hatches of the year after a long winter. They are almost always mistaken for caddis due to their fluttering wings and profile. The tiny grayish-black nymphs wiggle endlessly in the early winter until they reach the bank and crawl along the snow. Browns love to hunt the perimeters, and these are ideal food sources in the cold temps. Though tons of egg-laying adults will be on the surface, the browns will usually be packing away the nymphs just below. In the colder temperatures, trout seem to take

▲ When you rummage through your fly boxes, if you had but one fly to fish for seclusion-loving leviathan browns, it would be a giant Kaufman's or Brook's stone fly resembling a big black meaty *Pteronarcys*. Credit: Author

forever to feed on them, since they are just waking out of a long metabolic hibernation. The long drifting times of the egg-laying females sometimes cause a long, complex inspection to take the dry fly, thus making the intervals of dry fly interception by the browns seem much longer than normal. This hatch also has a great tendency to induce very small rise forms that appear to be smaller fish, but some of the biggest Browns will barely scratch the surface when taking the fluttering adults as they come to lay their eggs. A dropper of a wiggle stone or soft hackle stone is ideal for imitating emerging stoneflies under the surface.

Regardless how you rank your insects, the stonefly is a meaty, buggy-looking creature of gourmet delight that will always catch *Salmo*.

## The Complex Caddis Conundrum

Throughout fly-fishing history caddis flies have been treated as if they were less important than mayflies. They have been the drab sisters, disparaged or ignored, in the literature. On the stream they have been a puzzle that anglers have chosen to neglect all too often. But for what reason? Certainly not because

of the relative value of these insects to trout, nor because of the relative value to fly fisherman on the trout stream.

—Gary Lafontaine, *Caddisflies*

▲ The ever-challenging and fidgety caddis: a flyfisher's delight or tragedy. Credit: Albert Pesendorfer

To many anglers, these words come to mind when browns are fixated on caddis: "skunked . . . can't figure which form they are taking . . . they refused everything!"

To me, being skunked by caddis hatches has been a constant source of inspiration in an almost perverse sort of way. Having a trout refuse my fly while observing incredible feeding activity on the surface or subsurface was the inspiration to write *Selectivity*. This book addressed how to decipher the code of imitation, presentation, and the reasons a trout will refuse your fly. The joy of creating new patterns and approaches is paramount to the fly-fishing experience, especially when it comes to the enigmatic caddis.

In the early 1990s, my new laboratories were the waters of Lower Michigan and the finicky Muskegon River tailwater, where we chose to build our fishing lodge and resume the past twenty-three years of my life pursuing its trout, steelhead, and salmon. Like the tough rivers of my past that did not easily render up their secrets—the Letort, the Delaware, Silver Creek in Idaho, and Hot Creek in California, along with other magnificent rivers around the world—the Muskegon was a unique beast all unto its own.

The Muskegon grows big browns. With water temperatures that border from icy cold to marginally warm, it imparts a high amount of eutrophic energy to the food system, which creates such a diversity in aquatic and terrestrial vertebrates and invertebrates, that it can baffle fly anglers because they have to make so many choices on a daily and monthly basis. Its browns are often preoccupied with midges and small caddis, with bugs sized #18–20 being their major food source.

Carl Richards started fishing Michigan's Muskegon River in 1959, and he introduced me to it in the mid-1970s. This river had terrific caddis fly hatches but no one could consistently catch fish, even when the trout were feeding on the caddis all around us.

When we did catch fish we took some fat, strong, well-conditioned trout, for the river is rich in caddis. Twelve-inch fish shaped like footballs would put up a great fight, and the larger nineteen-inch cruisers would keep anyone's adrenaline going all evening. There were plenty of fish, and plenty of bugs, but we

▲ Muskegon browns, like this one caught by Geno Kelly, grow to massive sizes and have such a diverse smorgasbord of food sources that it would boggle the mind of any trout in any other part of the world. Credit: Author

could not sort out which flies the fish were taking, and we were frequently skunked.

—Dick Pobst,
*The Orvis Pocket Guide to Caddisflies*

My good friend and angling partner, Dick Pobst, summed up the Muskegon caddis experience perfectly above. My journey into the Muskegon and its selective brown trout started on a long, broad, magnificent riffle-and-flats stretch of water known as Carmichael. It is here through toil, misery, sweat, and tears that I renamed it the "House of Pain." In this humiliating and frustrating stretch of water, I watched hundreds upon hundreds of trout rise during the caddis hatch, night after night, only to go home skunked, bewildered, and ready to break my fly fishing rod over my knee. It was here that I met the other master of the modern caddis fly world—the late Carl Richards. To this day, although he grows older and less mobile each year, I still have the honor of fishing with Pobst, and reminiscing over how a river can imprint so powerfully on the inquisitive mind as it ponders the enigmatic conundrums that only caddis flies can bring.

The "House of Pain" is a magnificent piece of water about a half-mile long and a hundred yards wide. It starts with very fine gravel and food-harboring vegetation for a good hundred-yard stretch, which was the home to some of the most significant mayfly and stonefly habitat one could ever imagine. It then drops into a very long, slowly-meandering, weed-filled flat that is the perfect foraging and inspection station for wise brown trout to carefully nitpick over their daily fare. The caddis flights of *Hydropsyche* and *Cheumatopsyche* were massive, beginning in May and peaking in the late summer from August through October. Here along the flats in the summer evenings is where I started the frustrating hair-pulling and endless fly-box searching. It became an obsession beyond comprehension, but added much to my education on trout selectivity.

In every bit of spare time I would be glued to the vice, looking to tie perfect imitations of the caddis pupae, ovapositing adults, or quad-wing spent spinners that littered the water in incomprehensible numbers. Here the *trutta* would just pick the surface up and down the flats morning, noon, and night, ingesting hundreds of caddis every day.

The annals of modern caddis fishing by Pobst and Richards were just being written at the same time I was trying to crack the code. Before them came the magnificent work of LaFontaine, which explained so much about caddis, and especially about emergers. Here he emphasized the "air bubbles' that caddis pupae give off

▲ Tail waters, as here on the Missouri River in Montana, are especially rich in plankton good for caddis hatches. Credit: Mike Tsukamoto

while surfacing. His addition of the Antron sparkle material around the pupa, simulating the air bubble ascent, was a major revelation.

Carl Richards was a magnificent thinker and bug madman that had aquarium tanks in his basement full of caddis, mayflies, stoneflies—you name it. If it swam and trout ate it, he was studying it. In his caddis investigations he never noticed any air bubbles coming from caddis pupae as they ascended to the surface to emerge. In one interesting evening as our 4x4s were parked along the Carmichael flats road, we enjoyed a bottle of Knob Creek bourbon well into the night, discussing the peculiarities in Muskegon caddis hatches, and how the brown trout and its big fat rainbow cohorts responded to the hatch. After a few drinks, Carl would always come out and say, "there is no such God-damned thing as those air bubbles—that's a bunch of bull crap!" Carl didn't think much of or care about LaFontaine's investigations, and subsequently wrote his own book on super caddis hatches.

The Carmichael Flats and San Juan riffle, another part of the Muskegon I named closer to the dam, were the perfect venues for long, complex brown trout rises to inspect every single detail of the emerging caddis pupae. In our stomach samples we found that the trout favored pupae almost 80 percent of the time, since they had a good amount of biological drift and were much easier to pursue than ova-positing, popcorn-bouncing, egg-laying female caddis. But brown trout did favor the diving females, since females would either deposit eggs by bouncing into the surface, or by diving under the water to attach them to rocks. Here the diving caddis pattern was very lethal and in this moment air bubbles had more significance than in the emerging pupae—thus I now tie these patterns with the bubble effects of Antron.

The Muskegon was most importantly associated with the development of the teardrop Antron trailing shuck. Craig Matthews, another Michigander/escapee who lived right up the road from me, and left for West Yellowstone, immortalized the Antron tailing shuck in other patterns like the X-Caddis. Eventually Antron/Z-lon was adapted for use into all types of mayfly emergers.

What made the brown trout of Carmichael Flats so difficult in the long run was the amazingly slow, long, weed-filled flats that allowed the trutta to cruise up and down for several hundred yards. Here they discriminately picked off ascending pupae, pupae struggling in the surface meniscus, bouncing and diving ova-positing female "popcorn caddis," and of course the quad-winged spent female caddis, which inspired a complex series of presentations unlike conventional mend/drag-free dry fly techniques.

The caddis hatches here made such a strong food imprinting, for such a long duration, that the only thing that compares might be on spring creeks where trout feed almost exclusively on midges or crustaceans. For example on the Big Spring in Pennsylvania, in the old "ditch" days when the hatchery was blowing effluent clouded with tremendous fecal matter of chironomid red larvae, the scum was the ideal food source for the *Mancasellus* cress bugs that trout would subsequently consume by the hundreds. To catch the gluttonous browns that lived there, it was necessary to imitate and lift your exact detailed patterns off the *Chara* weed and float them into a narrow funnel of a feeding lane to catch even an ultra-picky twelve-inch trout.

## Caddis Hatches and the Spatial Niche Marginal Water Connection

There is a statement that has appeared in one form or another so often in angling literature that is widely believed by fly fisherman: caddis are becoming an increasing food form because growing pollution and wider use of pesticides are taking a higher toll of the relatively fragile mayflies, while sparing the more rugged caddis flies.

The reason for the increased preponderance of caddis flies in our streams is due to the increase of organic pollution of civilization, giving many filter-feeding *Tricoptera* species, the net makers, a competitive advantage over mayflies. Many net-making caddis, such as *Hydropsyche*, are more abundant because nutrient-laden currents now deliver greater quantities of drift food into their feeding nets. This is an interesting observation and I for one am glad to hear that our tampering with nature has had at least some benefits for aquatic insects and trout.

—Gary Lafontaine, *Caddisflies*

*Tricoptera* caddis and *Salmo trutta* have a unique bond in that they are both maximum adapters and infiltrators into marginal niche environments. *Trutta* are known to eat just about anything in their environment and tolerate great ecosystem extremes. Caddis similarly eat a great diversity: leaf particles, decaying animal matter, algae, and woody debris bacteria all comprise their daily fare. They go about their day along the rocks collecting, shredding, scraping, and piercing. Whether they are spinning nets, building cases, or predation foraging, they are nice meaty morsels available to brown trout that occupy the same habitat.

## The Sedge Shroud

A good lesson to me came on the chalk streams of the River Test and other more affordable Avon waters back in the 1980s, when I fished them for a whole month. Downtown Stockbridge is a magnificent quaint little village with boutiques, small pubs, and an Orvis shop. In the smoking bar of the historic Grosvenor Hotel, debates

▲ Having already been a disciple student of Vince Marinaro, the modern American chalk stream Letort legend, and practically reading every book on entomology published, I studied up on aquatic insects in England and tied patterns to match the hatch British style. Credit: Ken Takata

between Halford and Skues took place about the relative merits of the dry fly versus the nymph. Throughout downtown, tiny conduits of diverted spring creek water from the main River Test, which they called "carriers," held gigantic brown trout. Many people would feed them bread, and catching them was off-limits.

As we walked in the back of the Greyhound Inn, which had a private beat of water along the river innkeeper Andy McDowell introduced me to the first emergence of the *danica* mayfly. The next day my guide, a very cool and relaxed young gentleman who worked out of the Orvis Company's Nether Wallop Mill and had a good working knowledge of the trout's behavior, drove us in a Range Rover toward the Timsbury beat on the lower Test. Once we got there, a soaking rain started up and we sought refuge in the ghillie's hut, which was a beautiful old-fashioned thatched roof masterpiece, well-stocked with dark stouts and ales, and delicious cucumber sandwiches with smoked salmon. While waiting out the rain, we chatted about the differences between American and British chalk streams, and how American anglers practiced catch and release fly fishing, which had not yet caught on in 1980s in Hampshire. In this case, our ghillie was all for it and did

not mind us returning the beautiful brown trout that rose freely to a well-presented fly.

English mayflies had different names than in the Americas. Pale Wateries, Iron Blues, and Tup's Indispensables correspond to America's Sulphers and Blue-Winged Olives. I asked our young guide Ian about the sequence of hatches that we'd experience that day. "No need to worry, mate, and not too much fuss over the bugs, aye. Put on a size 14 parachute dry that you have the most confidence in and that should do the trick. Our trout don't fancy themselves for too much exact imitation, so you need not worry." Apparently, all the effort I put into tying the exact imitations of the insects was all for naught. A size 14 Adams parachute received a positive nod from Ian: "Good choice, mate." I then wondered whether almost every angler that ever set foot on those waters fished a size 14 Adams.

In River Test tradition, one can only fish to an actively-feeding surface-oriented fish from a downstream position. Almost immediately upon arrival on the stream, a good brown trout rose, and Ian pointed the direction to place my fly. With one simple cast and one simple rise, a beautifully-colored sixteen-inch brown trout sucked in the Adams. "As I told you mate," Ian said, "our fish aren't picky like your American trout and will rise on command." One trout after another came to the net with zero refusals, which almost made these browns crazy easy to catch. After retreating to the Gillie's hut after another afternoon shower, we got a little "pissed" (inebriated) as we passionately exchanged stories about different American and British tactics.

It is strictly banker's hours between nine and five on the chalk streams. This is mainly a result of the biology of the ecosystem's cold water slowly warming up as the sun rises over the trees, which starts the mayfly hatch. Once the sun goes down below the trees, the mayflies tend to diminish with the four or five hours of sunlight.

As I was departing I couldn't help but notice the swarms of caddis, mounting a huge spinner flight in the lower stretch of the beat.

"So tell me about the caddis," I asked Ian.

"Caddis? Not quite sure I follow you mate. You mean sedges?"

I nodded, pointing to the prolific sedge hatch going on along the stream.

"They can be quite a nuisance—in a blizzard at times—but not quite sure the trout fancy them. And besides, I'll have you back to the pub loading up the mugs with our ales, bitters, and stouts by then, so need not worry about the sedges."

For the hell of it, I asked Ian if I could go downstream and investigate the caddis swarms. Sure as I imagined, the trout were boiling the water destroying the ova-positing females and sipping pupae in the film with slashing rises and gulps everywhere. I put on a LaFontaine sparkle caddis pupa and allowed it to drift and twitch down the slow run. Within seconds my new HLS Orvis rod was bent over with a hefty twenty-one-inch *trutta*. Ian the Ghillie could not believe his eyes and was very interested in my sedge pattern as he watched from afar. "Keep this to ourselves, eh? Most Gillies and anglers know nothing of the sedges, nor care to, since they are after-hour hatches and the chef at the Inn would be upset if we were late for dinner—eh?"

What I witnessed that evening was a massive swarm of egg-laying *Brachycentrus subnubilus* Grannoms—or Mother's Day caddis. They love the rich, ice-cold, weed-filled waters of the Hampshire chalk streams and build little chimney cases as larvae. Along with *Hydropsyche* caddis, the Cinnamon and Grannom sedges can be "super hatch" emergences. I pulled out my streamside mini pocket sein—the sheer abundance of the biological drift of pupae boggled my mind.

Today, given the pollution, agricultural over-fertilization (especially in Britain), and human encroachment of development into the countryside, mayfly hatches have dwindled as caddis hatches have increased. Today the sedge is a very important fly in a British brown trout fly fishers'

arsenals and continues to evolve. Good friend and author Terry Lawton has pursued UK salmon and trout for years, and he has seen a massive change to the fragile chalk streams of England, as well as the ideology of the British fly angler when it comes to hatches:

The fishing on most English rivers is controlled and managed by clubs, which believe that rivers must be stocked to keep the members happy. Individuals, including Halford, were proponents of stocking rivers, often unnecessarily, and many will have read Harry Plunket Greene's book *Where the Bright Waters Meet*, and its harrowing story of the destruction of the little Bourne Rivulet (the uppermost tributary of the Test) by filling it full of stock fish. Today the more enlightened clubs have seen the error of past ways and are reducing the number of fish stocked.

In the UK, many people start to fly fish for trout and think that they must then start fly fishing for salmon. Why? Snobbery to a degree. I think that they think the salmon is a worthier quarry and so carries more status. In a similar way there are still clubs that restrict fly fishing to dry fly only with a complete ban on fishing nymphs. Seeing a fish rise through clear water to take your high-floating dry fly and then turn down with it in its mouth is a truly wonderful and exciting experience. It is the excitement that makes many go for a hook set *before* the fish has had time to turn down. Equally exciting and wondrous is seeing a big mayfly such as an *Ephemera danica* hatch. When this happens quickly and smoothly, one minute there is no sign of a fly and the next there is this wonderful large fly floating by as its wings dry. Will it get airborne before a trout eats it, or worse, it is attacked by a damsel fly?"

Finally, one only need fish a giant tailwater like the Missouri, Delaware, Muskegon, and other freestone and spring creeks during a massive super caddis hatch and watch this extreme, refined selectivity exhibited by brown trout picking larvae off the rocks, attacking submerging pupae, or pouncing on bouncing or diving females as they lay eggs. Also, the photophobic likes of *Tricoptera*, where heavy hatches usually occur towards evening and cloudy rainy days.

## Midge Magic

I never fully realized the importance of midges— *Chironomidae*, *Simulium*, and crane flies—until I fished the Pennsylvania and Montana spring creeks along with the large eddy pools of the Catskill and Taconic mountain range freestone rivers like the Beaverkill in New York and the Housatonic in Connecticut. My baptism

▲ Any lover of *Salmo* would be very happy someday to retire in this magnificent realm of Iceland where brown trout and Atlantic salmon have found the ideal conditions for their existence. Credit: Arni Baldurson-LAX-A

by fire with midge hatches was a painful study in how *trutta* can go from eating large mayflies and stoneflies to foraging heavily on barely-visible size #28 midge adults and pupae. But the true importance of midges was fully revealed to me when I fished the Big Laxa River in Iceland. If you are a lover of *Salmo,* Iceland is like dying and going to heaven.

Besides being the ideal ecosystem of freestone and valley spring creek rivers with ideal temperatures from warm ocean currents, the Laxa absolutely magnificent for geographic beauty. The landscape is garnished with geysers and volcanic mountains. Snowcapped peaks, luscious green moss lichen, and grass wetland valleys with wildflowers dot the rich sheep and cattle farms. Lake Myvtan (Midge Lake), emanating from spring sources at the Laxa's headwater aquifers, has the perfect nutrient fertility and ideal conditions for black fly *Simulium* midges, which form amazing mating flights for weeks on end and nourish the entire food chain, including Harlequin and Barrow's goldeneye ducks, geese, and storks. This biofertility also

produces some of the most spectacular brown trout and Atlantic salmon fishing in the world today.

With such huge midge hatches, the brown trout and salmon parr/grilse here totally key onto its incredible abundance and grow to amazing sizes. To both *trutta* and *salar,* a tiny twitching riffle-hitched tube fly imitates skittering of the midge adult activity and is *the* lethal fly here. Though many larger *trutta* tend to be carnivorous in nature, which often ends up being the case as they grow older and hunt larger food forms, it is inversely common here to have consistent twenty-two-inch-plus browns feeding on midges all day, thus the necessity for a sturdy midge pattern and heavier tippets. The Laxa is a prime example of the consistent fixation *trutta* will have for maximizing caloric intake on a given food source at a given time.

*Diptera* occur in extremely fertile waters, especially in the absence of mayflies and stoneflies. Usually, tailwaters with severe flow fluctuations will eliminate the more delicate mayfly populations, and midges will thrive in greater abundance. Spring creeks also harbor massive midge

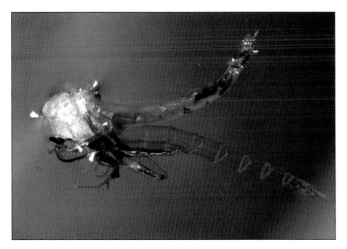

▲ *Diptera* emerger and adult. Credit: John Pierson/Mike Tsukamoto

*Chironomidae* and *Simulium* midges grow to the larger size 14–16 range. Here they are staple fly patterns for the stillwater fisherman and the classic "buzzer midge" has evolved to new standards for stillwater brown trout fisherman. Brown trout usually conduct the most substantial midge feeding activity during the period from late afternoon into evening as waters warm. On sunny days, if shady areas are available at nearshore bluff ledge pools and under hanging trees, the midging will take on a furious space all day. During these brief periods when the pupae float in the meniscus preparing to split their sacks, and while the adults are unable to take flight immediately after hatching, the midges skitter helplessly before they free themselves from the water surface and are very vulnerable to the trout. Imitations of both midge forms are equally attractive to trout, and a pupa dropper of below a midge dry will often bring success.

As for adult midge coloration, the black-and-cream spectrum is usually 90 percent effective on all freestone and tailwater-like spring creek waters. The larvae can be anywhere from a light green olive, black, or to extreme red for the bloodworm species that like to feed on fecal matter. In the summertime and late fall the midges will be a cream to whitish color, and anglers can mistake them for the *Trico* hatch.

Also, as anglers heavily utilize many world-class brown

▲ A well-fed Icelandic brown. Credit: Jim Klug-Yellow Dog

hatches due to weedy and sandy soil environments that collect detritus materials over a longer period of time, due to the lack of flow that can flush river substrata very quickly. *Diptera* are also very fond of fecal matter that is usually found in the effluent of hatcheries that may be located at the source of spring creeks.

On large Stillwater lochs in the UK and elsewhere,

trout fisheries with catch-and-release or restricted regulations, the *trutta* here will be exposed to a great degree of sophisticated fly patterns that imitate mayflies, stoneflies, caddis, and midge patterns. But if you seriously look at the anglers who pursue the hatch-matching scenario, most tend to flick fly patterns in a size 12 to extreme size 18 range. Perhaps fewer than 15 percent of the anglers will venture into the size 20 or smaller categories with 8X tippets—thus many larger, more selective sipping browns seldom meet a fisherman.

Midge feeding can be a learned behavior from the experience of getting hooked by the larger, more common fly patterns. In addition, due to the brown trout's long compound and complex rise forms, especially on long flat still waters of spring creeks and tail waters, and also on the large slow pools of the classic Catskill freestone river, the long presentation times, coupled with leaders up to eighteen feet long, can make midge presentation nearly impossible at times, giving the trout the full advantage of an angler's mishaps. As for the young-of-year *trutta* and *salar*, *Diptera* are "manna from heaven," as their midge buffet is available as soon as browns and atlantics break free from the embryonic sack and start feeding.

### Crustacea and Mollusks: The Supercharged Protein

Squid, shrimp, amphipods, urchins, crabs, and krill all inhabited the oceans, seas, fjords, and rivers during the Cambrian period 100 million years ago. By the end of the Eocene glacial age they thrived in substantial numbers when *Salmo* evolved. There is no question that serious imprinting to this abundant food source has been occurring since before the existence of *Salmo*. Atlantic salmon and sea trout, along with browns on spring creek and tail waters, will often target crustaceans, and in some places the tiny creatures comprise 90 percent of a salmonid's diet in some waterways.

### FRESHWATER CRUSTACEA

Salmonids mostly feed on the freshwater scuds or shrimp in environments that have substantial vegetation. *Gammarus* and *Hyallela* scuds are the most prominent along with *Misys* and *Dioporia* shrimp, which usually emanate from coldwater impoundments from the Alleghenies to the Rockies. *Trutta* can be extremely selective about these food forms, necessitating exact imitations.

In similar waters, crayfish will often utilize the food chain and become lobster-like edibles that no brown trout can resist. On my home tailwater on the Muskegon and Michigan, the freshwater scuds and crayfish make up a large part of the brown trout diet when the mayfly, stonefly, caddis, and midge hatches are not present. Crayfish also become an important food source during their vulnerable softshell crayfish molting season beginning in June and lasting through the summer.

▲ The Scud. They are protein-packed superfoods for *trutta* on spring creeks and tailwaters. Credit: Andrew Steele Nisbet

To make the brown trout–crustacea connection even more difficult or often impossible to crack is the *Daphnia*, or water fleas, common to most tailwaters. Here on my rivers in July and August, *Daphnia* emanate from the reservoirs in massive numbers, and the trout will filter-feed them like a whale does krill. A *Daphnia* imitation would probably be about an impossible-to-match size 42. Cluster patterns would be the only way to go, but alas, these are not effective.

Scud imitations have evolved immensely since the invention of the Killer Bug, Grey Goose, and other simple round/slender curved patterns. Very selective *trutta* feeding on scuds and cress bugs can go to into intricate feeding rituals like Galapagos woodpecker finches. Darwin discovered they were dislodging insects from trees and branches by using twigs, sticks, and cactus needles. An amazing task for a reptilian modern dinosaur that birds are by all respects. The highly adaptable browns have learned to maximize or greatly speed up their foraging and caloric intake on crustacea, primarily scuds and cress bugs clinging to vegetation, and in a unique way of their own. In my *Selectivity* book I mentioned a very large brown on the Letort spring run named "the juggler," who would charge its head into a patch of watercress, *Elodea*, or *Chara*, and then retreat downstream to a very particular position in a narrow, sandy, clutter-free channel to intercept the delectable scuds, much like an angler doing the boot shuffle on the San Juan River in New Mexico. Here they will scuff their boots into the substrata, dislodging red worm annelids, nymphs, and *Chironomid* larvae for opportunistic trout who took up feeding channels right below their waders.

In very clear spring creeks and tailwaters, due to the complexity of crustaceans' anatomy, fly designers are creating intricate patterns with cutting-edge materials like Kiley's Scud skin and Gammarus Foil. One of the key elements in imitating crustaceans is the grayish-greenish translucency of the body, as it matches identically which each river's unique coloration. One discriminating detail that I have found is the amber back blood veins, which I imitate with an amber vinyl rib in all crustacean patterns. From a prey identification standpoint, keep in mind that scuds are free-swimming organisms that are easily detectable by trout.

## CRAYFISH

When thinking of crayfish, we often think of bass fly patterns, rather than their significant relevance to the brown trout, especially the larger *trutta* who relish them. These *Astacidea* crustaceans, or miniature lobsters, are a mind-bogglingly rich food source full of protein. They are not

▲ Sculpins and crayfish share the same habitat and are like rib-eye steaks for brown trout. Credit: Kevin Feenstra

fond of polluted waters and thrive in highly calcium carbonate rich rivers, especially spring-fed creeks as well as more acidic freestones and tailwaters. Studies have shown time and time again that *trutta* forgo cold water oxygen comfort in favor of massive digestion of food sources and will tolerate the higher water temps found in some larger freestone rivers to fulfill this massive caloric overload.

Crayfish dwell along the bottom structure feeding on decaying trees and animals, and hide in the same reclusive rock and bolder territory that brown trout and sculpins love. They swim quickly with their back tail noisily pushing water, which acts like a dinner bell for large trout. In the soft shell molting states, when the crayfish shed their exoskeletons in order to become larger, they are vulnerable, easy-to-digest, and highly sought after by trout. A crayfish can live through up to a dozen molting periods.

Through the summer on the Muskegon River, brown trout will gravitate toward very shallow waters just above ankle deep near springs in the nighttime, feeding on the crayfish and poking their heads around rocks and little crevices. There is a period of almost two months when

larger *trutta* are almost impossible to find, while they are robbing the shoreline of soft-shell crayfish. Fishing these imitations at dusk or early-morning hours is a killer.

## Terrestrials: Bastardized *Trutta* Candy

Anglers first developed terrestrial imitations in two prime *trutta* frontiers; first in the Catskills, and then the chalk streams of Pennsylvania's Cumberland Valley. Louis Rhead came here to the Americas in 1883 as an illustrator and artist of books. Rhead was the first sketcher of mayflies, stoneflies, caddis, and other insects, spending hours alongside the Catskill Rivers. He was an entomological John Audubon, and his book *American Trout Stream Insects* (1916), was the first concise treatise on the landborn subject.

Though Rhead received much criticism for his often bizarre insects that sometimes resembled Disney-style animation characters, he tried to put exact realism—almost too much realism—into his commercial imitations. Many of Rhead's contemporaries considered him to be a snake oil salesman of trout flies who failed to acknowledge the

▲ Brown trout grow massive and colorful when feeding on crayfish. Credit: Dave Jensen.

▲ A cow country spring creek terrestrial box. Credit: Author

establishment or the achievements of the British/Catskill dry fly elitist school. He made molded facsimile lures and flies and sold them from his studios in the Bronx. If you look at today's modern terrestrials, they use a ton of new synthetics like foam/rubber legs, plastic eyes etc. In this way, Rhead was the new world's first progressive terrestrial maker.

Today's terrestrial angling in summer is a seven-continent affair. In some cases, like out west on the big rivers, it can become totally exclusive with the proverbial "hopper/ dropper" setup—Hopper on top with a nymph below. Often the Hopper or large stimulator dry becomes the targeted feast or strike indicator alarm on this deadly combo.

### Pennsylvania: The American Chalk Stream Terrestrial Incubator

Pennsylvania's Cumberland Valley and State College's "Happy Valley" has a very special place in my soul. I doubt that any other place has had a more profound impact on my thought process and the quest for selective, fussy brown trout. I first read about the world famous Letort Spring Run and Falling Springs in an article written in the 1970s about their huge, selective, wild brown and rainbow trout in Vince Marinaro's documentation of the "Caenis/Trico" hatch. As a food and beverage director at the Washington Sheraton in the early 1980s, my Georgetown apartment was ninety minutes from the legendary Falling Spring Run. I was shaking with awe on the first day I saw these gentle little limestone jewels: they were God's perfect creation for a selective trout, and I was blessed just to feast my eyes on them for the first time.

The valley's spring creeks and their hypnotic charm have provided me with decades of memorable encounters with its unique and selective trout inhabitants, even though they have been altered by development and are now a far cry of their former selves. They have fostered friendships, mentors, some of the best and most difficult days of trout fishing I could ever experience, and were always a special place to retreat to from the bustling pace of the big city.

But the real importance of the Pennsylvania limestoners to modern American fly fishing was when the rivers ran full and lush with vegetation in the summer as they serenaded through the fertile farmland and lush meadows. There were alive with grasshoppers, crickets, beetles, ants, lady bugs, and many other terrestrial critters that would easily fall into the spring creeks as a stiff wind kicked up, cattle grazing near the creeks pushed and knocked them

▲ The warm and humid mid-Atlantic summers are ideal for terrestrials on Pennsylvania's Big Spring Run. Credit: Mike Tsukamoto

in, or farmers plowing activity stirred them up— helpless prey for prime brown trout.

## Vincent Marinaro: America's First Modern Terrestrial Master

If there are truly forefathers of the contemporary American thinking man's fly fishing, we must pay dues to the brilliant Vincent Marinaro. He, along with Lee Wulff and Art Lee, are legendary giants in the art and science of *Salmo*. Vince's writings and observations parallel the importance of G. E. M. Skues, and his masterworks *A Modern Dry-Fly Code* (1950) and *In the Ring of the Rise* (1976), gave us everything that could be new, enlightening, theoretical, and practical, in the progression of the brown troutsman. With his sharp and analytical mind, and the time he spent along Vince's and Fox's Meadows along the Letort observing, casting, and studying the ecosystem from top to bottom, he echoed in the footsteps of the British greats: Skues, Sawyer, and John Waller Hills.

In *A Modern Dry-Fly Code*, he broke new ground with fly concepts and presentations, particularly the terrestrial arena. They were as unique as the Cumberland Valley Limestone Spring Creek/chalk streams. American trout anglers had their foundations on the broad, fast-flowing freestone streams, with river-specific techniques. If the Catskill fly angler would have driven past the tiny, weed-filled Pennsylvania limestoner, they would have kept going, wondering how a trout could live in such a weedy,

low-lying place, until they put their hand in the icy cold 48 to 51 degrees F waters, saw the mayflies hatching, and looked at large wild trout straight in the eye. These weedy, low-lying streams in the humid summer farmland were prime nurseries and incubators for the terrestrial insects that *trutta* found delectable.

The Letort gave up many three- to five-pound, highly introspective brown trout, for Marinaro, Charlie Fox, and Ross Trimmer on hoppers and beetles. The combination of stream flows, overhanging security structure, weed channel flow alignment, and proximity to terrestrial shoreline incubators, all played a major role in forming the trout's cunning sit-and-wait kill artistry on the Letort's terrestrial buffet.

In Marinaro's last and greatest book, *In the Ring of the Rise,* he became the ultimate theorist and documented the world of selective brown trout of the Letort and the Au Sable in Michigan, two rivers that I am proud to continue to fish to this day. Vince's words still haunt me when I walk these waters:

Subjectively, it is very difficult to say what a trout is thinking when he inspects and selects. All discussions about selectivity are only superficial. We can only speculate on his mental process. We must continue to defend on outward manifestations for clues to his preferences in selecting certain flies. The trout has not changed. His fundamental nature is still the same, no

▲ Vintage Kodak print from my mentor in my youthful days. The late Vincent Marinaro on a day when I served as his net boy. Credit: Matthew Supinski

matter where you find him. He behaves the same in freestone as in limestone waters; the same in rough as in quiet water. He inspects, drifts with the insect, and selects in rough, fast water, the same way that he does in quiet water. In the rougher, faster streams he operates in a somewhat smaller space-time frame. It is only a matter of degree, not of his nature. He is still the same deadly accurate hunter in pursuit of his prey. He is a kill-artist whose hunter skills are cultivated and refined from babyhood; without them he would die. His relentless pursuit of a victim is a startling study of concentrated deadlines. His way of life is a perpetual search-and-destroy mission.

Today the Letort is, as it was sixty years ago, still the most difficult trout water on which to find success, even for the most advanced trout angler. Taking a selective wild brown trout on the Letort is a major accomplishment. In *A Modern Dry-Fly Code*, Marinaro described the Letort very practically:

What shall I say of the Letort? Certainly it is beautiful, not with the wild beauty of our mountain freestone streams, decked out in their garish display of laurel and rhododendron, but rather with the calm and serene beauty of pastoral scenery. Nestled in a little valley, with gently rolling hills on both sides, it meanders

slowly and evenly, its placid surface hardly ever ruffled even by the westerly winds which prevail thereabouts.

The Letort is a hard taskmaster and does not treat lightly any violation of dry fly technique. Any suggestion of drag, heaviness in the cast, or thick gut is magnified many times on such a calm surface.

In Marinaro's *Code*, for all practical purposes he put the importance of terrestrial insects of a trout's diet in a very strategic category. As I mentioned how Rhead and Hewitt touched on them and introduced their heresy to the stoic school of dry fly purism, Marinaro's low-lying farm creeks teemed with grasshoppers, beetles, and a multitude of terrestrials. Here he perfected his Letort-style hoppers, his tiny jassids, and ant imitations. He was constantly viewing his insects and terrestrials and their imitations from every angle and light source, in a desperate attempt to examine and define what the trout sees with terrestrials:

A close examination of many species viewed against the light, will disclose some surprising things. Consider, for example, the startling fact that in two different species of the same family, the black and the red ant, there is a tremendous variance, the former being absolutely opaque in the body and the latter glimmering and glowing as though lighted by some inner fire.

Even allowing for the high magnifying power of the trout's eye, which is easily duplicated with a magnifying glass, there is no apparent translucency in any degree in the black ant. Obviously these two must be dressed to attain different effects.

The Japanese beetle and the grasshopper belong in the opaque category. So too do the jassids. All of these except the caddis are terrestrial-born and bred—thus how much then, is translucency worth in the imitation of insects upon which trout feed?

*A Modern Dry-Fly Code* was novel in that for the first time patterns were developed not just to please the eye of the angler or fly tier, but to find out what made sense to the trout. He created Quill-body hoppers and green drakes, worked feverishly on wing design and silhouettes, and analyzed every aspect of the nymph, emerger, adult, and spinner forms. He took midge fishing to a new level and even played entomological horticulturist by trying to transplant green drake nymphs from Penns Creek back into the Cumberland Valley spring creeks, which were losing their large ephemera hatches through grazing and habitat destruction. Marinaro's *In the Ring of the Rise* characterized the exact rising trout sequences as simple, compound, and complex rise forms.

Prior to his death in 1986, I had the fortune of having him mentor me in the stalking of the ultra-selective wild *trutta* of the valley. He became a fly guru to me in that I was for the most part "a groupie stalker," who drove this curmudgeonly man crazy. I believe he entertained my advances, in the hope that I would eventually go away. He taught me much about the world of terrestrials, minutiae, and spring creeks—I even have a selection of his jassids and midges. He is without doubt the greatest selective trout mind to ever walk the planet. In that and his works, all trout fishers owe him much veneration and respect.

### "Terrestrial-ites" and the Hopper Infatuation

As much as I love the late Datus Proper and his work, and the fact that I got to know him in Washington, DC from

▲ "In my experience, trout have not been very selective when feeding and grasshoppers fishing is not delicate, but it is exciting, A big grasshopper just right under the bank of the Montana meadow stream in August is likely to produce a response that can be heard by your fishing partner to bends down river."—Datus Proper, *What the Trout Said;* Credit: Doug Danforth

our National Capital Trout Unlimited chapter and fished alongside him on the Pennsylvania limestoners, I often continue to disagree with half of what he's written, as much as I love the other half of it. Through his brilliant insight into so many facets of the fly imitations and what trout see and think, I often see his observations as being very parochial and traditional, whereas my observations come from three hundred days a year on the water as a guide.

It was the wild and ultra-selective brown trout of the Letort and Yellow Breeches that initiated the whole secret terrestrial society. But as climate change enters the future, we will see a pronounced increase in the percentage of terrestrial insects that love the humidity and prolonged warm autumns, leading into early mild winters, or so they predict.

Secondly, *trutta* have shown time after time that their adaptability is paramount to their millennial survival and dominance. As waters warm, the greater availability of terrestrials over longer periods of time will make these imitations more important for the angler. Thirdly, the terrestrial game is very complex given the morphology of the insects themselves. The high-tech synthetics available to incorporate into the newest imitations, lead to ever more sophisticated designs. Although Datus Proper

▲ The upper Yellow Breeches and its wild browns, which get crowded by hatchery trout. Credit: Author (top); Mike Tsukamoto (bottom)

found trout to not be discriminating about hopper designs, in my experience the complete opposite is the case. In *Selectivity*, I addressed the various colors of hoppers based on woodland versus open meadows, and how local climates and temperature can all affect the way they are presented—plopped, skittered, smashed, danced off the banks, etc. Then there are those long compound and complex rises a brown trout will make on many freestone and spring creek rivers. Marinaro described these instances, which will drive a hopper angler insane on spring creeks, with close inspections and refusals, only to subsequently accept or refuse—all in the same drift.

Right alongside the Marinaro and Fox school, who hung out at the old Yellow Breeches shop in Boiling Springs, Pennsylvania, were the two Eds. Ed Koch was a Cumberland Valley legend. A passionate author, lecturer, fly shop owner and connoisseur of the two extremes of fly fishing—midge fishing and large terrestrials. In *Terrestrial Fishing*, a legacy book dedicated to the Cumberland Valley school of terrestrial selectivity, Ed wrote:

For Vince Marinaro and Charlie Fox, they had the water to themselves in the early years, save for half a dozen of others and the regulars who spent many frustrating hours in quest of the elusive native brown trout. Charlie knew every trout, where it lives, when it fed, and what it ate. For several seasons he and Vince have pursued a huge brown, who when hopper season came, had become a thorn in Vince's side. No matter what fly was presented and no matter how perfectly presented (and if anyone was capable of perfect presentation, these two were), the hopper-feeding brown eluded them.

So here again we see how *trutta* can painfully agonize even the most sophisticated anglers. The terrestrials and the inability to match them with standard old-school patterns, drove the Letort regulars nuts with late nights at the vise creating detailed buggy contraptions to fool the elusive wild browns. This pushed Marinaro and others to new levels of tying mastery, as Ed Koch recounted:

He went to work on a hopper imitation. This was a challenge he was determined to win. He returned to the stream several days later armed with his new creation: the Pontoon hopper. Bill Blades and Dave Whitlock would have been green with envy. It looked more like a hopper than the real thing, but Vince found out looks weren't everything when the new creation cast like a bear. Undaunted and even more determined, he set out in quest of the elusive brown. With effort and a little change in casting technique, he was able to control the new hopper.

For the next few weeks every encounter was the same. Finally one morning the climax was at hand, though neither angler knew what was about to happen. As always, Charlie went upstream to his watching station. Vince cast while Charlie relayed instructions. The trout rose to the hopper and begins a backward drift and inspection Vince anticipated the usual reaction (rejection), but suddenly the nose broke the water, the hopper was inhaled, and Vince reacted. He realized at once that the weight and strength of the huge Brown were far more than he and Charlie had estimated. They had guessed the trout to be 26 to 28 inches and seven or eight pounds. Thoughts of victory, I'm sure, flashed through Vince's mind. The pressure from the rod lifted the trout near the surface, giving Charlie and Vince their first close-up look at the fish. It was much deeper in body than either realized. Charlie moved downstream and Vince up stream when suddenly, with strong strokes of the huge tail, the Brown began to bore for the bottom. Vince applied all the pressure he could, but the trout continued to dive for cover. It finally made it to the undercut bank, shaking its huge head and sending throbbing impulses along the line into Vince's rod. Vince felt the line go slack and just as suddenly as the fight had begun, it ended.

I could have only imagined how disheartened Vince was, with his hands still shaking after such a powerful encounter. We all have witnessed that moment sometimes in our lives. I believe this started the whole passion of the leviathan brown terrestrial fixation. Eventually the Letort Hopper became Ed Shenk's signature as patterns started to become more intricate with refined legs, bodies, and colors to match the terrestrial hatch.

Perfection came to the smaller terrestrials like ants, ladybugs, and tiny leaf hoppers, also known as Jassids. These he employed when a firm identification could not be made, and became one of Vince's signature terrestrial patterns tied in size 24. It is a very simple fly using a jungle cock for the back and sparse hackle.

Back in the good old days the Letort regulars were a very secretive society, a sort of brown trout Knights Templar. Many a day I'd drive two hours to watch the legends of Fox, Marinaro, Schwiebert, Lefty Kreh, and Trimmer from a distance on Fox's meadow, since I was not part of their clique. Each was trying to outdo each other and also had a real attitude and opinion about what the others thought of the extremely introspective and sometimes impossible wild browns of the Letort. It still amazes me to this day how one type of fish could have such a powerful influence on the way one conducted one's life and to drive anglers to insane levels of unfulfilled passion with only glimmers of closure and victory.

## Enter the Leviathan *Trutta* Master: Ed Shenk

Ed was a true lunker hunter who foraged with a very calculating mind. Originally a geological survey analyst in Washington, DC, his private recreational mastery of Cumberland Valley spring creeks was a feat that he took to new levels, perhaps more so than probably any other living being. His fly patterns for these waters probably exceeded any of the other legends for their sheer practicality and ability to fool the most selective and also often impossible monster *trutta*. I first met Ed at a TU weekend at the Allenberry and watched him move up the upper Letort from the Bonny Brook Road Bridge, fishing all day long on his hands and knees. He was developer and practitioner of the small five-foot rods necessary at times to fish through the brush and wood piles.

Ed was known for four patterns that are still deadly to this day: the Letort Hopper, the Letort Cricket, Shenk's Deer Hair Sculpin, and Shenk's Cress Bug. As the years went on and Ed had fooled more and larger leviathan Letort brown trout, he became known for his pursuit of a specific large brown he named "Old George," which he details in his book. We will revisit Ed Shenk's trophy hunting in Chapter 8.

Along with the writings of Letort regulars, another great terrestrial book came out by Gerald Almy, and more recently, *Modern Terrestrials* by Rick Takahashi and Jerry Hubka. Thus our appreciation for terrestrials has become more

▲ Ed Shenk. Credit: Cumberland Valley Tu/PA Fly Fishing Museum

sophisticated, in tandem with the availability of today's modern foam and synthetic materials. But if anyone was to take the credit for this land-born revolution, it would be *Salmo trutta's* inquisitive and confounding habit of always being willing to experiment with new and unusual food forms.

## Potpourri Fare Affairs

From the invertebrate standpoint, stomach analysis has shown brown trout to ingest just about anything, including twigs, pieces of plastic, and other junk that has found its way into its riverine surroundings. Whereas 95 percent of aquatic invertebrate and vertebrate prey have well-defined patterns, one the most vexing of all is deer fly adults and larvae. On my homewater, the Muskegon River, the deer flies on the water race about at what seems like 70 miles an hour by May. The bugs have an incredible ability to hover close to the surface near drift boat hulls and anglers. Off the surface, trout will leap frantically to intercept a deer fly, which is almost impossible to imitate, as are dancing caddis. Sunken patterns twitched on the surface or false casted in the air elicit no interest whatsoever.

Hellgrammites and Dobson flies are also nice meaty chunks of prey, and when obtainable in high quantities can be a very formidable staple of the *trutta* diet.

The beautiful electric blue damsel fly just spells trout food to huge browns; an epic video from New Zealand showing them feeding by porpoising dramatically into the air demonstrates the brown trout's tenacity and ability to capture prey no matter how impossible the circumstances.

I was able to capture the brown trout's amazing ability to intercept prey in the air when Tom Harman and I were filming our *Selectivity: Trout* DVD. On a Minnesota spring creek called Trout Run, during a Mother's Day caddis hatch, the browns were leaping full body, two feet in the air, to grab all the female egg layers as they were either ready to land or about to take off.

Tadpoles, snails, and annelid worms also can comprise a significant portion of the *trutta*'s diet and should never be ignored. The San Juan worm or the squirmy fly is the typical example of a wiggly annelid worm that crushes even the most sophisticated big brown trout on occasions.

## Vertebrates: Riverine, Lake, and Fusion Habitats

Being very privileged to now live and professionally pursue my passion in the Great Lakes freshwater wonderland of Michigan, I can now more clearly see the vast adaptability both brown trout and Atlantic salmon use to conquer and freshwater river and lake ecosystems in search of available

▲ This sturgeon strain of brown trout from Michigan is a prime example of the fine line between resident niche and migratory urges in *Salmo* behavior that continues to perplex many admirers and scientists who study the fish's behavior. They are at the right place at the right time, even in winter. Credit: Jeff Cole/ Rich Felber

seasonal prey. Also, spending time as a boy in Poland's Baltic corridor, an ecosystem almost identical to Michigan, and growing up in yet another very similar Great Lakes habitat in New York State, I can now see clearly how chameleon-like the predatory creature *Salmo* can be, as well as its uncanny ability to forage on a vast array of vertebrates in all sizes. Pennsylvanian leviathan trutta hunter, Brian Judge, stalks lowland marginal rivers with big streamers that have strong vertebrate bait fish driven browns.

The Sturgeon River in the Northeast index finger of the mitt of Michigan is beautiful, cold, and swift-flowing, with limited and extremely difficult access, so don't waste your time here. In this area also lies the hallowed Au Sable river watershed, which is much more angler-friendly. Both have prodigious leviathan brown populations.

The Sturgeon flows dangerously through deep, lush forests of conifers, maples, birch, and cedar. Bogs give its water a deep, rich, tannic stain. Its course contains type two rapids with lots of boulder rock and gravel—ideal *trutta* habitat. Its aquatic insect life includes mayflies and stoneflies as it eventually winds its way down into Burt and Mullet Lakes through prime, wild, scenic river flows. It eventually reaches Lake Huron by Cheboygan and has an amazing ecosystem link between swift-flowing river, cold, fertile lake systems, and eventually the 750-foot deep inland freshwater sea that is Lake Huron.

In the fall of 2010 on the Big Manistee River, Tom Healy was fishing for migratory Chinook salmon from Lake Michigan with his guide Tim Roller. They were tossing

hardware thunder sticks when an enormous brown struck, which turned out to be a forty-one-pound new world record. Now in the news, people wanted to come to Michigan to catch enormous world-record browns. But there was a serious problem brewing, unbeknownst to potential new tourist fishermen.

Michigan's Great Lakes salmonid abundance is massive, especially with wild Chinook and Coho salmon. They dominate the fall, spawning on rivers in startling quantities and aggressively taking over spawning niches. The *Seeforellen* browns that do very well in other Great Lakes states are high Bavarian Alpine lake fish that grow to massive sizes. Wisconsin has their *Seeforellen* program at full stride and they now own the newer world record from Lake Michigan at forty-three pounds.

Michigan's Great Lakes brown trout program revolved around the strictly hatchery-bred *Seeforellen* fish. After dozens of years of reproduction in hatcheries, the fish became very genetically limited. A good friend and fishing partner, biologist Gary Whelan, described Michigan's *Seeforellen* as "so inbred that they forgot to learn how to swim."

Hence his mission to find a hearty migratory strain going back to the 1890s roots of the first Great Lakes *Salmo trutta* invasion. The wild Sturgeon River strain was the perfect migratory brown trout that fit a multi-foraging profile with dynamic growth and the capability to dominate a watershed. In the Sturgeon system there are resident wild browns, as well as migratory browns that will descend into the depths of Burt and Mullet Lakes to feed off bait fish in

▲ Migratory ocean and lake Brown trout in Tierra Del Fuego and Great Lakes do much better due to the fact that there is little natural salmon reproduction or competition. Credit: Jessica DeLorenzo

the winter months, as the waters go on into Lake Huron. They then take advantage of prime riverine foraging when the giant *Hexagenia* mayfly is a substantial food source, along with smaller trout and baitfish that form a complex food chain ideal for the adaptable *trutta*.

Could this system grow the truly mammoth-sized brown trout Michigan was looking for to satisfy its world-record billing? Is there a fifty-pound *trutta* lurking somewhere between Lake Huron's deep fertile icy depths and the headwaters of the Sturgeon? Possibly so, but most importantly, the wild adaptable genetics are instilled in the strain along with the incredible diversity of food sources and habitats that can be optimized during conditions when one habitat might be too warm or too cold to provide maximum growth.

Given these super-*trutta* ecosystems on the Sturgeon, the Baltic Sea estuaries, lake/river systems in Patagonia, Tierra Del Fuego, and elsewhere, these types of waterways could be exact replicas of *Salmo*'s initial evolutionary birthplace. Somewhere between ocean briny fjord lake estuaries, large lowland rivers, and forested mountain streams, *Salmo* began and continues to flourish even though migratory and temporary residency occurs with Atlantic salmon in the ocean and sea-run browns. But for the freshwater-dwelling *trutta*, the Sturgeon River has the maximum dose of aquatic vertebrates and invertebrates of various sizes and degrees, based on the current growth needs from fry to parr to extreme adult phases. These migratory highways provide the ultimate growth and dominance coefficient factors necessary for a vibrant and healthy population. In *Ecology of Atlantic Salmon and Brown Trout*, the Jonssons came to similar conclusions:

The size spectrum of the prey consumed may influence the growth rate of the fish. Although Atlantic salmon and brown trout feed opportunistically on seasonally varying prey types, there is a general tendency that the fish take larger prey as they grow. If larger prey is unavailable, the fish will gradually cease growing. (Mittelbach, 1983). But, there can be exceptions associated with ontogenetic (occurring during an organism's development) niche shifts such as in some Lakes where brown trout shift from zoobenthos to zooplankton freely, as they grow larger and older thereby escaping potential pelagic predators (Jonsson and Gravem, 1985; Schei and Jonsson, 1989). In such cases both the energy content and the availability of the prey change with the habitat shift. For the fish, the profitability of the prey depends on its energy content relative to the amount of energy needed to detect, pursue, handle, and digest the prey. The most profitable prey is that which gives the highest net energy gain per unit time.

They explain spatial niche feeding regimes as follows:

Within a population all individuals (*trutta*) are not active simultaneously. Experimentally, (Alanara et al. 2002) show that individual brown trout made sequential use of foraging areas, with dominant individuals being active at the most beneficial times of dusk into the early part of the night, while subordinate fish fed at other times of the day. However, the degree of overlapping activity times between high-ranking fish depended on energetic demands. At low temperatures when requirements were low, the temporal activity patterns of top ranking fish were synchronized with foraging concentrated at the preferred times. When temperature was raised to increase energetic requirements, activity patterns showed strong temporal segregation: the most dominant fish remain predominantly nocturnal, where second ranking fish became more diurnal.

These scientific tidbits do not come as any surprise to many trophy "*trutta*saurus" hunters, which we will eventually realize in the night fishing game addressed in more detail in Chapter 8.

## The Sculpin Craze

Foremost on the list of aquatic vertebrates is of course the sculpin and darter. Its early imitations from Ed Shenk and Dave Whitlock using deer hair and cropping the patterns into a V shape, and the Muddler Minnow from Don Gapen, are the most fished streamer imitations gaining in popularity. The sculpin is the ideal prey for *trutta* and parr Atlantics, since its habitat preference mimics the *Salmo* riverine lifestyle almost identically in its lifestyle of hide-and-seek predators.

Sculpins are benthic predator/ambushers that love the same rocky gravel substrate, and cool, fertile, flowing waters that *Salmo* inhabit. They share identical spatial niches and eat almost the same aquatic insects. It is no wonder that often when both are scavenging for food, they have head-on collisions with each other, but the *trutta* will always be the victor.

The mottled freshwater sculpin is the most common and is distinguishable by its olive-brownish-green body with large pectoral fins and black or brown blotched spotting. Along with its taste for aquatic insects it also consumes fish eggs, scuds and cress bugs, and smaller pinhead minnows and trout fry—again, identical to *trutta*'s preferences. They also prefer the same water temperatures as the larger brown trout, from the upper fifties to low sixties.

With their large pectoral fins anchored on the bottom, they tend to rest pointed up on the bottom, constantly surveying the benthic structure for movement as they swim

▲ An image of a Muskegon sculpin caught by Kevin Feenstra. Credit: Kevin Feenstra

in small spurts, pounce on their prey, and hide while they digest. Their perfect body mottling with the bottom makes them very difficult to find by the untrained eye, and even at times the *trutta* themselves hover over them unaware, until the sculpin moves.

Darters look very similar to the sculpins and have an almost identical lifestyle and foraging preferences, but are more colorful. The rainbow darter is very colorful and also a very popular aquarium fish. Most of the minnows are in rivers and streams having back eddy/ shoreline areas with slower, shallow, slacker flows, flows foraging on plankton, and aquatic insects. Chubs are the most common—both in Europe and North America— and constitute a nice delicacy for larger brown trout on the hunt for meat. They are bright silver and grey, which is easier to detect.

There are possibly thousands of minnow species worldwide, and nearly all of them form an important part of the brown trout's diet. My first experience of this was when I used salted dead minnows as bait when I was a boy, swinging them on a fly rod. Smaller yellow perch, bluegill,

and gobies also add substantially to a carnivorous brown trout diet in still waters.

Sucker fish—hog nose and red horse, along with sucker minnows—feed on midge larvae in many tailwater rivers and streams, and provide a very substantial part of the brown trout diet. In my home waters, the Muskegon River, the massive midge population supports a large population of suckers, whose sucker minnow offspring and eggs subsequently allow *trutta* to pack on huge pounds.

In the very fertile salmonid river systems of the Great Lakes, where natural trout and salmon reproduction is very high, salmonid sac fry, fingerlings, and parr are highly important to the diet of larger, carnivorous *trutta*. Brown trout have always been notable for their cannibalistic tendencies. Where you have high degrees of salmonid natural reproduction, you also have the eggs associated with that reproduction. When the Chinook salmon are spawning in the fall, or the steelhead are spawning in the spring, brown trout will form predation lines below the gravel. Also in river systems like New York's Muskegon, Manistee, and Salmon rivers, and other Great Lakes rivers, the significant sucker spawn from late April and into May attracts massive numbers of larger brown trout, who ingest this yellow caviar in great quantities.

Finally, small frogs, snakes, freshwater eels, and newts can contribute substantially to diets of larger *trutta*. Although these morsels are unusual and not often commonly associated with *trutta* behavior in its predation preferences, it nonetheless baffles the mind what they will hunt for in the hunt for their next meal. When it comes to predation on the very wild side, there are stories of gigantic *trutta*saurus consuming small ducklings, geese, moles, mice, mink, and small birds. Their aggressive tendencies have been known to take advantage of anything that moves and swims. We'll address this in Chapter 8.

## Gluttony and the Satiation Issue

Sometimes a brown trout just cannot get enough to eat. The brainwave signal that is closely tied into the human stomach that sends a note to the brain to stop eating is not present in *Salmo*'s physiology. We thus see brown trout and Atlantic salmon being known to be taken in fishermen's nets in Norway weighing sixty to ninety pounds.

We have all seen brown trout that grow so fat that they are shaped like footballs. This is usually during extreme prey availability. In Michigan and elsewhere, we have a *Hexagenia limbata* hatch that allows trout to grow fat fast. In big lake and sea systems, *Salmo* hunting schools/pods consume massive loads of sardines—alewives, herring, smelts—you name it, which allows them to become grossly obese. Back in the 1970s, a fourteen-year-old boy captured a thirty-six-pound brown trout by hand from the Logan River Reservoir. He was strategically positioned in front of a narrow trash/seine net at the bottom of the reservoir where every known imaginable biological drift would pass through. This allowed the massive *trutta* to eat continuously twenty-four hours a day, seven days a week, fifty-two weeks a year.

Ichthyologists throughout the world have often found giant brown trout in lakes and rivers with distended or exploded bellies lying dead along the shoreline. This has been seen several times in the Great Lakes in a sign of extreme predation to the point of death. It is during these very extreme growth surges that a fish's anatomy cannot keep up with the prey intake and us has extreme problems growing to match the amount of food being ingested.

Population density in rivers and lakes also explain growth rates and obesity levels in a very logical fashion. Population density and food competition, is inversely related to average trout size. In highly fecund rivers with massive amounts of reproduction and optimum conditions, as on the Au Sable River in Michigan where the rivers are loaded with brook trout and brown trout in the five-to-nine-inch range, density seems to be a negative factor, since the food supply can only support so much of the population. Again, the Jonssons addressed this tendency in their comprehensive book, *Ecology of Atlantic Salmon and Brown Trout*:

What is the mechanism behind density-dependent growth and reverse growth in rivers? Newman (1993) found that that the fish use the best foraging sites available, and as the density increases, the fish are forced to use less profitable sites. This results in decreased growth but also an increase variation in size. Orbital results from a three-year study of a brown trout population showed that growth to age 1 was significantly reduced for a year class which is about four times as abundant as another cohort study year class. Here the reduction in growth was not due to a decrease in the growth of all trout but due rather to an increasing number of slower growing fish. Search for food may also drop if the energy cost of finding and consuming food is higher than the energy gain of feeding.

So, what can an angler learn from all this scientific information? Basically, if you want more fish in a smaller size, concentrate on the more class-A, blue-ribbon, very cold, and prime reproductive sections of the upper rivers, where size is smaller but population is greater. If you are on the hunt for a trophy leviathan brown, the lower, more marginal sections of river where there is less trout density, as on tailwaters and spring creeks that border from the cool to warm transition periods, these areas will usually hold the largest brown trout due to fewer fish, the more diversified prey, and the fertility of the waters.

In many ice-cold tailwaters that are more oligotrophic, like the Neversink River in the Catskills, the larger brown trout will not take up residency in prime river structure or begin aggressive feeding until the waters in the lower reaches of the river warm to the upper-fifties and mid-sixties.

As with the story of vole predation in New Zealand and Argentina by gluttonous browns and rainbows, or during cicada hatches when fish almost get to the point of exploding stages, the brown trout, due to its curiosity and constant hunt for dominance in its feeding niche, will often put itself at risk for physiological gluttony damage, because it just can't say no to another item of prey. This has allowed them to become evolutionary successful, since overfeeding can sustain organisms through food drought periods. Overall *Salmo* is a very balanced creature in terms of its ability to cautiously scan and forgo unfamiliar predatory experiences, but at the same time exhibit the curiosity to adapt to new food forms as they become available.

▲ Massive Muskegon River *truttasa*urus. Credit: Author

# 7. Tactics and the Chase: The Introspective *Trutta*

A brown trout's senses, DNA encryption, past experiences, and "evolutionary modifications"—which are forever ongoing—define the scope of its behavior and adaptability.

I have often been an admirer of the laws of coincidence and circumstance that environments play in modifying behavior. Pioneered in psychology, the nature vs. nurture debate is a scientific, cultural, and philosophical inquiry about the root causes of human culture, behavior, and personality. Nature is often defined in this debate as genetic or hormone-based behaviors, while nurture is most commonly defined as environment and experience.

So, in our case, if you took three wild German brown trout fry from their ground zero indigenous German rivers like the Wiesent in the Black Forest, and placed them in western hemisphere environments—a mountain freestone river, a spring creek, or a large boulder strewn tailwater—would their characteristics and behavior change dramatically, or are brown trout true to their genetic codes wherever they are placed?

What seems to be a constant is that their true personalities would still dominate and only adapt slightly to their unique environments. It's tough to reshape and mold millions of years of adaptable genetic codes and continual modifying behaviors. As we have discussed niche habitats in the previous chapter, let's look more broadly at more associated river type environments and how *trutta* fit into their ecosystems. The Jonssons scientifically categorize here in their work:

An often used model to simulate potential available habitat for stream living *Salmo trutta* use the "physical habitat simulation system (PHABSIM), by (Milhous, 1989). Estimates available for habitat are for species and life stages as a function of discharge. It requires information about water depth, water velocity, bottom substratum, overhead cover and habitat preference curves for the species in question.

*Salmo* habitat is often size and age structure related. The smallest and youngest parr typically exploit shallower areas closer to shore, and older and larger parr switch to faster and deeper stream habitats as they become larger.

However in small streams, brown trout can be distributed along the entire stream transect. In larger streams, juvenile brown trout are typically located along the bank areas, as large individuals often exploit deep, slow flowing pools and water velocities farther from shore.

## The Classic Global *Salmo* River: The Freestoner

One of the most prominent classic *Salmo* tropisms is an affinity for boulder-strewn, rocky, or gravelly rivers that run through moderate gradients, vary in flow from severe to calm and placid, and are cool and fertile. This goes for *trutta* and *salar* alike. Perhaps 80 percent of *Salmo* rivers worldwide make up this habitat and were the optimum conditions for them to evolve millions of years ago.

Browns and Atlantic salmon are synonymous with mountainous valley freestone rivers. The first documentation of fly fishing by the Romans of the local Vardar River

▲ Metamorphic rock in all sizes and forms are the ideal spatial niche environment for *trutta* on Maryland's Savage River. The river evolved from extreme pressure and was carved by water and into various-sized boulders, stones, and gravel over millions of years. Credit: Mike Tsukamoto

inhabitants in the Dinaric Alpine range of Macedonia took place on freestone Rivers. As with the American hallowed Catskill school, and the western fly fishing new age frontier angler, these types of habitats all produced our humble fly fishing beginnings. The sound of waterfalls and rapids cascading through rocky volcanic boulders, and spring brook tributaries winding through dense green forests of ferns, are indescribably beautiful sights and sounds. Brown trout use freestone rivers in their entirety as they form complex tributary systems of various flow inputs and emanate from mountain brook springs, tributary creeks, spring creek underground aquifers, tiny bog rivulets, and spate runoff waters channeled through geologic craved rocks, forming ideal *trutta* habitat.

Freestone river environments change by the minute—evolution in hydrodynamic motion. Their ecosystems vary throughout their lengths by physical parameters and trout food availability of food. These general ecosystem interactions occur from internally in the river and from external forces. It is here where the shredder insect, *Pteronarcys* stoneflies, tear down the first decaying leaves and forest organic matter. Then the *Hydropsyche*—the caddis and mayfly collectors—share in the optimal plethora of organic matter. Each river system in the world is unique, which is what makes fly fishing and chasing brown trout rivers fascinating.

Most freestone rivers start off very sterile or oligotrophic, emanating from underground caverns void of oxygen, but with extremely pure water, as they hit the rocky gradient forests, tundra or river valleys. Light, oxygen, and organic matter start to add eutrophic fertility, and start the food chain. The coloration of freestone rivers usually come in two types. There are the Alpine—like rivers of mountain origins that have the crystal-clear, bluish—green opaqueness that makes them emerald jewels. You can find them in Slovenia, Italy, New Zealand, and Switzerland, some of the rivers of the Gaspé in Québec like the Grande Riviere and a few out in the Rocky Mountains of Colorado. California's Smith River, with its very low nutrient load, has primary influences of volcanic and calcareous rocks and pristine clear quality, as does the Bonaventure River of the Gaspé. Here you can see fifteen feet down into pools as if they were a shallow foot.

For brown trout to become extremely comfortable and successful in a freestone environment, it should possess a combination of all the various ecosystem variables: food fertility factors, physical characteristics such as fast riffled gradients, long slow Valley stretches and deep Eddy Pools, and excellent gravel for natural reproduction. Freestone rivers have no shortage of this. But even for the adaptive brown trout, the freestone river can be a harsh place that perfects a trout's skill level for survival and dominance. This is most embodied by the Alpine rivers of Europe, the

Kashmir range of India, the mountainous terrain of Kenya, and even the highest elevation streams of the Appalachians and Rocky Mountains, where *trutta* have carved out new frontiers due to their dominance and adaptability.

Freestone brown trout are not "pushovers," as many people think they are—quite to the contrary. I described the extreme visual and spontaneous predatory instincts of freestone *trutta* in my *Selectivity* book, on a Maryland river in the Catoctin Mountains named Big Hunting Creek as an example, where its trout must master fast river flows for food detection, tolerate droughts and floods, and constantly be aware of predators in the shallows that often go undetected due to the volatile and fast-flowing surface water which distorts the trout's vision. If spring creeks embody stability, freestone rivers facilitate chaos and the refinement of a *trutta*'s adaptability skills.

The Beaverkill, Willowemoc, and Ausable systems in New York; Kettle and Pine Creeks in Pennsylvania; the Housatonic in Connecticut; and the Big Hole and Madison in the West are classic American brown trout freestone river systems ideal for analysis. Here, each freestone habitat variable we discussed facilitates the *trutta*'s need to be "in the right place and at the right time," to take advantage of optimal water temperatures and flow, seasonal hatches, available food sources, cover, and nocturnal feeding, procreation, and nursery habitat territorial dominance. The diversification of ice cold forest habitat emptying into wide open valley and meadow sections offers great diversity in water temperature, fertility, and holdover habitat with prime feeding opportunities. Nursery water propagation and adaptability in migration corresponding to seasonal foraging opportunities are important. When these waterways exist without dams, they provide the ultimate migratory highways.

Brown trout in the freestone thoroughfares are masters of capitalizing on the environment when it comes to holding prime water habitats for seclusion, as well as using big shady boulder pools, woody debris, and undercut banks, which you will find throughout these systems in vast numbers regardless of how small or big the river capillaries will be.

Larger freestone systems often support multiple species of trout. Brook trout, rainbows, marble trout in Slovenia, and related salmonids such as grayling can all inhabit the same river system harmoniously. To the individual personalities and tropisms of each fish, they exist harmoniously mostly through their spatial niche habitat separation which is quite universal. However, *trutta* is the master of niche capitalization and food forms as they constantly seek out ideal conditions at any given locale, traveling perhaps dozens of miles in these river capillary systems to forage the best resources. However, due to its migratory roaming tendency it does not usually have a long-term effect on other species.

▲ The brown trout like this Patagonia beast can sometimes come to dominate waterways at certain periods of time. Credit: Jim Klug/Yellow Dog

It is in my humble opinion that any wild trout today is a terrible thing to kill just because it was not the original indigenous population. The proverbial "live and let live" should be more broadly examined as a wild brown, rainbow, brook, or cutthroat trout territories intermix and don't fit the historical molds and models they used to.

Often a significant indicator for disfavor and eradication of a certain species is the establishment of a non-indigenous and hyper-dominant species. Unfortunately and most often the dominant and highly migratory *trutta* is often difficult to measure by biologists, especially in the vast freestone river system trout population densities. Despite modern electroshocking in pounds per hectare modeling evaluations, due to the *trutta*'s elusive and ever-changing migratory character, these estimates are often flawed and only relevant when taken over a long period of time. With the complex freestone river systems and capillary networks, where the *trutta* migration is ongoing throughout the season based on food availability and habitat factors, its population estimates are very tough to gauge. Thus a given sampling might be totally skewed and handicapped if taken at the wrong place and the wrong time, which is often the case in these rivers.

Many times very large brown trout turn up on sections of river where they "should not be," when categorized by traditional blue ribbon trout stream standards set by parameters in fisheries' biology models. This perhaps intrigues me the most about *Salmo trutta* and makes them very frustrating to manage. I am proud that my home state of Michigan uses wild brown trout strains to acclimate when stocking river systems, since "wild genetics" are the masters of adaptation, which inbred hatchery genetics cannot duplicate.

There are some very large, wild nomadic brown trout from the Beaverkill/Willowemoc/Delaware interchanging River system network that are only occasionally caught by the rare night fisherman or boy plying a fly tipped with a worm under a bridge or at Junction Pool. Their special quality and adaptability to run up tiny less than inches deep tributaries to spawn and venture into marginal waters deemed almost impossible for survival, are the keys to the vast success of the freestone rivers that offer outstanding *trutta* abundance at any given time of year. Only through modern era radio telemetry and GPS tagged monitoring, are we beginning to see the complexity of habitat pursuit in these vast systems.

## The Tailwater/Freestone Component/Trutta Highways

In the past, I and other authors have treated tailwater rivers and freestoners separately. But having fished them and guided on them for fifty-one years, they are essentially the same beast. Throughout the world, tailwaters are perhaps 95 percent total freestone rivers that had been dammed for

One tendency today in the fisheries management world is to eradicate certain species in favor of an indigenous species. This secular purist indigenous viewpoint occurs in brook trout waters of the East Coast of North America and rainbow trout and cutthroat of the West. Often brown trout are eradicated due to them showing up in high numbers of the population versus the indigenous species. Time and time again this purist indigenous restoration ideal usually fails due to the extreme dominance and persistence of the brown trout to be apex predators and dominators.

As in the 1980s, the brown trout of the Big Spring in PA were electro-shocked out of the upper "ditch" to allow the indigenous brook trout to have a competitive free domain, even though browns wanted to dominate. Similarly, in the indigenous brook trout waters off the Appalachian range in Virginia along the Skyline Drive, these spectacular jewels figure in highly in protecting their indigenous prominence in fisheries management. However Blue Ridge Mountain Rivers have been overrun by wild brown trout stemming from lower elevation streams and often their population is slightly greater than the indigenous brook trout. But through it all the two still coexist in perfect harmony, as brookies push further up the ecosystems in spatial separation.

▲ The Delaware River system, with its west, east, and main branches, looks like a massive spring creek/freestoner with reproductive potential and navigability for brown trout. Credit: John Miller

hydropower, or water reservoirs on existing freestone rivers. Aside from the ice-cold water input, from a geological and ecological standpoint, freestones and tailwaters keep the same structure.

Tailwaters are freestoners on steroids. But steroids as you know come with a double-edged sword. Most are built through mountains or steep gradients cutting through the rocky morainal terrain, where the dams and impoundments have the most effect in storing water. Thus the beautiful combination of boulders and gravel structure gives these rivers the classic riffle/pocket/pool/tail-out format. The bottom draw cold-water influence thus changes the river system forever by often unleashing very cold subterranean limestone ground waters like on the South Holston and White River tailwaters. As a result many tailwaters take on the look of spring creeks with the tremendous weed growth, which foster swimming and clinging mayflies, scuds, and cress bugs.

The lake or reservoir impoundments add the fertility dimension to often very dystrophic and sterile freestone systems. Thus having a combination of photoplankton and zooplankton, which greatly feeds a number of aquatic invertebrates including caddisflies and scuds. Pelagic baitfish spills often occur when reservoirs are flooded. From a benthic standpoint, when heavy-duty hydropower turbines churn shad, alewives, and other sardine-like baitfish, as on the White River in Arkansas, the additional nutrients provide tremendous growth rates for the carnivorous browns.

On the negative trophic side, hydro dam peak electricity generation can cause abuse to freestone rivers by scouring the benthic structure, depleting insect populations, and stunting potential natural reproduction. Some river systems like the Delaware have drastic changes in flow, especially in the fall of 2017 where it was dropped to 95 CFS and thus put major damage and stress on spawning brown trout.

But overall their benefits create leviathan brown trout fisheries where they didn't exist and can have long-term positive effects in increased mayfly populations to the detritus and organism fertility emanating from the reservoir. Also since the highest elevation in gradient points are usually selected for the dam builders, what lies below a tailwater is a usually long, very flat, and placid river flow system that brown trout highly prefer. Think of the dams being built at the riffles of a river which always signify gradient, and you will get a picture of why brown trout love them so much. The exceptions are in very high elevation short stretches of tailwaters between dams where white-water canyons and rapids exist. But these are the exception rather than the rule. The manifest destiny of *trutta* will find a way to dominate all of it given the chance. The great diversity of habitat and food fertility allows *trutta* to truly develop its ideal lifestyle. Being the masters of extremes, brown trout are happy to capitalize on the baitfish factor at high flows, and the clarity of low waters during midge hatches.

## Drift Boat Hunting

Since a good amount of trout fishing is done from drift boats and power jets on big rivers, let's look at this very efficient way to cover lots of water. It can put the fly angler in great positions to make excellent casts and presentations, and allows long, drag-free drifts with dry flies and nymphs. But as perfect a vehicle as it seems, it also is a huge deterrent to very selective brown trout, given the trout's sensory mechanisms. Since I guide from a drift boat or jet boat, I could not live without one, especially on big tail water rivers, but I have learned to use them, and often look for ways to use them more efficiently. The boats will cause problems for all the major trout sensory areas at one time or another, so here are some considerations.

When you or your anglers are casting, remember that you are at a very high profile. The sunlight's reflection will cast longer on the water and for a greater distance than wading. When the trout is looking up at the high-floating wings of the mayfly as it comes into its vision window, your head and body will also be highly visible on the edge of the bent refraction window that allows a trout to see around corners. As for shadows, the bottom of a drift boat is easily detected if the trout is at deeper level, which gives it an expanded window of vision.

The sound imprint is also very pronounced with your boat. Dropping anchors and clanging the bottom sends massive vibrations. Oars hitting the surface or the side of the bow create vibrations and ripples. Your feet stomping on the boat's bottom also leaves a great acoustic footprint.

So given all this for thought, here is what to do best. If you can get out of a drift boat and approach selective trout by wading at a lower profile, do so. Be very careful when lowering the anchor; do it slowly. Always look at which direction the sun is to your profile and limit the shadows.

Drift boats also have unique beneficial aspects. When anchored, they often create seams and creases in the current flow below the boat downstream, funneling surface food were trout take up feeding positions. Anchors scraping the bottom have been known to create a San Juan shuffle. In this instance the benthic dwelling insects become stirred up as part of the biological drift. Often trout will come very close to the drift boat, since the bottom of the boat is perceived as wooded security structure,

and also becomes a shady refuge area for the trout. In addition, the boat's hull and oars are great attractors for egg-laying caddis and stoneflies, in addition to giving off human heat from its passengers, which attracts mayfly spinners on a cold evening. If you ever wondered why mayfly spinners hover over the top of your boat or head and are otherwise nowhere else to be found in the river, it is a result of this thermal situation.

## Spring Creeks: *Salmo*'s Posh Domain

Fly fishers who are enamored with spring creeks worship them as God's special brew, as a Wyoming preacher once labeled them. In all my writings I constantly pinpoint that wonderful description since they run at a constant perfect temperature year-round, have the ability for trout to feed in them 365 days a year, and are not subject to extreme velocities in flow. Their ideal vodka-clear waters allow you to see the trout in its predator-prey relationships vividly, unlike the many thunderous, tannic-stained freestone rivers. Spring creeks embody the passion and lifelong pursuit for the selective fly angler—especially where brown trout are found.

If there were ever "Ground Zero" waters of foundational importance, it would be the meandering, weed-filled chalk stream spring creeks of England. The founding fathers and mothers of early fly fishing crafted the art form on these placid waters, such as Dame Juliana at the nunnery near St. Albans in Hertfordshire, on the River Avon. Her writings in the 1486 *Boke of St. Albans* on fly fishing tactics and fly patterns for Avon's *Salmo* were the true first treatise to ever exist in modern civilization. Fly patterns made with exotic bird feathers and leaders of perfectly entwined horsehair made fifteenth-century fly fishing not too far from what we do today.

As our sport continued its iconic development later in the 1800s with the historic mental jousting of Halford and Skues on the British chalk stream of Hampshire country and its fabled Test and Itchen Rivers, wild resident brown trout, sea-run strains, and Atlantic salmon all transformed the angling art into a highly passionate pursuit of individual styles. Halford, with the gentleman's proper dry fly approach, and Skues's promotion of the subsurface nymph, thus forming the everlasting debate that still divides our sport today in beautifully drastic complements; from matching the hatch on the surface, to fishing large articulated nymphs and streamers.

This spring creek foundation was elevated even further on the benches of the Letort Spring Run, as the limestone legends of Marinaro, Fox, Koch, Harvey, and others created a complex web all brought to you by *Salmo trutta* and its whimsical capricious ways as we discussed in the last chapter. Things haven't changed much and even to this day on the Letort, fish are just as super selective as they were a century ago.

▲ Spring Coulee, in the massive spring-filled *trutta* mecca of the Driftless, Wisconsin. Credit: John Flaherty/Author

Spring Creek brown trout are at the highest echelon of selectivity's dynamics, and will humble and torment even the most accomplished angler. Fishing spring creeks should be more appropriately summed up as "hunting spring creeks." For here every selection of tackle, fly, approach and thought process, must be carefully weighed and examined—careless bumbling through the Spring Creek meadows and trashing the water, like on a Freestone River, just doesn't work here! Spring Creek anglers are elitists—purists—anglers that have gone to a higher level of appreciating the sport. These creeks are not for everyone, nor should they be.

Limestone spring creeks are loaded with alkaline calcium carbonate, $CaCO_2$. This, along with other nutrients is a powerful stimulant to start the whole food chain process starting with aquatic vegetation—elodea, duckwort, chara, watercress, etc. Here begins the plankton growth, setting the right conditions for aquatic insects and other benthic invertebrates.

Limestoners percolate from the exposed subterranean caverns lying at the bottom of mountain ranges where volcanic rock upheavals took place. Here they gush from the valley floors at a perfect 48° to 53° F water temperature and remain that way year-round, despite heat waves,

subzero winter temperatures, droughts, and floods: perfect for a brown trout with year-round predatory tendencies.

Valleys between mountain ranges, perfect pastoral livestock grazing areas, fertile soils, prime farmland, and the "Amish Springs Factor" I call it, are good ways to find spring creeks. It's truly amazing how the Amish farms from Pennsylvania to Virginia and Tennessee, from Ohio to Wisconsin and Minnesota, have all settled in fertile valleys surrounded by spring creeks. Here cows and sheep graze through the gentle flowing meadows as brown trout sip tiny mayflies and eat helpless terrestrials in the summer. The *trutta* utopia here is in the water's tranquility and stability. Only during extreme flooding of the valleys, usually from hurricane systems, will disrupt the stable waterway harmony of spring creeks. The limestone valleys of England's Hampshire, Pennsylvania's Cumberland Valley, the Shenandoah Valley of Virginia, and the Driftless area in Wisconsin/Minnesota, extending to the Paradise Valley in Montana and Sun Valley in Idaho, all have one thing in common: extremely selective spring creek brown trout.

Wherever spring creeks are found in the world, civilization and the *Salmo* is embodied in them as part of the lifestyle. Native Indian base camps were always found close to them for their wonderful year-round source of pure, clean, subterranean water that provides food for wildlife and fish year-round for sustenance. Army camps in the various wars dating back to the Revolutionary and civil wars used them for their drinking water in strategic locations in valleys where the enemy could be seen from a distance. Here British soldiers on the Yellow Breeches in Pennsylvania washed their stark white wardrobe, which eventually turned yellow from the alkalinity and thus the river got its name.

The "Amish Springs Factor" highways here in North America usually will find spring creeks dotted alongside them. Historic highways such as Routes 81, 11, 30, and others dot a trail through limestone pastoral farm country, where buggies and horses, turn-of-the-century barns, and iconic buildings and churches accompany the limestone legacy. Always an indicator of the springs are the spring houses, the proverbial provisions storage units that use the cool thermal springs in the summer and warm effect in winter to house the precious cured meats, root vegetables, the churned butter, and cheese wheels that provide sustainability for a culture that doesn't have modern appliances. They are usually located on a spring branch and many a large leviathan brown was pulled from these

structures. All along this Amish Trail you will find towns and roads named after the springs such as Springfield, Boiling Springs, Bellefontaine, Warm Springs, Mineral Springs, and the list goes on of indicator names revealing the jeweled Spring Creek gems.

The crystalline spring creek waters are conducive to *trutta*'s wariness of predators due to wide open spaces and the moist soils that transmit vibrations, along with their extremely detailed evaluation of natural and imitative fly patterns that must be perfect for deception. Due to spring aquifers always being such prized real estate for agriculture and drinking water facilities, they are also prime targets for state and federal hatchery builders to have a constant supply of year-round ideal water to grow trout and salmon. Find these hatcheries and you'll almost always find spring creeks. Browns love the waters below the hatcheries for the massive midge and Crustacea output of the nutrients. Also a good hurricane low pressure system coming up the coast or inland and dumping inches of rain almost always lead to an opening of the hatchery gates, spilling helpless pellet-fed juvenile trout to carnivorous leviathan brown trout waiting below. From New York's Caledonia Spring Creek, to Pennsylvannia's Spring Creek in State College, to

▲ Although *Salmo trutta* has come to inhabit even hostile regions, the spring creek environment is ideally suited to their needs, where they can grow quite large, like this specimen caught on a midge pupa imitation on the Kickapoo, Wisconsin. Credit: Jack Flaherty

Iowa's Spring Branch Run, the browns below the hatcheries can be the most difficult and discriminatory epicurean feeders around.

Another iconic Spring Creek, Big Spring Run near Newville, Pennsylvania, once had a massive state hatchery at its source and its wild indigenous brook trout coexisted with rainbows and browns in a niche spatial separation environment. But it was always the larger browns that carved out a nice dominant feeding lie for themselves in peculiar places to dominate the predator food chain.

Enter here the amazing Silver Creek in Idaho. It showcases the classic feeding styles of spring creek leviathan browns despite competition. It is an oasis in the vast Sun Valley arid desert. The valley below scrapes the top of huge subterranean aquifers fed by surrounding mountains to create a high-altitude spring creek like no other in the world. The vegetation and ecosystem support one of the highest densities of insect life of any trout stream in America.

Its browns grow to very large sizes. Big twenty-inch-plus fish will sip and gulp in the backwater sloughs just like in the spring creeks of Paradise Valley in Montana. A plethora of aquatic mayflies from brown drakes to tiny olives, not to mention the meadow grasses and with its terrestrial insect buffet, feed the selective fish who are careful and take their time when foraging.

The *Tricorythodes* hatch (tricos), is massive here. Every day from summer until late fall, the emergers, maters, and spent spinners blizzard from dawn until the high noon sun. It is a protocol affair—very structured and regimented as the fish population attends to its daily feeding needs. Pods of rainbows and brown trout will take positions in small schools on the shallow runs, waiting for the spinner flights to fall and the meal to begin. Dominant fish jockey for position and try to protect the prime feeding lanes. But the occasional big brown bully crashes the party and pushes out all the rest of the submissive rainbow and brown feeders.

But the big *trutta* seem to be the most selective/reflective feeders and adept at intercepting the prime mother loads of backwashed, spent spinners. In the reverse spiraling sloughs, the heavy accumulation of spent spinners and lack of current flows, makes these big bruiser browns nearly impossible to catch. The slightest intrusion on these current-less waters, casts a warning signal as soon as the fly and leader casts a the slightest shadow. Thanks to their gluttonous predisposition, they are maximizing their "cost/benefit" analysis of the daily metabolic equation. They act like channel catfish on the Susquehanna in Pennsylvania, carpet-vacuuming feeding machines.

To be successful with these fish, they are on the hunt for double/triple spinner patterns, maximizing prey efficiency. I fool these leviathans on a size 12, long-shank hook with a cluster "trico bomb," tying two females and one male spinner, using clear and black bodies with peacock thoraxes and organza for the wing material. Also, I put a good curve in the bend of the hook, to imitate the burnt up and spent form of the fly on the water.

▲ A big brown feeding on mayfly spinners. Credit: Dave Jensen

Stalk and hunt your trophies by watching and observing with less casting—the twenty-five-inch beast of a brown you hook of a lifetime will be just as surprised it took your offering as you did! So when confronted with garbage-feeding spinner vacuum cleaners—whether it be on the Bighorn, Silver Creek or Delaware, each large fish will maximize its movement to the surface and capture multiple insects in a highly specialized way.

## Spring Creek Stealth and *Trutta*'s Magnificent Perception

Given what we know about the brown trout's vision, vibration, and motion detection capabilities, it would pay off in great dividends to study the greatest angling predators of all—the great blue heron. These amazing fish hunters can teach fly anglers more about approach than any book or video. The stalking heron is a magnificent display of everything the fly angler can hope to be when approaching very wary, fussy, and selective trout. A heron's strength lies in its slowness, blending, extreme patience, and stealth.

Habituation and assimilation are extremely important predatory attributes. All dominant predators (flyfishermen being one of them), use this for stealth, cloaking and to create calm before the act of predation. In psychology it is "the gradual decline of a response to a stimulus resulting from repeated exposure to the stimulus." Having guided clients for trout over twenty years and fly fishing for them since I was young enough to remember, I can tell you how important it is to slow down and blend in—also create "a quiet time" break. Watching the old-timer sit on the rocks, smoking his pipe, as trout sip tiny blue-winged-olives on a long Catskill Eddy pool, is a classic example of habituating. The fly fisher must slow down and blend in. Bright-colored clothing is for magazine covers only! As the fly fisher stages motionless or near that state, it will not alarm the trout scheme of vision and its sensory receptors.

The heron soon learns the four R's of predation—REFRACTION, RIPPLES, RAIN, and REFLECTION. Paying attention to these and capitalizing on them in your approach, since they distort the trout's vision, gets you into tight sight fishing and hatch-matching situations, giving you a greater degree of success with extremely fussy fish.

Shadows and the predator's reflections will put down trout very quickly. Raindrops on the water are a blessing and a curse. When sight fishing, it makes the discernment of the trout's movement and feeding pattern hard to see. For the bipolar shy/aggressive brown, it gives it more comfort as it surface window is distorted. Conversely, the condition makes it tougher for predatory advances and distinguishing surface insects for identification. In these situations, even the fussiest trout can accept poor fly presentation and imitations. I recall a day filled with rain on the Delaware tailwater in the junction pool, whose trout are known throughout the world as being the most fussy. In the steady rain they took my Blue-Winged Olive emergers with reckless abandon. Such careless behavior rarely happens on the Delaware. The distorting ripples from waves and wind has the same effect both for prey and predator.

Refraction only applies when the heron or fly angler is at a high profile and very close to the surface. Here a heron learns how to compensate by moving its head from left to right, up and down, to compare the angles and depth perception and to bow its head not to be seen. The same applies to the angler, who should stay as low as possible by kneeling, squatting, or on all fours.

The detection of sound by fish is linked through two sensory systems, the inner ears and the mechanosensory lateral lines. Given the fact that the brown trout evolved in dark forest and ocean environments—often with less than optimal light, hearing and vibration sensation played a more important role than vision. All *Salmos* have a close proximity of the inner ear location to the swim bladder. Gas densities in the swim ladder are much lower than that of its watery environments, thus compressing the swim bladder gas through sound waves.

*Salmo* also have neuromasts below the skin surface, which are hair cells that detect motion. Pores will hook-up the prey/predator movements to the fluid inside the lateral line canals, where change in water flow are detected, translating into sonic abrasions. It's amazing to watch a pool of freshly-stocked trout—or newly-migrated salmon swimming in a school up from the ocean or lake. It is as if every movement and action change is perfectly synchronized in accordance with perfect spacing between fish occurring—you see this in a school of aquarium fish, and large schools of pelagic bait at sea. This is a result of water flow information reaching each fish through the lateral line at precisely the same time and distance, resulting in perfect choreography.

In summary, the neuro-sensory organs of all *Salmos* are carefully linked, allowing them to detect prey and predation very easily. Since we are talking about selective spring creek browns, notch up these sensory advances of each fish even more slightly.

## Spring Creek Approach and Presentation

Brown trout on spring creeks manifest selective behavior as a lifestyle due to the relative ease of feeding and less urgent frequency. Also, Spring Creek trout will just shut down for long periods when alarmed by predators, such as fly fishers and avian attacks. Aggressive phases are usually during a heavy hatch, nighttime, or during a time when a plethora of summer terrestrials become available, such as grasshoppers, beetles, tiny ants, and cicadas. But these aggressive phase occurrences are few and far between. Slowness and ease are the hallmarks of the spring creek trout—the pursuing fly angler must adopt the same habits.

There is an age-old battle of approach philosophies dating back from the English chalk stream/spring creek methodology. It was common practice to fish a dry fly only upstream to rising fish. As more and larger spring creek waters were discovered like Silver Creek in Idaho, some European spring creeks, Montana and New Zealand spring creeks, anglers discovered that the larger waters were best suited for the use of downstream fly presentations, like the down—and—across reach cast. Here, the highly-selective fish required the use of long twelve-to-eighteen-foot leaders with very fine five-to-seven-foot tippets, so the fly comes into the trout's window first, long before the fly line. Also, drag is eliminated and reduced by very long drifts, especially when combined with a puddle cast and downstream stack-mending.

However, this tactic also has disadvantages. Approaching from the downstream position allows the angler to be cloaked as the fish faces upstream. If the angler comes from upstream while fishing downstream, part of the angler's body or fly rod will penetrate the refractive window of the trout's vision, thus alarming the trout and triggering passive/dormant behavior. Regardless of which

approach you desire, a very low, stealthy profile and infrequent false casting are the keys to success. Walking softly—sometimes tiptoeing around on elbows and knees—is necessary for extremely spooky wild brown trout. Good knees and patience are required—knee pads under your waders also help. When the famous Ed Shenk of Pennsylvania's Letort stalked trout upstream from the Bonny Brook Bridge, he did it on his knees, and only for very short stretches.

You don't jump out of a vehicle and just start fishing a Spring Creek. Having a plan of attack and familiarity with its trout behavior is paramount. My approach to Hot Creek in California, in the wide-open high valleys of the Yosemite range, will be different than from wooded spring creek in Pennsylvania or Trout Run in Minnesota. Since they are usually low-lying valley waters in open spaces, shadows become important, as well as your footsteps on the wet, swampy pastures. The overall mandate on spring creeks is to slow everything down, keep it small and minimal, and visualize your presentation before you actually present it.

## Spring Creek/Tailwater Dry Tactics

Since the trout's feeding channels between vegetation columns are usually narrower, the trout's inspection window is usually shorter and limited. On bigger spring creeks,

▲ Bob Cramer makes a low, stealthy approach on Virginia's Mossy Creek.

move and wade slowly into a down-and-across casting position. However, the word slowly cannot be more critically emphasized. On bigger waters like Silver Creek or Henry's Fork, it might take a good ten minutes before you get into a position not to disrupt the fish feeding.

It is critical to understand Marinaro's simple, compound, and complex rise forms. During a consistent and somewhat frequent emergence of Blue-Winged Olives or Sulphers, the trout will set up the most advantageous feeding station and take adults and emergers in a simple rise form. If the fish has a long inspection area of feeding—wider creeks and feeding lanes—the trout will revert to compound rise feeding, especially during sparse hatches, or occasionally to available terrestrial insects. Complex rise forms usually occur to larger mayflies, quickly-moving egg-laying caddis and stoneflies, or to large terrestrial objects like grasshoppers and cicadas. Since the frequency of let's say a giant Sulpher *Potamanthus* mayfly—size 6—is often rarer, but does occur, the brown trout's radar alarm is very high. Equally so with twitching and skittering big grasshoppers.

Before an extremely wary large brown makes a decision on a highly-scrutinized food form, it will look for a few discerning characteristics that will cause it to follow it downstream, turn back to its original lie, only to follow it and pursue it again, and finally take or refuse the natural or imitation. A fly fisher imparting a simple twitch, quiver, at the right time, or side swimming motion to the fly, will pull the attack switch on for a cautious and highly speculative trout. Here is where *trutta* selectivity goes into overdrive and really puts on a show. Some anglers loath the challenge, some will pull their hair out in frustration, and others like me will get the popcorn out and watch the show!

## The Benthos-to-Meniscus Strata Approach

The object of fly fishing, whether wet or dry, is the catching of trout, not anyhow, but by means refined, clean, delicate, artistic, and in a sportsmanlike sense that are fair to the quarry and fair to the brother angler.
—G. E. M. Skues

The above passage pretty much sums up Skuesian dogma. With his masterworks *Minor Tactics of the Chalk Stream, The Way of the Trout with the Fly*, and *Nymph Fishing for Chalk Stream Trout*, Skues lays out the anthology for selectivity. His observations, tactics, fly patterns, and empirical theories on trout behavior are to this day the bible for our sport. It is a little pity that most modern-day fly fishers have no knowledge of this genius.

Skues's incredible observations of how brown trout see each detail of the fly's form, silhouette, and definition, as well as trout feeding behavior, rise forms, and the underwater world of how browns see nymphs, are light years ahead of anything observed today. He invented the first "stomach pump" by using a marrow scoop. To Skues, fly fishing for brown trout was an intellectual extension of his incredible bright and analytical legal mind. It was the intellectual chase and drama of the pursuit that made him the first founding father of selective brown trout. But it is his beloved nymph fishing he will always be remembered for.

There has been so much written about the nymphing game in the past century and a half that it seriously boggles the mind. From the most simplistic applications to the highest echelon pinnacle of modern "tight-line/Euro" nymphing refinement, much of it can be quite intimidating. Nevertheless the extreme effectiveness of nymphing will forever dominate the brown trout fly fisher's arsenal.

However, sticking to my guns and staying on point, my goal in my *Salmo* treatise here is not to reinvent the proverbial "nymphing wheel," but once again relate to the nymphing nuances that pertain to my subject matter. There is no question as I frequently mention, that *trutta* definitely influenced the amazing writings of Skues and Sawyer. Here, progressive nymphing masters like George Daniel and his book *Dynamic Nymphing*, as well as the most current complete manifesto of the always insightful writings of Jason Randall, with his newly-released *Nymph Masters*, have much in common with classics like Schwiebert's classic, *Nymphs*. Fortunately for the angler, current practitioners have micro-analyzed nymphing techniques, mystique, and deadly effectiveness to perfection.

The classic "piece of the pie" chart as seen in Cecil Heacox's work *The Complete Brown Trout*, indicates that nymphs comprise 90 percent of the brown trout's diet. This predatory prowess applies highly to brown trout on several levels.

It is no secret that *trutta* is a master of seclusion and has an affinity for camouflaging itself between rock crevices and gravel substrata. Also its photophobic tendency to retreat from life as much as possible favors these areas that are open to twenty-four-hour predator feeding regardless of the weather outside. Needless to say, nymphing and brown trout go together like bread and butter.

With this tropic tendency, they also love feeding in slower currents—much slower than its cousin the Atlantic salmon that uses the boulder/rock substrata to cushion flows even in the most volatile riffles, rapids and runs. In Heacox's 90 percent rule, he also shows that mayflies comprise 90 percent of the brown trout diet. As we know today this is not always the case in the brown's diet, which will be a total function of its habitat and maximum caloric intake which could result in the extreme as 90 percent being in the shrimp and cress bug spectrum, or terrestrials, as we often see in highly fertile spring creeks and tailwaters.

In addition, as Jonsson and Jonsson mentioned in their masterpiece, *trutta*'s preference to be a "sit-and-wait"

▲ Nymphing is the bread-and-butter approach to the photophobic brown trout. Credit: Torrey Collins

predator often favors this prime feeding lie/current-based positioning to intercept nymphs that get caught up in the bubble line flow. Find the strategic interception points and you will find brown trout nymphing nirvana. Here, look for shallow-to-medium depths and small/rocky/boulder pocket water directly below a white foam bubble line, and you will find these prime taking lies.

Again, with an application to its trophic tendency, as mentioned in earlier chapters, the brown trout does not like to come in physical contact with its habitat—meaning though it closely secludes itself amongst the rocks, undercut banks, and dead falls, it usually will never touch them in its breathing, swimming, observing and predatory state. But it has a tendency and high degree of accuracy in picking off food items off of the bottom, rocks, woody structures, and cement bridge pylons, by dipping its head downward vertically and picking and shredding its prey free from their habitat if necessary. This is more so a common occurrence in the *trutta* predator profiles than other species of trout.

## Tight-Line Euro/Slavic Nymphing

Other than the two-handed Spey revolution that is still occurring in its renaissance of the last two decades, no other form of fly fishing has taken on such an amazing grip than Euro nymphing. Manufacturers have created many rods, lines, and fly patterns in the last decade to support this extremely effective trout presentation technique that has taken the industry by storm.

Being in the right place at the right time is the key to much of life and creative opportunity. In the early 1980s I stumbled upon the early forms of Euro nymphing totally by accident. It was the summer of 1980 and I was fresh out of college with a three-month Eurail pass from my parents to sow my adventurous oats in the land of my ancestors, along with a culinary apprenticeship. I still had uncles, aunts, cousins, and grandparents in Poland and Austria that I had been dying to see since I was a little boy.

It was on a June day in the wonderful resort mountain town of Zakopane, Poland, high up in the Carpathian Alps.

▲ Fly-fishing master, Dave Karczynski, stalks Poland's Carpathian Alp waters, Ground-Zero for Euro nymphing, and its cherished browns: *pstrąg potokowy.*
Credit: Arek Kubala

It is the home of the Gorale mountaineer folk, "Polish hill-billies," as Dad called them; he came from the aristocratic northern Pomeranian/Prussian elite. The Gorale mountain folk were very creative; everything they touched was a work of art. From their Podhale style architecture of beautiful wood engravings to thatched roof A-frame mountain villas, their intricately-colored Easter eggs, custom fiddles and bagpipes, festive stitch celebratory embroidered "parzenica" dance outfits—whatever they touched, they had a distinctive mountain flair. Their delish smoked sheep cheeses, mountain air dry-cured meats and sausages, hunters' stews (bigos), and smoked trout were delicacies to die for.

The Carpathian Alps have hundreds of miles prime freestone rivers and tributaries, with beautifully-colored, spotted brown trout (*Salmo fario major*—like the ones in the French Pyrenees). Known locally as "*pstrag*," they were found in gorgeous rivers like the Dunajec, where the world championship of fly fishing competitions has been since held.

One day on a mountain hike with several cousins and a young lady friend I met, we came across several Gorale men fishing in a beautiful little mountain stream tributary. The rods were beech saplings finely whittled and lacquered with some German monofilament attached to the tip—sort of a Tenkara dapping cane pole. Their intricately-woven caddis larva and mayfly nymphs handmade of silk and ladies garment fibers were amazing. They would fish fast boulder-strewn riffles and lead the line with the current, setting the hook often on any tiny bump they felt. Needless to say I saw them catch dozens of trout and stuff them in fern-lined pouches and baskets for their dinner tables. Little did I know I was witnessing the first crude type of Euro nymphing, which has now become a craze throughout the world.

When speaking in Polish to one of the Gorale, I noticed they had quite different accents from the northern part of Poland. They explained to me that fly equipment was a luxury item almost impossible to come by in those still communist Soviet bloc countries, unless you had American dollars and bartered on the black market. Thus they had to make do with what they had and occasionally got a hold of a Western Europe fly fishing magazine for inspiration. It was a pretty cool thing to witness, needless to say.

Thus these crude beginnings eventually evolved into highly-effective nymphing techniques that were further enhanced by the Poles, Czechs, Slovaks, and French, and taken to world fly fishing championships where numbers and measured inches of fish is the deciding factor for victory. It is now the standard technique in all world fly fishing championships and has recently been perfected further by the French using twenty-foot leaders and eleven-foot 3-weight rods. In essence it has become monofilament nymphing, a tactic the famous Pennsylvania fly-fishing master Joe Humphreys wrote about in *Fly Fisherman* magazine back in the mid-1980s.

The reason deep-bottom dredging/tight line/Euro nymphing is so effective on brown trout is that it presents the fly "in the fish's face" in living spaces between the rock crevices and gravel benthos substrate. It is essentially high-stick/tight-line nymphing with direct contact to the bottom strata, and is highly effective in mountainous, rocky, boulder-strewn rapids, riffles, and runs. Much of the world championship competitions were hosted in Europe where the mountain trout streams of the Alps had high numbers of brown trout populations and grayling, though due to their harsh environments, did not hold extremely large fish. Thus the numbers game was the key. On big tailwaters, where long, drag-free drifts with indicators are needed, and in very weedy-bottomed spring creeks, the Euro game is not applicable except in a few "clean" rocky gravel slots.

The technique was introduced to the US national team in 1997 when the United States hosted the competition. A Polish angler by the name of Viadi Trzebenuia, a former Polish world champion, became enamored with the beauty of the American trout streams of the Snake River Valley and decided to coach the Americans in this highly-effective technique. It is now replacing strike indicator nymphing at alarming rate, but has its effectiveness range of the close to mid proximity presentations.

Josh Miller, Torrey Collins, Nanda Sanise, and Aaron Jasper are die-hard *trutta* Tight Liners—they live and breathe the down-and-dirty tight-line nymphing gig. They, along with the author, pragmatically break down their presentations as follows:

- Ten- and eleven-foot delicate-tipped rods in the 3- and 4- weight range seem to be the norm these days. Long leaders with very little to no taper and a short line is the key to having as much direct contact with the bottom.
- True fly casting is not involved here but a refined vertical lob-tuck cast penetrating to the bottom is the key—all in keeping a vertical presentation with the rod tip leaving the line at a low profile and a minimally slighter faster speed than the current. Here you are bouncing and slithering the fly presentations close to or on the bottom, using your rod tip to gauge depth and allow " bump and slide" maneuvering as to not get snagged.
- Keep constant tension and feel the bottom and effectively lead your flies downstream and setting the hook often and every time you feel a pause or hesitation, which can be minimally slight at best. Position sets or "lifting" sets are common at the end

▲ It takes time and practice to learn the lethal subtleties of sighter tips. Credit: Aaron Jasper.

of the drift before the line is quickly put back into another drift. Since the technique is mostly in faster water, the trout often hook themselves with the help of the current, but it is an extremely "sixth sense" learned technique that becomes more proficient with use.

• The most common rig is a series of nymphs directly hooked from the shank in tandem, or as droppers with the main heavy weighted anchor fly—usually a large stonefly. Weight is incorporated into the flies, usually woven into the body or as bead heads in gold, tungsten, or copper, or with jig bead head nymphs. The "twenty-inch" separation rule allows for less foul hooking and "wrapped up in line" battles.

• "Sighter tips," are usually orange and green amnesia or poly background materials make for your built-in indicator into the line, that lets you monitor the slightest take in the meniscus to detect even the slightest takes. Serious anglers prefer different levels in the leader system where these sight indicators are set.

Torrey Collins, a fly shop guru in Connecticut on the Farmington, further elaborates on integral leader dynamics:

Currently I like a tapered butt section of clear Amnesia mono about 10 feet long (5-foot 15-pound, 3-foot 12-pound, 2-foot 10-pound, or substitute a 9-foot 0X leader if you don't want to tie up a butt section), tied to an 18-inch mono "sighter" with two to four colored sections (I like bi-color Cortland Indicator Mono in the .012–.009 inch range) with a 2 mm tippet ring on the bottom end of it, and to that normally attach 5–7 feet of 5X–6X fluorocarbon tippet—5X is typical and is a good choice if you are just starting with this method. Deeper water and fishing further away both require longer tippets, smaller streams/shallower water dictate a shorter 3–5 foot piece. I put a 2 mm tippet ring on the end of this long piece so as not to eat up this section every time I have to add new tippet to the end of it. I tie my final two fluorocarbon tippet pieces to the tippet ring, one about 18–24 inches for my heavier/ anchor fly on it, and another about 4–8 inches for my smaller/lighter dropper fly. I use the same size tippet to my anchor fly as the long piece above it, and the dropper fly is tied to the same size tippet, or maybe 1/2–1 size lighter. The smaller the dropper fly, the more I'm apt to use a lighter tippet.

If you don't want to tie up your own leader, there

are some excellent pre-made ones available. Rio makes an excellent Euro leader that has a 9–10 foot milky white butt section with a 2-foot colored sighter section and a tippet ring on the end of it, and then you just add a long piece of tippet to that.

Lighter tippet catches more trout . . . *sometimes*, but not necessarily for the reason you might think. If you use all thin tippet below your sighter, you decrease water drag and increase the sink rate of your nymphs, so they get to the bottom faster, and without having to use super heavy flies. Even reducing your tippet by only one "X" size significantly reduces hydrodynamic drag (dropping from 4X to 5X decreases water drag by about 35 percent according to my engineer friend). Thinner tippet is also more flexible, which allows your flies greater freedom of movement, so they present more naturally.

How thin is thin enough? You'll have to experiment to see what works for you personally, but I'd go as thin as is practical for the conditions and fish size. For normal-sized flies and trout, I would recommend 5X–6X as a starting point, giving you a good sink rate combined with reasonable break strength and abrasion resistance. Match the fly weight/size to the tippet diameter. Lighter flies require lighter tippet to properly sink them. A ten to eleven foot 2–3 weight rod with a soft tip is ideal to cushion your tippet against break-offs if you like to fish lighter tippets.

Torrey further insists you keep these points in mind in your approach:

- Start close to the bank and progressively work yourself out in two-to-three-foot intervals and feeding lanes.
- Keep moving, "run and gun," make a few casts and move on—be careful not to take a spill in the fast rocky waters since you are concentrating so intently on your site indicator and paying little attention to what you're walking over. Fish every tiny nook, cranny, boulder pocket holding lie, top middle and bottom of the runs where you think trout would be holding. The key is to have your line in the water as much as possible and fishing and dissecting almost every foot of the water. It is nervous fishing, with the goal to catch as many fish as possible—not the quiet sport of contemplating the rising trout and planning to execute a cast. This is competitive stuff, Olympic-style fishing, with the goal to catch as many fish as possible.
- Fly selection should be a mix of attractors and extremely accurate natural presentations. The "hot spot" bright fluorescent thread or dubbing is often added to Euro bead heads. Often the attractors will bring in the fish only for it to see a very realistic-looking nymph, Browns especially will key in on this. The "Frenchie nymph" is a perfect example of combining a natural-looking pheasant tail with an orange-dubbed gold bead head—it won the world championship for the French team, thus its name. Depending on hook regulations, you could use a crustacean, mayfly, and caddis combo, with a creeping deep-weighted large stonefly to imitate the entire biological drift.
- While practicing extreme attentiveness to your sighter indicator for bounces and takes, keep an eye out for any nymphing activity of trout flashing on the bottom as they often do in faster water to take a fast flowing nymph in the biological drift. In these faster water environments, trout feed quickly and frantically. Finding the right "hotspot" is often the key to success.

Before the Euro invasion, myself and others in the "old school" days used the fly line "tip" indication nymphing method prior to indicators. I recall as a young boy watching the tip of your line twitch or move when the fish took your wet fly or nymphs. Sophistication came in putting a piece of orange or red glow bug yarn at the tip of the leader fly line connection to help facilitate strike indication, or orange loop connectors or attaching adhesive foam was used. Here, split shot was and still is used above and below the nymphs was a way to get to the bottom quick. This technique worked well to imitate not only dead drifting imitations but swinging mayflies and stoneflies that naturally behave that way.

Keep in mind that the highest degree of tactical efficiency is definitely accomplished with the Euro technique due to the direct tactile and visual contact. The more we venture into the realm of high-stick nymphing, we can push our distance level a little further but we will lose some strike sensitivity. Also positioning wrapped weight and split shots in and above or below sequence with the nymphs will also inhibit strike indication.

One serious downfall of the Euro technique is premature "hookulation." Most people do not discuss two other downfalls of the Euro technique whatsoever, since it takes away from the allure and glamor of the technique. "Lining or flossing" fish, is a technique for the less informed, as an accidental result of nymphing using long fine leader tippets where the leader "flosses" the mouth of the steelhead like threading the needle. When the line tightens up the angler that sets the hook. With this constant hook setting of the Euro technique, this occurs a lot more often than most anglers will admit.

Another downfall is snagging or foul-hooking fish. Though

▲ Master tight-line nympher Torrey Collins on one of his home waters, the classic freestone Housatonic in Connecticut.

it is not the goal of the Euro nymphing technique, which predominately will get the nymphs in the mouth or somewhere near it, foul hooking does occur. Frequently it is due to a fish rejecting the nymph at the last second and bumping the line with its body, nose, head, or tail.

As for these implications in correlation with nymphing for brown trout, the often extreme caution a *trutta* will exhibit in examining its prey or artificial fly, foul hooking often occurs—especially when primary holding lies are targeted repeatedly over-and-over by the relentless vertical drift staccato and the wise *trutta* scurries to the side to avoid the nymph. But this is just a side effect of the technique and not a valid tactic unless you are a poacher. I will tell you that in the early Slavic development, poaching was a necessity to survive and put food on the table, thus part of the reason for developing this technique.

The foul hooking becomes more prevalent in very low waters where the fish are stacked head-to-tail in runs of oxygenated water, and also during extreme heat and drought periods. Lining will occur when brown trout are in a passive dormant state, as water temperatures are

warming in the summer, and are continuously opening and closing their mouth to take in more oxygen. Here they will get into the faster riffle pocket water that is so effective for Euro nymphing.

In conclusion, Slavic tight line nymphing is a highly-effective fish-catching technique, perhaps the most lethal of all. If you are proverbially "hooked" on catching lots of fish of fish and occasionally a monster, in big numbers, which is what this competitive fly fishing technique was designed for, Euro nymphing is for you. It is a calculated, "mine sweeping/carpet bombing–like" presentation of brutal efficiency, thus its extreme popularity, especially in competitive fishing, and well worth one's time to practice and learn.

### Sink Tipping, Strip Teasing, and Brook's Pot-Shooting Methods

The invention of sinking lines has revolutionized the sport of deep-water nymphing and streamer fishing. Prior to that, lead core and wrapping lead was the makeshift method. Today, sink tips that vary from completely sinking to front end wet tip sinking to neutral buoyancy sinking have now become a complex "grain" brain drain.

Nevertheless, sinking lines keep the flies down for longer periods of time, and gets them down faster, especially in swifter water. On the disadvantage side, they are often difficult to control with a high degree of accuracy, due to the various sink rates and how undulating currents affect line depth penetration. All too often the lines will drag along the bottom, thus dragging flies with it in an unnatural presentation. By upstream and downstream mending and other various techniques we will discuss, one can have greater efficiency in all water conditions from heavy flows, to still waters, to slow and meandering tailouts.

From a stealth and presentation standpoint, brown trout are just as snooty as some fly fisher purists. As they become more selective and have been hooked often, especially in catch-and-release waters, tippet shyness is a given. A glaring thick, black or brown sink tip coming through the predator window will often startle a cautious *trutta*, especially in very clear, serene waters like a spring creek or tailwater, or aqua-blue freestone waters. These waters exist in Italy and elsewhere in the Dinaric Alps.

There are at least two highly effective techniques that allow the fly presentation to creep and crawl. The first is the Brooks "pot-shooting" discussed in his excellent book *Nymphing for Larger Trout*. The other is from Gary Borger called "the striptease," as described in his treatise *Nymphing*.

In the pot-shooting method, the angler drags a quick-penetrating, heavy-tip sink line through the primary holding and feeding lies in strong, boulder-strewn rivers, such as Brooks's beloved Madison. It is a dragging technique with the casts targeted above the pothole lie, a tight mend upstream to allow it to sink, and a high-stick vertical presentation that finishes with a gradually-lowered rod tip to allow the fly to thoroughly cover the pothole feeding lie. The angler must envision each pothole feeding lie and properly target and time the cast to control the sink. The strikes will come very abruptly and violently and are usually indicated by a tug on your line and on the hand controlling it. This is not selective twitching for more subtle takes. It was designed for big browns in swift rivers where the fish must make split-second decisions to crush or pass up a fly. Using sink tips, the angler can control the line with upstream, downstream, and stacked mending toward the nymph, and by raising or lowering the rod tip as you feel the line cruise through the rocks and crevices where brown trout like to ambush their prey.

When dealing with brown trout taking large stone flies in graveled waters of all speeds—fast, slow, medium, and still water—Borger's striptease method can be the ideal nymphing presentation. It is also a live presentation method that fishes the nymph like a living insect.

A sink tip of a more neutral buoyancy tapering down to a heavy tip will allow you to regulate the movement of the nymph better. Once you make the cast and achieve the desired depth, fold and overlap the line in the palm of your hand in four to five inch sections with a steady crawling motion from the from thumb index finger to pinkie. This imitates the crawling of large stoneflies as well as some of the larger mayfly nymphs that are burrowers and crawlers. During the presentation, the angler allows the line to drift free, followed by short strips of the line to bump the nymph toward the bank or the surface, thus provoking a brown trout or Atlantic salmon's "sit-wait-move-strike" predator attack movement, which usually comes firmly and violently, just as when stripping a streamer.

## Indicator Nymphing: The Glorified Bobber Salvation

Prior to Euro nymphing, the strike indicator revolution took fly fishing by storm. It ranged from early crude beginnings of small twist-on styrofoam types, greased yarn balls, and larger Styrofoam indicators, balloons, and frankly anything that can float and carry the weighted flies below. The high-stick indicator method, with as much line and leader off the water just to allow a float to properly dead drift the presentations, is still one of the most effective ways of nymphing.

When comparing Euro nymphing to float indicator nymphing it is a tale of two polarities. The depth penetration and strike detection of Euro nymphing is almost hyper accelerated and the fish often doesn't have a chance and is caught quickly. On the other extreme, indicator fishing has probably an 80 percent effectiveness, especially when coupled with split shot weight. Here the delay in penetration and transmission of the take can often be delayed into reaching the indicator, and an angler may miss many strikes, since extreme line control is required to create the tension necessary to administer a strike, but not so much tension that it would interfere with a nice, smooth, dead drift. Once the indicator does go down the fish is almost always hooked through the tension of the water, thus very little foul hooking goes on, but many fish-hooking opportunities are also lost.

Upon presentation the cast can be immediately mended upstream to allow the fly line to always stay above the indicator and to reduce drag. The steady upstream counterclockwise or clockwise mends, can allow the indicator to float dead drift for considerable distances in the current. In tailwaters and freestoners, a dead drift of the indicator can be achieved up to forty to fifty feet at a time. These long drifts can be achieved by letting out very tight clockwise and counterclockwise circular mends off of your rod tip through terse wrist movements, depending on the flow of the river.

▲ High-sticking the boulder "pot shot" method on the Upper Cattaraugus in New York. Credit: Andrew Steele Nisbet

One thing I particularly enjoy about the indicator system is your ability to manipulate the fly with these upstream, downstream, and sideward mends. They give the nymph more natural and creepy crawler swimming suggestions that can often entice a very fussy *trutta*. Often a few twitches of the rod tip at the end of the long drifts, watching the indicator twitch, can make the difference in the strike or a yawn from the *trutta*.

Placing split shot in the leader can be critical, depending on the flow and penetration. Some prefer split shot above tandem nymphs, others prefer a split shot between the two. I prefer to use a series of tag system droppers off the mainline with the weight at the complete bottom to allow for the nymphs to sway and move more freely in the current from the terminal mainline. Here you could also place the flies vertically at the desired depths. Also in this scenario when the fish takes the dropper nymph the strike transmits directly to the indicator, versus being impeded by any weighted split shot. The general rule is that the length from your nymph to the float should be one and a half times the depth.

Keeping your nymphs floating downstream below your indicator above it is just a matter of mending in the appropriate direction. Your indicator should "tick the bottom" at a slant, thus indicating proper depth penetration.

## Hopper Dropper/Dry Dropper

This rather new and popular presentation—I say "new" meaning widespread adoption during the last two decades (even though Brooks introduced it in the 1950s)—is an instance of having your cake and eating it too, which literally translates into fishing the entire spectrum of the trout feeding meniscus.

Two schools of fly-fishing practice brought this technique into the mainstay arsenal that it is today. Keep in mind fishing tandem flies is as old as perhaps Dame Juliana in the book of St. Albans. But as the turn of the twentieth century brought more regulations to fly fishing and general angling restrictions as a whole, the tandem series was often eliminated for a single hook/barbless artificial fly, especially on catch-and-release waters. The first known established catch-and-release waterway in the United States was in the 1930s on a small spring creek called Beaver Creek near Hagerstown, Maryland. More recently many states, provinces, and countries allow two flies to be presented, some up to three, some have no limit at all. However most are still firmly limited to one hook in fly angling situations.

The Catskill school of Gordon and Hewitt were the first to explore the dry dropper presentation. Taking a hint from the multi-wet fly brook trout meat swingers,

▲ Floating a large Wulff, stimulator, Royal Trude, or parachute Adams, with a nymph dropper like a pheasant tail below is very productive when drift boat fishing on larger rivers and spring creeks like the Bighorn and Big Hole. Credit: Steve Galleta

their collaboration would employ large floatable spiders like Hewitt's Neversink Skater, with a dropper of a traditional wet fly that did not spook the new German brown immigrants. The true nymph designs were just beginning to catch on in the new Catskill school with Gordon's correspondence with Skues and Halford in England. The first innovative flies came from the banks of the Neversink upstream from Hewitt's Big Bend club. The gentleman's name was Ed Sens, and his family owned a farm along the Neversink. He modeled his first nymph designs off Gordon's Quill Gordon. One could just imagine the effectiveness of a Neversink Skater dry with any Quill Gordon nymph dropper on those historic waters.

What really popularized the dry dropper craze was the Montana/ Yellowstone/ Wyoming/ Snake River summertime hopper fishing. Guides looking to get the clients into big hookups would run a prince or pheasant tail nymph off a hopper or Club Sandwich foam terrestrial and have alarming success. Often the main focus is on the dropper nymph. Using a large floating attractor dry fly as your indicator is often a smart choice, when fluorescent indicators can spook ultra-alarmed *trutta*, and also fish occasionally targeting the indicator—here your indicator has a hook and I can't tell you how often the dry is targeted even though it was never meant to be more than just as strike indicator.

In gentle flowing spring creeks and tailwaters, where brown trout selectivity is at its highest, using a more natural-looking dry like a Sulpher emerger with a tiny Pheasant Tail, or a Griffiths Gnat with a sunken midge pupa, which addresses the highly-effective minutiae category, can be deadly for both spectra of the dry and submerged presentation. This dry dropper technique is indispensable in less-fussy waters like trout clubs and private spring creeks, where fish are often fed pellets at both levels and there is little current or flow.

## How *Trutta* Observe Blind Nymphing

As far as brown trout are concerned, you are dealing with two ends of the feeding spectrum—subtle and deliberate. Very selective browns are quick to pass judgment on heavily-fished catch-and-release waters, where the trout will see common fly patterns like the Pheasant Tail over and over again. Here, repeated carpet bombing presentations (i.e. tight lining), over and over again can actually spook or turn off highly-educated and selective brown trout.

However as *Salmo* species—both browns and Atlantic salmon—grow older and larger, they approach flies with slower attack speeds instead of the quick, frenzied take of younger fish. That is why anglers employ the Euro technique in competitions where catching tons of small to medium range trout will win the prize. A large brown trout will examine every detail of an imitation or natural, and once they make a commitment to take a fly, will usually do so in a very firm and solid fashion. Often an angler will set the hook too early, and in the wrong direction, which is not downward and to the side against the current, but directly upstream with the lifting upward motion—this will blow the hook set 90 percent of the time. Premature hook setting, which unfortunately the Euro technique employs, and not allowing the fish to put its mouth over the nymph or food item in a thorough fashion, which older, larger browns usually do, results in many lost opportunities. I can't tell you how many times myself or my clients have prematurely "pulled the gun" on both the nymph and dry fly setting the hook when it comes to larger fish.

Here is where the strike indicator system has its highest value, since our hook setting is usually very clearly defined and the bobber indicator goes down and stays down until the angler pulls up for the hook set. These are almost 90 percent assured takes and hookups. The indicator system also allow for longer presentations from the longer drift periods that can be achieved through tight circular mends and stacked mends. These longer presentations suit a brown trout just fine since there compound and complex surface rising to dries, which Marinaro described so beautifully. Long drifts and inspections of nymphs is paramount in slow meandering waters of impeccable clarity. The quick drift and jerking hook setting of the Euro technique does not allow for these inspections.

Indicator fishing also allows for a long line game. The new two-handed 3–6 weight switch rods of eleven feet that are becoming increasingly popular for this purpose. It is a cane pole bobber fishing style, where long lines can drift with an indicator down a big river, allowing the angler to get far away from its prey. Brown trout are often very spooked by drift boats and close wading situations, especially on large clear tail waters. Keep in mind the Slavic technique was invented and perfected in fast-flowing Carpathian Alps mountain waters, with high tannic stain and turbulence.

In conclusion, to be successful in your blind brown trout nymphing, size up the habitat and perceived selectivity index of your prey prior to choosing the appropriate technique. Be competent at all three; Euro, sink tip, and indicator, and apply them where best suited. Your brown trout success ratio will increase dramatically.

## Classic Skues/Sawyer Sight Nymphing

You must cultivate an eye for water and an eye for trout. This gift is not easily attained: in all cases it requires practice cycle and some never acquire. They can be learned by nine people out of ten it is learned by what seems easy but it's hard: looking at the water. Looking at it not like we were casually examining it's intently, boring into it, determining to penetrate its hidden recesses. You must make up your mind that if there are trout in the River you will see them. Trout are dim, uncertain and nearly invisible.

You learn in time where to look and what to look for. You must not expect to see a whole trout, outlined as though lying on a fishmongers slab: any fool can see that: but what you have to train yourself to pick out shadows. You will waste time on stones or gravel or sticks, or such—like, it is remarkable how you improve and nothing improves you so quickly is being with someone who is good at the game.

—John Waller Hills, *A Summer on the Test*

Ninety percent of the food that comprises the diet of a brown trout, salmon parr, or landlocked adult is found subsurface on nymphal invertebrates and other vertebrates. This constant biological diversity is what inevitably imprints returning *salar* to take the fly. For ultra-selective spring creek brown trout, it could approach the 98 percent mark, when you really ponder the challenges presented. As a spring creek trout grows larger, it becomes more photophobic; its predatory alarm system is higher as a result of its deeper lies it forages in the deep underwater world for its daily fare. Nymphs, larvae, scuds, sow bugs, sculpins, dace, darters, chubs, and other small trout fry become its main food source.

Sight nymphing for browns was perfected by Skues and Sawyer as previously mentioned, on relatively shallow, crystal-clear chalk stream waters, which allowed observation of feeding trout. In *Minor Tactics for Chalk Stream Trout*, G. E. M. Skues summed up the value of the deadly nymphing technique with an accurate imitation:

> The next I tried was a blue-winged-olive. There was a hatch of this pernicious insect one afternoon. The following pattern is always a failure with me, and in anticipation I have tied some nymphs of appropriate color of body, and hackles with a single turn of the tiniest blue hackle of the Merlin. This enabled me to get two or three excellent trout, which were taking blue-winged-olives and nymphs greedily under the opposite bank, in which, or rather the first of which, like their predecessors, and refuse to respond to a floating imitation.

Here, Skues realized that despite the visual hatch of blue-winged-olives, 70 percent of the activity of feeding fish was taking place down below. He was possessed later in life to find the ultimate blue-winged-olive nymph, which eventually came down to using a Pheasant Tail dyed olive.

Sawyer's killer bugs and buzzers, along with his Pheasant Tails, made extremely selective brown trout look gullible and feed comfortably on his patterns. There is a saying that "some flies catch the fisherman, and a small majority catch the fish!" This could not be more true than for the Sawyer

▲ Frank Sawyer was a true master of spring creek sight fishing who took nymphing to a new level with his slow and steady stalking of the River Avon, pheasant tail nymphs, and long *Pezon et Michel* parabolic taper bamboo nymph rods. Photos: Terry Lawton

nymphing system. Since Sawyer trimmed and cultivated the weed growth along the Avon River as its River keeper, he examined thousands of natural *Ephemerella* and *Baetis* nymphs, and learned of their simplicity of design with pronounced body segmentation, which the pheasant tail fibers emulate. He wrote:

My studies through the years have led me to believe that if one were to make an artificial to imitate all the underwater creatures on which fish feed, then hundreds of different patterns would be needed. Actually the representations of nymphs could become as involved as it is with surface insects to such an extent that would be far too complicated for the average fisherman to understand.

In all branches of angling, simplicity is an aim to be pursued, and simplicity can indeed be adopted in both dry fly and nymph fishing. So perhaps I look at things from a somewhat different angle. Through the years the fish have been the judge of my artificial nymphs I have constructed and by reasoning things out I have come to the conclusion that the view of the fish must have primary consideration.

—Frank Sawyer, *Nymphs and the Trout*

Sawyer was an advocate of the slow and steady approach. When I nymph spring creeks for wild browns, his words always echo in my head. As I have learned by trial and error, you must approach each piece of water in microcosms, dividing each piece of the river into small beats. Our tendency on rivers is to roam and wade till you're blue in the face and fishless, always thinking there is a monster lurking around the next bend. This is not the appropriate way to fish spring creeks.

Here, each piece of water can hold a large, selective brown trout, even though none are perceived to be there. On spring creeks, the sheer number of fish lying in total disguise and shelter is amazing. With all the weed growth and undercut banks, dark channels, etc. there are hundreds of fish and sections of a fertile spring creek fishery that you often walk past looking for the "honey hole." On one of my favorite spring creeks in Wisconsin, it took an electro-shocking biologist fish survey to teach me this lesson.

One day years ago, I was fishing and exploring a section of Timber Coulee Creek By my estimation that particular section did not have a very high crop of trout, and I usually headed past it in a hurry to get to more productive waters. All of a sudden I heard the rumbling of a gas powered electroshock generator buzzing upstream from me by the fish biologists from the DNR. To my amazement I could not believe the size of the browns and brook trout that were slowly coming to the surface from the shock and the electrical currents of the generator. They were hiding everywhere under the vegetation. I was totally humbled, shocked and amazed how that stretch I thought to be void held so many fish. My approach here must have been too quick, as I sent the fish scurrying for cover before my casting ever began. I learned my lesson to approach this area with a whole new attitude in future days. Sawyer again sums up simplicity and the obvious, which often eludes us:

Nymph fishing, if you are to be successful, is indeed a matter of being careful. It is not just the business of throwing a nymph all the likely places and hoping the fish will take it. You turn yourself into a hunter and, with all the keenness of a stalker after a stag, figure wits and your eyesight against the facilities and faculties of the wild fish. It is not an art to be acquired in a season, or, for that matter in a dozen seasons, for it to be truly a nymph fishermen is a very necessity to know something of the habits of the fish and, even more, of the habits of the creatures on which they feed beneath the surface. Nymph fishing is indeed technique of its own, and the casting of the artificial so that it appears attractive and not disturbing is an art one must learn only by experience.

Sawyer mentioned quite frequently the importance of what he described as the "induced take," which provides a natural movement like lifting, twitching, and creating a lifelike feel to the nymph presentation, which all too often fooled the fussiest Avon browns. His patterns concentrated on the swimming and wiggling nymphs (Sulphers and Olives) most common to chalk streams and tailwaters, as well as clinging and burrowing mayflies that inhabit the silt of the spring creek. He wrote that his "Sawyers nymphs—pheasant tail" have the profile of an "in the round" silhouette and how a brown trout sees with extreme detail his underwater drifting or swimming prey, with legs tucked in. Once again Sawyer alludes to the selectivity conundrum that all fly fishers eventually succumb to—"I have no idea why that fish took that fly—it looks like hell, it resembles nothing, but that fish wanted it in a big way!—go figure." Thus we have the fly patterns that make no sense to us, but makes incredible sense to very fussy trout.

Sight nymphing is hunting—plain and simple. Bilateral and extremely acute vision is required. Stalking at low profile out of the sun's shadow is a must. And having the patience to study the patterns and behavior of a large, selective brown trout is paramount to nymphing success. There are two phases of sight nymphing—deep/mid-water presentations, and surface nymphing to "bulging and tailing" trout.

In deep benthic presentations, it is important to get your nymph down well in advance of the trout's lie. This can be done either by weighting the nymph or by using a tungsten green split shot a foot or so above the fly, or by tying weight in the form of a bead head or copper ribbing into the fly itself.

Nymphs are presented dead drifted, twitched ever so slightly, or "raised and twitched," by slow-swinging the nymph toward the surface and in front of the fish, to imitate the rising emerger. With the new tight-line switch rods, like my Thomas & Thomas eleven-foot three-inch and Orvis, Scott, and Sage's new-era light switch rods, you can feel and glide your nymphs/soft hackles with extreme delicacy and manipulation. Most trout will use a small twelve-inch feeding window or lane. An extremely selective nymphing trout won't move very far to the side, down

▲ A nymphed-up beauty by Joe Goodspeed of Thomas & Thomas Rods. Credit: Hoe Goodspeed

or up, to take the fly. On rare occasions you will see them move more than several feet.

If you have very good vision, you can see your nymph, or "guesstimate" where it is in the drift. Better yet, I came up with a system of using "Sighter Nymphs." They are basically orange Pheasant Tails, tied with dyed orange pheasant tail, copper wire, and a copper or gold bead head. I try to match the weight of the fly with the natural looking one I wish to ultimately present—so if the natural is not weighted and has no bead head I have ones that weigh about the same density as the natural I am about to choose. When I cast these I time the amount it takes to penetrate the water to the depth or where the trout is feeding from (point A), to its interception/take spot (point B). So here for example, I now have approximately eight seconds, for instance, that I know my nymph will be in the strike zone and thus I could concentrate on peripheral binocular vision to watch for the trout's mouth to take the fly. When I see the quick opening and closing of the mouth take, I set the hook. This works particularly well for very tiny minutiae nymphs in the size #20 range.

With bilateral vision, you can watch the nymph and trout at the same time. A taking or interested trout, will do several things to alert you that it is interested. Once spotted, it will initially make a slight movement toward the

imitation. Its ventral and pectoral fins will start pulsating and beating slightly. And of course, your focus should be on the white mouth opening for a take. Be warned that sometimes a trout's mouth will open close to the insect imitation, only to refuse the fly or eat a natural.

One mistake sight nymph fishermen make is to set the hook too early—thus pulling it out of the fish's mouth. A slight delay when you see the mouth open will be to your advantage. Set the hook with rod at low profile and to the downstream side, so it is secure in the side of its mouth.

Other trout-specific behaviors become apparent when you see a trout grabbing artificials or natural nymphs. Sometimes it will glide downstream and circle the nymph- in an ultra-complex form discussed in the surface takes. *Chironomid* midge larva nymphing browns will pick the artificial and natural by pushing the nose right into the sandy bottoms or gravel, or very close to it. Scud and sow bug feeding trout will often pick them off the Spring Creek vegetation, or shake the vegetation with body and mouth to dislodge these protein-infused delicacies.

During a hatch, when spring creek brown trout are, "back and tail bulging" the surface, they're usually feeding on stillborn and emerging nymphs in the surface meniscus or slightly below it. Fishing these imitations is difficult and requires a detection measurement system. A section of orange or red monofilament leader butt or fly line tip is sometimes already made by the line manufacture. Adding a small piece of fluorescent yarn or foam—very tiny, mind you—into the leader will allow you for greater detection. One of the oldest and stealthiest systems is to lubricate the leader with floatant all the way to just several feet before the surface nymph. Gary Borger made this technique famous when midge fishing on Stillwater Lakes. When the leader goes down quickly, set the hook! The timing of the bulging rise is important, as to when to start the drift of your imitation. Be very gentle and careful in your hook setting as to not to spook or foul hook the bulging trout.

Knowing the biological drift of your river intimately is paramount for successful nymphing. These naturals will dictate the shape and silhouette of your nymph designs. Carry a safe stomach pump and use it when you are in a difficult situation. But use the device carefully and properly by always lubricating it with water and not penetrating it too deeply into this trout's stomach—more of a throat pump I would say.

Some words of caution need to be applied when on the sight-nymphing hunt. We most often turn our attention to the main channels of biological drift in the most primary of taking runs and holding lies. But on spring creeks and tail waters alike, due to the uniform temperature of the water and meandering vegetation channels which spread out the current flow sometimes uniformly, large trout can be sitting just about anywhere. Quite often they are right at the shoreline next to the undercut banks right by your feet and under your armpits. Target the predator foraging profiles close to shore and eventually work your way up to the main channels. Also very common on tailwaters, especially during *Isonychia* and drake hatches, along with stoneflies, many of these nymphs like to move toward the shoreline to crawl upon rocks, boulders, or logjams before they hatch. Thus the trout are hanging tighter to shore, where you walked into the tail waters even though most rising activities are taking place in the main bubble line channel.

I learned this lesson when writing *Selectivity* from Johnny Miller, a.k.a. Master of the Delaware. Here we found twenty-inch brown trout in the middle of a sunny July afternoon in less than a foot of water, hugging the bank looking for *Isonychia* nymphs.

Finally, use "the slow and steady" hook-setting method, since many midges have small hook gapes and usually don't penetrate so well, particularly in the large, cartilaginous kypes of trophy brown trout.

## Egg Nymphing: The Butt Candy/Caviar Fixation

One only needs to visit the Salmon River or Oak Orchard off Lake Ontario in the fall, or Lake Michigan's Pere Marquette River to view what the egg buzz is all about.

There are those very few and far between times that I call "*trutta* stupid-isms," when browns lose their cautious, predictable demeanor and become clumsy and crazy for a particular food item. The egg binge mode is one of these instances. They throw caution to the wind and become aggressive enough to feed right next your wading boots when the gluttonous binge of egg protein from larger salmon, steelhead, and other trout spawning becomes abundant. Due to this extremely rich protein source and availability, even though browns will have multiple hatches like Quills and Sulphers at the same time in spring, or caddis and blue-winged-olives in the fall, they will target the egg orgy in a very predictable way. Here is where they are most susceptible and often caught by bait anglers using spawn sacks, since they will

▲ Resident and migratory browns will target the larger orange to reddish pink/apricot eggs from Pacific and Atlantic salmon, sea run brown, brook trout, other resident trout, and hucho. Browns and Atlantic parr seek out the smaller caviar of grayling, whitefish, shad, and particularly suckers with similar intensity, especially on Great Lakes and Baltic rivers. Credit: Author

swallow the eggs quite readily for the chewy, odiferous delights.

Egg-feasting browns will usually position themselves at the gravel ledge drop-offs, and one can easily distinguish them by their very nervous behavior, white mouths and triangle-spotted tails, versus the forked tails of salmon. They will get extremely animated and into a frenzy when the gravel is being dug by the female spawners, unleashing clouds of silt into the current. This spawning preparation of digging gravel redds will unleash amazing amounts of nymphs and larvae of aquatic insects from mayflies, caddis, and midges, along with eggs. The actual spawning affair itself will unleash these clouds of silt and male sperm, which are very easily identified. You want to make your presentation of the glo-bug, bead, or Otter soft-milking egg right behind the spawning activity for trophy *trutta*.

Several nuances must be addressed. The predating browns will be very cautious not to get too close to spawning fish—especially the larger-kyped and aggressive male salmon and steelhead. I have witnessed on too many occasions smaller browns coming downstream half dead with a big chunk of flesh taken out of their middle torso. Browns love to scavenge for eggs in the early dawn low light hours, during rain storms, or right at dusk. Not all browns will be totally fixated on the eggs, as some will be totally focusing on the nymphs and larvae, or other immature baitfish, leeches, eels, etc. that partake in the frenzy. One of my favorite patterns is a bright Kelly green *Rhyacophila* caddis larva. In spring creeks they are fond of red *Chironomid* worms.

An egg and nymph/larva dropper always is the way to go. Also beware of undulating shelf confluences that usually exist below gravel bars and cause an undertow/counterclockwise revolving upstream current in these unique areas. Here the browns head will often sit facing downstream with tails pointed upstream, to intercept the reverse current upswelling of the biological drift.

The best technique to use during this process is the Euro nymphing technique. If you must use an indicator, tie on a large natural stimulator stonefly, parachute Adams, or rope twine, which blend in much better. There are now clear "Thingamabobbers" that do a pretty stealthy job, or poly white indicators that match the foam flotsam. Long leaders and usually tungsten split shot between the two fly offerings are necessary, to allow them to bounce slowly above the gravel. Even though I refer to these times as a "stupid-isms," the browns can be extremely cautious and very shy of the fly line or strike indicator—thus I firmly believe in watching the sight fishing take, of the white mouth opening and closing quickly. These browns are not firm conviction takers and spit imitations in an ultra-second, thus the Euro technique is more favorable.

## The Mid-Strata Chase: Classic Wet Fly Swing

If any presentation could truly describe the initial brown trout developmental moments of fly fishing as we know it today, this was it. Its inspiration again brought to you by *Salmo trutta*'s predator foraging profiles of "sit-wait-chase." Whether it first appeared in Macedonia, or in the more refined empirical laboratories of the English chalk streams, its genesis was a pure "chuck-and-chance-it" affair. Here the angler tied feathers or fabric to a hook and string of some kind, and cast, tossed, or dapped in a flowing river. As the current took the line and fly, it broadsided in the downstream flows, and eventually turned in an upstream-swing style. Somewhere in the drift or swinging turn upstream, the brown trout or Atlantic salmon would swipe at the fly from instinctual imprinting. This pure predatory response to target something living and moving away from it by the fish, is still the basic framework of fly fishing that is most universally used and easily accomplished. That is my crude explanation, since I have yet to encounter an explanation of such. Since those crude primordial moments, we have since learned to manipulate the presentation with all sorts of mending, rod positioning, sink rates of the lines and leaders, etc.

Ask any brown trout or Atlantic salmon fishermen today about their most cherished and rewarding presentations, and many will say "swinging wets/soft hackles." It is very cool way to fish. Whether it is done on single-handed or two-handed rods, using the new-age lightweight switch rods, what is so dynamic about this technique is the fish must make a concerted effort to target the fly, follow it, and then almost always annihilate it. There is no confusing or constant hook setting like the Slavic/Euro technique. Here, when the trout or salmon strikes your fly—they most often and certainly hook themselves. What usually follows is a frenzied, breathtaking, strong aerial battle, almost as if your *Salmo* can't believe it worked that hard to take something that they shouldn't of have, now that they feel the hook. Though fish caught on the nymph can fight equally as well, the wet fly swing take is the proverbial "gotcha take," and the fish's response is " I'm getting the hell out of here fast," as witnessed by its relentless fight on the fly rod.

Mid-strata presentations work well with *Salmo trutta* for a variety of reasons. The caution and awareness *trutta* exemplify usually puts them in a command of their waters and primary lie/habitat positioning. Their binocular/peripheral/vertical vision planes are always on high alert for prey and predators, whether it comes in the form of the dead-drifting nymph, a swimming emerging aquatic insect, or a scurrying baitfish or sculpin, it's uncanny how the brown trout manages to find and target whatever is thrown its way. Their high predator alarm senses could be the main reason why they are so difficult to catch at times when compared to rainbow or brook trout.

*Salmo*, both *trutta* and Atlantics, which we will explore later, like to strategically set themselves up in the middle strata, keeping one eye on the surface and one eye on the bottom, albeit strategically over boulder gravel/rocky structure, and adjacent to further protective lies, such as logjams and undercut banks, bridges, etc.

Browns are also excellent identifiers of interception points where the biological drift accumulates, like in the back eddies of a series of cascading riffles, or in the inner seams of back-circling currents, usually formed on the inside and extreme outside of the river bends, like they do on my home rivers of the Muskegon, Manistee, and Pere Marquette tailwaters. I could literally go down fourteen miles of river and pinpoint and target the brown trout interception points that will almost always be full of browns with no rainbows, even though my river consti- tutes a 50-50 percentage mix of the two. Once prey is unleashed in these interception points they are not subject to the extreme flows of the biological drift, thus they are allowed to exhibit whatever movement they may have in their behavior: swimming, twitching, crawling, bodily pul- sating, etc. The brown trout has learned to identify these subtle, or sometimes not-so-subtle motions in these envi- ronments and pounce on them quickly. Thus the wet fly swing brings out the quick grab predatory instinct in them, more often than just a dead drifting nymph.

My experience with both rainbows and browns has led me to the conclusion that the brown trout, being the more concealed and elusive sit-and-wait predator, sets up in more ideal taking lies to observe something moving past it at a slow or fast pace. Rainbow trout on the other hand seem to be forever preoccupied by searching and scavenging in the biological drift, and move around a lot in their predator foraging profiles. You could see this on underwater videos of the two species when nothing is really going on in the biological drift. Brook trout also will do the same as rainbows. Brown trout will move around and scavenge relentlessly for prey—especially if there is a major feeding opportunity hatch for instance, that they must capitalize on very quickly. But is their overall prefer- ence to wait, target, and execute their strategy quickly and efficiently. Whether this is the browns' thirty million years of evolution versus a rainbow trout, or twenty more than a brook trout, only nature, Darwin, and God can make that behavioral evaluation.

## The Simple Classic Wet Dynamics

Why this technique is so much loved is because of its simplicity in execution. In the nymphing tactical complex- ity that we explored earlier, there is no need to make a "mountain out of a molehill" with the wet fly technique.

Pure and simple, it is a down-and-across cast, with the belly of the line leading the fly to swing on the drag, as the rod leads the line and creates tension to move the fly broadside across currents and swing upward at the end. This simple trigger mechanism for the fly almost always catches fish. With a series of "folds," as A. E. H. Wood described mending in his greased-line method, you can manipulate the fly by up- or down-stream mending, to sink or swim the imitation at the desired rate, or level depend- ing on what is being imitated, such as struggling baitfish or emerging mayflies and stoneflies. Keeping the rod tip close to the surface allows you maximum line surface friction and instantaneous strike detection and hook-ups.

## Soft Hackle Wets: The Parkinson's Twitch and Operation Clockwork

I learned the importance of imparting action by coinciden- tal encounters while watching elder fly masters practice their art form as a youngster. By asking annoying ques- tions at barber shops and fly shops when I heard or saw anything related to fly fishing, my thirst was quenched for knowledge. Nobody back then liked pain-in-the-butt nosey ten-year-olds, walking into a snobby boutique fly shop back then. I was scorned by sales-oriented propri- etors going right at the jugular of distinguished-looking country gentlemen. Today, "kids are cool," and "the future," and proudly displayed. Back then it was an elite ole' grumpy gentleman's club; even women were scorned! My only fly shop was twenty miles away at one of the first Orvis shops in the country—Reed's, in Williamsville—a wealthy suburb of doctors, lawyers, and old money, where there was no room for a factory neighborhood ethnic kid like me to be poking around with pocket change.

But my wet fly tactics were often hit-or-miss chance-it affairs. Besides pestering my dad for more information, which quickly became frustrating due to his Polish stub- bornness, I ventured out to gain more knowledge by watching very lethal angling old men that fished near the bridges of downtown Arcade, New York. Here was a small, quintessential Americana village of Victorian homes, a turn-of-the-century train station, and little stores and restaurants dotting the village. There was an ice cream stand next to one of the bridges and my dad would often drop me off there for hours for the ice cream and fish at the same time. It is here I ran into "that man with the hat and the pipe," as I called him when I referred to him while talking to my dad.

Here was the classic stereotypic "Fedora Flea Flicker," as distinguished dressed-up fly fishermen were referred to. Fishing his cane bamboo rod with his wicker creel basket, he would swing his tandem wet fly concoctions with extreme lethal prowess. It seemed every time I turned around he had a fish on as I continued to get skunked. It

▲ The lovely Cattaraugus Creek meandering through the valleys and foothills of the Alleghenies of southwestern New York is a perfect example of eastern freestone River architecture influenced by springs, various rocky strata elevation bluffs, and tributaries. It is here in the mid-April off-color snow runoff waters of a Sycamore tree pool that I caught my first trout on a Quill Gordon wet fly, a gorgeous red-spotted kyped fourteen-inch male. Little did I know that my crudely self-tied fly was imitating the emerging *Ephemerella* subvaria Hendrickson mayfly that began to take flight on that warm April afternoon. Credit: Andrew Steele Nesbit.

drove me absolutely nuts because I could just not figure out the "method to the madness" for his success.

One day as he was walking back to the car, a spiffy 1960s Jeep Wagoneer, I mustered up the gall to say I've been watching him and asked him what the secret of his success was. I also asked if I could look at his fly box. To say that I was soiling my pants as I trembled from my bold inquiry would be an understatement. First without a word but just a grumble, as saliva dripped down his pipe still in his mouth, he showed me a beautiful metal fly box that had a "W" logo—which later I found to stand for Wheatley. From the Catskill tradition, which now had a firm legacy in the Allegheny foothills, the classic wet fly was king.

Then, in his curmudgeonly grumbling utterances, he basically told me he was fishing two wet flies and twitched them throughout the swing—"You are fishing too lethargically, my lad, and you must move around more and cover the stream," he grumbled. He accused me of sitting by the bridge abutment and being too lazy to move, like the villagers who would come down and fish with worms. "Your dad didn't buy those waders for nothing kid. Use them!" he scowled. Well! I beg your pardon, sir, I said to myself,

since he hurt my feelings and sort of insulted me, but which I did take notice and admit. It is perhaps because I saw a hatchery truck once dump some brood stock brown trout in that location one spring and managed to catch a trophy one there, that my stubborn habit brought me back to the same spot.

But during our encounter, I couldn't help but notice his constant hand trembling and headshaking. I think I was onto something here. The next time I watched him swinging his wet flies with such impeccable casting and covering every inch the water, I saw his hands shake the entire time. Here, by coincidence, I cracked the code of the wet fly Holy Grail. In hindsight as I matured in the game, he was imparting a living insect twitch and movement to his soft tackle flies adorned beautifully with webby Hungarian partridge feather hackle tied in at the head, which made his flies swim with such wonderful motion and pulsating movement. By shaking his rod hand wrist gently up and down, with what I call today the "Parkinson's twitch," his technique was more lethal than just employing the dead drift swing.

Emerging aquatic insects and tiny baitfish will display

▲ The magnificent urban tailwater of the wild brown fishery at Maryland's Gunpowder River, which is perfect for soft hackles. Credit: Mike Tsukamoto

this stuttering motion and movement. Also if you ever wonder why you occasionally catch very selective trout when reeling in your line at the end of the day's fishing, it is because the stuttering motion of winding reel imitates the emerging insect.

Based on the advice of my old timer mentor, I began to break the water down into incremental parts and cover as much of it as possible. As I grew older and began to read more magazines such as *Field & Stream* and *Outdoor Life*, they always talked about fishing a spinner or a crank bait Rapala using the "clockwork countdown" method, which makes sense, and gives you the discipline to break down every piece of water.

But, as I began to read more intellectually provocative magazines like *Fly Fisherman*, and through my own experience, I discovered that this method of thorough presentation can be further applied by targeting primary and secondary lies by making sure your presentation runs broadside through them at just the right sink depth.

Keep in mind a few simple rules of the game when employing this technique:

- Start close to shore or from your drift boat and progressively work your way out. Fifty percent of the fish sometimes lie right at our feet or oar lock.
- Longer leaders are a blessing when swinging flies, for you do not want the fish to see your fly that usually sticks out like a pink flamingo. Thus the new-age fly lines in New Zealand grey and dull greens/olives blend in with the water much better as do the tippet materials from the Maxima chameleon to the clearer greenish/tan/clear fluorocarbon. The worst thing you can do is line a fish prior to the fish seeing your wet fly, which is often the case when leading the line on a downward bulging swing.
- Target certain predator foraging profile sites that take us off guard and by surprise, such as summertime close to shore sites scavenging for soft shell crabs that browns like and also picking swimming nymphs that are shore bound migrators (*Isonychia*). Thus you'll be targeting skinny waters sometimes with no current or minimal flow which would normally get no attention.

Tactics and the Chase: The Introspective *Trutta* • **139**

- Prior to fishing a run pool or set of riffles and rapids, make a mental note of where you think your fish are lying in a waiting position to strike your fly and envision the attack. Most importantly, fish and swing through thoroughly, allowing for pulsating and stripping as they hang time dangling and of the drift. Too many fishermen pick up their line quickly to swing again before thoroughly allowing the presentation to exhibit itself. Remember larger brown trout have slower attack speeds, especially on cold, foggy tailwater mornings, and will exhibit a more cautious curiosity that would allow them to follow the fly and often refuse the offering before eventually committing. This can go on for several casts.

## Lifts, Takes, and Tucks: The Leisenring/Sawyer Nexus

The brown is a master of prey perception, as often the tiniest movements either elicit a strike or refusal. Though many will say these techniques belong in the nymphing category, here we have basically a simple styled fusion between the moving wet fly and the dead-drifted nymph; both imitate critical parts of the biological drift. Both of these manipulating presentations are almost identical and initially started with nymphing techniques, as we covered above. Here, an angler imparts slight movement to the wet fly presentation, as this can be the proverbial "icing on the cake" to induce a trophy brown or Atlantic.

Enter James Leisenring and, again, Frank Sawyer, each representing opposite sides of the pond at the same time—the crucial 1940s developmental period when the world was at war. Sawyer was the brilliant sight-nymphing master ghillie of the River Avon Officers Club, whereas James Leisenring lived in Allentown, Pennsylvania, and fished the classic beauty of the Brodhead Creek in the Poconos. Each were subsurface masters and pretty much perfected a method to entice a predatory-minded, sitting-and-waiting trout who was inhabiting a perfect intercepting lie, to move and take the fly as in the wet-fly style.

Leisenring's knowledge was gained through correspondence and time on the water. He became an associate and pen pal of G. E. M. Skues, with whom he exchanged many ideas about nymphing.

Leisenring's presentation was a more down-and-across, dead-drifting style approach, with a slight swing. When the fly reached the diagnosed or observed trout holding and taking lie, the rod was paused, or raised slightly to accelerate the fly toward the surface, thus duping a trout into thinking that it was an emerging insect, which would

▲ Leisenring's Broadheads, now home to a new master, talented Henry Ramsay. Credit: Henry Ramsey.

trigger a predatory strike. By raising, lowering, or stopping the rod, this controlled the rate of ascent, and his visual swinging technique started to have lethal effectiveness, especially on the vodka-clear, rapidly-moving waters of the Analomik section of the Brodhead.

Sawyer, on the other hand, who mastered the art of sight nymphing on British chalk streams, would employ the low-profile/sometimes-on-his-knees approach from the downstream position. Here, crouched over, he would use an upstream reach cast–nymph tuck presentation, mainly because fishing downstream on the chalk streams was taboo and ungentlemanly. Also due to the extreme clarity of the spring creeks, approaching from a downstream position was much more advantageous, versus the brawling freestone waters of the Brodhead that distorted surface vision. As the fly penetrated the holding position of the trout, Sawyer would raise or swing the rod tip to the left or right, depending on streamside bank position, or lift it, to imitate the swimming nymphs of the *Baetis*, and pale watery Sulphers. His sleek nymph designs, such as the Grey Goose and the Pheasant Tail, imitated the swimming insect with its legs tucked under the abdomen.

As for my subject matter, these presentations were spot-on perfect for our stereotypically "always looking up" *Salmo*—both *trutta* and *salar*. Brown trout awareness can never be described as tunnel vision, same as an Atlantic, and their predator profile programming has always been oriented toward movement detection, particularly to the meniscus. Thus the lift and the induced take are for the most part identical, except that Sawyer's method imparted more horizontal and vertical inputs of the lift, rather than the more strictly vertical lift or pause of Leisenring's.

## Swinging New-Age Articulated Wets and Wiggle Nymphs

Within their natural habitat aquatic insects move! They move around on the bottom of the stream: they swim from the bottom to midstream; they ascend from the bottom to the top. When they break through the surface tension, they move while shedding their nymphal shucks. If we are to simulate the naturals correctly and fish them effectively, it is not enough to design artificials of the insects as we perceive them when they are immobile or dead. —Doug Swisher and Carl Richards, *Emergers*

Besides the No-Hackle innovations of their masterpiece *Selective Trout*, Swisher and Richards stumbled upon more interesting insights into how prey is perceived and actually functions in the wild habitat. It was again my good friend and mentor, Carl Richards, who diagnosed the the nymphs' swimming movements and brown trout appeal.

The wild brown trout–filled Rouge River and Muskegon River tailwater were a hop and skip away from his office. The preliminary work he did for his masterpiece books were done on these thinktank laboratories. I would often see him sitting on the banks or in his car sketching images of how insects move and how they were perceived by his beloved brown trout. He would constantly seine the rivers, take stomach examples, and fill his river water jugs and coolers with live insects to bring them home to his elaborate aquarium tanks, where he photographed and studied their movement. After Carl, Johnny "Bugsy" Miller of Delaware and Muskegon fame did the same and produced the amazing insect images in this book.

Coupled with his passion for one of the most perfect brown trout spring creek systems in the world—the Au Sable of northern Michigan, where Marinaro ended his final writings with such superlative accolades, Carl's ever-probing mind never stopped till the day he died.

Though Doug Swisher brought the brilliance and organizational glue that to the relationship, Carl personally could be credited for initiating the new era of articulation, amongst many other things. We often point to the East Coast (Pennsylvania/New York etc.) for being such innovators in the fly-fishing legacy, which they were. Not to discredit these brilliant schools and legacies in the least, but the more I investigate and the more I live here, Michigan's prolific trout and salmon inspired genius in so many people, and in so many ways. Michigan was and still is a major fly-fishing milestone of invention, right along the lines of the Catskill dry fly, bead head nymph and foam terrestrial revolutions. To address the tactics associated with these swimming and moving aquatic insects, Carl Richards wrote an amazing book called *Emergers*.

Mayfly nymphs crawl, swim, or float to reach the surface. The swimming is accomplished by undulating the abdomen up and down in a vertical plane. This movement flips the fringed tails up and down, and both actions provide propulsion in a dolphin-like movement. Mayfly nymphs do not use their legs to swim, although they sometimes crawl through the water. The very fast-swimming mayfly nymphs have interlocking tail fibers that enable them to make rapid sprints. These minnow-like swimmers hold all six legs tucked under their abdomens. The more clumsy swimmers, such as *Ephemerella*, hold their forelegs forward, out, and down. In either case, the only time their legs move is when the nymph stopped swimming and reaches out to grasp or perch on some object.

Carl's early articulated wiggle nymphs were designed by the inspiration of the *Hexagenia* mayfly, called "wigglers" in Michigan. They were a very popular bait fishermen

▲ Brian Fleischig, avid disciple of Richards and owner of Mad River Outfitters, makes ready his AuSable boat for a float down the *trutta*-filled Mad River in Ohio. Credit: Author

used for steelhead and brown trout by putting these large nymphs on a hook and drifting them in the rivers. In my designs, I use a fusion of modern materials and naturals, leaving the loop for the back tail hook abdomen loose and unrestricted, to give the proper part of the anatomy lots of wiggle room Also in combination with a tiny tungsten head that acts like a jigging head motion, you can truly manipulate my wiggle nymphs exactly like the undulating naturals of the fast-swimming *Isonychia*, Gray Drake, *Leptophlebia* and other mayflies. It is again through *Salmo*'s curiosity and infatuation of moving prey that makes innovations like these so deadly on brown trout and Atlantic Salmon rivers.

The exclusive Zanesfield Rod & Gun Club in Ohio, where a hefty price tag allows you to fish beautifully-connected spring ponds in a very natural setting, opened my eyes to how brown trout—even hatchery-raised specimens—behave in the midst of other competitive species. This club is very rare in the fact that they do not feed the trout once they are stocked in the spring ponds. Since the headwaters of the Mad River run through them, they possess adequate scud, sow bugs, mayflies, and midge hatches, as well as all sorts of baitfish. In one particular stretch where brown, brook, and rainbow trout occupy on an equal share of the real estate, it was highly akin to having a bunch of puppies in a kennel, and when you tossed

in a doggie treat, in this case here a fly presentation, you could quickly see the alpha personalities separate from the subordinates. When I tossed in a small sculpin imitation, very quickly a larger eighteen-inch brown trout zoomed right in for it, only to give it a quick look and casually move away with a "not interested" look on his face, since many of the club members fish almost exclusively woolly buggers and muddlers of some sort. However the brook and rainbow trout would come in right after, a little slower to get out of the gate, muddle around the fly for a while, pick and nip at it, until one got hooked up.

Fishing the articulated nymphs and wets involves an across-stream cast at a slightly down-stream angle. An initial quick mend or two upstream, followed by a pause, and then sending a downstream mend to create the bulging broadside swinging tension, is the start of the articulated game. As the fly begins its broadside path, employ continuous twitching of the right hand with the rod tip close to the surface of the water as possible, to retain tension and movement. Occasional lifting of the rod up and down jigging style, will cause the tungsten head to jig and bobble. Occasional short and tight strips and pauses, after the jigging, will make the fly come to life. With the constant line tension implied, browns will almost always hook themselves due to all the line tension and the irresistible fly movement.

One of the biggest problems with this technique is the use of a far too light tippet. I always advise at least 2x and 3x tippets, regardless of the clarity of the water, since your tippet is not under scrutinizing inspection—targeting the swimming nymph and intercepting it is the trout's total focus.

These techniques work extremely well for the large swimming and burrowing mayflies, especially ones that will swim to shore to crawl up, like the *Isonychia* and Drake families. Also in the springtime, many of the trout and salmon rivers are full of young, newly-hatched parr and other tiny baitfish that swim with a high degree of casual display. Though they tend to stay tight to the banks, the schools of these tiny prey will eventually meander out into the main currents, especially during midge hatches. Large browns and landlocked Atlantics alike will explosively target them with huge surface disturbances. Often your mayfly wiggle nymph is confused for faster-swimming baitfish vertebrae, thus be careful not to set the hook too hard—having a light tippet could end up costing you a Leviathan *Salmo*.

## The Topwater Meniscus Conundrum

All too often we place too much importance on just strictly what is above the water line and not enough attention to what is in it or just immediately below the liquid tension zone. It is in this mysterious transitory zone that the hair-pulling hatch-matching conundrum occurs.

In an effort to decode the most confusing scenarios a topwater *trutta* angler will find themselves, I'm diving straight into the masking hatch scenario, which is so characteristic of brown trout surface feeding. Swisher & Richards, Arbona, Caucci, and Nastasi, all alluded to this scenario in their writings on selective hatch matching. This is when there were several different types of aquatic insects on the water, but the trout are keying in on one specific insect or stage of emergence/egg laying—i.e. emerger versus spinner, thus making exact duplication more difficult.

In its basic form a trout may be selecting tiny size 18 Rusty Brown Sulpher spinners, which are very difficult to see, especially in tannin-stained waters. These can be on the water at the same time as the first night's emergence of the much-larger Green Drake or Sulpher adults, which they seem to be ignoring much to the surprise and dismay of the angler. Similarly in the fall, when massive numbers of tiny Blue-Winged-Olive *Pseudocleon* are on the water, the trout can be keying in on similar-sized size 24 midges or tiny brown flying ants in the same sizes. By seining the meniscus, an angler can eventually, through time on the

▲ *Salmo trutta* pay particular attention to the meniscus. Credit: Dave Jensen

water, decipher these dilemmas as the rise forms usually signal the feeding code.

However, the puzzle is often not the topwater matching dilemma, but what is in the meniscus or below that the brown here is inspecting. A classic example of this happened to me and to many others on the ice-cold Downsville section of the upper West branch near Deposit. Here in the middle of July, regardless of atmospheric temperatures approaching 100 degrees Fahrenheit, the frigid water temps coming out of Cannonsville reservoir will start out at the low 40s in the morning and warm to the upper forties to low fifties once the sun and heat penetrates it. Large brown trout will be feeding profusely and can be almost impossible to catch at times due to the tremendous number of natural Sulphers on the water that are struggling against the icy temps to emerge. Thousands of adult duns were floating by untouched, yet the trout were feeding on something else—stillborn emergers paralyzed by the surface tension.

I've seen a similar scenario during the pale morning dun hatch on the Western spring creeks of Montana's Paradise Valley, such as Nelson's and Armstrong's. Here these beautiful yellow adult sailboats seemed to be everywhere and the trout feeding heavily, but not on them. This is why you hire a good guide for someone that spends a lot of time on the water. By repeatedly sampling the meniscus, you will notice the tremendous amount of stillborn nymphs coating the under layer below the floating adults. This is primarily an ice-cold tailwater and spring creek phenomenon, or early spring on freestoners, which hinders the nymph-to-adult metamorphosis. This is also the case on slow, flat meandering waters, which do not allow for the propulsion of the nymph to crack through the surface meniscus, like they can in faster riffles and boulder-strewn rapids, where the nymphs use the hydro propulsion to launch them into the air.

A greased-up, articulated Pheasant Tail with a tuft of folded CDC in the head to emulate the emerging wings and a tinge of yellow in its thorax, fished solo or as a very short subsurface dropper with a dead drift and an occasional twitch in the film meniscus will often do the trick. But all is not that simple when it comes to *trutta* and their uncanny ability to focus on the not-so-obvious prey opportunities. During the filming of my *Selectivity: Trout* DVD, it was a stifling 99 degree F day at the end of September, which is a rarity for the Paradise Valley in Montana, especially when they had a foot of snow the week prior. With no wind the heat was baking me, and I just had to retreat up to my chest in the cold, spring-fed waters to avoid heat stroke. The trout were rising in intervals all day long, with absolutely nothing coming off the water. Thanks to my handy pocket-sized stream seine, and the director allowing me cool-down breaks, I would

walk into the pool up to my chest to lower my body temperature. Meanwhile I poked around the meniscus with my seine. What I found was a hodgepodge of leftover shucks from early morning *Trico* and tiny Blue-Winged-Olive emergers, bits and pieces of spinners, midge pupa shucks, and ultra-tiny brown flying ants. All were in that tiny 26–32 size range that were impossible to distinguish just by visualizing the water from above.

Later that week as the heat wave continued I bought a snorkel and mask at the downtown Bozeman Walmart, and put my eyes right in the meniscus. All this "crud and junk" was just on the downside of the film, and thus many of the rise forms I saw were subtle, barely-budging rise forms, where the backs and tails of the "untouchable" huge browns were breaking the water while their heads were firmly glued in the meniscus. Later that evening at the vise I tied up size 24 sparse stripped peacock herl and three barred micro fibbet-tailed "shucks," which basically looked like a piece of nymphal case. The next day while filming I caught two large twenty-one- and nineteen-inch "untouchable" browns. A careful stomach pumping revealed that their bellies were full of shucks with the occasional *Trico*, tiny BWO, and a scud here or there. Keep in mind it was late in the season and most of the hatches were over, especially after a short window of snow and freezing temperatures before the heat.

Taking the complex masking to more bizarre level, the extremely sophisticated browns of my Muskegon tailwater, which is almost too food ultra-rich, do some crazy things in the spring and summer of the year. Since our tailwater dam is both a bottom and top spill operation, lots of surface water off the Croton reservoir can spill into the river system through the gates, especially with a 6-inch rainfall in the middle of summer. When this happens all kinds of biological drift from the reservoir enters the tailwater below, which our *trutta* are keen to utilize.

All June long we have tremendous mayfly hatches of every sort. Large bugs like Drakes, *Isonychias*, caddis, Cahills, and Sulphers are all thrown in the mix—besides the gazillion midges and micro caddis. This overwhelming variety can make hatch-matching quite a difficult proposition. For the past several years, trout would come to the surface and rise to what appears to be nothing, "phantom risers" I have since dubbed them. The rise forms and gulping is so characteristic of midge feeding that the first thing you do is try various sized midges in different colors and states of emergence—that's what an astute season dry fly fishermen would do on any given river in the world.

But with the constant surface and subsurface seining, by myself and a good friend who fishes three hundred days a year, eighty-two years young: Bob "Brownie" Mansel, we came to learn of the *Daphnia* effect, similar to what happens to the tailwater is in Colorado with the *Mysis* shrimp.

▲ A brown trout bulge-rise feeding. Credit: Dave Jensen

Tons of yellow/orange microscopic protozoan *Daphnia* fill the underside of the meniscus, which the brown trout will come up and gobble just like a midge hatch. A single brown can consume thousands of them a day; thus, putting a few strands of yellowish orange "dubbing" on a hook has very limited success in hooking these fish when there are so many naturals.

Another common occurrence in rivers throughout the world is the springtime "pinhead/micro baitfish"—aquarium guppies look gigantic in comparison. With so many different types of fall fish, pinheads hover the surface in search of phytoplankton, where brown trout feed on them almost exclusively. This can last for weeks, despite heavy hatches of mayflies. They are particularly heavy in tailwaters and lower sections of freestone rivers that have warmed to marginal temperatures. Sipping nutrient-dense minnows with such little effort is both a luxury and a delicacy that *trutta* cannot resist, and these types of waters often hold trophy brown trout.

Thankfully for the average angler targeting specific hatch periods, most brown trout are reasonable beings and will concentrate on these super hatches like the Hendricksons, Green Drakes, Sulphers, etc., since such easy prey are so abundant.

Though quick to pounce on its prey in the most savage way, as we'll see in the next chapter, brown trout tend to prefer a lazier, more cautious approach, and take advantage of an easy meal when it becomes available. Thus, anything stuck or floating in the meniscus, or its underside, is a prime target, as evidenced by the brown "bulge rises." Stillborn mayfly nymphs, caddis pupae, etc. are all prime meniscus targets. But when browns are in these ultra-selective meniscus-feeding modes, when exacting imitation does not seem to work, a large stimulator Royal Wulff or Neversink spider pattern can turn the trick, thanks to the curiosity and the unpredictably predictable nature of the *Salmo trutta*.

One need only compile stomach analysis of a brown trout over the season and see its uncanny penchant for the bizarre and unusual, which often doesn't make any sense at all. I have found leaf particles, twigs, pieces of plastic, small colored stones, and part of a McDonald's hamburger wrapper, in the belly of *trutta*. Being ultimate adapters, browns are quick to exploit new food sources or at times be confoundingly wary of abundant hatches like a Green Drake or *Danica* mayfly hatch. They often need to take a day or two to adjust to the new food supply like hoppers and cicadas. This is the schizophrenic tendency the browns have, drawing a fine line between obsession and repulsion.

## Surface-Feeding Rhythms

Larger browns will surface feed at a leisurely pace given the general modes of operation of its daily routine. A particular brown will dominate a certain turf or fiefdom with several clear channels adjacent to each other, and an escape niche, usually an undercut bank or a wooded deadfall nearby. A large alpha dominant brown will be surface feeding here when a hatch is in progress. Once a somewhat steady size 18 *Baetis* hatch starts, for example, the large alpha trout's first move is to take up the most leisurely feeding lane, combined with a shelter niche like an obstacle or overhanging branch tight to the bank. Such lies often inhibit the fly fisher's presentation, especially if the fish has been caught before and is very wary. These exterior obstacles usually produce very large brown feeding lies, since they are almost impossible to catch there. Coincidence sometimes has it that big trout are produced from these tricky areas due to lack of angler success at these points . . . or, do big selective browns seek impossible, shelter-driven lies intentionally? The verdict will always be out on the subject, due to the fact that they are coincidental.

Once you have diagnosed the degree of difficulty, angle, direction, and type of cast to be used in the situation, the second step is to establish some consistency in surface feeding, as the fish finds a comfortable feeding interval. Once the fish senses no bells/whistles/alarms of intrusion, patiently and quietly remain still and in position to execute your contemplated cast. You are very close to victory. If you have timed your arrival with the peak of the hatch emergence, the fish may have a rare moment of clumsiness.

But timing is everything. If you wait too long, that drizzle of rain and clouds might give way to sun and the BWO hatch will be over. Blue-Winged Olives are very fond of low light conditions, coupled with a light rain or drizzle. This can occur on spring creeks in the middle of winter or on a fall afternoon. The key is to be there at the optimum time, when the fish is most adventurous and feeding steadily. The telltale sign that things are winding down in a hatch period is the decreased frequency of surface rises, indicating refusals to even naturals.

Here switching to nymphing scuds, sow bugs, and Pheasant Tails, or BWO nymphs is a good choice, even though there are still a few Blue-Winged Olives left on the water. This is the comfort zone browns tend to go to, since surface feeding for long periods of time exposes them uncomfortably.

## Dry Fly Approach Variables

Forget flog-casting to death—it pays to have a planned approach in the meniscus game with the persnickety

▲ Throwing a puddle cast, or a "sweeping to the left or right reach cast mend," as Roman Moser does here, can give you a somewhat of a downstream reach cast—as you fish upstream—which can buy you a little more drag-free time during your presentation. Credit: Albert Pesendorfer

*trutta*. Line drag will affect your fly, particularly on spring creeks, tailwaters, and fast freestoners, where the weed channels send undulating currents into the surface, and tail-out pool lips create all sorts of backswirls, eddies, and unnatural hydrodynamic movements. This is especially important on longer drift inspections, for which *trutta* are notorious. Also given the fact that your window of presentation may be only a few feet, with your main section and leader butt falling on the aquatic grasses near the feeding channel or boulders near shore, or eventually being dragged there, these issues complicate things immensely.

If the trout is making a simple rise, you can afford to come upstream, from the downstream position, which shields you from predatory alarms, as long as you keep a low profile. Your cast must be precise at the first get-go, since you might not be allowed a second chance.

Conversely, the advantage of coming from an upstream position going downstream and presenting a down-and-across reach cast, is usually the only way to go for ultra-selective spring creek/tailwater browns. In this situation, the fly comes into the fish's window first, before the tippet material, thus the trout will focus all of its effort on scrutinizing the imitation and less time scrutinizing, or "being disappointed" as Marinaro put it, by a dragging fly, even

though to you, the drag might be almost imperceptible. On big spring creeks like Silver Creek, the River Test, and a host of others in Patagonia and New Zealand, you could get out and wade and move into position slowly. On the limestoners of Pennsylvania, Wisconsin, and Minnesota you have to pick trees, shrubbery, or other obstacles to shield your advances from upstream as you descend on a fussy trout.

These are a given for spring creek dry fly fishing. But the single most important delivery item is the leader. Spring creek and tailwater leader tapers must be specially selected if you stand any chance of hooking ultra-selective fish on 6X–7X tippet. They must have a firm, long, and heavy butt section, tapered down quickly to allow for five to seven feet of light tippet.

## Attractors: Breaking the Boredom

Although the brown trout's selectivity dictates proper fly silhouettes, size, and color, there is no question that when Theodore Gordon was tying up his famous Quill Gordon designs, he was directly influenced by more selective brown trout than by the easier-to-catch brook trout.

One of the most common areas for attractors to work well for browns are fast-cascading freestone rivers with

▲ Attractors do not realistically match anything in particular, but the combination of color and design suggest a food source. These can be very effective in certain environments like big Montana rivers like the Missouri, where Pennsylvanian legend Tommy Baltz admires his *trutta*. Credit: Mike Tsukamoto.

broken surfaces that distort vision and speed up a predatory response. In these cases the attractors catch the attention of a trout much quicker than a simplistic and sparse imitation. They are also beneficial in that the angler can see them above the water better than a trout can see them from below.

Browns relish two basic types of attractors—the types that suggest a certain category of insects, as well as types that do not suggest anything in particular but feature stimulating colors. Two examples would be the Royal Wulff (Coachman) and the Bivisible.

As mentioned above, they work particularly well in fast-flowing freestone river systems, where movement and silhouette of the fly are perhaps more important than exacting imitations. However, the greatest use for them is in the "curiosity killed the cat" category, when brown trout are bored to death with constant similar imitations, as is often the case in heavily fished catch-and-release waters like the Delaware or Missouri. When nothing else is working, something totally different and presented in a bizarre situation often brings success. As a guide, I can't tell you how many times I scratched my forehead and uttered the following words to a client: "No way—I can't believe the fish took that thing!"

Keeping with the bizarre and unusual, these flies work very well in newly-prospected waters in virgin territory where the browns might have never seen a fly, for instance in the mountains of Kashmir or regions of Patagonia that are yet to be explored. These bizarre and unusual patterns are so different from what the wild trout there feed on, they elicit strike responses from the sheer novelty standpoint, or because these fish have not yet established a selective predator profile.

The other category is the more suggestive attractor—like the Adams or the Stimulator. If fly anglers around the world had but only two dry flies to fish, it would definitely be these two mainstay patterns. Here, body wing profile is everything. The Adams suggests mayflies—Drakes, Hendricksons, *Isonychias*, Quills, BWOs, etc.—the list goes on. The Stimulator suggests stoneflies and caddis. This pattern will catch fish anywhere and anytime, but is especially effective when timed during the particular of emergence of these hatches. When I fished the hallowed chalk streams of England's River Test and Itchen, out of all the flies the ghillie had the opportunity to suggest, it always came back to a parachute Adams.

Finally, the common rule for attractors is they will work well on waters that do not get a lot of fishing pressure. But then again, given *trutta*'s unpredictable nature, it might just be the first fly you might want to go to on your first casts regardless of water.

## Summer's Manna from Heaven Presentations

To say that brown trout have a love affair for exotic terrestrials is an understatement. As many humans have a

▲ A fly fisher imparting a simple, well-timed twitch, quiver, or side-swimming motion to a fly will draw a strike from the cautious and highly speculative New Zealand brownie. Here Baltz's para-nymph imitates the meniscus food perfectly. Credit: Ross Purnell

curiosity for extra-terrestrial/UFO/Yeti–type stuff, *trutta* love to violently crush big hoppers and cicadas, despite maintaining their cautious guard.

*Trutta* are "control freaks" and dominating creatures of their niche habitats and are the so-called experts of their realm. They know every nuanced behavior of mayflies, caddis, aquatic vertebrates, and everything that dwells in their realm. But when the seasonal "creepy crawly freak show" terrestrials show up, they can at first be somewhat alarmed and cautious.

Marinaro's complex rise of Letort brown trout fame, or as I put it, the "I'm not quite so sure" rise forms, usually occur to larger mayflies, and definitely to large terrestrial objects like grasshoppers and cicadas. Since a giant size 6 Sulpher *Potamanthus* mayfly or an occasional grasshopper in a deep forested stream lacking open pastures and meadows are so infrequent, their sighting will trigger a *trutta*'s alarm. Before an extremely selective trout—usually a larger one—makes a decision on a highly-scrutinized food form, they will look for a few discerning characteristics that will cause it to follow it downstream, turn back to its original lie, only to follow it and pursue it again, and finally take or refuse the natural or imitation. Sometimes a slight twitch to the fly triggers a response.

Here is where complex selectivity goes into overdrive and really puts on a show. Some anglers will loath the challenge. Some will pull their hair out in frustration. And others like me will get the popcorn out and watch the show!

## The Minutiae Component

Usually when the doldrums of summer kick in and the heat around the globe gets turned up, fishing for *Salmo*—both *trutta* and *salar*—can slow down tremendously. After the plethora of the super mayfly and stonefly hatches of spring and early summer have deposited their nymphal seed for the next year, the lull in surface feeding is almost a brief respite.

Here is where the late summer–early fall daytime midge game and the nighttime meat game are most effective. This is the period where the *Tricos*, tiny BWO *Pseudocleon*, and midges emerge in quite a regular fashion, often unnoticed by anglers chasing bass and warmwater targets. As icing on the cake, the miniature terrestrial sprinkling of beetles, jassids, and flying ants can rev up a brown trout's appetite even while it is focused on proper oxygen and water temperature refuge. On ice-cold spring creeks and tailwaters that is not a problem. But on the broader freestone rivers, the brown trout must now use its adaptability to combine all feeding opportunities in a perfectly-balanced equilibrium with suitable temperatures.

▲ Big browns, like this beauty, love flying ants of all sizes. Credit: Aaron Vanderwall

One of my favorite times of year is the dog days of August, when the still nights are occasionally broken up by a passing and welcomed thunderstorm, and crickets, hoppers, and cicadas create their chirping buzz. To an ever-foraging brown trout, the end of summer is a time of extreme busyness, like the squirrel gathering acorns, as they too must prepare for procreation by gaining as much weight as possible for the spawning ritual. Whether they must pack in tons of *Tricos* and terrestrials during the day, or hunt mice and other fish by night, they are now fully focused on the hunt.

But August's doldrums are rife with devils in the details. Amongst all the natural diverse aquatic edibles mentioned above, one significant terrestrial food source becomes an addiction and hardwired to brown trout's daily daytime feeding: ants. For no known scientific reason, when they fall on the water they are the true "manna from heaven."

The windy days in late summer or early fall produce massive winged brown flying ants from size 14 to as small as size 24. Their abundance on spring creeks, tail-waters, and wide-open freestone valley rivers can border on flotsam overload. I have witnessed steadily feeding, simple-rise-form-gulping browns during a heavy *Trico*, Pale Morning Dun, or Blue-Winged Olive spinner fall, go out of their way to sip the tiny ant delectable. Many theories are strictly folklore, such as "they have a nice taste to them," or "their buggy tentacles are too irresistible to ignore." Whatever it is, they are a consistent and powerful food source that is often difficult to see, since they can be perfectly masked in the meniscus with their dark colors and flat-flushed profiles.

Here a streamside seine when wading can save the day. Also, the rise forms to these more plentiful terrestrials are simple and deliberate, unlike the complex rises and uncertainty larger hoppers and cicadas might elicit.

### *Trutta* Kryptonite: Hopper/Ant Dropper

Given all these diverse summer and fall offerings, a terrestrial on top and an ant dropper is a perfect way to explore the options. Also varying the depth of your dropper can have very lethal implications. During the ant flights, I'll use a larger surface #14 HI-VIZ ant, with a smaller sunken ant, since there is not much buoyancy in ants once submerged. Another option is to have an ant and a tiny Blue-Winged Olive spinner a foot apart to mimic the surface biological drift, or a larger ant and a smaller ant, since they both comprise the surface drift.

In the masking hatch situations when you have a Trico hatch, tiny rusty BWO spinners, ants, and midges all at the same time, have pre-tied tandem combos of each ready. Remember to scale down dropper tippets to match the appropriate fly size.

When beetles are on the water, they can go from quite thick in wide-open valleys like in the days of Marinaro on the Cumberland Valley spring creeks during the Japanese beetle invasion of the 1940s, to a sparse occasional sprinkling, as on mountain freestone streams and tailwaters. In these situations a black beetle with a fluorescent sight indicator on top of the fly, tied tandem with a scud, sow bug, caddis pupa or midge pupa dropper can be irresistible for even the most ultra-selective browns to ignore. Studying rise forms is one of my passions. On a double-floating dropper system, I have often watched a trout go back and forth between the two before making a selection. Though this is rare, it does occur. I have also had a double fish hook-up on two different dropper flies, when fishing to a pod of steadily surfacing and aggressive takers.

### Chucking the Terrestrial Meat

Grasshoppers, crickets, and cicadas make up the meaty threesome that browns cannot resist once habituated to their presence and the first daring attack and gulp brings a soothing sensation to the throat and stomach. It only takes about a day or so for them to adjust and strategically place themselves next to undercut banks and under overhanging grass. Here will be the ultimate hunting lie that will produce until autumn's first frost eventually wipes out large land creatures of unbelievable nourishment.

It is interesting to see how different brown trout have developed different terrestrial predating preferences and behaviors. Some like terrestrials moving in swinging helplessly across the current. Others like them twitching and dead drifting. Some like them totally dead drifted and examine them for long periods of time, like we mentioned above in Marinaro's complex rise. On Michigan's Pere Marquette, guides pound browns to death all summer with all sorts of creepy terrestrial-looking patterns, and on Montana's rivers with "hopper/droppers." So varying your presentation from dead to twitch drift makes sense to browns that build up a high degree of selectivity wariness in these cases.

I once learned the secrets to successful terrestrial fishing by an old curmudgeonly Pennsylvania angler who specialized in the Cumberland Valley and State College limestone spring creeks, whom I nicknamed "the bushwhacker." The bushwhacker always picked hot, humid days, with a strong breeze blowing. The sign of a cold front coming through that day was always a best bet to get the heat and humidity to stir up the bugs and then blow them in every direction. He would often drive around from creek to creek until he found a farmer cutting hay or gathering with their tractors. His name came from his wading staff antics and how he walked up and down the creeks and smashed the overhanging shoreline vegetation to dislodge hoppers, crickets and whatever else was there. This was

▲ Mike Batchkie tossing terrestrials from a drift boat floatables on Michigan's Pere Marquette. Credit: Author

a primitive form of natural chumming but boy did it drive the fish into a frenzy.

I described my use of the "bushwhacker" technique in my book *Selectivity*. In hindsight, some might think this is an unsportsmanlike practice. However, in all ecological seriousness, we were doing no harm and perhaps messing with one billionth of the land-based insects in those fields. If anything, the browns there got a feeding buffet to enjoy!

Another technique he used was to carry a butterfly net and capture a bunch of hoppers and put them in a plastic container poked with holes. He would sit on the bank smoking a cigar and chum/throw hoppers (note: check local laws regarding chumming) into interesting undercut banks scenarios and watch how the trout behaved. They often revealed the spot of a lunker leviathan Brown that came crashing out to smash the hopper. He was a total catch-and-release fly fisherman, and his empirical practices were observations and amusement.

In wide-open Western rivers with broad, sweeping prairies and arid climates filled with grassy fields on rivers like the Yellowstone, the Snake and others, hoppers are the mainstay food and the fish are less dubious about targeting each and every one of them. Once the giant *Pteronarcys* salmon fly is gone, large meat hunters transition over to hopper mania.

When fishing hoppers and cicadas, I try to target a natural presentation by casting into a grassy bank, and pull my fly off quickly into a "drop and plop" landing. I then strip, twitch, pause—repeated many times, as you're going directly across current or slightly downstream. This technique often locates fish, which sometimes swipe at the fly and miss, or at least reveal themselves and show a surface orientation but no take. I then usually drop down in fly size and dead drift a smaller, sparser Letort Hopper, rather than the more-detailed Whitlock Hoppers or the new Ken Moorish foam and rubber creations.

It is important to pay attention to the color, silhouettes, and sizes of the hoppers and cicadas in your area. *Orthoptera* and *Arthropoda* come in different colors and might have total different sizes and coloration from one valley to the next.

Other than slinging big streamer meat, the pursuit of big browns with this terrestrial phenomenon is about the coolest thing. Make sure you use heavy tippets, preferably 1X and 0X. If fish are extremely tippet shy on dead drifts, you can drop down to 3X but no further. Setting the hook too early and pulling the terrestrial out of the fish's mouth is a common mistake. Let the fish take it in and set your hook firmly with the downward strip set. Profile-setting the rod

▲ The lovely limestone Spruce Creek in Pennsylvania provided a memorable day of cicada plopping next to the bank. Credit: Harpster family

straight up into the air will usually blow the hook set and pull the fly out of the fish's mouth. If refusals come often, check your body shadow and profile, or change flies, tippet size, and tactics. I have conjured up very large brown trout with bigger hoppers only to eventually catch them on a tiny sparser size 12 Letort hopper with a long dead drift and complex rise.

Similar tactics go for cicadas. *Magicicada* is an amazing giant monster that invades rivers and creeks on a thirteen-year and seventeen-year cycle in eastern North America. They are sometimes called "locusts," as cicadas belong to the taxonomic order *Hemipteran* (true bugs), suborder *Auchenorrhyncha*, while locusts are grasshoppers classified to the order *Orthoptera*. Cicadas detect seasons by evolutionary genetic codes and important clues about where trees are in their growth cycle from the composition of the roots they feed on. What will baffle scientists forever, and perhaps the cicadae themselves, is how they keep track of how many years have passed.

Cicadas drop in rivers, usually in their clumsy flights between trees, in search of other mates. Also, violent storms and brisk winds in the summer make them pop up on the water. Ideal terrain is open grassland combined with tree patches, which allow wind to move through the trees. Rivers such as the Green River in Utah, Montana's Madison and Big Hole, and New Zealand rivers, along with all the other Eastern and Midwest freestoners and spring creeks, are ideal places to find them and hungry browns in waiting.

When fishing cicadas you have two types of responses—the aggressive pulverizing take, or the inquisitive poking and following. The aggressive takes become more assured as the trout have had one or two meals of these meaty delicacies. Alternate dead drifting and twitching, with the "plop and splat" on the water, which will transmit to the browns' delicate lateral line vibration sensory system.

## Fishing the Dry as a Living Insect

In my "four systems go" checklist of how a trout views your surface presentation, wing silhouette as the result of refraction's "bending around corners," meniscus body profile and segmentation, color/ultraviolet hue, and finally motion and movement, allow the fish to distinguish and be comfortable with their designated program feeding choice.

Back in my early days an excellent book came out by an unorthodox genius—another great Catskill man named Leonard Wright. As with G. E. M. Skues, he rattled the cages of the dry traditionalists, and definitely got people's attention. Wright's genius and laboratory was the waters of the Neversink, a river dear to me because of our family's summer cottage on its lovely waters. Most fly fishing literature was geared toward mayflies, and generally neglected stoneflies and caddis, which move around a lot, flutter, twitch, dive up-and-down to lay eggs, etc. If you ever fish the Neversink with its big, deep, rocky pools and cold, crystal-clear water, insect life can be sparse and limited, especially in the upper waters above the reservoir. Though it has great hatches, they do not endure for significant periods of time.

▲ Wright was quick to identify the Brown trout's infatuation with quick, jittering prey movements with the fluttering caddis. Credit (tie and photo): Jim Haswell

Focusing on a bug's movement, Wright's famous design, the Fluttering Caddis, was one of the first new highly buoyant, slanted tent–winged imitations that an angler could skitter and twitch downstream-and-across, which is so unorthodox from the classic mayfly dead drift. Wright spent hours observing trout in slashing rises, which most often targeted the high movement of caddis and stoneflies. This pattern was part of a whole new age of fluttering dry flies such as the Stimulator, Wulff series, Bivisbles, Trudes, and Goddard caddis.

My first experience with the fluttering caddis was at the laboratory stream of my youth, the Wiscoy Creek in western New York's Wyoming County Appalachian foothills. This stream had tremendous natural reproduction of wild brown trout back in the 1970s. Literally every pool you fished you would drum up two or three native Caledonia/Seth Green strain German *trutta*. Granted, most were in the nine- to eleven-inch range, but the spring-fed freestoner could also produce twenty-inch browns when leviathan hunting at night.

It was already midsummer. The classic hatches had long gone except for the occasional yellow drake or giant stonefly. The *Tricos* were the only consistent hatches, but as the heat became more oppressive, it was a quick early-morning affair. Upon my visit to Reed's Orvis shop in New York, I noticed a box of Wright's Fluttering Caddis featured on the counter in cream, brown, and black. Of course I had to have some.

The next day in the pure sunshine and heat of the afternoon, I tied on a cream fluttering caddis in a size 12 and cast it down-and-across with a twitching skitter. The smaller browns that were still out in the afternoon demolished the fly on what seemed like every other cast. I believe a lot of this was due to the novelty of someone fishing this way, since the creek was catch-and-release and received pressure from skilled fly anglers.

But back in the early seventies, caddis were still a new frontier and very few people knew how to imitate them. In the summertime one can often see trout leaping in the air for damselflies, butterflies, and moths, since food sources are scarcer and less obvious. Movement once again is the key trigger in the ability for the fly to be greased up and maintain a non-sinking profile.

## The Sedge Curse Presentation

Nothing can be more frustrating to a dry fly fishermen who is well-versed in all the hatches and stages of emergence, and well-prepared to match whatever comes his or her way, only to be stifled by a behavior of a natural that is almost impossible to imitate. We have all seen it before: trout jumping up in the air to grab egg-laying caddis, hovering above the water but never seeming to touch it.

When I set up my lodge on Michigan's Muskegon River, Carl Richards and Dick Pobst were making history with their caddis book treatises. Though they came up with impeccable designs and identified all the insects thoroughly, besides the occasional mention of a twitch or skitter, lift and jig in your presentation, they discussed no casts in particular.

One of the biggest dilemmas is during the caddis ovapositing flights where the females drop their eggs. Here the females hop and skip like a ping pong ball going back and forth. Extremely selective tailwater trout quickly pick up on this movement, particularly the larger browns. To keep a dry fly constantly dropping back and forth, up-and-down, is a difficult endeavor.

Thus I came up with the "Statue of Liberty" cast in 1998 out of sheer necessity to get clients into trout during this very difficult period of August through September. It has two parts: The first is to imitate the egg laying, and the second is to imitate the diving and ascending female caddis who deposit their eggs on the river bottom and then try to quickly swim up.

Anglers can execute this cast by using long leaders up to eighteen feet with heavy butt sections to manipulate the fly that quickly taper down to very fine tippets. After drying the fly on a series of false casts, you raise the rod completely vertical into the sky with your armpits completely exposed upon delivery of the cast, just like the Lady Liberty holding up her torch. This will allow the fly to hop and skitter airborne and touch down one or two times. Usually a very motion-oriented Brown will slam the fly in the first or second hop.

Then through the drift, by raising the rod high and doing line-lifting wrist-curl mends upstream, you can still get the fly to come off the water, but by that time it usually begins to soak and get wet. Again, the longer leaders allow you not to overpower mend and lift the fly all the way back to you in the air—be gentle and delicate.

Finally, two things occur at the very end of your presentation. As the flies are directly downstream below, you can lift it several more times to create the popcorn caddis effect. This part of the drift is very deadly, since trout will take up station below your boat or body wading position, since you have created a seam that fish will blend into to feed.

Eventually the fly begins to sink. Allow it to do so by sending stack mends directly at the line downstream to allow the fly to go under. Once at the end of its sunken drift, pump your rod and raise the tip to imitate a submerged caddis emerging to the surface. With this one presentation you could imitate all the phases of motion-oriented caddis and stoneflies in a very effective manner.

▲ Massive White River Arkansas *trutta*saurus, taken by leviathan hunter Tommy Lynch with his masterpiece "Drunk and Disorderly" streamer. Credit: Lynch

# 8. *Trutta*saurus: The Ultimate Kill Artist

Although the sometimes introspective *trutta* is often labeled as a sit-and-wait predator, in the "pounce-kill-hide-digest" mode, they are highly skilled at ambushing prey by day, and especially at night. Larger carnivorous *trutta* set up specific ambush niches or hunt in packs to accomplish the task of eating smaller fish. But large brown trout from all parts of the globe eat rodents, snakes, small ducks, and other carnivorous terrestrial delectable items. From the Catskill mountain freestone rivers to English chalk streams, from Kenya to the Himalayas, and from New Zealand to Patagonia, *Salmo* unleashes the lethal killer that lies within in a savage and bloodthirsty fashion. As the old trout bum saying goes, "A brown trout will eat anything that doesn't eat it."

A whole new era of younger millennials and Gen-X'ers have taken the "meat-slinging game" of fly fishing streamers to a higher level in a way that has revolutionized the sport. Once considered the noble pastime of gentlemen in tweed and bamboo rods, armed with traditional Quill Gordon and Adams dry flies, fly fishing for decades was a purist/hatch matcher's "flea flicker' game in the true British tradition. But a new "bad ass breed" of long-bearded, finger-stripping, heavy metal aficionados plying ten-inch articulated "streamer chickens" and stripping them like mad with killer movement is taking on the traditional "quiet sport."

Much of this phenomenon developed on my home rivers here in Michigan, with a strong east coast saltwater influence, as well as the Montana, Pennsylvania and Arkansas connection. It is a damn cool gig and one that will change your appreciation for what I like to call

▲ A barbaric, prehistoric Michigan *Salmo* predator. As with sturgeon, many anglers don't realize *Salmo* are modern dinosaurs dating back fifty million years ago. Credit: Author

"*truttasaurus*" as my mentor Vince Marinaro once labeled it, being the ultimate primal, killing, predatory machine. What is not commonly associated as *Salmo trutta* prey can now be lumped into the "road kill" category, a term we developed in Québec and I introduced in *Selectivity* to describe the massive, articulated, meaty streamers that gigantic *salar* take in the doldrums of summer. These are fly facsimiles of things we pick off of roadside pavement and out of car grills.

With *Salmo*—both brown trout and Atlantic salmon—one must acknowledge their refined curiosity and extremely vicious predatory habits toward anything small enough to fit in its mouth and stomach, even if by piecemeal. Often the out-of-touch traditionalist anglers label this category as bizarre folklore. I can surely tell you that is not the case, and that such predation happens more often than you think. Here one can attest to the vole hatch of rodents in New Zealand and how giant leviathan *truttas* hunt them down viciously.

## First Encounters of a Carnivorous Kind

This leviathan *trutta*saurus murder mystery takes place in the lovely pastoral Conewango Creek Valley Amish country not far from my uncle's place in the Chautauqua wine region along Lake Erie, while on summer vacation as a boy. Keep the lights on while you read it!

It was the summer of 1972 and I was a fourteen-year-old boy with a hard-working dishwasher job in a local diner on Grand Island, New York where we lived. I got a much-deserved three week vacation to spend with my Uncle Mike and cousin Richie at their Lake Erie shoreside home, high up on a wine vineyard bluff overlooking beautiful sand dune beaches. Each day we would play soccer and volleyball on the beach, fish for white bass and sheepshead drum off the power house pier at Niagara Mohawk Power where my uncle worked, and eat fresh oysters on the half shell with smoked whitefish chowder at the beachside fish shack. In the evening we would have awkward rendezvous with girls on vacation. After years of repulsion and avoidance of the opposite sex, I was just beginning to get curious about them.

Aside from all the coming-of-age experiences I was enjoying with my older, hipper cousin Rich, the true underlying goal of that summer vacation was to explore the small spring-fed brown trout streams a short drive away in western New York's mysterious Amish country. Not far from the horse-drawn buggies and carts clapping along the roadside, there was a psychic spiritual community along the breezy shore of Cassadaga Lake known as Lilly Dale. It was a spooky place of weird-looking old Victorian houses where practicing witch covens, palm readers, clairvoyants, fortune tellers, occult worshipers, Druids—you name it, all gathered. When we drove by in my cousin Richie's chrome-bumpered, spit-shined Chevy Impala, we got weird creepy looks from these people. To good old-fashioned Polish/Austrian Catholic altar boys like Rich and me, these mysterious freaky people were nevertheless highly intriguing.

If this unusual atmosphere was not enough chilling excitement alone on our way to Amish country trout streams, we encountered the icing on the cake. While on a *Starsky and Hutch*–like rubber-burning adventure on the back roads, we discovered a very bizarre occurrence—a "gravity hill," near an old creepy eighteenth-century graveyard where only Amish buggies would go by.

Once at "gravity hill," Rich would get to the bottom of a gently ascending hill, stop the car and put it into neutral and all of a sudden the car would climb the hill on its own accord without my cousin touching the gas pedal or steering wheel—this was now turning creepy as hell!—but way too much fun. (Authors note: Upon my further research, there are locations throughout the Appalachians/Allegany foothills where this phenomenon exists. It said to be a result of optical illusions of terrain elevations, where the horizon is obscured and non-vertical growing trees give the impression of going uphill on what is actually a downhill slope. Whatever it was, it was way too cool!)

All these eerie, creepy happenings were fusing together perfectly for a river monster fish hunt. As our hunt began, my uncle Mike had a small clue and lead. An acquaintance at work fly fished the streams at night, like many Allegheny "*trutta*saurus" angling hunters did, and said there were leviathan browns as long as your leg in those streams that attacked anything and everything. It was folklore type stuff; like all ghost sightings or Sasquatch hunts, nobody ever seems to catch them.

My uncle made good on his promise to take us camping for a few days in the Amish country near the Cassadaga and Conewango creeks, where the big browns lived. We set up our campground near the village of Randolph on a farmer's property where my uncle frequented for unbelievable corn, tomatoes, cherries, eggs, free-range chickens, and grass-fed beef. The creek ran right past the barn and had excellent big trout habitat with under-cut banks, log jams, and small bridges that a river monster *trutta* might secure as its home, if it truly existed. Casting Letort hoppers by day and picking up the gorgeous eight-to-thirteen-inch brownies that lived in the creek, I knew from reading Jim Bashline's *Night Fishing for Trout*, that the real deal monsters fed at night. Since my uncle didn't fish much, he came along as the flashlight guy and also as the emotional support guardian, since I was still afraid of venturing out into dark, hostile woods by myself. My cousin Rich was not a big fisherman and preferred to stay at camp reading car magazines by the campfire and sneaking beers from my uncle when he could.

▲ The night game has since changed dramatically with high-tech headlamps. Here Aaron Vanderwall shows a night monster catch from the Au Sable in Michigan. Credit: Vanderwall

After difficulty seeing my line and the biggest muddler minnow I could buy in those days on my first night of fishing, I heard all kinds of strange noises by the stream and was always imagining red electric eyes following me wherever I went. "What was that?," I would often yell out nervously and frightened as hell—but I always tried to maintain my cool composure. "That was probably deer—don't worry," my uncle said. He didn't tell me until after the trip that the farmer said there were larger numbers of black bear this year who ventured down from the nearby Allegheny National Forest.

At about 1:00 a.m., I saw a small critter swim near the surface to the other shore near a huge deadfall in the creek, only to be followed by a huge wake and sudden thrashing and boiling of the water, reminiscent of a crocodile attack! I was scared shitless and ran out of the woods like hell to the car where my uncle was already inside, smoking a cigarette and listing to his Polka music from Pennsylvania on the car radio.

"*Znalazlesz cos?*" my uncle asked in Polish—*find anything*? I could barely catch my breath and was trembling

and couldn't talk since I ran so hard back to the car. "Whatever it was scared the hell out of me," I said. "Let's get out of here and back to the campground NOW!"

The next day we took a ride after my morning fishing and drove to my uncle's favorite Amish roadside market stand along Route 394. There they had the finest Amish homemade cheeses: Muenster, Emmentaler Swiss, Colby Jack, and others. The orange-cased Muenster was my favorite and I ate it with butter on fresh Amish bread that was to die for. We bought sausages, baked goods, and potatoes that we threw in tinfoil for the Dutch oven pit back at the campfire we made.

The Amish couple were clad in their traditional white shirts and blue overall bibs, the father with his hat and long beard, the mother in a white bonnet and dress. They had a couple of boys a few years younger than me who noticed the hip boot waders I was wearing. "English boy like to fish, eh?" they asked me. I told them I was after a big brown trout and said I heard something back in the creek below the bridge last night where the giant tree that fell in the water created a huge pool. "It scared the crap out of me—it chased something on the surface of the water and looked like a crocodile attack," I nervously explained. "Ja . . . bet it was a really big German." (They called the browns "Germans," as was confirmed later in life when I fished the Baraboo spring creek near Amish farms in the Driftless area of Wisconsin, where the Amish there called them the same.) "We are going out hunting for them tonight with our spinning rods . . . come back tomorrow, English boy, and we'll let you know what we found," they said with a boyish cockiness. Their words had me in suspense and I believed I was onto something in my search for the river monster brown of a lifetime.

After another night of being afraid of everything I heard in the woods, I realized the night fishing gig wasn't my proverbial "cup of tea," and I stuck to morning hopper fishing, where the only thing I learned not to fear anymore were the cows that followed me wherever I went. But returning to that Amish stand the following day I saw the two Amish boys back by the hut in back of the produce stand by a buggy cart—they were cutting something up. I saw the spinning rods propped up with a big hooks and split shots above it. I saw the smiles on their faces and their constant giggling.

Then, to the amazement of my eyes and sitting on a bunch of ferns with ice blocks near it on the flat cart, was my river monster—a true *trutta*saurus brown of at least ten pounds—a giant leviathan—I gasped with awe. "There is your river monster, English!" the one boy exclaimed. "We use field mice we capture and put them on hooks and reel them in along the surface. We caught him just after midnight and the full moon allowed us to see him waking water where he was hunting—*Ja*? This big German had a small undigested duckling bulging from its belly, huh English boy? Look at the guts and stomach here . . . probably what you heard him eat the other night when you were out eh?"

To say I was truly awestruck and astonished by that viewing was an understatement. The folkloric mystery of big browns eating things that go bump in the night was now a case solved. Later in my twenties when I visited the English chalk streams of the Test and Itchen, an old ghillie told me of the big brown that chased ducklings, snakes, and rodents by the mill dam in the upper River Itchen, which I talked about in *Selectivity*. My fishing partner Ash said, "Bollocks!" to the old ghillie, who was known to drink a wee bit too much Scotch. I replied, "I'm with ya, ole chap!—show me to this monster."

## The Carnivorous Brown: Early Beginnings and New Age Mastery

Today, thanks to its pioneers and their techniques, "slinging

▲ A prime *truttasaurus* hunting lie for all the obvious reasons: shelter, spawning gravel, insect/bait fish foraging areas. Credit: Author

meat" has become a subset of the fly fishing passion for leviathan *trutta*. Large trophy brown trout rivers are not everywhere, and factors that give rise to trophy fisheries in the wild are usually in situations where trout densities are lower, such as marginal waters and certain tailwaters that have extremes in flow regimes and temperatures. These favor the true alpha adaptable survivors that maximize foraging with migration and changing ecosystem conditions.

Some river systems like the Au Sable in Michigan, the Big Horn in Montana, and some spring creeks of the Driftless area in Wisconsin and Minnesota are magnificent brown trout ecosystems with a tremendous density of wild fish due to ideal water quality and spawning conditions. Each of the year classes thrive in abundance and thus compete heavily for available food, which can vary at times of year.

The tremendous abundance of ten- to fourteen-inch fish in the systems makes for incredible fishing. But the truly large *trutta*saurus leviathans lie in the marginal lower downstream sections, where they find unique foraging opportunities based on migratory adjustments to capitalize on fertile food sources in these areas where most trout don't do well due to adaption inability. In my constant anthropomorphism analogies, it's much like athletics. Millions of kids around the world start playing soccer and football, but only a few will become Ronaldo or Tom Brady–type players, or in this case truly giant *trutta*saurus browns.

> What is the mechanism behind density-dependent growth in rivers? Newman (1993) suggested that the fish use the best foraging sites available, and as the density increases, the fish are forced to use less profitable sites. The reduction in growth was not due to a decrease in the growth of all trout but rather in an increase in number of slower growing fish. Brannas et. al. ( 2004) found that an aggressive behavior was most beneficial at low and intermediate densities, and non-aggressive behavior was advantageous when foraging at high fish densities. Finstad et. alst (2007) demonstrated that increased shelter, measured as the depth of interstitial spaces in the substratum, explained 24 percent of the variance in growth performance, indicating that habitat quality influences growth rate.
> —Bror Jonsson & Nina Jonsson, *Ecology of Atlantic Salmon and Brown Trout*

It stands to reason that positions lower in the river systems can often dictate larger predator habitat areas and more diversification for ideal and vacant feeding lies.

### Early Pioneers of the Streamer Game

In Joseph D. Bates Jr.'s excellent treatise on Atlantic salmon, *Fishing Atlantic Salmon*, and his streamer book,

*Streamer Fly Tying and Fly Fishing*, he extols the virtues of streamers and bucktails when it comes to *Salmo*—both browns and Atlantics. "Bucktails or streamers are useful as salmon flies, particularly as a 'change of pace' pattern when salmon can't be tempted with anything else. In extremity they often are successful, especially when the fish have been shown so many classic patterns by so many anglers that they will only react to something unusual."

Colonel Drury in a 1969 issue of *Fly Fisher's Journal*, describes the dual nature of *Salmo*—in this case Atlantics and why they take the streamer. But it also addresses the brown trout's "prey or aggression" tendencies when striking beastly-looking flies:

> In the autumn, the situation is complicated in the fact you are dealing with two distinct categories of fish. There is the fresh fish which may, depending on conditions in water temperature, behave like a spring fish or summer one, and there is the stale fish which, as the spawning season approaches may, particularly if a cock, come on the take again. When the stale fish are interested it is generally in a large fly, irrespective a water height or temperature, they will often grab it with a ferocity that almost pulls the rod out of one's hand. To understand this "killer" take one must remember that the male salmon parr—(juvenile 8–14 inches) can fertilize the eggs of an adult female salmon and that, if allowed to do so this precocious youngster will take part in the nuptials. They (the cock fish) will kill these potential interlopers if they can catch them and this explains why a large fly

▲ During my guiding adventures off Torch Lake and Michigan tributaries, large articulated streamers have elicited violent strikes from male *Salmo* that were chasing salmon and brown trout parr. Credit: Author

which superficially resembles a salmon parr can be so effective.

But much of the meat slinging game for *trutta*, regardless if you enter in aggressive territorial dominance issues between larger and smaller fish, is about prey. For instance, for a leviathan holding under a prime undercut bank prey-ambushing structure, who will lash out and crush a smaller naïve juvenile looking for a new predator niche, what we are talking about in this chapter is killing prey for alpha growth consumption.

## The Northeast Connection

Amongst the many early prototypes, in this author's opinion the first could very well be a Québecois named Charles Langevin and his lethal Mickey Finn streamer. That simple three-color rainbow trout parr pattern brought my very first streamer-caught brown trout in a Western New York/Allegheny Mountains foothill stream when I was twelve years old. I'd picked up the fly in a box of old dusty flies at the bottom of the counter at a local bait shop. The owner sold me all three of them for a dollar, since he said no one was using those "Frenchie flies." Langevin developed it sometime in the late 1800s, and it proved deadly on the large brook trout and landlocked salmon lakes. He named it after a Chicago bartender named "Mickey," who would slip drugs into a woman's drink for seduction.

As I talk more of these early phases of streamer development in the landlocked salmon chapter, it was the Herb Welch/Carrie Stevens rainbow smelt baitfish imitations of the ghost patterns from the Rangeley Lakes District, Maine—the black and grey versions—that gave the fly fishermen the first meaty intricate streamers meant to be food, versus the more visual aggressive motivator of the Mickey Finn.

But Brooklyn played an important role in the baitfish streamer design when Preston Jennings crafted his beautiful Iris and Lord Iris streamers, with a color motif similar to a Jock Scott and more along the lines of salmon feather winged imitations. Since most New Yorkers eventually migrated north to fish for Atlantic salmon in the Canadian Maritimes and New England, Atlantics were always on the mind of Catskill brown trout fanatics.

## Sculpin Power

If any singular inspiration had the most powerful influence on streamer design it would be the riverine prey that browns and Atlantic salmon like to eat the best: the sculpin. This meaty V-shaped creature of the dark, rocky crevices inhabits and loves the same areas brown trout like to call home. It is the ultimate sit-and-wait predator, just like *trutta*, and its mottled appearance camouflages it beautifully among its surroundings. Its large pectoral fins allows

it to anchor firmly and observe its entire predatory field. It has a wise old sage humanlike face, with large mouth and froglike eyes. It is capable of effectively ambushing its prey such as tiny scuds, small crayfish, and aquatic insects. It tends to hop from spot to spot like a leapfrog attacking, then camouflaging itself.

Things were brewing in the 1930s. Materials such as marabou and deer hair taken from a buck's tail were influencing streamer development, just as with the strung hackle-winged flies. Don Gapen of Minnesota was passionate about Nipigon migratory brook trout, also called "coasters," which were ravenous baitfish eaters coming off Lake Superior. Don's inspired sculpin pattern that spearheaded the modern streamers of today was the infamous Muddler Minnow. With its thick deer hair cone/V-shaped head and slender body, it was the perfect sculpin imitation for coaster brook trout when they came up the river.

But then the golden age of fly-fishing inventions came in the 1970s and 1980s. Russell Blessing of Pennsylvania came out with a new pattern based on the standard English woolly worm, and thus the woolly bugger came about. This is probably the most revolutionary fly in the streamer category still used today with deadly effectiveness.

Around that same time things were brewing at the vise on the Cumberland Valley limestone springs of Pennsylvania. Ed Shenk was a Letort Spring Run legend, but to put it simply he was just a very "fishy dude." If Marinaro was the probing mind, Charles Fox the soul and river keeper protector, Shenk was the guy that caught fish in times and places where no one else thought it possible. He was also a master fly inventor and probably spent more time fishing subsurface with nymphs and streamers than the other Letort legends.

He took the V-shaped, spun deer head to a new level with his masterful Shenk sculpins. I was first introduced to these by Harry Murray of Virginia while on my way down to fish the new spring creek fishery of Mossy Creek when it first opened up to the public back in the mid-1980s. I would always stop by Murray's pharmacy/soda bar/fly shop for a much-enjoyed sermon by Harry, who always had the best fishing prognosis for your condition and the best prescription for what ailed you. He was a preacher of the highest order and his gospel was how to be the best fisher of fish. He spent much time on the Cumberland Valley in Pennsylvania, had learned the ways of Letort regulars, and brought them back to the Shenandoah Valley as the spring creek legacy was starting in Virginia.

"You have to have some of these in black-and-white, Mossy Browns are gulping these like pulled pork on a bun, son!" As he dumped a few of them in my hand, which of course I immediately bought "because Harry told me to." In the water, the marabou tails and the spun heads had had the exact silhouette of the sculpin, which a large killer *trutta*saurus brown could not ignore. I fished these on Mossy in all the deep channels and undercut banks, and below the little cattle crossing bridges with deadly efficiency.

Eventually, I fished the Bonny Brook section of the Letort and caught my largest brown on Ed's black sculpin. I would always see him on his knees fishing upstream from the bridge with his cress bugs and sculpins and his small five-foot bamboo rods. He was a stalking master similar to Frank Sawyer and caught some very large browns, much to the amazement of the other Letort regulars. His tale of the hunt to catch the behemoth brown he named "Old George" is a wonderful story of streamer hunting so typical on small spring creeks. It is told in his masterpiece, *Ed Shenk's Fly Rod Trouting*:

As usual, Old George fed at dusk, dropping back down the daybreak or shortly thereafter. It's surprising just how much the fish knew about his surroundings. He knew every bush and tree that grew along the stream. For instance, for three mornings in a row I saw the big wake move downstream at exactly 5:45 AM.

On the fourth morning I was in a position to intercept them, when right on schedule the action started. I was hidden motionless in tall grass where old George would pass four feet in front of me. I still wasn't quite sure the size of the fish, so this was going to be a good opportunity to look. As the fish passed me, he must have recognized something wrong, because he bolted and headed for home at great speed.

Shenk was one of the first to understand the large leviathan feeding behavior of spring creek browns and their love for the sculpin in the same secluded places. He, along with Frank Sawyer on his beloved River Avon, noticed that large browns sit and wait in dark, secluded places in ambush points at night and would also not feed for several days if they captured a large carnivorous prey. *Trutta*saurus browns are also creatures of habit and tend to control a certain section of stream just like a mobster crime boss controls a specific neighborhood.

In the hunt to create the ultimate sculpin streamer pattern, back in Michigan, creative fly-tying working the brown trout–rich waters of the Pere Marquette River were

▲ The New Zealand Matuka streamer with parallel barred rabbit strip imitates the unique gill shapes and undulating motion of the sculpin. Today Feenstra and Lafkas in Michigan, Holsten, and Schmidt in Arkansas, and the Pennsylvania Cumberland leviathan hunters: Brian Judge, Neil Sunday, and Dusty Wissmath, take sculpin power to a new level. Credit: Kevin Feenstra

busy at their fly-tying vices. One of them, Tom Naumes, and creative anglers like Dave Ellis took a New Zealand Matuka and put a Muddler deer head on it.

Dave Whitlock of White River brown trout fame was a master of invention. Credited for developing the Whitlock/Vibert trout-hatching box implanted into gravel for creating a simulated wild in-stream egg hatching capability, besides being a great fly angler, he was an incredible sketch artist, fly creator and warmwater species fly-rod innovator. He took the deer head Muddler/Matuka variation from Naumes, and developed the Whitlock's sculpin, inspired from the Michigan connection. This was all leading up to a new era, once again pointing back to Michigan.

## Kelly Galloup:
### The New Age Michigan Meat-Slingin' Era

After such master works as *Selective Trout, Hatches, In the Ring of the Rise, Nymphs, Matching the Hatch, Caddis,* etc., another masterpiece was about to change the way we look at trout feeding behavior. Michigan guide and master trout bum Kelly Galloup, with the technical literary aid and trout proficiency of co-author Bob Linsenman, embarked on a stunning new look at big, meaty, audacious-looking chicken streamers that in the past would have been confused for bass or pike flies.

*Modern Streamers for Trophy Trout* was one of those books that came along with dramatic impact and changed the meat slinging art form forever. I met Kelly prior to his cutting-edge book when still in my old hotel corporate days and writing my first book, *River Journal: Pere Marquette.* Kelly, a guide on the Pere Marquette. like his father, was unmistakable by his brash, bodybuilding good looks, charming personality, inquisitive nature, and naturally gifted for figuring things out. He came up in the wet-fly swinging old-school that was popular with all the Pere Marquette guides from the traditional English school. Back then we all explored the giant *Hexagenia* mayfly hatch and were often swinging flies before or after the hatch. Kelly was inspired by the Houghton Lake Special, a black-and-white Silver Hilton–style fly that was favored

▲ Kelly Galloup and Bob Linsenman were always conducting research on the *trutta* kill artistry. As does Pennsylvania leviathan *truttasaurus* master, Brian Judge. Credit: Bob Linsenman

by longstanding Pere Marquette legends like Simmy Nolph and others.

Kelly was always pushing the envelope and watched bass fishing shows to figure out what triggered a fish's aggression. He was impressed by a bass master–type episode, where they pummeled the fish into going deep by throwing crank baits, to drive them into a predatory aggressive frenzy, which eventually elicited a strike. One day Kelly, armed with a Shenk's White Sculpin, drummed up a huge brown trout on the Boardman River right in the middle of the afternoon in a similar bass-fishing style.

He and his fishing partner Jerry Dennis were constantly tweaking patterns by tying them bigger and gaudier. Kelly also took to scuba diving a lot of rivers to look at trout predatory lies and structure that brown trout like to use for their ambushing sabotage points.

After opening the Troutsman Fly shop in Traverse City with Russ Madden, who was another masterful streamer pioneer, the Pacific salmon invasion became a full-blown frenzy. To the true Troutsman followers, this was viewed with disdain and scorn, since the salmon would often bring out undesirables engaged in a snagging conquest of unsportsmanlike behavior. Kelly and a few others turned away from the latest craze of hunting the Pacific transplant salmon that now infested all these brown trout waters, to totally focus on trophy hunting big *trutta*saurus leviathans.

By giving the salmon "lining" guide trips to his other guides to pay the bills, he strictly wrote his own rules for fishing the *trutta*saurus brown trout, while guiding his passionate clients. By fishing the hatches and streamers, and traditional wet fly swinging, he would take leisurely lunches and naps and fish in a gentlemanly fashion, which was missing from the salmon carnival craze. He fished on the upper Manistee/Au Sable and other systems that have migratory barriers to the salmon populations.

Eventually Montana caught his fancy, since it was the blossoming brown trout mecca of the world with such famous rivers as the Madison and Big Hole. He then bought the Slide Inn on the Madison and continued to develop large, articulated streamers. He pushed the limits with such bizarre names as the Sex Dungeon, Boogieman, Stacked Blondes, Zoo Cougar, Butt Monkeys, and Barely Legal, just to name a few, sounding more like the lingo a prison turnkey would hear, let alone a gentlemanly astute fly fisher.

After developing rods for streamer fishing such as the Bank Robber, and perfecting stripping techniques, most of the new-school hipster streamer junkies of today all look at him as the Theodore Gordon/Vince Marinaro "godfather" of the streamer school of trout fishing.

## Salty Origins: Mark Sedotti

The East Coast tradition of hunting stripers and bluefish inspired alternative pelagic baitfish patterns from the simplest to the most complex. Bob Clouser Minnows and Lefty's Deceivers form the mainstay of pelagic baitfish patterns that were easy to tie and had good motion and movement. With his amazing array of breathable synthetic materials, Enrico Puglisi made baitfish fly patterns come to life like never before. Watching these baitfish streamers move in the water embarrassed even saltwater hardware throwers with their lifelike qualities.

Mark Sedotti is an East Coast surf master who casts big flies to predatory fish. He took all the motifs from the masters and fused them together into a perfect big baitfish pattern known as the Slammer. But to the East Coast and Midwest trout fly fisher and guide, hatch matching, traditional nymphing, and maybe fishing a muddler or Woolly Bugger–style Matuka's was the extent of their traditional streamer repertoire.

Sedotti pushed the "big and bigger" envelope. By using seven-to-nine-inch flies to seduce large White River Arkansas twenty-inch-plus browns at a time when a four-inch streamer was considered big, he busted open a whole new world of streamer design. What Sedotti did was to provoke the extremes of *trutta*saurus aggression

▲ Paul Zagorski's streamer "meat locker." Credit: Author

while acting as the guardian of its coveted ambushing niche. Here the new game was to determine how big was too big. At first, many experts thought his visionary patterns would be great for pike or muskellunge.

Sedotti influenced Russ Madden, who was then working at Kelly Galloup's Troutsman shop in Traverse City. Madden pushed the 4.5-inch long standard limit to 8 inches with Sedotti's "Slammer" East Coast flies. The Michigan boys originally thought they were too big, but when they started seeing huge browns chase them, it blew them away, and inspired them to call the flies the "screaming Jeezus" streamers, since every time they saw another trout give chase they would say, "Jesus! Did you see that one?"

Madden started tying flies in large sizes like his Kraken and Circus Peanuts, and introduced them to friend Alex Lafkas, who then embarked on the same journey and eventually took these massive streamers to the White in Arkansas, where they now spend their winters chasing the massive world-class fish of that tailwater.

Thus the new age Double Deceiver era, based on Sedotti's Slammers, pioneered a whole new series of color combinations in just the right amount materials that Midwesterners Mike Schmidt of Angler's Choice Flies, and Mark Loughead of Motown Flies continued to refine to perfection. Thus Sedotti and Galloup spurred the Michigan "Mitt" invasion of the world record Leviathan waters of Arkansas's White River. Forgoing the old standby sculpin in muddler patterns, it is now big game fishing with 8–9-weight rods, sinking lines in all various tapers and sink rates, fifteen- to twenty-pound test tippets that dominates the big *trutta*saurus trophy chase.

## Tommy Lynch: Decoding the *Trutta*saurus Predator's Mindset

As Kelly pursued Montana browns with articulated streamers, the Pere Marquette was breeding an intense new breed of trophy *trutta*saurus hunters. Enter the night-owl bat-vision genius and passion of Tommy Lynch. Starting as a guide with Pere Marquette Lodge doing the traditional salmon and steelhead gig, Tommy learned, as many brown trout addicts eventually do, that nymphing on spawning gravel held no allure or room for creativity. It was the aggressive and predatory leviathan brown hunt, much like a muskellunge gives, that inspired Tommy. He spent every guiding and leisurely moment studying how a *trutta* attacks the fly with large roadkill streamers through all seasons and water conditions. Despite perfecting his almost fanatical streamer tactics on his beloved home waters of the Pere Marquette, Manistee, and Pine, with jaunts to other migratory leviathan waters of northern Michigan and the country, he took the "Tommy time magic" on the road to the White River in Arkansas. But the magic and draw of the night game to the heart and soul of *trutta*saurus and its dark killing machine primal hunting instinct is what still takes Tommy to probe *trutta*'s highest predatory levels today.

## Tactical Phases of the Streamer Meat Hunt

The big streamer game is all about provoking fish to hunt and pulverize a large articulated monstrosity of a fly, whether it be to eat or protect territory. No matter what size your brown trout are, for all practical purposes, the *trutta*saurus truly think they are invincible badass apex hunters who react to provocation when we throw those ghastly things we now call streamers in front of them. Therein lies the excitement of it all. For practical purposes to categorize your hunting approach, we will explore the four main phases.

The beauty of brown trout river domain is their varied and unique habitat and natural brilliance. From small spring creeks and tailwaters to massive freestone systems, not to mention little conduits and cemented carriers and channels that run right below little towns like in Stockbridge, England or cow country villages, large brown trout will inhabit the most amazingly diversified water types

As the hydrodynamic currents and flow of rivers interact with its structural components, predatory ambushing points that *trutta*saurus dominate and become big because of these unique fusion areas. The bottom strata, shoreline profiles, and mainstream obstacles are as diverse as each river is unique. These unique features blend together to form the perfect tonic for the leviathan hunter.

Much has been written about where to find large browns and hunt for them. As Dr. Bob Bachman's PhD dissertation studies from his treehouse observatory station on Spruce Creek in Pennsylvania showed, the feeding and seclusion behavior of specific big brown trout are usually localized into dominating territory river stretches that vary in size and duration. Thus they venture into all types of habitat on a foraging escapade by day and at night in the summer, like Ed Shenk's "Old George" as well as my "Mr. Big" Brutus on the Letort, which I described in my book *Selectivity*. These fish are especially apt to guard their territories, in particular during the prime predatory foraging seasons of spring and summer. The famous and unique migrations of *trutta* usually take place in the fall and winter for spawning and avoiding harsh winter scenarios, which often turn out to have benefits in stillwater feeding opportunities when upper river areas may be jammed with ice.

A prime alpha predator hunting niche, for instance a deep run with a perfect woody debris logjam next to a fast gravel section or large undercut bank, can develop an appetite for and most likely a dependency on other fish and animals in carnivorous *trutta*saurus browns. Perfect places to start for looking for these ambushing points would include woody debris sweepers, large boulders, and rock piles that create pots or buckets, as well as islands and side channels that create a fusion of divergent flows merging together to form a seam. River tributaries, back eddies, drop-off shelves—especially gravel bars dropping off into deep pockets with counterclockwise circling undertows—are prime baitfish accumulation areas, since they funnel and concentrate vast amounts of the biological drift of insects and crustaceans. Find the smaller trout, baitfish,

▲ Tommy Lynch displays the effectiveness of his "drunk and disorderly chickens." Credit: Author (top); Lynch (bottom)

sculpins, darters, etc., and you'll find *trutta*saurus. Thus if all indications point to a predatory big trout "condo," work it hard and provoke the take. A big *trutta*saurus must take advantage of the easy prey food item no matter what time of day, since often the energy exerted into hunting can eventually catch up with its metabolism and work negatively against the fish's ultimate goal of maximizing growth and alpha spawning dominance.

The provocation game is all about casting and stripping, meanwhile the potential for provoking and agitating the aggressive predatory strike can be possible at any time by covering all the aggressive niche habitat water thoroughly. Streamer stripping is hard work and it is physically challenging to go whole days with a result of turning just a few fish. Getting a large one in the net is well worth the effort to the new and veteran meat-slinging fanatics. Much of the game is "wall banging"—casting to shore structure and banks and stripping, with jerks, jigs, and pauses. Target backeddies, gravel rollers, tributary mouths, seams, and drop-offs. A large predator could be in any of these areas at any given time, so don't spare the casts.

## Individual Trophy Hunting

Guides and passionate anglers who work their home water trout streams know every single rock, logjam, and benthos feature of the waters they see daily. Over time they learn to identify a specific trophy fish in the same territorial locales. Here is when the general casting to cover every specific lie turns into a named individual target. These big browns are often given names like "Old George," like Ed Shenk's Moby Dick pursuit, "Scarface," and "Blind Eye," as described by Frank Sawyer on his River Avon.

In this scenario it is important to study the habits of the fish in its predatory pursuits. They remain dormant in their lunker condos until the urge to feed comes about. If they capture a large prey, they can go several days without ingesting food, thus they seem to have disappeared. Once the satiation diminishes and they are back to leaving their lies at certain times, hunting at night and early mornings. These fish are also very sensitive to different patterns and colors. They often ignore the flies that have fooled them in the past, and display a remarkably violent refusal behavior. This type of hunting is usually best in small spring creeks and rivers where the prey is sight fished and its predatory pursuits can be visually documented.

In the trophy-hunting tight waters game, unlike the perpetual casting of provoking strikes from all different lies in big water, the less you cast the better. The more time watching and observing, noticing trends in the fish's feeding and migratory behavior, are all part of forming a database in the angler's mind of what to do next and how to adjust after failure. New and exciting streamers sometimes suggest themselves from these observations.

## The Baitfish Hatch

I had my first taste of the "alewife hatch" back in 2004 on the big, wide-open waters of the Delaware River system in the Catskills. It is a river I have fished since I was a young man in the 1980s and the tailwater was all about hatch matching mayflies to ultra-selective trout. Pioneered by Al Caucci and Bob Nastasi in their epic work *Hatches*, to be successful here you had to imitate the Hendricksons, Sulphers, *Isonychias*, and Drakes to perfection. But when I arrived at our family's summer cabin in the Catskills one July, the Delaware was at critical flood stage. Meeting up with a guide I employed at the time, James "Coz" Costolnick, who worked salmon and steelhead for me in Michigan at our lodge, and his summer business on the wild brown trout rich Delaware. "Coz" met me at the West Branch fly shop where he worked, and immediately took me to the fly bins packed with four-inch white streamers. "We are going to need a few of these, Supinski," he said. I was taken aback. I am usually figuring out and pulling my hair out at the intricacies of size 18 Sulpher emergers and tiny BWOs at this time of year, and this made no sense. "They are spilling water like hell over the Deposit reservoir spillways—alewives are everywhere in the river and the big browns are hammering them," he said. "Let's grab a dozen and get out of here to get some donkeys!"

Normally, if you could drum up one big fish in a day on a dry it was considered a good day. By taking Teeny sink tip lines with fifteen-pound tippet on, (6X was the norm), you would cast these white deceiver/Clouser type imitations into the grass back eddies along the shoreline and turn twenty-inch fish in almost every likely-looking spot. The water was highly stained and they were tight to the bank in heavy flows hammering trapped schools of these very confused baitfish. That day we put nine browns over twenty inches in the net! It was more like striper and bluefish fishing than the selective trout mind games usually found on these waters. As soon as the spill gates stopped and the water cleared, these fish went right back to being their snooty selves.

A similar scenario exists on the southern tailwaters in the Holsten, Smith, Watauga, and Clinch TVA dam electro power generating tailwaters. But nowhere is it more prominent and grows more world record browns than on the White River in Arkansas. Here, with their tremendous power generating capacity, the turbines grind up and spit out shad from Bull Shoals Lake and the *trutta*saurus that eat them are notorious. Large articulated streamers pique the aggression of the fish on the hunt here. Covering all the water, especially the walls and banks, brings results when the water is "CFS up and On."

Other similar baitfish scenarios exist like on the Great Lakes tributaries when the migratory Pacific salmon and steelhead fingerling hatch during spring time and the larger browns will chow down on them. Also smelt and emerald

▲ Master brown trout expert Paul Zagorski with a beast from White River. When the turbines are generating, shad escape the reservoir and are often crushed, creating gigantor *trutta*saurus like this one. Credit: Alex Lafkas

shiner migrations enter into the lower river systems and stimulate the baitfish hatch. Here, a tandem fly rig to imitate a school of distraught bait, coupled with an alternated stripping and jerking retrieve while close to shore, is a key technique to imitate parr and catch big fish.

## Spawning Aggression

This final phase will take place in the fall and early winter when *Salmo*—both brown trout and Atlantic salmon—are getting near spawning or are potentially in the process. Here you are triggering the alpha dominant territorial niche aggression by trying to stimulate the intrusion of smaller trout and salmon trying to get in on the procreation game.

Keep in mind a small ten-inch *trutta* or *salar* is actually sexually mature and can fertilize a twenty-four-inch female's eggs. Thus to a large kype-jawed male keeping his territory free of aggressor intrusion, a large double deceiver with a two-toned profile (white below/gray or brown top ) imitating a smaller trout or salmon smolt or parr, and deeply dredged and swung through territorial gravel areas and staging lies, will bring violent strikes. This technique is now my go-to plan when I target landlocked Atlantic salmon on Michigan's inland glacial lakes and the Northeast landlocked fisheries in the fall. The large landlocked male will behave just like a big aggressive brown trout, as I discovered for myself the first time when an eighteen-pound *salar* crushed a seven-inch Double Deceiver. Previously I would never have considered trying such a fly.

## Sculpinating: Old School Shenk Style

Ed Shenk received his inspiration from the marabou flies he had used in junior high school. Another inspiration, the Fledermaus streamer tied by Western angler Bill Schneider, influenced Ed's "chewy flies" concept of how the trout like to hold onto the marabou and muskrat fur and chew on the fly before spitting it out. With the deer hair spun head concept launched by the Muddler Minnow, Shenk put all these together for the deadly Shenk Sculpin that proved irresistible to the trout of the Letort and Montana.

I experimented with three versions of Ed's presentation technique to imitate the natural as much as possible. I casted it upstream, let it sink in slowly like a helpless prey, and pumped the rod and stripped line, occasionally bouncing and jigging off the bottom to imitate a bouncing and resting sculpin. By keeping a tight line I had direct contact with the fly and was able to set the hook on any type of grab or take.

Another variation using a cross-stream cast swam the fly above his targeted leviathan, and rested and twitched off the bottom in front of its nose to trigger a reactive compulsive take.

Other times I would slap the sculpin down hard near undercut banks by crawling up on my knees and chest, and literally "tease the monster out of the cage." Spring creeks allow you to do this with their deep, undercut banks, small cattle-crossing bridge abutments, and stills.

Shenk employed other techniques such as the "crawfish crawl," where he would find sandy patch channels and gravel areas and twitch the pattern like a crawfish stirring about the bottom. Most of these fish were sighted targets, which are quite obvious on the crystal-clear limestone waters of the Letort. He would often cast the sculpin downstream from the fish, strip it feverishly upstream as it went by the peripheral vision of the large brown, and then dead drift it slowly backwards downstream, to have the fish turn and follow it, only to finally, slowly strip it away as the fish approached, which often would elicit a violent "gotcha" take.

Shenk's approach on Letort was always a low, stealthy profile. When I watched him above the Bonny Brook Road and other areas of Marinaro and Fox's Meadows, he spent as much time getting to the bank to fish as he did fishing. He realized the vibration sense of the wary trout and walked like a heron just to get to the stream. When changing locations he would ease away very slowly toward any designated spot, and thus was a study that all streamer anglers on small creeks would do well to emulate.

## The New Age: The Sex Dungeon/Drunk-and-Disorderly/Double Deceiver

The large fly game was inspired by hardware fishermen and jointed lures like the Rapala. Few know that Louis Rhead, of Catskill fame fused together the Normark/Norwegian lure in the early 1900s. I still recall the time when I visited the Rivers Test and Itchen, and walked into the Orvis shop in Stockbridge in the mid-1980s. I looked at the English edition of the Orvis catalog in their store and admired all the different types of flies: Iron Blues, Pale Wateries, etc., and noticed that the few streamers in the catalog were labeled under the heading "Lures."

Given the fact that catching large brown trout was the ultimate goal by every angler, dry or wet, there was now a unified movement of designing and presenting flies that stimulated the aggressive predator attack of wise old twenty-inch-plus browns that would not take a size 14 Hendrickson.

Without doubt the three most lethal modern-day streamers originate from three main motifs. Kelly Galloup's Sex Dungeon incorporates rubber-legged articulation and a Shenk Sculpin–like spun deer head that pushes water and air bubbles. Though Kelly wasn't aware of Shenk until he read his article in *Fly Fisherman* magazine, the two had separately embarked on perfecting the V-shaped sculpin body. Kelly's Wooly Sculpin predecessor for the Sex

▲ Lynch with his box of chicken "Drunk and Disorderlies," which shows the havoc they wreak. Credit: Author

Dungeon followed along the lines of the other Shenk/Whitlock/Naumes V-shaped models.

Tommy Lynch's Drunk-and-Disorderly, named for how the streamer stumbled through the water, used the Dahlberg Diver "hammer head," similar to the digging motion imparted by the tongue on a Rapala or a Flat Fish lure. His deer hair spun head gave the wobbly diving motion that big brown trout could not resist.

Finally, the East Coast–inspired Double Deceiver had a tremendously lifelike swimming action of a baitfish that is like no other streamer. Its bucktail and saddle hackle undulate and give a swaying movement. Thus on baitfish-rich impoundment tailwaters, this streamer is the king of the pack.

Lynch and Galloup analyzed every scenario, every season, and every condition to the utmost detail before they sized up their approaches to fly design. For them it's all about clarity and flow of the water. Lynch does not believe in changing a fly as often as Galloup. The best approach is to have confidence in knowing that there are fish in the designated interception niches and to deliver persistent, probing presentations that a large brown eventually cannot ignore.

High spring runoff and flood stage water will dictate larger patterns fished tight to the "wall/shore" where baitfish will be easily captured in the slack eddies. Black, chartreuse, orange, pink, and yellow colors hold up well against stained waters. Here the fish is more or less looking up against the silhouette in close range due to very limited visibility. In clear water conditions, the fish can see through the entire water column, thus the olives, grays, and whites hold up better on low-water streamer fishing.

Kelly's "jerk, rip, and strip" is perfect for fishing streamers that have a weighted head or weight added to the shorter leader system. This allows a pause for the streamer to slack and die in an undulating, jigging motion. Tommy's steady short strip with rod down pumps the fly in tight, short grabs, pulsating the Drunk-and-Disorderly into a wobbly motion with a tight line. Here he dives and works the streamer, as opposed to jigging and bouncing with the "rip and strip." Both are equally effective and based on fly design more than anything. By varying speed, teasing the fly into different movements, and pausing for a crippled dead drift/injured movement, you can bring on the bite trigger violently as the predator brown senses vulnerability.

The "two-handed burn," where the angler puts the rod under the armpit and rapidly retrieves a streamer with both hands, triggers the ultimate predatory aggression, like the childish taunt of "Nah, nah, you can't catch me." Here you can see a large brown going long distances to crush a fly, then often stopping at the last second, resulting in a shy and disappointed refusal. When fish are on the kill mode in early spring and high water, starting off the retrieve in the fast burn and then immediately halting for a slow dead drift can trigger violent crushes. In the fall, in clear water conditions, where they seem to "nip" at that the fly, or called the "fall gerrhh," like a puppy mouthing a small plastic milk bone, short steady twitching strips, followed by dead drifts, only to repeat again short twitching sometimes turns the aggressive bite.

Another technique for when the fish shows up to the fly but refuses to take it, or chases it to the lift up, you can "tease it up." If the fish lingers for a few seconds around the fly you just pulled up to cast again and seems disoriented, immediately lift and splat the streamer down and strip wildly, with a sudden pause and dead drift in the immediate area. This will usually seal the deal with the fish glued to the steel. If you pause and wait to repeat again, it almost always allows the fish's aggression to dissipate, along with its interest. But on Atlantic salmon, that pause can work wonders.

Though the modern streamer game is a very aggressive approach, triggering and provoking a fish to strike which usually happens quickly, I have found that on cold tail waters especially, bigger fish need a little time to "rev up" and are not always immediately responsive to a large fly presentations. Thus, fishing the fly with a slower, deep-dredging motion, and in holding lies not normally targeted such as the middle of the river or one-third the way out from the bank, often produces in colder and less-clear waters. Many anglers have the patience of a housefly, immediately jump to the conclusion that there are no fish, and halt their casting. Confidence, determination, and a steadfast commitment to provoking to take is much more powerful here than fly pattern, color, or how you choose to fish it.

Habituation, notification of an intruder, culminating in arousal and triggering the bite, is the natural progression in *trutta*saurus streamer fishing. Since much of the tailwater game is done from drift boats rowing and occasionally anchoring, if three boats go down the river in tandem, it is usually the last cleanup boat that scores the fish, as the first two invoke habituation and then arousal, basically chumming them up for the second or third boat to grab the kill.

In 2015, Blane Chocklette, a Virginia musky guide, began tying and experimenting with multi-segmented articulated streamers that emulate the natural swimming and movement of baitfish more than any pattern that came before it. Using anywhere from four to seven jointed articulations, his fly can be tied to emulate any baitfish, particularly smaller stocked rainbow and brown trout, which are large and easy meals for giant *trutta*saurus hatchery truck pillagers. I have had tremendous luck with them imitating sculpins, baitfish, and smaller trout, and especially in aggressive trigger colors like white, black, and yellow. Tied in olive to imitate crayfish movements and natural river baitfish like dace, they are extremely effective and well worth the time.

## Fusion Tactics When the Going Gets Tough: *Trutta*'s Unique Adaptability

Stripping streamers all day is hard work. On the average if you turn a few fish and get one or two really big ones it's been an awesome day. As with two-handed Spey swingers for steelhead, the streamer junkie is afflicted with the passion for the aggressive take. Most of the diehards will only fish that way once they taste the aggressive tonic. But sometimes you get caught up in real lulls in the action, depending on certain scenarios I have found.

In tailwaters and spring creeks that have extreme food biodiversity overload, like an insane crustacean population, hatches so thick the surface water turns into minestrone soup—like during the *Hexagenia* or Gray Drake mayfly hatches on Michigan's rivers, or blizzard *Simulium* midge flights like on Iceland's Big Laxa, the brown trouts' unique opportunistic predatory adjustments will cause them to strictly focus on gaining as much caloric intake of those foods, versus chasing a big streamer. Though

▲ Though big browns can be as predictable as a dog barking at a doorbell, they will often go the other way and elude canny anglers, especially on heavily-fished tailwaters. Here Ken Collins shows a tricky Ontario Grand River stunner. Credit: Ken Collins

there are the rare exceptions as when fishing a streamer before, during, and after hatches, which will take fish that have been "pounded to death" by fly anglers, for the most part understanding the waters you are fishing and using appropriately-timed technique can give you a thinking man's advantage.

Though all streamer addicts have their own preferences as we have discussed, the best advice is to mix all systems up frequently, especially when fish are off the bite. These tactics often work for me especially on heavily-fished tail-waters and smaller spring creeks. Usually if you're walking the banks and seeing lots of wader footprints, you aren't alone, just as drift boats pile on top of drift boats in big tailwaters like the Delaware and Missouri.

But just because there is lots of pressure doesn't mean everybody knows what they're doing. Most leisure fly anglers are creatures of habit and sheep with fly rods. They do exactly what they were told at the fly shop or what their last guide told them to do. Also keep in mind that most guide boats will have at least a few inexperienced anglers; that's why they are hired for their services. I often welcome rivers that are full of guide boats on a particular day, because I know that the fish will most likely be seeing the same presentation over and over, the neighbors might not have the skills to pull the trigger, or the fish will become very habituated and off the bite.

Your best approach here is to wait until the armada has been launched downriver before you decide to be the "cleanup angler," which often works wonders on rivers full of drift boats like the White, Missouri, Delaware etc. This is especially so in the high-stakes game of provoking an aggressive strike, which often big browns don't need to do every day. Keep in mind a good big baitfish, sculpin, smaller trout, or huge crayfish can keep a *trutta*saurus stomach quite happy for days. Even though you've marked your fish, and you know exactly where that monster is lurking, the fact that it doesn't show for you on the day you are fishing does not mean it is still not there. It could be enjoying a large meal or perhaps was just put down by a bunch of clueless anglers who startled it.

Leviathan brown trout are products of the angler's conditioning, thus constant angling pressure shapes the type of presentation a fish will respond to as a result of repeatedly-observed tactics. If "rip-and jerk" stripping is the most popular on a particular river, try something completely opposite, like dead drifting, bow/arc upstream dredge casting and slow-swing twitching.

For successful streamer stripping, whether by pounding the bank from a drift boat or wading a run, move very quickly and cover the water thoroughly. Probably 90 percent of streamer techniques employ constant casting and coverage to produce great results. For big *trutta*saurus that have been caught or duped into "pricking the steel," their aggression may err on the side of caution. As an angler you should consider slowing it down, taking breaks, and blending in, just as a good sight-stalking nymph or dry fly spring creek fisherman does. It can't hurt, and it has often produced extremely large trout at the craziest times of day (bright sunny afternoons), when the typical "gun and run" game was not working.

Also keep in mind that *trutta*'s aggression can be turned on as quickly as it is turned right the heck off. Just as spill gates from a tailwater reservoir can produce a baitfish overload, it can quickly shut the faucet. Thus, the best advice is to hire not "just a guide," but the "top gun" that knows, loves, and lives the game. Also, ask a lot of questions of people that frequently streamer fish the rivers and streams, think outside the box, and are prepared to present something totally different than what is customary. That approach will serve you well no matter where in the world you are fishing.

## Casting, Setting the Hook, and the Fight

When casting heavy sink tips and large, meaty, double-hooked articulated flies, the novice can wind up in the emergency room very quickly. This is no place for a nice tight loop, elbow tucked in tightly like a British gentleman. Opening up the loop and letting the heavy line extend all the way back is the key, with your arm out slightly to allow the casting plane to avoid ears, your guide's head, and back of your own head. You're basically slowing up your back casts, allowing it to stretch and load the fly. I often use a water load technique where the entire line touches the water on the backcast and is easily lobbed forward with a maximum amount of rod tip loading. It is advisable to generally slow down your cast and to be more deliberate, to ensure proper loading and clearance.

In smaller, tighter streams a heavier triangle taper line can turn streamers over with a roll cast or single spey cast, and a measured amount of line can consistently and repeatedly probe the bank.

We often "blow the hook set," which happens for veterans as well as novice streamer anglers by "pulling the trigger" prematurely. Lifting the rod tip and hauling back into the air is another. Or just the plain visual thrill of seeing a large fish attack your fly gets the nerves all jittery and hence we get too excited and pull the streamer away, not allowing the mouth of the fish to get a good "chewy bite" over the fly and engulf it, either at the head or on the tailing articulated hook. This is a common problem when seeing a large twenty-pound Atlantic salmon come up to take a bomber dry fly on the surface.

A good hook set is a continual strip strike going into the middle and butt of the rod tension, not just the tip, which allows the barb of a big hook to penetrate the cartilage jaws of a large *trutta*saurus. Keeping the rod down at a low

▲ Ensure that the hook is set during the fight by keeping the rod low, paying attention to the rod angle, and adding a few extra strip tugs or sharp hook sets, as Dave Karczynski demonstrates here. Do not assume that a hook is set on the first try, or that it is permanent. Credit: Arek Kubala

profile to the side of the jaw and keeping a steady pull to one direction will allow for firm hook penetration. If the fish immediately changes direction once hooked, anglers must adjust the tightening position or the line will go slack.

If the fish comes at the streamer going downstream from an upstream lie, setting the hook to the side of an upstream will produce the opposite direction that secures the hook. If it comes from under the fly, a sudden pause or slacking will allow the fish to inhale it. Never pull it directly upstream from the downstream take!

## Mousing: The New Age Night Game

Night fishing really allows you to produce large browns on a consistent basis—especially in the summer after all the major large bug hatches are gone, when large browns feed almost exclusively at night. In Michigan, the *Hexagenia* mayfly hatch starts at dusk and runs through the night, bringing out throngs of sophisticated big bug dry fly anglers. I believe this phenomenon is the precursor to a big brown's nighttime habitual feeding mode that will serve it well until the fall, where their migrations and spawning and also those of salmon and other lake-run spawning migrators soon preoccupy its lifestyle.

Jim Bashline's book, *Night Fishing for Trout: The Final Frontier* (1974), which I mentioned earlier in this book, inspired me as a high school youth who just got his driver's license and worked a summer job on a second shift painting tractors in the John Deere factory. I often left the factory at eleven o'clock at night and headed right away to my local trout stream to pursue the nighttime quarry armed with a quart of Genesee cream ale beer and an imagination running hormonally wild with visions of leviathan *trutta*.

Along the banks of Oatka Creek, New York, a lovely cold spring creek that held good populations of large browns, I was scared shitless on many occasions when things would go bump in the night and scare the living hell out of me. I was awarded with the occasional beautiful brown over twenty inches, but many other respectably sized fish as I plied the waters with large black stoneflies. Bashline himself had a pattern called the Sleepless Night, with a peacock herl body and a black wing with a large pronounced silhouette. I swung it broadside in the traditional Allegheny Mountain wet fly swing.

On the wooded spring creeks of Michigan, the canoe hatch is prominent all summer on the Au Sable, Pere

▲ Some of the earliest bulky-winged wet fly night patterns, such as Jim Bashline's Sleepless Night and Michigan's Houghton Lake Special, all have a black/red/silver ribbing motif. I caught this Pere Marquette brown with such a fly. Credit: Jim Haswell (top); Batcke (bottom)

Marquette, and other rivers that hold large numbers of trophy *trutta*saurus. Often the only time you could fish for them is late evenings into the dark. Fortunately this is the time when these giant beasts of darkness choose to feed on large *Pteronarcys* stones, other trout, and baitfish, frogs, snakes—whatever they can get their mouth around, which actually is quite as large as my Amish leviathan of the night at the beginning of this chapter.

The wooded forest environment of Michigan's sandy soil spring creeks and the primordial forests of New Zealand are ideal breeding grounds for the tiny field mice or vole of the north woods, the *Microtus pinetorum*. These nocturnal creatures make their homes along the tree trunks and banks of Michigan rivers and often fall helplessly into the water to swim back to shore. They are frequently destroyed in a violent surface kill by large browns lurking and waiting for these perfectly edible steaks. Hence the "mousing" game begins at night in summer, after all the big mayfly hatches and low warmer day water makes the browns dormant by day, and *trutta*saurus aggressors by night.

Tommy Lynch has taken the night-time gig to new levels and has evolved the sport with intricate observations never fully understood by anglers in the past. At night, Tommy explains, "Anything that splats the water signals *kill it, I want it*," to a carnivorous predator lying in wait. That kill-artist aggression is triggered by that strong disturbance on the water by the mouse, streamer, or large stonefly stimulator pattern, as the angler combines sound, feel, and whatever limited sight he or she has for night stalking.

The night mouse grab is usually strong and with conviction, but an angler should give the fish time to come up under and behind the large edible and be given enough slack to inhale it. "When anglers tell me they 'bumped some nice fish at night, but didn't hook any,' that meant they were fishing too tight and not allowing the fish to take it," Tommy explained. Usually a slightly higher rod with a semi-taut line and steady swimming/waking with gentle twitching will usually do the trick. Allow the line to pull heavy and firm prior to setting the hook, to let the fish mouth your imitation.

In mousing, every pool, run, and riffle, has its own type of mouse movement presentation based on speed and depth. In deeper pools, you want your mouse or large *Pteronarcys* to make a lot of commotion; usually the fish are holding deep. When fish are tight to structure like undercut banks in trees, often just sliding it naturally off the structure or shoreline and gently creeping it will have a more natural appeal. In shallower riffles in pocket water, an immediate splat followed by a few subtle "V" wakes is all you'll need since the fish are ready in shallow hunting positions. Often tossing it in the tailout above the riffle gives the fish more time to see the prey coming.

When fishing in or just below the surface at night, what a brown sees upward is quite a bright sky. Diffused through light from the stars and whatever moon phase is present, your flies will show up as a dark silhouette. Color will really only show on bright moonlit nights. That could be why the white-bellied mouse by Tommy Lynch fishes better on those types of darkness levels.

Keep in mind that both browns and Atlantics have extremely well-developed lateral lines that sense vibration in the slightest degrees. One can only imagine how sensitive the *trutta* senses are. Thus it is very important to move even more delicately and quietly than you do in the daytime. When three or four guys go to a river at night and work their way down mousing, the last cleanup guy is usually the most successful, because the first couple of guys startle the fish and thus the fish eventually habituate and go back on the prowl, this time even more stimulated.

## The White River *Trutta*saurus Streamer Legacy

The Ozarks cast a tremendous mystical vibe on you when you first visit this special place. It all begins with some of the cleanest filtered limestone spring water on earth emanating from the foothills near Madison County and traversing the entire Missouri/Arkansas limestone belt. With towns bearing the names of Limestone, Eureka Springs, and Valley Springs, this enchanted land of underground water in lakes was a haven to prehistoric inhabitants that built stone dwellings along the White River and its tributaries to set up farming and fishing camps. The diversity of wildlife enticed early French trappers and fur traders in the eighteenth century.

The project for the Army Corps of Engineers and the Tennessee Valley Authority to provide hydropower on a scale similar to Niagara Falls commenced during the grand age of dam builders. With the building of the Bull Shoals and Norfork dams, the warm water ecology of these rivers was transformed into an icy cold, crystal clean trout mecca. The US Fish and Wildlife Service set up a hatchery at the Norfork facility to aid in the transformation to stock millions of rainbow trout to ease the pain of the beleaguered bass and warm water anglers. It was a new age that began earlier because of the federal flood act legislation that spread from the Catskill Mountains on the brown trout rich Delaware system.

With anglers enjoying the tremendous rainbow trout angling, Dave Whitlock and his cohorts privately introduced brown trout into the system in the 1960's with his famous Whitlock/Vibert boxes to help hatch fish in a somewhat turbulent environment of power generating fluctuating flows. Anglers preferred the easy to stock and grow rainbows. Whitlock's introduction as well as the federal hatcheries' introduction of a few plantings of the

Scottish Loch Leven strain did well in the larger river systems. Soon the quietly-brewing wild brown trout fishery would reveal itself.

In 1972, a 31.5-pound brown became the North American record taken from the White River. The browns were never protected and often overlooked as incidental catches, but they were soon to steal the world stage and shatter record after record. From 1977 to 1988, record thirty-four- and thirty-eight-pound brown trout came from the White. But it was in 1992, when a forty-pound leviathan from the little Red River shattered the all-world record. Now Arkansas was now the *Salmo trutta* mecca on steroids.

Regardless of the flow fluctuations from power generation, the White River and Little Red River tailwaters are year-round 47 degrees F spring creek–like waters—perfect to grow large *trutta*saurus giants. Hence it was no coincidence that the new era of power-generating hydro dams, which Bull Shoals typified in their new TVA/Southern Power hydro-masterpieces, that the ever-adaptable and opportunistic niche feeding *trutta* would take advantage of them like a cunning predator ready to pounce.

John Holsten is a guide who lives and breathes trophy White River browns on the streamer. He has seen every transition of the fishery and lives this White River *trutta*saurus nirvana every moment of every day. Today pounding big, articulated streamers and mice at nighttime is the gig for another forty-pound world record that is only casts away from eventually happening. John shared his knowledge and his perception of how the White evolved with me.

To Holsten, it is a vast and dynamic tail water habitat that has been known for its large, aggressive, but at times "sneaky" brown trout. Water releases from the hydroelectric facility at Bull Shoals Dam can vary astonishingly from 700 cfs to 26,000 cfs, and commonly requires instant changes in rigging for both nymphing and streamer enthusiasts alike. Holsten admits that prior to the articulated streamer revolution in Arkansas (2009–10) the river was most commonly nymphed by fly anglers in all levels of water release. Not that there weren't any streamer enthusiasts, but it just seemed that once the four-to-seven-inch articulated streamer appeared, the phenomenon greatly increased the success ratio for fly anglers in Arkansas who were looking to release the fish of a lifetime. During the lower water releases, "Swinging" Sculpin and Muddler variations can be very effective especially in the evenings, as these fish are primarily nocturnal. The mouse patterns pioneered by Lynch are also extremely effective at night in lower water.

Clan behavior—packs of fish of like size hunting together—is a common occurrence during the mid- to high-level water releases on the White, as well as the

tailwaters of Tennessee, Virginia, and Delaware, which hold massive wild trout populations. Holsten has found that the feeding behavior of the larger fish has become significantly more aggressive, especially during daylight hours.

Holsten and Patrick Fulkrod have shared their theories with my observations on how tailwater brown trout feed often in packs of similar-sized fish. This "group feeding"

▲ As winter approaches spring, trout need to put on weight through heavy predation. Due to their procreation bonding instincts, anglers can often catch 22–26-inch spawning-age fish in tandem, like the pair here caught by guide Patrick Fulkrod's clients on the South Holston. Credit (top and bottom): Fulkrod

correlates with studies that Bror and Nina Jonsson note in their *Ecology* book. Brown trout and Atlantic salmon schools often hunt baitfish in groups based on a hierarchical structure stemming from body size and alpha dominance over other year classes. This behavior has been documented from Scandinavian lakes and rivers to Dinaric/Balkan Alps rivers. There are several theories as to why this happens.

One is that similar-sized fish specialize on similar-sized prey; just as smaller food items will be more appealing to smaller fish, larger prey appeals to dominant carnivorous fish. Also the spawning ritual takes place in the fall as larger alpha dominant fish will school up in clans together for spawning territorial rights.

Another explanation for this behavior is the theory of maximization of efforts, or the "two minds are better than one" mentality. As *Salmo* hunt in the big lake and ocean waters to corral schools of pelagic fish, and body slam them into a stunned and paralyzed frenzy, this can often convert to river predation, especially on big tail waters, where there is specific niche dominance in drop-off shelves, trench pockets, and pool/tail-out structure lies.

The new streamer practice of fishing large, articulated meaty chickens has now begun to spread to every river and tailwater in the world where large carnivorous leviathan brown trout are found. I have heard accounts of large marble trout in Slovenia targeting perfectly the streamer invitations, as well as in the epic brown trout rivers of Patagonia and New Zealand.

The wild brown trout waters of the Delaware and Big Horn systems in New York and Montana respectively, once traditionally known for strictly hatch-matching or indicator nymphing, are now experiencing streamer infatuation as it is spread by guides and anglers looking for a trophy of a lifetime. Nothing will get your juices flowing like watching a *trutta*saurus attack a streamer.

## The Put-Grow-Aggressor: Domestication to Wild Predator

Though we place much emphasis on wild fisheries, as we should, the "really wild" environments don't quite exist anymore since urbanization and development have encroached on wild fisheries at alarming rate. Take the historic Letort Spring Run of the Cumberland Valley, and you will now see suburban shopping malls, Home Depots, fast food chains, and industrial parks in the meadows where cattle and sheep once grazed in a beautiful pastoral setting. This is occurring all over the planet where brown trout and Atlantic salmon once thrived in the wild without any disturbance.

Thus it is important for government agencies to protect and enhance fisheries where possible with stocking and habitat enhancement. Categorizing streams' further potential to have sustainable populations of wild fish, slot limits,

put grow and take fisheries, due to limited ecological capacity, or combination of both, is thankfully becoming more the norm these days. Thus carefully recognizing a marginal river's capacity to produce or hold over strains of trout and salmon is vital to the future of *Salmo*.

One thing is for certain. The incredible resilience and adaptability of brown trout to exist in conditions which are thought almost impossible for survival is the uncanny fifty-million-year dinosaur product of evolutionary perfection. Throughout the world in city and urbanized settings, little streams running through culverts and ditches right through town often have wild brown trout strains that had been totally forgotten and are often discovered after accidental chemical spills, or stream survey projects from an environmental pollution safety standpoint. These startling discoveries can occur anywhere that the original domain and distribution of *trutta* has been ingrained for millennia. Hence, placing more emphasis on "holdover fisheries," which tend to do well when environmental conditions like cooler summers and ample rainfall benefits year-to-year survival. With climate change rearing its ugly head, this is often a crapshoot that biologists must juggle from year to year.

Michigan and other states are now experimenting with using wild, century-old German brown strains taken from waters that had adaptability reinforced conditions, and stocking semi-wild fingerlings to infiltrate streams, carryover, and grow large. This progressive approach is the desired method for holdover, versus the domesticated hatchery mutants that many states dump in. Stocking the smaller fingerlings will allow wild imprinting sooner and allow them to hold over to grow into large, aggressive browns. The smaller fingerlings do not become ingrained and domesticated as larger yearling fish do, and hence do not have it as "good for as long" eating pellets in comfortable concrete raceways with no danger from predators or harsh environments. Stocking these yearling hatchery mutt fish usually makes them "fish out of water" once stocked, and thus they cannot adjust to wild conditions as easily as smaller fingerlings of wild genetic stock can.

Hence, Michigan uses the original German strain of Gilchrist Creek for smaller spring creeks, and the migratory Sturgeon strain for bigger rivers with access to open lakes and other river systems, thus enabling them to hold over, grow large, and become top gamefish aggressors. Below is a story of how *trutta*'s true adaptable and aggressive nature only takes a short time to unleash the *trutta*saurus potential.

## Rocky Bad Attitude on Virginia's Tye River

It's fascinating to watch and observe the habits and personalities of brown trout, but particularly with hatchery trout. Even though they are labeled as dumb pellet eaters, browns can't be called such as my story unfolds. *Trutta* can have a stubborn and arrogant demeanor no matter where you find them.

The upper Tye River in Virginia's Shenandoah National Forest is a beautiful, cascading freestone stream. I fell in love with its Montana-like feel. With a wide-open valley of Angus and Holstein cattle grazing and tall mountain peaks, it has a "big sky Montana in the Blue Ridge" feel. Its upper waters in the higher elevations have wild brook trout. But as it spreads out into a valley, the state of Virginia Fish and Game stocks tons of rainbow, brown and brook trout—some brood stock browns that often push the five- to six-pound range.

On a trip with my dad Antoni, we arrived by coincidence on "stocking day"—an absolute freak show of anglers lined up shoulder to shoulder, armed with Velveeta cheese and corn kernels. I sat on a stump and watched the circus commence. Smaller rainbows and brown trout were caught as fast as they were thrown in by the hatchery buckets. When the locals strung up their limits and were quickly packing it up, I struck up a conversation with the Virginia Fish and Game stocking workers. Some were biologists that were watching the frenzy. One said to me, "I have one special prize in here—let's see if this boy finds a home!" He laughed. He went into the hatchery truck tank and pulled out about an eight-pound, kype-jawed brown trout, that long surpassed the brood stock days. Once they carefully put it in, after shaking its head in disbelief that it was in the new "wild" environment, it swam downstream almost immediately for a deep hole that had a huge boulder the size of a small swimming pool like it knew the new territory well.

The poor fella found a nice trough on the downward side of the rock and just hunkered down. If this fish would be able to talk to me, it would say, "WTF am I doing here? I had it good in that hatchery, fed three square meals a day, and had all the female brown trout during breeding season I wanted!"

I was curious about that old boy for days as I fished the smaller, wild brook trout headwaters of the Shenandoah National Forest on a short four-day vacation when I worked in the hotel business in Washington. Each evening, I would return and see that big kype-jawed brown in that same position next to the huge rock. He seemed to have a scowl of disdain on his face.

One evening, as I sat and smoked a cigar on the rock watching some Quill Gordon mayflies, a local cheese bait slinger was plying the depths of the pool, looking for one last dumb hatchery rainbow to nail his power bait. Sure as I can say, "Velveeta," he had a nine-inch rainbow on the line. All of a sudden and out of nowhere, that big brown trout came alive and swam around the rainbow and nailed it. "Holy Shit, that brown just nailed your trout," I said to the angler as his fish swim away in the mouth of the brute that broke his line. It was like witnessing a shark attack. That was the coolest thing I ever saw—that old dog could hunt!

The moral of the story is that even institutionalized hatchery trout eventually learn to hunt—some quicker than others—but the urge is the forever there. Never underestimate the innate genetic predatory power of *trutta*saurus, no matter where or what bloodline it comes from.

▲ Cannibalistic browns eat smaller rainbows like minnows. Here a rainbow double D engulfed. Credit: Author

▲ Credit: Author

# 9. The Regal Atlantic Salmon: The Nomadic Leaping *Salmo Salar*

*I*f ever there was a fish that throughout history held a piscatorial god-like status even to this day, it most surely is *Salmo salar*. As the brown trout was quickly being appreciated and valued for its ultimate elusive, deceiver personality, the *salar* was equally swelling the ranks of its sporting and culinary reputations as "the king of fish." Civilization's appreciation is matched by no other fish. Now that we have covered all the most pertinent intricacies and eccentricities of its cousin the brown trout, let's delve into the connection between the two. Besides all the similarities I described in the opening chapters of the book, three little anecdotes over the years have firmed up my claims of their strong bond.

## Back to the Treehouse

In the streamside treehouse of my youth on the Wieprza River dream world laboratory, I would watch the newly-arrived Atlantic salmon from the Baltic and the resident brown trout going about their business of hierarchy niche exploration. There was a good deal of the proverbial "push and shove/move over" jostling going on with two alpha dominant fish in a very small environment. Through these close quarter situations, the joint immediate need requirements revealed themselves. As one was a migrator there to spawn, the other; *trutta*, a daily forager gathering food for its survival, they blended together in a way most fish don't seem to have with one another. Often a surface-feeding brown trout would sip gently in the tail-out of the pool right next to a twenty-pound kype-jawed Atlantic, who somehow didn't seem to care the other fish was so close by.

Both *trutta* and *salar* would amazingly swim simultaneously very close together like kindred spirits, when the water levels were very low and they all huddled directly under the main current bubble line in a very tight unison as if they were from the same clan bloodline, which they are. Sometimes the browns would dominate the upper

▲ The only time there would be disruption in the pool harmony between the browns and Atlantics was when they accidentally rub each other. As I dicussed In my early chapters, one of their negative tropisms of tactile feeling discomfort. Credit: Author

end of the pool and the Atlantics the lower tail out. But most of the time, the Atlantics loved the upper throat water near the fast riffles, leading into the pool, since with their large pectoral fins they could dominate the faster currents and preferred it, since the scavenging, nitpicking Browns were always sniffing around for a leisurely meal. I was too young to really understand the dynamics of what was going on, but it's clear to me in my memories now how the two blended together so harmoniously.

## Selective/Introspective Peculiarities

Once my fly fishing matured and I came to know *Salmo salar* better through the writings of Lee Wulff and Colonel Joseph Bates, I took yearly trips at different seasons for salmon migrations in the Gaspé of Québec and elsewhere in the world. I've come to understand how the Atlantic salmon and brown trout's curiosity, stubbornness, and baffling behavior were so uniquely hardwired. My fascination with the connection between the two kept driving home in a way that I simply could not ignore.

Perhaps most intriguing was how an ocean-going fish could revert back to the whimsical behaviors of the brown trout hunting mentality. Since it was on a migratory mission solely for the purpose of procreation, real interest in foraging had no place, since ingesting food for all practical purposes is nonexistent here. Many anglers, such as Lee Wulff, maintain that the natal stream development explained their feeding behavior of taking the fly, due to the riverine biological drift stimulating that feeding drive curiosity.

In my book, *Selectivity*, I compared the three stages of *salar* migration to Freudian psychoanalytic phases. I described the first run phase of early spring/June as the ID phase, where the fresh-run Atlantic salmon, chrome silver and dripping scales from the sea with sea lice, was like a "bull in a china shop," and would aggressively attack a Blue Charm or Green Highlander fly with reckless abandon. Due to their sophisticated visual rods and cones adapted for pelagic bait hunting, they were at this stage still focused on the green/blue ocean spectrum, which explains how these color motifs in fly patterns are so successful.

Once settled into the incubator riverine pools, they now must adjust to their new holding pattern environment until fall comes, when they are fully gravid with eggs and sperm. They now must realize that certain behaviors will have consequences, such as humans experience in the ego state of development. So, running around and chasing Green Highlanders or Double Deceivers becomes much less important than procreation.

## Are All Atlantic Salmon "Takers" to the Fly?

So here is the eternal question that continues to baffle anglers wherever they find the *Salmo* nexus. Yes, the aggressive tendency to take the fly exists even during this procreation period, but perhaps less than 50 percent of that migration is apt to take the fly and be the "alpha takers" that make the trophy column. Similarly, large trophy brown trout may stubbornly refuse to take a fly fisher's offering, no matter how perfectly presented. Biologists know that many brown trout die of old age, having been never caught.

But is this disdain to take the fly a result of being caught before, learning avoidance techniques, or having superior sensory perception? Or is it a learned response as part of its DNA-inherited behavioral structure? Therein lies the *Salmo* conundrum.

Thus, it is so important for us to practice catch-and-release on these alpha takers, since their aggressive tendency is firmly implanted into the next generation, to breed more fly takers and have sport. How many lodges on how many salmon camps have thousands of Atlantic salmon in the pools only for the anglers to return back to the lodge completely fishless or to have two- or three-catch days amongst a dozen anglers? There are quite a few I tell you!

Being a lodge owner of a salmon camp, no matter where you find them—from the Canadian Maritimes, Iceland, Scotland or Europe—it can be a very humbling and frustrating affair when rivers are chock-full of salmon and they refuse to bite. This is the daunting proverbial black cloud that hangs over the anglers who spend a fortune to entice their bucket list once-in-a-lifetime catch. Hence the lodge owners must keep the motivation and eternal optimism of both the client and the guides/ghillies focused day after day. I once went five days straight without a take despite thousands of salmon in the river system.

The exception is massive wilderness river systems in the Kola Peninsula of Russia or Labrador, where migratory runs are a result of an extremely compact and condensed population of several year class/seagoing salt fish jammed packed into pools and runs, and abnormal continuous and high hook-ups can occur. For angling success elsewhere, due to the highly hierarchical niche dominance Atlantic salmon will display, it is safe to say that the great majority of Atlantic salmon angling scenarios have a tremendous amount of uncertainty and short windows of opportunity for angling success.

My thoughts here turn once again to the Gaspé of Québec and a very famous River guide of Scottish descent name Austin Clarke. Austin is one of the last of the proverbial "gentlemen's gentleman" Atlantic salmon ghillies, who has taught many protégés. He has witnessed the glory days of massive numbers of fish ascending the rivers at a time when all the salmon greats killed fish, including the venerable Lee Wulff. Much of the conquest and kill was a result of the machismo bragging rights of conquering the fish of a thousand casts. To fool one on the fly, and even more so the complex and difficult task to land them, often on very light pound test material, bamboo rods, and tackle that seems underclassed for twenty-to-forty oceangoing beasts, was and still is quite a feat. Thus, the kill gives the angler superhero qualities when they bring the fish back to camp to pose for the conquest and hang the replica on the wall.

But as Austin saw the value of every salmon, through the years he became more perplexed by how someone can kill such a precious and most perfect specimen of nature that travels thousands of miles to its the exact homing location, all through its biological time clocks and masterpiece of creation.

"You see that man over there, he is the head of the Atlantic salmon control commission in our district. He killed a thirty-six-pound female last year that was ripe with eggs, took the fly aggressively, and was foolish enough and had the gall to brag about it for months on end. Sad, very sad and ignorant," Austin once told me as we sat on the bank, looking for that perfect fly to tie on, when the salmon in the pools wanted nothing to do with anything of our selections.

"By killing that female, he killed how many hundreds of potential 'fly-taking' Atlantics, since it only can be reasonable that somewhere in that DNA structure the aggressive genetics are transmitted to the next generation?" Austin reasoned. In hindsight, this makes logical sense, but impossible to prove unless we can interview a *Salmo*. Given Darwinian evolution and its constant motif of survival of the fittest and adaptive behavior that almost importantly favors procreation of success, it stands to reason most Atlantic salmon should have nothing to do with the fly if they want to procreate successfully and return to the ocean to feed once again.

Could this aggressive "fly taking" gene, which provoked this fresh run beauty taken on the Alta of Norway by Lakselfan on a tube, be an aberration of evolutionary hierarchical dominance gone to a self-defeating level? When it comes to the larger scheme of Darwinian survival success, that same alpha dominant tendency is a double-edged sword where victory and annihilation have a borderline fine thread. That alpha dominant tendency will be the key to attaining the pole position in a spawning battle of competitiveness and allow future genetics to be firmly implanted by dominating a pool, a specific spawning area of river, and keeping all potential threats to the individual interest at bay. But this tendency can also get the fish killed if it becomes too aggressive and takes a fly of a would-be killer angler, thus its gene pool could be snuffed out.

▲ A magnificent Norweigian *salar* taken by Valgerdur Erla. Women have been masters of salmon fishing since the days of Dame Juliana, as modern *salar* lady virtuoso, Joan Wulff, has demonstrated over the decades. Credit: Arni Baldurson/Lax-A

## *Salar* Curiosity on Steriods

What I found most fascinating about *salar*'s aggressive and curious foraging tendencies, which it has in common with brown trout, became fully apparent on the Gaspé rivers in the late summer/early fall stages of September. Here as the leaves were turning, and the nights were getting colder, the Atlantic salmon would get darker with their beautiful spawning colors, rotund and deep-girthed bodies, and marbling spots. Here the true *Salmo* curiosity became full blown, as the fish entered the superego stage just before spawning. Usually the water was quite low, the fish had been pounded to death by salmon anglers all summer, and the fish had started to behave like very inquisitive brown trout. They had now been the river system for six months and were excited to get on with spawning.

Since *Salmo salar* return to the exact area of their natal birth rivers and do not die after spawning, they can return to the ocean and make repeat spawning migrations, unlike the Pacific salmon. Thus it would be very interesting to note of these multi-spawners, what aspect of their riverine habitat environment they retained after going back to sea and returned to the same area over and over again.

This time of year exhibits a more playful and curious Atlantic salmon behavior not usually found in the initial fresh run spring phases, when they strike a fly aggressively and with firm resolve, just as you would expect a pelagic baitfish predator to do while hunting in the ocean. Once in these incubator pool environments, does a *salar*'s curiosity turn its behavioral whims and mannerisms to act like old, wary brown trout, who are always probing and inquisitive, yet stubbornly shy and elusive?

In my *Selectivity* book, I have a long tale about orange eastern newts, the Doddi Orange salmon fly, the timing of the newts' daily forays into the river, and the Atlantic salmon's extreme preoccupation with the red/orange color spectrum as their sexual organs develop. Was the orange newts' presence coincidental with salmons' optical irritation by orange colors, resulting in the willingness of the Atlantic to accept this fly? We may never understand, but only enjoy the prefect angling opportunities.

My thoughts here turn to an empirical laboratory I had on the Grand Cascapedia River 'Forks' pool one late September while fishing to a very large kyped male. This fish was positioned in the same part of the pool on a daily basis and was extremely reluctant to accept any fly offerings. It seemed to have a high degree of curiosity toward particular-sized brownish-orange leaves blown on the surface by the strong autumn winds in late September on the last days of the season. It would come straight up to the surface, mount its giant large kype underneath the leaf an inch away in the meniscus, and follow it back in a very complex rise form, which Vince Marinaro described. It

▲ The classic *salar* wets and bombers. Credit: Author

would float vertically underneath the leaf for a long period of time until it cleared the pool and the fish would return back to its holding position. The guides told me this would happen day after day, as it exhibited a strong curiosity akin to a brown trout in a large Catskill river pool.

I casted, dead drifted, and twitched every possible green, red, and orange bomber I could to "the Maple leaf" salmon, only to have several long inspections but no take.

But like a bipolar switch had just been flipped, on my final day there, I put on a large orange and white deer hair bomber contraption that I devised over a couple of Scotches the night before—aptly named "the maple leaf." I added some ugly rubber legs to it and dead drifted and twitched it. The drift ended with a violent explosive take on a very cold rainy day.

Similar stories, such as the previously-discussed white Ephron Hatch and white Muddler Minnow on large male salmon during the fall mayfly hatch, again reinforces my link between Atlantic salmon and brown trout; not only from a morphological and genetic perspective, but from very curious behavioral alignments stemming from the blood bond of the rivers.

## The Big Laxa Minutiae Conundrum

If I have one place to live or die and go to heaven, it would be magnificent Iceland. This geological wonder of stupendous natural beauty is a *Salmo* chaser's paradise. Its Big Laxa/Lake Myvtan *Salmo* river ecosystems is one the world's most phenomenal natural wonders, which I mentioned in the prey chapter. Volcanic activity carved out craters and channels of lava flowing north to the Atlantic 2,300 years ago, which formed an ecosystem rich in nutrients beyond comprehension. Bubbling mud pools, geysers, and mineral springs from geothermal caves and lakes provide ultra-plush spas and resorts for the tourists as they enjoy the summer's constant daylight and perfect weather. On one side you have volcanic activity and cones and craters, surrounded on the other side by lush green grasses, wildflowers and grazing sheep in the rich pastoral setting. Underground springs that filtered through the volcanic rock percolate into a clarity that is amazing—perfect rich *Salmo* waters.

The Laxa has a deep blue color with amazing clarity and aquatic richness like a giant spring creek with all the alkaline-loving vegetation of watercress, chara,

▲ When looking at the water during these phenomenal Lake Myvtan river system midge flights, you see nothing but rise forms of brown trout taking midge clusters in the meniscus. Also amazing to note is that very few people fish for trout here since Atlantic salmon are the crème de la crème. Credit: Arni Baldurson/Lax-A

elodea-all swaying back and forth as you look up at the snowy-capped volcanic rock peaks and the azure-blue sky. But through all this natural awe, the Laxa has one of the heaviest populations of wild browns, sea trout, and Atlantic salmon in an unfathomable mix anywhere else in the world today. Emanating from Lake Myvtan's dense plankton environment, and with constant springs feeding the system, the conditions are perfect for tremendous fertility and the midge Simulium flights previously discussed.

The Laxa's brown trout have plump, robust bodies, sharp teeth, and gorgeous leopard-like spotting. Browns in the four- to five-pound range are very common, with many fish approaching larger sizes. I had the pleasure the other year fishing with a Thomas & Thomas eleven-foot 3-weight "Contact" rod swinging size 14 Soft Hackle midge pupae and size 16 cluster Griffiths Gnats dry/dropper combos. One could easily catch fifty brown trout in an evening to the point of bordering on insanity.

I first learned of the extremely selective nature of the salmon in the long flat beats of the lower River. Art Lee talked about them in his fabulous book "Riffle Hitch." With the Laxa's slow, meandering, broad waters, the Atlantics here have tremendous inspection times for everything in the biological drift. Unlike fast, thunderous rivers where the fly is usually taken on the swing in a convincing manner, the Big Laxa salmon look at your fly in the same manner that large, selective Letort or New Zealand browns carefully inspect size 16 ants.

On the Big Laxa, the fly styles are tiny size 14–18 little tube trebles and doubles that have black/blue and a tinge of yellow or orange. With the incredible inquisitiveness of the salmon here and their willingness to take their inspections to a more complex/compound degree, minutiae satisfies their curiosity.

Much of these complex fly offering inspections must stem from their natal experience in river feeding, where midges are the key to a healthy life for a parr that can spend up to three to five years in the river before migrating to the ocean as a smolt. I believe that is why the quivering riffle hitch adds a little uniqueness to your presentation. The constant twitching and waking, much like midges do when they hatch, when done properly by infusing a needle hole into the side of a tube, brings long follows and the belated take, when the salmon puts his mouth over the surface fly as it is engulfed, as you patiently wait for the line to tighten. Using very light fluorocarbon and pound test in the Laxa's environment of weeds and very sharp volcanic rock shelves will test an angler's abilities to fight a fish. Often your riffle hitches will catch trophy browns on the same salmon presentations. This presses my case here of how Atlantic salmon and brown trout are so closely aligned, even though one is a visitor to spawn and the other is a resident.

▲ A Laxa Atlantic salmon arsenal. Tiny tubes, trebles, and doubles often pique the curiosity of *salar* that are driven from natal imprinting to aquatic midges and ayflies. Credit: Lax-A photo

That minutiae conundrum later proved to be the key one summer on the Dartmouth River of Québec. It was a very hot and dry summer, not typical for the Atlantic rim shoreline, which usually gets a good dose of rain as it hits the Chic-Choc Mountains close to the coast, which is the final leg of the northern Appalachian Trail. My guide and I were praying for a take to the fly by a salmon. It was bordering on nervous compulsive behavior and insomnia. On day three we had not even a wink by the gorgeous Atlantics, which were stacked like cordwood in the pools of low water and waiting for a good storm to come through. Even though we had cold nights had good water temperature ranges, their dour, passive behavior was getting a little old.

Nevertheless, my guide Gordie, a wonderful Scottish chap who was always optimistic, decided to head as far up into the Dartmouth River system as possible, where cold water and fish "bored to tears" would eventually succumb to a fly offering. We tried every pattern under the sun: traditional Undertakers and Blue Charms, Sunray Shadows, you name it. We then went to the unorthodox bastardized "road kill" patterns—forget getting the fish to take, we outright spooked the living hell out of them!

Sitting atop a pool that was absolutely jam-packed with salmon, my guide and I would drink a few Labatt's beers, smoke a few cigars, and just enjoy the beautiful August weather, talking about the glory days of June long gone by. Staring at several very large male "Croc" fish at the top of the pool, I noticed one giant kype-jawed male turning and looking at something in the drift that caught his curiosity. My brown trout–influenced mind was always hardwired into matching the hatch, and this upper stretch of the river had a particularly good *Baetis* Blue-Winged Olive hatch, and I saw smaller parr and other resident brook trout rising to them in the early morning hours. Could this giant oceangoing Brutus of a *salar* be looking at Blue-Winged Olive nymphs? Not possible, I thought, living in my bizarre hatch-matching fantasy land.

I thought to try a tiny size 16 double hook Collie Dog that I had laying at the bottom of the box left over from Iceland. It was stark black and silver, and I could add some olive-dyed partridge soft hackle with my hand vice and traveling tying kit—about as minimal in the Scottish tradition as you can get. Gordie had an uncanny ability to deal with my whimsical eccentric presentations that made no sense but sometimes came through like a grand slam in the bottom of extra innings. "What the hell, Matt, your guess is as good as mine," Gordie mumbled, as he looked at his watch to make sure that we caught the last call at those Québec saloon ballet shows—probably our only sure thing on that given day. The new chef was going to leave us meals with a frown face magic marker on the tinfoil to be heated up in the microwave, since we were always late for dinner.

Dropping down to six-pound Maxima fluorocarbon was a risky proposition when dealing with twenty-to-thirty-pound Atlantic salmon. But strapping a Turle knot to this minute insanity was the only way to properly present the fly. After many traditional wet-fly swings starting at the surface and slowly working my way into the mid-depths with upstream folds and mends of the line, I noticed that the last drift caught the curiosity of the male as it gave my fly a side view glance. Due to the hot sun I could've been seeing a desert-like mirage. I presented the cast and swung the fly exactly as the one before and my line tightened with a "fish on!"

I was shocked! Gordie was on the verge of cardiac arrest. Twenty-five pounds of giant, marble-spotted, kype-jawed, *Salmo salar*, launched and cartwheeled into the air as my large arbor LOOP reel went into drag-singing euphoria. Three jumps and we were off to the races, running down the bank, all the while knowing that six-pound test and a size 16 double fly wouldn't hold very long. After one more amazing jump that Brutus had in him, my line went limp. I was dejected as I reeled in my line and saw my fly was still there and everything was intact. But landing a giant ocean fish on a tiny fly was just not to be. The greatest thrill of all was to know that I cracked the code and persuaded the fish to take a BWO nymph on the swing, brown trout style! It was yet another episode of the *Salmo* selectivity connection further engraved into my growing conviction.

## A Godlike Fish Etched in Primitive Art

Legends, folklores, mythology and worship have been etched in time with the nomadic *salar* wanderer's return to the rivers since the day Cro-Magnon man laid eyes on them. Their river migrations resulted in tribal camps, caves, outposts, dotted strategic intersections, and tributaries of rivers all over the Europe wherever *salar* made their homeward pilgrimage. The *salar* is etched in Gaelic

▲ French village along a onetime *salar*-running river; their restoration is slowly coming together to bring their historic runs back to when Neanderthal man worshiped the life-saving provisions of these nomadic fish. Credit: Aaron Jasper

folklore amongst ancient druids. In North America, the Mic Mac and Abenaki Indians sustained their winters off the runs of *Salmo* and their beautiful folklore tells of the demi-god salmon and other revered animals like beaver and whales, which mythically taught the Indians culture and protected them from danger.

Waiting for the *salar* to return to the rivers started somewhere around twenty thousand years ago during the age of Cro-Magnon man. It was a great dawning of a new man that was then sweeping across northern Europe; from France to Spain, to the Baltic corridor. Each dawn was a journey into discovery and awe. *Salmo salar* and *trutta* eventually fused with man's need for subsistence as people built villages on *Salmo* rivers. Today castles and famous lodges stand where primitive man's fishing caves and fire pits stood.

In *Selectivity*, I introduced the reader to the upper Paleolithic period in the Dordogne area of France, between the Loire and Pyrenees mountains, which was as perfect a landscape early man could ever have ever found—it was a green-forested Garden of Eden. The Dordogne River, with its dozen or more tributaries, flows through a series of steep cliffs, gorges and fast-flowing rapids with breathtaking scenery. As the river runs the valley, it becomes a lush wonderland of fertile pastoral farms, orchards, wineries, and wide-open spaces. Every tributary river back then was teeming with *Salmo,* as most villages were built around them. Perigord, one of the main gastronomic districts of France, is located here with its vineyards and truffle-rich woodlands. Along its tributary, the Vezere—a beautiful river unto itself, lays the cave dwellings of Lascaux and Les Eyzies and the world of pre-history's rock art shrines.

In a series of amazingly-detailed paintings, the first known depiction of *Salmo* took place. A beautiful artistic display of an Atlantic salmon or sea trout, by some Cro-Magnon fisherman, embodies the admiration and worship these fish were given. On the floor of this particular cave, known as "L'Abri du Poisson" its full-body profile and kype show remarkable detail. There are noticeable signs and areas along these rivers that early man modified pools and channeled tributaries to capture the once-massive Atlantic salmon runs of these rivers in these enchanted mountains and forests.

One can only imagine the crazed excitement and elation early man would have had to witness a massive onslaught run of Atlantic salmon swirling, swarming and leaping in a jam-packed pool. It must have been the ultimate manna from heaven! When the Roman legions conquered this

▲ Constant fly presentations and extreme annoyance prey suggestions are necessary to pique natal imprinting to juvenile food forms, and big ocean prey food motifs. Niche hierarchical dominance irritation and sometimes pure luck all enter into a successful Atlantic salmon fly presentation. Credit: Author

massive area, then known as Gaulish Aquitania, they dubbed the salmon *"salar"*—leapers—for their ability to jump high waterfalls, while migrating upstream. The earliest writings by Pliny, in the era of Caesar Tiberius, noted that the people of Gaul called them *"Salmo,"* and had no greater love for a fish—it was like the worship of a god. Roman legions brought back pelts of smoked salmon and traded them in open-air markets for gold; it was prized as highly then as it is today.

The passion for the "king of all fish," as Atlantic salmon is known, reigns supreme wherever they are found or exported. No other game and food fish creates more generated sportsmen and culinary currency per person than this noble warrior.

A ton has been written about *salar* and the fly-fishing passion they inspire, but *salar*'s mysterious nomadic ocean life of migration and elusive predation is the true shrouded veil of their existence. Scientists and commercial fishermen know their two main foraging feeding grounds off Greenland and the Faroe Islands, and also have sketchy, broad migration routes to its natal rivers and streams, but their day-to-day life is a mysterious journey known only, and incompletely, to scientists who track them through radio telemetry and GPS, which affords brief glimpses into their lives.

Saumon, Lax, Semga (French, Nordic, Russian terms for them), no matter how you say it, will turn heads and dilate eye pupils from gourmet chefs, world destination tourists, and fly fishermen like no other subject matter.If there is one "Holy Grail" in the piscatorial world, these fish are it!

Today, the northern European corridor of Cro-Magnon man's rivers still harbor wild "truite fario"—brown trout, grayling, and sea-run brown trout, but *salar* are nowhere near historic levels due to population growth and habitat destruction. But thanks to Europe's massive restoration of indigenous Atlantic salmon waters, a continent-wide effort to reestablish the mighty "Saumon Atlantique," of centuries gone by, are seeing salmon beginning to swim up the great rivers of the Rhine, Rhone, and even the Thames again. Left over from the French glory days, the Brittany district still maintains small migratory runs of indigenous Atlantic salmon that have survived until today.

## Evolutionary Predisposition to Cracking the *Salmo* Code

As I detailed the *Salmo*'s evolutionary and historical journey in the opening chapters, the poor man's Atlantic salmon—brown trout—and the noble prince of fish—*Salmo salar*—had evolutionary diversifications in habitat but not in verve and temperament. In segmenting

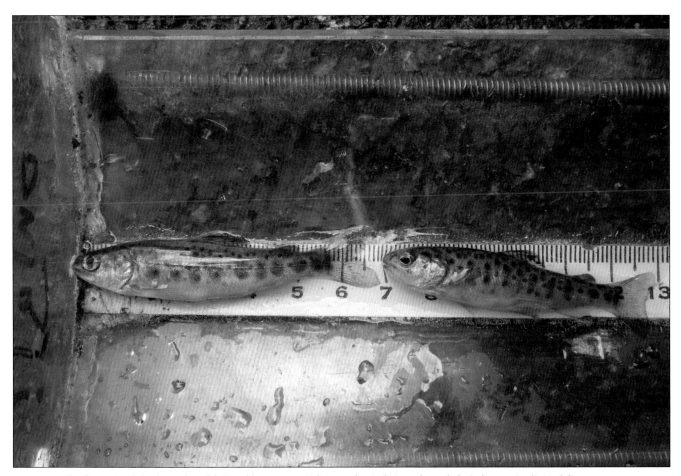

▲ A New York Salmon River hybrid cross breed (left) and brown trout (right) note the similarity and morphological nexus. Credit: Verdoliva

and studying genetically unique population distributions throughout the temperate zone—Arctic rivers, oceans, and seas, and the split between North American and European origins, no other group of fish have raised more eyebrows or arguments as the genetic link and evolutionary separation of these two species. But cross breeding between *salar* and *trutta* does exist in the wild and is more prevalent than previously known.

Fran Verdoliva, New York DEC/Salmon River coordinator off of Lake Ontario, which was once indigenous *salar* habitat, has documented rare natural reproductive hybrid brown trout/Atlantic salmon parr in the wild. Mating has taken place between a female salmon and a male brown trout, but there is a 90 percent or higher rate of deformities and mortality in development, and the offspring that do survive are sterile.

How does all this scientific information benefit the *Salmo* fly fisher? It suggests that Atlantic salmon and brown trout are so closely related, that our techniques for presentation may have overlapping themes and qualities for both of these hyper-selective specimens. To view and treat them as the same quarry will benefit anglers immensely, just as it has changed my perspective and success with *Salmo*.

Whether we fly fish Québec's Gaspé Peninsula or Iceland's Laxa, Michigan's Torch Lake landlocked Atlantics or its cousins in Sweden, the strong genealogical similarities are cause for a global perspective with varied presentations. Yet, breaking it down, they are as much alike as they are different. Herein lays the conundrum and complexity of selective presentation. I have always said that when you fish for Atlantic salmon, "you must think like a brown trout, and vice a versa." It often works! Our riverside observations and experience often explains this and rewards us.

## *Salar*'s First Founding Disciples

Back to Dame Juliana Berners, who wrote the *Treatise of Fysshynge with an Angle* in the Book of St. Albans in 1495. Her empirical laboratory was on the River Avon with browns, Atlantic salmon, and sea-run browns. Her very detailed instructions for coloring horsehair for leader tippets by season shows experience with the selective nature of *Salmo*. She also learned to discern *Salmo* species–specific behavior, which still applies today.

The salmon does not bite on the bottom, but at the float. You may sometimes take him, but it happens not very seldom, and with an artificial fly when he is leaping, in the same way as you take trout or grayling.

We shall speak next of the trout, because he is a very dainty fish and also a very greedy biter. He is in season from March to Michaelmas. He is found on clean gravel bottom and a running stream. You

may angle for him at all times with a running or lying ground line: except in leaping time, when you use an artificial fly.

In the last passage, Berners already understands the difference between nymphing (ground line) and dry fly opportunities during a hatch. Thus, *Salmo* selectivity was already well known back in the 1490s.

Through the eighteenth century, fly fishing for *Salmo*—browns, Atlantics, and particularly sea runs—gained in popularity throughout England and Scotland. Stewart, who published the *Practical Angler*, fine-tuned the art of the wet fly swing. In Scotland, lake or "loch" fishing with a trio of wets became the norm and the first fly-fishing competitions started on these lakes. During the Revolutionary War, British officers found colonial rivers to be loaded with brook trout and salmon and fished for them ardently. Early officer-sportsmen like Sir William Johnson and Joseph Banks, were the first known writers and proponents of the art of the fly, primarily fishing for salmon in Québec and upstate New York regions, where New York's Salmon River had wild indigenous populations. These fish have since gone extinct, but are now coming back.

Perhaps no other celebrity angler delved into the world of Atlantic salmon more than the legendary Lee Wulff. Only I quote the master himself, speaking on the paradoxical nature of Atlantic salmon:

The essential differences between angling for an Atlantic salmon and for other game fish had their beginnings long before man ever thought of fishing. Over endless years in the slowly changing world, nature's pattern has fitted this salmon into its own special niche, bestowing upon it interesting traits and characteristics quite at variance with the conception of how a fish should live and act.

The salmon is anadromous. The rivers are his nurseries and the sea his major source of food. In the flowing fresh waters the young salmon find suitable nourishment and hiding places and the streams become crowded with their numbers. (Nature) Having brought these great, swift fish back to the rivers after sea sojourn of ravenous feeding, it was essential that their appetite be curbed lest they try to live on their own young, which formed the greater share of the available food, and so contribute to their own extinction. So we find great hordes of salmon, ranging in weight from a few pounds to more than 40, settling into the freshwater pools, sea-fed fish which the rivers themselves could not produce except by sending them out to board on the bounty of the sea.

Fishing for a fish devoid of hunger, a fish larger and stronger than its surrounding waters could produce, confined to narrow pools and river channels where he cannot escape the site of the fisherman's fly. The appetite of these returning, mature salmon are curbed to very great degree but not so completely that they, on rare occasion, will take a fly bait. Therein lies the paradox they create.

Wulff was the first to truly dissect the crux of the Atlantic salmon challenge for the fly angler, whose audience was rather small but growing. Back then it was the aristocratic pastime of royalty, wealthy families, diplomats, and corporate moguls. Many beliefs about the *Salmo* enigma were knowledge passed down from father to son in the ghillies' ranks. River-dwelling families kept secrets about the

Atlantic salmon's behavior and techniques, but none have gone on to pen their knowledge into a book like Wulff.

Lee's Houdini-like ability to go to places in the Atlantic salmon world, make observations and descriptions, and catch difficult fish on light tackle and small flies, made his first book the bible on the subject. Usually traveling as a guest of a famous lodge, estate owner, or passionate salmon angler, his *salar* insights from time spent on the rivers cracked the shrouded veil of folklore and theoretical myth that misrepresented *salar*.

Many in Europe, the United Kingdom, and Canada became salmon ghillies as young boys like their ghillie fathers and grandfathers—many never even finishing grade school—so for them, the art of writing was out of the question. Also, Wulff divulged many of their family secrets and flies. The situation is still the norm in Canada and Europe, were salmon ghillies are full-time professionals and treat their craft as a winemaker would his special reserve. Each farmer has a theory and practice on the time-honored tradition of how to rotate crops and soils, but how many farmers actually write books on farming? So goes the knowledge of the salmon ghillies.

Perhaps the most powerful chapter in Wulff's book deals with the Atlantic salmon's selectivity. Few have been so bold as to deal with this issue. Many ghillies had diverging opinions, but Wulff laid out deductions that were simply magnificent:

If it could be proven absolutely that he Atlantic salmon never feed in fresh water on their spawning run, there would be no attempt to tie flies as insect imitations. If it were not extremely difficult, if not impossible, to prove that they do feed at all in fresh water, then salmon fishing would not be the remarkable sport it is. In truth, scientists say, Atlantic salmon returning to fresh water cannot physically digest food, though he may try.

▲ The "*Salar* Buddha," the late master unmatched Lee Wulff. Art Lee is today's living *salar* legend. Credit: Catskill Fly Fishing Museum

Consider these returning hordes of fish which have fed in the sea to such advantage. Is there anything in fresh water to approximate the vast shoals of shrimp or capelin, or herring, they are custom to feed upon? Salmon rivers have little to offer except a few insects, a fair quantity of salmon parr or lesser trout, and the eels, large trout, kingfishers, mergansers, and others already preying upon all the smaller forms of life. If the salmon tried to maintain their strength by feeding, they would not only clean up almost all the immature salmon but would eat all the small living things on which the Parr and small living things hunger for. To say that they do try to feed in fresh water but are balked by their size cannot be true. Trout of 5 pounds and larger managed to feed quite regularly, but smaller salmon, swifter and more able physically, are always empty-stomached. Fish a 6-inch smelt through a pool, and trout after trout will try to take it. Almost never a salmon.

From a purely biological predation behavioral code deep in a *salar*'s DNA and operant prey conditioning, what Lee touched on was all-encompassing from a logical standpoint. But logic is often "thrown to the wind." Wulff again theorizing further on the salmon's curiosity and angler/ghillie myths and misconceptions, stated:

Salmon occasionally will chase and capture natural insects. Fortunately, they will, at times also take an angler's spurious imitation. What they do with the natural insects they take is still debatable. Most anglers hold that if the salmon does catch a natural insect he immediately ejects it. Others are certain he takes the fly for food. Their consistently empty stomachs tend to prove they rarely eat insects for, if they did, occasionally some of the less-digestible remains would be found inside their stomachs. Someone came up with the suggestion that the salmon take the fly into his mouth and squeezes out the juices of the bug, which he swallows, then ejects the carcass. These juices, according to the claim, contained vitamins a salmon must have if he is to stay alive.

Unfortunately for this theory, if we follow the same line of reasoning a little further, it becomes obvious that a thirty pound salmon would need six times as

▲ Master Spey caster Pete Humphries with a Russian Kola *salar* masterpiece. Credit: Mark Danhausen

much in the way of vitamins as a 5-pound grilse, and therefore, would have to catch and swallow the juice from six times as many insects. The bigger the fish, if the theory holds, the more likely he would be to rise to a fly in the more often he would be seen feeding on insects. Experienced salmon fishermen know this is not the case. They learned that five-pound fish are more readily rooked to the artificial fly and are more active in any apparent feeding than are the larger fish.

This was to this day truly groundbreaking theory, being put for the first time in a logical *Salmo salar* behavioral framework to inspire modern fly design and presentation. To every serious *salar* angler and newcomer to the sport, Wulff's bible is an absolute must read from start to finish.

Around the same time as Wulff's second edition (1983) came out, Hugh Falkus, the great British salmon mind, was writing his own Wulff-like epic masterpiece. *Salmon Fishing: A Practical Guide* gave yet more insight into the confusing world of the salmon as well as its whimsical and elusive nature. Falkus made some very interesting observations on the salmon's responses to the fly and categorized them into six groups:

1. Feeding habit—a deliberate take, frequently ascribed to a reflex action resulting from early river life as a parr.
2. Aggression—the "crunch take," a seemingly automatic reaction to intrusion into the salmon's territory.
3. Inducement—a response take primarily based on chasing and escaping quarry.
4. Curiosity—a gentle non-take in which the fish rises to or touches the fly with mouth closed, with no intention of taking the fly.
5. Irritation—a response, usually aggressive, resulting from prolonged aggravation such as the repeated casting over the fish.
6. Playfulness—behavior, such as bumping the fly or flipping it with its tail, in which the salmon makes no effort to seize the fly with its mouth.

Around the turn of the late 1990s, Atlantic salmon fishing was "the sport of nobility and the rich," and a billion-dollar industry. New frontier *salar* rivers on Russia's Kola Peninsula, as seen captured in that snowy image by English spey caster Pete Humphries, opened magnificent *Salmo* rivers that would yield dozens of often non-fussy salmon, unlike the traditional salmon rivers. With this renaissance, three great works came out again to give selective *Salmo* fishermen an even deeper insight into the world of this aristocratic and elusive king of fish. In 1970, Colonel Joseph Bates, released *Atlantic Salmon Flies and*

*Fishing*, another remarkable insight into the *salar* world. But when Joseph passed away in 1988, he had a conglomeration of previously undisclosed writings which his daughter, Pamela Bates Richards, was determined to bring to press, and in 1996, *Fishing Atlantic Salmon* became the new Bible about everything Atlantic salmon: fly history tackle, behavior—you name it! It was a masterpiece right from the start with its attractive fly plates tied by the best Atlantic salmon tiers in the world.

In 1998 the cerebral, jet-set, gallivanting master Art Lee came along to become without doubt the new "Lee Wulff" protégé. Lee was a master writer, a reporter and newspaper columnist turned "professional fly fisherman" as he put it, when he moved to Roscoe, New York. He had a brilliant mind and incredible talent for writing magazine article after article—I know, because I read and relished them all. As Northeast field editor for *Fly Fisherman* magazine, he, along with late wife Kris and her beautiful photography, enthralled a new generation of inquisitive *Salmo* fly fishers. His first work, *Fishing Dry Flies for Trout on Rivers and Streams* was an instant masterpiece since he had the Catskill brown trout dry fly laboratory right in his backyard. In 1998, *Tying and Fishing the Riffle Hitch*, took his Wulff-inspired method to new heights.

But from a *Salmo* selectivity standpoint, Art Lee's greatest contributions are his editorial columns for the *Atlantic Salmon Journal*. Here is the mind and soul of the passionate salmon addict at work, deciphering every challenge, problem and opportunity the Atlantic salmon experience brings.

In 2000 and 2001, two new Atlantic salmon masterworks were released, E. Richard Nightingale's *Atlantic Salmon Chronicles*, and a joint work by Charles Gaines and Monte Burk called *Leaper*, which was a beautiful masterpiece of stories about all the countries where Atlantic salmon exist. Nightingale's work had some good insights on selectivity, and here he criticized Hugh Falkus's six states of why salmon take the fly:

> Undoubtedly salmon do demonstrate a variety of behaviors at one time or another. Whether they can be properly be defined in terms of mammalian behavior is debatable. For instance, I have trouble accepting the notion that feeding behavior is simply a reflex response salmon acquires as in its early river life. Perhaps, the largest parr foods are insects. Parr never feed on shrimp or elvers or minnows as large as themselves. And what differentiates the rotation response from inducement or aggression? Or playfulness from curiosity?

In the prologue of *Leaper,* written by Joseph D. Bates Jr. and Pamela Bates, they discussed all the fuss about fly design, and put it into layman's terms:

▲ The indigenous *Salmo salar* natal rivers for the most part, were and still are the classic freestone/volcanic rock/classic snow run-off glacial rivers that embody the bulk of *Salmo salar*'s evolutionary waters. Credit: Arni Baldurson/Lax-A

If salmon will take such diverse items as bugs, insects, berries, twigs, worms, and even cigarette butts, why should we be so fussy about offering them carefully-dressed artificial flies in particular colors, shapes, and sizes selected to suit the conditions of the water, temperature, and so on? There is simply no pat answer—variables are too numerous and species too unpredictable. This is fortunate, because conclusive answers about fly selection and presentation methods would diminish the fun of fishing. The best one can do is to try to deal with varying conditions and likely responses and enjoy the challenge of discovery. Years of personal experience and reading the extensive angling literature can provide valuable insight.

Finally, breaking into the new frontier of how a passionate migratory *Salmo salar* guide views its enigmatic quarry, two modern books take a hard look at the new age of *Salmo salar*. In my book *Selectivity*, and Topher Brown's *Atlantic Salmon Magic*, we examined the empirical laboratory of the river and the interaction of the *Salmo* with its ecosystems. They are perhaps the latest evolving insights into how an Atlantic salmon behaves, written by guides/ghillies on the water three hundred days a year. We looked into the mind of the fish and shared the eternally-optimistic passion of being mesmerized in cracking the "taking" conundrum of the perpetually confounding Atlantic.

Looking at classic Atlantic rivers like the Grand Cascapedia in Québec, or the Ponoi in Kola Russia, the Alta in Norway, and Iceland's myriad of rivers, they are large river systems with a strong series of river tributaries and capillaries that often drain peat and glacial bog inland lakes and vast headwater spring groundwater systems that emanate from the mountains into broad valleys, eventually ending to sea. They have usually moderate to at times extreme gradient flows, large boulders, and rock-strewn pools for holding salmon incubating adults, and have vast stretches of propagation gravel in nursery waters for the fry and parr. Their aquatic invertebrate life can border on extreme richness with mayfly, stonefly, caddis, and midge systems, to less-fertile but pristine nursery systems.

As the rivers produce the necessary food for imprinting fry and parr to survive, they usually have a very good sustainable number of brown and brook trout or grayling in their ecosystems. Thus, the classic freestone rivers that had the largest pools, such as the Grand Cascapedia and York River systems in Québec, and the Alta and Kola in Europe, will usually produce the largest salmon, who in turn produce largest amount of alpha dominant offspring.

It is here in these massive ecosystems that the future of *salar* has the best chance of survival, which they have and will for millennia. Remember that *Salmo* evolved millions of years before mankind, and now must deal with any detrimental effects mankind is known to bring about to their natural order of things.

▲ Canadian Maritime autumn. Credit: Paul Marriner

# 10. Cracking the Bipolar *Salar* Code: Tactics and Presentation

The Cabot Coastal Trail and the Margaree Valley in Cape Breton, Nova Scotia are exhilarating places to be in October. Looking out at amazing vistas of the Atlantic Ocean and the Gulf of St. Lawrence, you can often spot the right, blue, and pilot whales that come to its fertile shorelines to feed on squid. But most breathtaking along the coast and up the river valley from the Forks down to the Seal pool, the maples here are ablaze with striking reds and oranges unlike anywhere along the Atlantic coastline.

Up the Margaree River valley is an amazing crown jewel of *Salmo salar*'s kingdom, as the tannic tea-stained waters ooze fog and steam on a crisp fall morning. The forest colors never relinquish their mesmerizing charm as the river runs through breathtaking cliffs and river valleys of Neoproterozoic volcanic rocks dating back 575 million years, and which have a unique montage of beauty all unto themselves.

But more pertinent to my *salar* quest at hand, is how amazingly these forest colors correspond to the orange and red mosaic marbling of the male Atlantic salmon's late fall spawning appearance. Its pinkish-white kyped jaws seem to yawn, as the male "crocs" stretch their mouths and they glide suspended in the low water pools. Curiously, later in the salmons' pre-spawn visual spectrum, these colors will correspond closely to the rod and cone color preference in the Atlantic salmon's retina.

Passionate Atlantic salmon fly anglers Peter Dean, Art Lee, and Colonel Drury all had one thing in common: they realized orange had a powerful effect on *salar*, especially late in the season. Dean developed his amazing orange prawn pattern, the Francis, in Iceland; Art Lee introduced the Doddi Orange; and the legendary British Colonel Drury created the General Practitioner prawn imitation. All had success with these patterns as an Atlantic's mind turned towards the spawning redds. There is something about orange/black and red—with a tinge of yellow, that piques a capricious *salar*'s interest in this intriguing, pre-spawn aggression phase. The famous Willie Gunn, tied by the eponymous Scotsman, embodies this lethal color code. I have experienced the power of these fly color combinations all too often on rivers throughout the world.

The Atlantic salmon's autumn pre-spawn phase could be most directly likened to a selective, moody, uncatchable brown trout's habits. It seems the more time an Atlantic spends in the river, the more it turns into a simulation of a large capricious and snooty brown trout. But we

▲ Robert Chiasson, a Margaree, Nova Scotia guide, proudly displays a stunning *salar*. Credit: Robert Chiasson

can identify this bipolar behavior and adjust our tactics, as we shall soon explore.

On an amazing fall day on the Margaree, I encountered a Micmac Indian boy who was crouching on a rocky bluff overlooking one of the pools. I asked him what he was looking down at from the bluff. "They are really psycho fish eh?—our people could never understand them— Micmac always called them *elue'wiet* (crazy). Bet they are tough to catch with your flies aren't they?" I could only give him an affirmative smile, knowing that *salar* would take my fly only when they chose.

## *Salmo* Selectivity in Overdrive

There is no question that while in the rivers, Atlantic salmon epitomize all the selectivity phases to extremes. Fresh out of the sea, their aggressive/active behavior is on steroids. They will smash a Lady Amherst or Green Highlander fly with the brutality of a shark or an orca. Once habituated to the river environment and in a holding pool, their selective curiosity will baffle even the canniest dry fly brown trout angler. If steelhead like to play with their prey like a cat, Atlantic salmon will play with your mind and break your spirit, as the Micmac boy observed. And later in their pre-spawning phase, they become dour, passive, and downright impossible to catch.

Picture this. You and your guide have the entire "Offie" Pool on the Gaspé's magnificent York River all to yourself. You are armed with every Atlantic salmon fly known to mankind. You can see approximately seven hundred or more Atlantics in the pool, ranging from eight to forty pounds. You cast from morning till dark. Result: Nothing, or maybe you get a few follows? If that is not passive obstinacy in the extreme, I don't know what is!

On the flip side of this equation, you are on Russia's Kola Peninsula, on the world-famous Ponoi River—perhaps the greatest Atlantic salmon river in the world. Here, massive runs of fresh salmon from the sea tarnish the salmon's reputation for fussiness. Double-digit hookups are the norm here. Often there is only one fly to use for weeks on end—a Willie Gunn tube fly. The sheer abundance of multi-year fish classes, causing aggressive reactions to the fly in ideal icy water conditions is the key here.

Eventually, all serious fly fishers eventually wind up being *Salar* fanatics. It's a natural "bucket list" evolution. They dream each night about encounters days before their Atlantic salmon trips like a pilgrimage to Lourdes or Mecca. The experience of being on an Atlantic salmon river is a euphoric high unto itself. They thrive in the most beautiful places on earth and have done so for millions of years. The sight of an Atlantic salmon swimming in a crystal-clear pool is enough to send chills of excitement down your spine. But deep in the mind of the ardent Atlantic salmon hunter, the excitement, enthusiasm and spirit of awe are the things that we can control. The uncontrollable items are the inevitable frustration and lack of success we experience, which is a given, whether we like it or not. Yet we keep coming back for that "mystery grab-that magical take," that washes all the frustration away in a flash.

There is a foundation of personality traits that build up when you are trying to focus and understand the mindset of Atlantic salmon—entire books are dedicated to this. For simplicity's sake I will stick to the facts and cut to the chase.

## The Accute *Salmo* Vision

Without writing a major treatise on what colors and silhouettes a trout or salmon sees, which we touched on in previous chapters, let's have a quick review on optic basics for Atlantics.

First and foremost scientists really don't know how a fish's brain perceives what its eyes see. The interaction between water and light is the distortion factor known as attenuation, which changes the intensity and color of the light. Two processes, scattering and absorption, change the way color appears at varying degrees of depth, viscosity, and clarity. So the deeper we go, the color red will eventually appear bluer and then terminate in black. The new florescent and UV materials in use today totally alter the standard color scheme when light interacts with water, and as a result, adding hints of these materials to modern-day flies has become an extremely lethal tactic.

So in shallow waters with plenty of light, as in a riffle of a river, the colors of your fly will appear pretty much as they do without water, and will gradually diminish towards the dark blue/black spectrum. Without getting into all the hundreds of intricate studies that scientists have conducted, it is clear that certain fish prefer certain colors, and this has been the overriding motif over the past centuries in designing *Salmo* flies. Research has also shown that very little light is necessary for brown trout and Atlantic salmon to see color as we see it. But one thing is certain—silhouettes and shapes are easily perceptible to fish, even though they'll will eventually be black at deeper depths or at night.

*Salmo salar*'s extremely sharp vision capabilities never cease to amaze Atlantic salmon anglers. Having monocular capabilities with rods and cones, they see the subtlest variations of color and movement. This may account for the success or failure of the thousands of Atlantic salmon fly patterns and their variations on a theme.

## Preston Jennings: *Salmo* Visionary

During the Catskill-based American fly fishing renaissance earlier in the turn of the last century, Jennings, along with the other progressive fly thinkers such as Gordon, Hewitt, La Branche, and Rhead, all contributed much to the understanding of how the new and elusive German trout invaders perceived the fly. But as with all fanatic brown trout anglers, Atlantic salmon is almost the next "must step" in angling challenges. Hewitt, a died-in-the-wool brown trout man, was the first to bring Atlantic salmon to the newly-created Neversink reservoir in the Catskills, and his efforts actually succeeded to the degree that he was able to fish for them in the upper branches as they returned in a spawning cycle. But unlike the migratory browns that were much easier on the take, the stubborn *salar* posed more challenges.

Jennings's genius in *Book of Trout Flies* (1935) was to look seriously at American insects and hatches and matching fly patterns and streamers with Atlantic salmon flies. His streamer patterns like The Murky Iris and Lord Iris were modeled on Atlantic flies. As Marinaro was to limestone brown trout, Jennings was an earlier contemporary to the northeast trout and indigenous Atlantic salmon experience.

▲ A Willie Gunn fly will entice any *salar* in the tannic waters of Russia's Kola, as pictured here by Arni Baldurson of Lax-A World Adventures. Credit: Lax-A

Through his intense examinations of naturals in the context of optics, light, and water interactions, he deduced that flies with color blends displayed a spectrum of colors, depending on light intensity at various times of day and night. This informed his theories on how *salar* see the fly." Salmon do feed in fresh water after their return from the sea. Salmon can distinguish colors, and are especially sensitive to red. Salmon take artificial flies which suggest natural food produced by their native river."

As for his first premise, almost all ichthyologists will dispute that fact, as anadromous salmon will completely shut down on consumption of prey once they enter the spawning river systems. Though the predatory response to snap at things is one of the main reasons they take the fly, ingestion of food for energy and growth purposes is pretty much nil. Jennings here was addressing the strike "feed" response I believe, or landlocked situations, as we will cover in the next chapter.

As most Atlantic salmon anglers know every river has its patterns and colors that the *salar* respond to best, so there must be some relationship between how they show the

color spectrum, and the viscosity, water composition, and average depth of the rivers, as well as the foods available to salmon there during their pre-migratory upbringing.

## Decoding Bright Fly/Bright Day Myths

This could be one of the greatest myths or bits of folklore where every guide on every continent will have their own viewpoints. Since I've been guiding for brown trout and Atlantic salmon and on the water for up to three hundred days a year for twenty-two years, I submit that my theories have the weight of experience.

Many British ghillies came up with the theory, "Bright day bright fly/dark day dark fly." Their rationale is that more glitter and brightness in the fly will show up better against an oppressive sun that scatters color spectrums. Personally I find no substance to this theory and can usually do better on darker flies on bright days, due to the blackness holding up silhouette better, making the fly more easily tracked and targeted against a bright sky's blinding object distortion.

My first truly "eye-opening" experience of *salar*'s incredible black fly/bright sun perception happened years ago on the Grand Cascapedia River. The famous Charlie Valley Rock pool was the hot pool for success the previous year. But when I eventually got to fish it, it was fishing very poorly and nobody had caught salmon out of it the entire season, due to new flow regimes from low water droughts. Also, there was a drastic flood in the prior year that realigned the river's substratum—thus changing the hydrodynamics for a holding salmon pool. The pool was not holding fish   plain and simple. All the guides knew it.

My friend, lodge owner David Bishop, always gave me the "short straw" on river beats, saving the good pools for the less-talented older and richer clientele, rather than Schally Wagg guides like me looking for cheap venues; talent I had, wealth I did not. Each morning he would hold a lottery and have the entire lodge anglers line up, play the lottery, and get their designated beat assignment for the day. It was a very nervous moment for some people, because it would mean the difference between success, and "oh shit, looks like we aren't going to catch anything today!"

Since rumors and guide gossip travels around the dinner table and cocktail hour as to which parts of the river were fishing well, versus and which parts were not, when David told me I was going to Charlie Valley, I already knew I was doomed, but didn't care. I just wanted to see it and take some pictures of it. With the death sentence sealed, I lit up a cigar, drank Perrier to fight the scotch hangover from the previous night, and hopped in a vehicle with my two less-than-enthusiastic guides. They knew I was "F'd," and that it would be a fairly easy day drinking coffee, chatting, and smoking cigarettes on the ghillie's bench speaking Québec ois-dialect French.

It seemed like the moment they got there, the guys were talking about having lunch—that is not a good sign. As I made ready my rod, tied on my own fly on, they told me" knock yourself out," it has been pretty tough here lately -eh!" I was not going to let their downer enthusiasm mess up my day—*Salar* rule #1: always have a positive attitude and consider it an honor to be on an Atlantic salmon river.

The water was low, and it was very hot and sunny. Not at all, "taking condition," for Gaspé Atlantics. My favorite fly on this river has always been the Undertaker, with a black-red/chartreuse butt mix. Starting with the large size 6 double, I began my swinging and stepping down the faster water above the rock pool with no luck—not a fish showing, and I could see there were no fish in the run's low water. As I approached the steep twelve-foot dropoff into the massive pool by the rock the size of the house, I decided to go really small—a size 12 double Undertaker—and to swing it at a very good speed right below the surface. Now the guides really thought I was crazy.

▲ The Undertaker fly has never let me astray; this chrome beauty took one on a stifling hot August day. When waters are low, the sun is out, and salmon are dour or "not supposed to be there," try a smaller and darker fly pattern. The proverbial "bright day/bright fly" never seemed to work for me. Credit: Author

"You might want to put a short sink tip on—that pool is very deep. Plus it is hot and sunny, fish will be holding as deep as possible," shouted my guide wunderkind.

"Nahhh . . . I'll stick with what I have."

They looked at me with that French-Canadian, "whatever, stupid Yank" look.

On the very second cast, as the fly swung near the surface of the deep drop-off, the taking fish exploded on the surface—I almost soiled myself! Fifteen minutes of intense battle yielded a magnificent chrome twenty-five-pound Atlantic female. The vision capability of that fish, being in the bottom of the deep dark pool, to see a micro black fly in the hot sunny noon hour, was absolutely astounding.

That evening it was the subject of much conversation at the Lodge evening happy hour—it felt like I was a prophet or something. I love this kind of stuff. I was totally written off by everyone, and became the underdog kid. Hence, regardless of what others are whining about, stay positive and experiment, or rely on tradition.

## The Evolution of the Salmon Fly Color Code

What is perhaps the most confounding mystery is what a *Salmo salar* actually sees in the fly for it to elicit a strike. Is it the combination of colors, fly silhouette, speed of movement, direction, or continual surface or broadside current orientation? Herein lies the key tonic to the often elusive grab. Thus the devil in the details lies in all of the above. But even as Lee Wulff so perfectly fused all the key biological ecosystem motif associations in his Atlantic salmon masterpiece, I continue to insist *salar's* true personality lies in the details of the blood bond of the river with its congenital twin, the brown trout.

Going back to the Macedonian red fly, and to the Dame Juliana Berners's fly fishing treatise, the verdict is still not out on what a salmon sees with flies. Nevertheless the design of a body with a wing is common to most Atlantic salmon flies of today, from the most simplistic to the most complex.

Through late 1600s Izaak Walton and Colonel Venables perpetuated the use of "gaudy orient" colors that were coming from the Far East. Turkey feather wings eventually were the predecessors all of today's modern hair wings. But as materials became more available from exotic birds from all over the Orient and Europe, the salmon fly evolved to a very complex medley.

It was in the mid- to late-nineteenth century that the magnificent renaissance of the salmon fly took place, as documented by George Mortimer Kelson and his book *The Salmon Fly* (1895). Known as "the high priest of the salmon fly," he brought a system and method to what has become the modern salmon fly and its variations on the theme.

As the British were once again the grand transplants of *Salmo trutta* throughout the world, the leisure time of the British officer allowed them to inspect local hunting and fishing opportunities, and thus discovered exotic birds and animal pelts. In his classic tome on *salar*, Col. Joseph Bates's *Fishing Atlantic Salmon*, looked into the tremendous diversity and beauty of several centuries of the artesian fly endeavors. He beautifully described what then in the past and is still today the crux of the *Salmo salar* fly:

> The classic patterns can be divided into two main groups. One is those addressed to hook salmon— which after all, is really what this is all about. This group is composed of many popular favorites still used today: The Doctors, the Rangers, the Thunder and Lightning, Green Highlander and Silver Gray. The other is those addressed as exhibition fly, sometimes called "vanity patterns." Often composed of rare feathers and complex design. Although these patterns were not necessarily intended to hook salmon,

many of them did. To put things into perspective, in this country around the turn-of-the-century a number of those most complicated patterns, including John Traherne's were offered for sale in fly shops by the dozen for little more than $.60 each. Regardless of whether the flies were intended to catch fish or to catch the favor of *Homo sapiens*, nowadays they catch collectors, who treasure them for their history, their beauty and their intricate construction.

This categorization opened a door for acclaimed salmon ghillies like Jock Scott and fanatical pursuers like Ernest Crosfield, Dr. T. E. Preyce-Tannatt, and Megan Boyd amongst many, to tie lethal patterns that caught fish. But looking back at all the inspired Scottish patterns of the Dee, Spey, and Tay styles, blending with the Ackroyds, it is a color orgasm fusion of artistic perfection, that to the eye of the beholder is sometimes overwhelming.

But to our subject, *Salmo salar*, as to why the fish takes them directly links back to the nexus blood bond of the rivers and of the hardwired *Salmo* predator behavior. Of all the various questions a salmon angler asks when he ties on a fly, the most important one is what exactly is the fish looking for?

## Identifying *Salar's* Ground Zero Preference: Any Color Works As Long As It's Black

One day at that time Robert Honeyman, fisherman at Bemersyde [on the Tweed], came down to the town, and asked my father if he would not come up and have a cast for salmon, as he knew of two or three lying in a stream [meaning a current in the river] which was overlooked by a high bank. He decided to go, and selected three or four flies which Jock had been dressing. "The water was low and clear at the time, so that the fish could be seen at the bottom. From the high bank where Honeyman placed himself he could see all that occurred. On the fly coming within reach of the first fish he gave a shout; the tightened line and boil on the water at the same moment gave the fisher the delightful sensation one feels in well hooking a fish. After landing it, the other two were not long in being laid on the bank." My father was so pleased, that he thought the fly should be named; and none could be more appropriate than the name of the dresser who had been so long in the employment of Lord John Scott."

> —George Forrest of Kelso,
> Scotland *The Fishing Gazette* (1896)

As we have seen with the Michigan and Catskill legacies for brown trout in the new world theatre, the River Tweed in

Scotland was one of those rivers of divine inspiration for the creation of the Atlantic salmon fly and its color dynamics.

The enchanted Tweed runs jagged across the Scottish/English border on its ninety-eight-mile journey to the North Sea. From four hundred million year-old volcanic activity to the more recent glaciation eighteen thousand years ago, the grand divine creator and chiseler carved out the river to form the iconic *Salmo* river adorned with beautiful rock embankment shoulders. Here the Old Redstone, Greywacke, and Cheviots all form an artistic mosaic along the river valley as it ventures to its mouth at Berwick, and opens up the sea to the *salar* journey. It is if the mythical Gaelic gods were watching the river course being carved out to ensure it had a large "S" formation as it emptied into the sea. As local folklore has it, the "S" was a sign to welcome the nomadic Atlantic salmon back home to these most perfect waters.

Along the river's journey, as with most Scotland *salar* rivers, you are fishing through ancient history, as the Scottish moors with their purple heathers are intermingled with pastoral sheep grazing farms, wetlands, and legendary castles like the one at Neidpath, which was attacked by Oliver Cromwell. A short hike will take you to the monument of the greatest Scottish hero, William Wallace, who was the inspiration for Mel Gibson's *Braveheart*. The Tweed has over fifty unique bridges that date back centuries from when the Romans encamped at Trimontium and crossed the river at Drygrange.

The annual return of *salar* to the Tweed was a food source for centuries, not so much today, as the runs have dwindled. There was a time when the smoked, cured and brined pelts of salmon were a delicacy for the Romans. The locals profited highly by sending them to several English kings and aristocracy. But for all symbolic purposes, the Tweed might've been the "ground zero" of the Atlantic salmon fly's color and design by a legendary yet low-profile Scottish ghillie named Jock Scott.

Being a guide/ghillie myself, we are definitely cut from an odd mold. It is as much of a calling as the priesthood, rather than a choice. Many guides and ghillies often talk of "living the dream—or curse." They come in all kinds of sizes, shapes, personalities, and intellects. Some have huge personalities, which I have been known to exude to my customers, as do several others I've met over my decades. Some may look at this as ego as being full of yourself. Yet the more I explore the mystery of why one would waste so much time and energy for such little profit to be a guide or ghillie, it all comes down to extreme passion; it is an addiction for which no cure is known. If Jock Scott fit into a mold it was a very low-profile one.

▲ The charming Scottish highland country side of a salmon river. Credit: Lax-A

Jock was living in the mid-1800s at a time when Victorian society and proper protocol and etiquette was its highest level. River ghillies were often known as rogues or peasants that were good poachers and could find the elusive *salar* and figure out what it was taking, or "gig" it with a gaff hook for the dinner table. Jock was known to be of big heart but not the smartest tool in the box. He was often labeled "somewhat trustworthy," which has described many guides in many different situations—whether it was for fabricating the truth or not showing up on time, etc. He often saw hard times like most guides do because he was so consumed with his passion—thus obviously planning was not his forté.

On a stormy voyage to Norway with Lord John Scott, he obliviously tied Atlantic salmon flies while the ship was almost destroyed by violent capsizing waves. The Lord himself commented that Jock should have been praying as opposed to tying.

Perhaps the greatest salmon fly ever tied, and named after him and his Lord, the Jock Scott is an amazing work of art and efficiency with all the most lethal color combinations that are still extremely effective today, in no matter what design profile. The black body throat and Hackle adorned by red, orange, yellow, with hints of blue and green was a masterpiece for the migratory king of waters.

Scott created a masterpiece not only that had aesthetic beauty, but extremely lethal salmon-taking color capabilities. There is an old saying among *Salmo* guides, whether you're on the hunt for salmon or brown trout, and it often is uttered as fly boxes are ready to be opened. As the fly choice for a first presentation is made, I can't tell you how many times I've heard the following come out of a ghillie's mouth: "any color will work as long as it's black!" Since that declaration could determine one's bucket list vacation of a lifetime, or whether a guide will be able to pay his bills and feed his family, the color black should have a monument built all unto itself in the angling world.

In hindsight, I look back on my first visit to the brown trout–rich Big Hole River in Montana, as I was armed with an arsenal of every fly and streamer known to mankind. I recall my enthusiastic young guide for the day, who didn't

▲ Jim Haswell's masterfully-tied Jock Scott. Credit: Jim Haswell

seem to be extremely knowledgeable, but knew where the leviathan *truttas* lurked. The first thing he uttered was, "put a black woolly bugger on."

This constant black fly motif again repeats itself constantly on the wonderful Atlantic salmon rivers of the magnificent Gaspé of Québec or Norway's Gaula and Alta. With legendary rivers such as the Grand Cascapedia, the Bonaventure, York, St. Jean, and so many more, any fly will work as long as it is black, the guides kept telling me. "Put on a John Olin—or an Undertaker," will be a common suggestion. Upon my inaugural visit, I had no idea what a John Olin was. It was a simple black fly with a gold body, silver tag, and yellow tail. It could be the crudest hair-winged double-hook concoction tied in two minutes, or a more elaborate and detailed tie, it didn't really matter. Later that I found out John Olin was a philanthropist, former honoree of the Atlantic Salmon Federation, and founder of Olin chemical. He used one fly exclusively in his quest for Grand Cascapedia giant *salars* up to forty pounds, which he caught on his fly. One cannot argue with that success. But to crack the black code we must search deeper to distant waters offshore, and also poke around in the gravel backyard of the natal river home of both *salar* and *trutta*.

## Cracking the Black Code

As we have seen, the common thread in the significant *Salmo* relationship between browns and Atlantic salmon is that they are known to be elite kill artist predators. And most of the time they rely on their sensory capacities to target their prey, much as do sharks. For instance, studies conducted on sticklebacks have shown that a red car going past an aquarium tank will stimulate the fish, which can be attributed to a correlation between male sticklebacks' red bellies, which indicate arousal and sexual aggression. The colors red and orange stimulate aggressive responses to the optic nerve of salmon, trout, and char. But what is important to note when looking at a very complex fly pattern such as a Jock Scott, is how the blending of all those colors will produce a hue or tonal effect to the general impression that eventually reaches a *salar*'s brain. Black is the least translucent color, which casts the best silhouette, and is clearly the most visible color for fish at any depth.

Since the inspired Jock Scott, so many subsequent flies have sported a similar color motif. Feather and hair wings like the Black Dose, The Sir Richard, Syd Glasso's Ballyshannon, Crosfield's Black Silk, the Dusty Miller, just to name a few, incorporate a black under tone background theme with Jock Scott–like color. The early Spey and Akroyds incorporate a dark/black theme like the Lady Caroline, Grey Heron, the Carron, etc.

Perhaps the deadliest modern-day fly on the Jock Scott dark/fluorescent/reddish spectrum is the Willie Gunn,

invented by the Scottish ghillie of the same name. It is particularly lethal in the dark, tannin-stained waters of Scandinavia, Scotland, and Russia. Along that theme, The Lord Mayor of London fly by Megan Boyd similarly employs that powerful orange-yellow spectrum. They are now tied in hair wings and tube designs and as Temple Dog designs, in which the hair is tied forward and then reversed and tied back for translucence, volume, movement, and water displacement. Today's modern guides carry boxes of them.

In those same boxes you will find another equally-lethal fly based on the same color motif, the Undertaker, tied by Warren Duncan of St. John, New Brunswick. If you die and go to *salar* heaven, and had but two flies to choose from for eternity, it would be the Undertaker and the Blue Charm. Along the blue-green spectrum the Blue Charm with its affiliates the Hairy Mary, Laxa Blue, Sheep series, Crosfield, and of course the Green Highlander, are our favorite early-season flies when fresh salmon arrive from the salt.

## Natal River Black Genesis

In their indigenous habitats of the Eastern Hemisphere, the "Atlantic trouts," as we have discussed earlier, browns and Atlantics, share similar river waters through spatial niche separation. When you catch brown trout and Atlantic salmon in the same river around the ten-inch size for instance, they almost look identical. Even an expert would be hard pressed to tell the difference. Since Atlantic salmon can spend anywhere from two to five years before smolting to the oceans, lakes, or seas, their day-to-day foraging behavior is almost identical to that of a brown trout. Although *salar*'s pectoral fins allow them to hold in much faster, more turbulent, and highly-oxygenated waters, and and they take up unique holding positions in the river systems, they are at this stage of their development pretty much the same foraging fish.

As *Salmo* have an affinity toward food on the water surface, the objects that show up best against a very bright sky or even in low light conditions are of particular interest to them, and black objects distinguish that silhouette better than any color. In the case of pre-smolt salmon parr of several year classes, they take up the faster turbulent lies due to their need for food, versus the returning adult's preference for slower, deeper pools. The spatial separation allows them to compete in the lie hierarchy survival. It is here we find the first indications of the black *Salmo* color code as an optic cue for food.

Prey confidence and conditioning comes in phases. As young *Salmo* fry hatch and emerge from fall and winter spawning efforts, the dark midges of spring and early summer, like the black Simulium of Iceland's Lake Myvtan and Big Laxa River, are their first food forms. Every time they

▲ This twenty-pound Michigan *salar* didn't fancy the dark color and provocative silhouette of this Green Butt Candy-Cane fly and crushed it! Credit: author

turn or rise to take a pupae or adult, the grayish-black theme becomes more ingrained. Later, emerging mayfly, stonefly, and caddis nymphs and larvae continue to condition the color response. Though many of the adult aquatic insects may turn different shades of light color such as white, yellow, and bright green, most nymphs and larvae are darker in color. Except for the East Coast Atlantic salmon river's bright green stone, which Lee Wulff imitated with his surface stone, or bright green *Rhyacophila* caddis larvae, 90 percent of the food spectrum is still dark; thus black is the ultimate *salar* fly color choice.

For the brown trout, which is a lover of dark boulder/rock hidden spaces and deep undercut banks due to its photophobic light sensitivity, things appear black deeper and with less light, which is the preferred predatory domain for *trutta*. Also, given his negative phototropic eye sensitivity, a study to determine how that determines a brown trout's orientation toward the black color spectrum would be amazing if it could be proven and accomplished. For now,

when a brown hammers a black sculpin or woolly bugger, it is sufficient scientific study for most anglers demonstrating the brown trout's strong affinity for this color.

Notwithstanding the fact that they will take all other colors, from olives to the lighter yellows and whites, in my experience there is much more hesitation and uncertainty when fishing these color combinations versus the reliable black.

## The Sargasso Eel Connection

Every gourmand, chef, fisherman, ghillie, farmer, you name it, knows how good eels are to eat. As a little boy we speared them on small tidal creeks along the Baltic in Poland. They were delicious smoked, grilled, or pickled like herring.

The Sargasso Sea, close to one thousand miles off the coast of Florida south of Bermuda, has an annual eel festival. It is a breeding orgy of these slimy creatures. Once the adults die off, the eggs drift forever into the Gulf

Stream and spew into the North Atlantic, then drift into the Davis Strait between Labrador and Greenland. Hatching into tiny black elvers in a couple years, the biological drift in this Gulf Stream is massive. They smack directly into the faces of migrating and newly arrived oceangoing salmon—either smolts or post-spawn adults returning to their feeding grounds. To say they feast on these would be an understatement.

Atlantic salmon and brown trout have one more common denominator in predatory foraging—an opportunistic orientation toward easy prey. Although silvery pelagic fish are high on their diets, the amount of work and energy expended to catch them must be significant. Just as a large stream brown gets lazy and ambushes a sculpin, mouse, or small animal by an undercut bank at nighttime, so will the Atlantics chow on anything that doesn't put them in competition with more ravenous killer hunters of the ocean like orcas, sharks, tuna, and anything that could put the big hurt on a nice delectable *Salmo salar*.

Thus many salmon-fly experts have always alluded to the elvers hatch as another black imprinting color factor—it makes sense and is tough to ignore. From my theory of foraging color preference building in stages, it fits nicely. One of my most deadly Atlantic salmon flies, the black leech Electric Candy Cane, has become a killer for Atlantic salmon on the Grand Cascapedia, and I eventually confirmed its value and lethality on my landlocked Michigan Atlantics.

But let's look at lamprey eels. This is a whole different beast, common throughout the North Atlantic, including the Baltic Sea. It is anadromous and runs into the freshwater rivers to spawn in the springtime. There is a huge problem with them in the Great Lakes system, since the Welland Canal was built and brought the lampreys from the Atlantic and Sea of St. Lawrence. In the new Atlantic salmon frontier of Michigan's Lake Huron, landlocked Atlantic salmon are big targets for the lamprey, which attach directly to the fish to suck blood and body fluids until the fish is dead. *Salar* are particularly vulnerable prey, as are all salmonids.

My experience with fishing large black leech patterns for *salar* has been a rod-jolting strike experience. It is as if almost they want to kill and crush it in retribution; they strike a black leech with firm conviction. Perhaps they realize the mortality implications of the parasite and their simultaneous migratory run with Atlantics in springtime rivers.

### The High Seas Predatory Hunting Ground

The dark and mysterious big ocean and sea hunting grounds of *salar* still remains quite the mystery for biologists. But due to modern technology, GPS radio tagging has indicated some of their migratory routes, and we now know that the main feeding grounds are often Greenland and the Faroe Islands and through the Baltic Sea. But it is still unknown how Atlantics use their predatory tactical skills on a day-to-day basis in this treacherous predator / prey environment. Just as brown trout become shy and elusive in the river systems as they try to maximize size and energy, the Atlantics also go about a certain degree of inconspicuous foraging in the nomadic high seas.

Foraging in the pelagic zones is the key for growth and energy maximization. Different prey occupy the seven different types of pelagic zones that go all the way down to the benthic area of total darkness. Light in these areas transitions along the blue-to-green spectrum, starting with light blue, medium, dark blue, and finally the grays and purples and into darkness. As we'll discuss later with salmon fly design, the blue and green spectrum has a strong influence on how Atlantics perceive their prey, which affects fly designs.

In the ocean Atlantic salmon feed opportunistically on various small mesopelagic fishes such as lantern fish, perlside, and barracudinas. They also take larger pelagic fish such as Atlantic herring, blue whiting, sand eels, sprat, capelin, and mackerel. Furthermore, they feed on squids, jellyfish, and all types of crustaceans and shrimps.

—Jonsson & Jonsson,
*The Ecology of Atlantic Salmon and Brown Trout*

Though *salar* can maintain attack speeds of up to twenty-seven miles per hour, and have the ability to hunt in packs, they come up from down under baitfish schools and push their bodies upward to slam and stun their prey, only to come back and pick up the disoriented and injured victims. Thus, hunting in the blue/green spectrum orients their optic focus in the open waters. However, they can also hunt in the darker mesopelagic spectrum for slower-moving lantern fish, which can form the bulk of a three-year class salmon's diet.

Vision acuity is a function of light variation and how much a salmonid exercises its variances and extremes. In the big oceans, Atlantics are all over the map in hunting capacity. They can dive down to depths of one thousand feet to hunt benthic crustacean/squid and diverse food forms when pelagic fish like herring/capelin are scarce and hard to find. All benthic food forms possess a chemical process known as bioluminescence, in places where light doesn't exist.

Atlantic salmon like to hunt in the upper surface waters where eutrophic nutrients are highest, along with pelagic baitfish, thus white streamers imitating baitfish are deadly as fresh Atlantics return to the rivers. Besides sardines, small sea urchins, crabs, jellyfish, etc., are also abundant

▲ *Salar's* male kypes are extraordinary prehistoric morphological masterpieces. Credit: Author

in the pelagic. For Atlantic salmon to go down to extreme depths to hunt, they must have amazing adjustments in their vision capabilities, which fuses with their sensory vibration perception for killer accuracy. In comparison, the relatively shallow world of a sixteen-foot deep river pool is really not that deep when compared to ocean depths. We frequently fail to compare the two ecosystems or consider the disorientation of fresh-run salmon into the rivers, who do not fully acclimate to them until later in the summer.

### River Color Phases:
### New Arrivals to Sexual Aggression

Fly selection is perhaps the most important aspect of fishing for fresh-run Atlantic salmon. Scientific studies have shown that fresh fish in from the sea, dripping with sea lice and tapeworms, show a particular preference for the blue/green light spectrum of colors, a function of its sea life from hunting the pelagic zones in the blue-green spectrum. This would explain why Green Highlanders, Blue Charms, and Sunray Shadows produce well at this time of the year.

Further studies have shown that as the salmon pod up in incubator pools to slowly grow their gravid milt and egg production, they shift to an attraction toward the black/ red /yellow/ orange color spectrums. This could be a function of two separate stimuli. The great majority of Atlantic salmon rivers run dark with a tea-stained tannic color. These conditions would greatly promote the color spectrum I just described.

Though in a minority, volcanic rock/calcium carbonate oligotrophic rivers such as the St. Jean, Pabos, and Grande Riviere of Canada's Gaspé, along with some of Iceland's and Europe's rivers, have few deciduous or marl bog influences. Thus they remain in the bluish/green pelagic zone water spectrum where green and blue flies are highly effective.

But as an Atlantic salmon's temperament in September/October and late fall turns entirely toward procreation, orange/red motif flies become deadly. These colors become extremely irritating during this stage of a salmon's physiology, as highly aroused salmon pool up in tight, competitive, pre-spawning river niches. At this time the

General Practitioner, Alley's Shrimp, Red Francis, and Doddi Orange are all extremely effective.

## The Complete Four-Phase Salmon Fly

By going through the various *salar* developmental stages and their corresponding colors, light levels, and feeding opportunities, it appears that salmon flies can be organized into three basic categories, with the color black being a common theme in each. Let's also look at the naturalistic side of this equation. Lee Wulff's amazingly lethal Ghost Green stonefly, as well as its many variations, is a surface-oriented parachute fly with a bright green body that consistently produces bright sea-run salmon. Starting in June a green stonefly—*Chloroperlidae*—emerges in good numbers on the northeastern Appalachian rivers extending to the tip of Gaspé. Does this natural emergence coincide with the blue/green vision spectrum of the Atlantics vision at this time, or does the natural itself do the job of stimulating the take? Or again, to play the devil's advocate, are the bluish/green waters of Québec's Grande Riviere, St. Jean, etc. part of the vision and fly preference equation? Regardless, we have green fly creations like the Pompier, Butterfly Green Machine, and others, and only salmon can tell us the exact reason why these patterns are so effective. The fact is, these flies catch fish!

Again on the naturalistic side of presentation, patterns like the Magog smelt, white and dark Wulff Muddlers, and the Alley's Shrimp, often resemble the baitfish and Crustacea that Atlantics encounter in the estuaries prior to river migration. If you ask any guy in the Canadian Maritimes about his or her "go-to fly," they will always tell you that it's a muddler. The silhouette of this fly resembles the sculpin baitfish/goby/stickleback that Atlantics can encounter as they approach the fresh water/salt water salinity estuaries, where these benthic fish love to hang out in the springtime, where warmer river waters heat up the colder estuaries, which also attracts baitfish schools.

## *Salar* Whisperings: Facts and Myths Debunked

**FACT:** Atlantic salmon want something they can't have!
The more obscure, elusive, exotic, bizarre etc., the fly presentation opportunity becomes, the better the chances for a hookup. I know this sounds quite strange, but when you least expect it, and you have given up on casting, the fish will take your fly, when it should not have. Their strong will to operate solely and obliviously to angler's presentations, only to turn on in a heartbeat, or when you're stripping your fly back to call it quits for the day, is usually the norm when fishing for Atlantics—or to take a totally unconventional fly pattern!

**FACT:** Atlantics are extremely surface oriented.
Again on this *Salmo* motif, similar to a brown trout, no one will argue this ageless personality disposition. We can only speculate about a variety of reasons for this behavior, so I will do my best to explain.

From the time they are born in the river to becoming small parr, their pectoral fins are a vital part of their physiology. These fins help them to jump incredibly high waterfalls and obstacles unimaginable by other salmonids, and allow them to anchor on to holding positions in very fast boulder-strewn rapids and runs that not many other fish could command. The love for faster, shallower, oxygenated, boulder/pocket water begins when the fish are parr, where surface orientation provides several benefits.

Here is where a good deal and majority of the aquatic insect life occurs. Hatching, egg laying, and darting nymphs and larvae are always present throughout the Atlantic salmon's juvenile river environment. From a survival standpoint, it also keeps them out of the larger deeper pools that are dominated by the Alpha salmon adults, and sea-run trout, and other native predatory species like native brown and brook trout. Here Atlantic salmon parr can be made a quick meal.

Thanks to the strongly programed and evolutionarily significant "life survival strategy," constantly referred to by John Malcolm Elliott in his excellent work, *Quantitative Ecology and the Brown Trout*, young-of-the-year salmon can survive due to this distancing from all its predators. In the lifecycle strategy, reproductive traits in populations such as brood size, size of young, distribution, growth, and survival all interact. Thus "looking up" behavior is learned behavior that is genetically transmitted due to spatial occupation. Given shallower water lies, predators from above like birds of prey—osprey, kingfishers, hawks, and eagles, etc.—tunes the young salmon's eyes to incoming predators, and also on the hunt for surface prey like hatching mayflies, stoneflies, caddis, or smaller minnows searching for the same.

**FACT:** Most Atlantic salmon are early migrating river runners.

Except for very short systems close to the ocean and lakes for landlocked Atlantic salmon, most fish start up the river systems as early as March for spawning in the fall and early winter. This lengthy "settling in" period to the river and pool life allows the fish to ponder and become selective; they have a lot of time to think about stuff, to put it simply. Given their already high level of curiosity, this circumstance makes them take the fly often enough to be a prize game fish. Late-running fish are still takers, but tend to get on with spawning activity more abruptly, since time is of the issue.

**FACT:** Atlantic salmon fly fishing is a study of time and patience.

This single factor is usually why many anglers are called yet few are chosen to experience the *take*, giving way to frustration when anglers describe their last salmon trip.

Often at angler's club meetings, I hear the expression at cocktail hour: "I fished for Atlantics once"—with the emphasis on "once!" But due to the fast, capricious arsenal of selectivity Atlantic salmon display, they will take the fly on their terms. For the numbers game, anglers are off with stripers off the Atlantic or Jackson Hole cut-throat trout.

## The Stratum Approach to Presentation: *Salar* Psychology 101

In modern Atlantic salmon fly fishing, there are basically four tiers of fly presentation. They are:

1. The classic wet-fly swing
2. The meniscus riffle hitch and mid-depth rubber legs
3. The surface dry
4. Deep-dredging "roadkill" streamers

Modern-day *salar* anglers have expanded the repertoire tremendously in the last few decades to incorporate unorthodox techniques that would have been frowned and scowled upon by the stoic high priests of *salar* tradition—which perhaps can be the most elitist of all fly fishing sanctums.

I was quite fortunate to be in at the beginning stage of the weird roadkill-and-rubber-legs phenomenon. Being a brown trout and Atlantic salmon guide for twenty years, and having fished for them for fifty-two, I have a lot of mileage under my belt. When confronted with the day-to-day tedium that *salar* can inflict upon its pursuers, one must think outside the box and sometimes apply unconventional tactics. I have never been a sheep with a fly rod following other sheep with fly rods. Presenting new flies and techniques to Atlantic salmon and treating them just like brown trout, is what I identify as a *Salmo* nexus. I cannot tell you how many new patterns I have developed with my fly tying travel kit at lodges throughout the world when nothing else was working.

## The Salmon Lodge Dynamics

Atlantic salmon are in the river systems to procreate and head back to the feeding grounds as soon as they can.

The fact that they take a fly is truly a mystical experience in itself. Having an innately brown trout mindset and predatory disposition, once back in its spawning grounds, the oceangoing Atlantic salmon quickly revert to being inquisitive, finicky, and playful *trutta*-like sporting creatures. Fishing the same traditional fly patterns, which ghillies and classic Atlantic salmon fishermen do, often habituates the fish to those patterns, and decreases their effectiveness.

Most Atlantic salmon in the top beat pools get too much attention from guides, anglers, and lodges after a few weeks. Once the fish are caught or pulverized to death by sloppy casts, guides will become bored to tears by the same stale traditional presentations. When you watch salmon all pooled up by the hundreds in these deep, cool incubator pools, you often see the males and females with their cotton candy mouths open wide and then close, as if they were yawning from sheer boredom. From a scientific standpoint this is surely a morphological result of cartilage growing and expanding, and also the need to take in more oxygen, especially later in the summer. Fortunately for our amusement, these "yawning/boredom" signals align with the time of year they are least likely to take your fly, leading many salmon fly anglers and guests at the Lodge to scratch their heads in frustration.

The mix of people at the classic salmon/trout lodge is truly enlightening; the allure and excitement of catching a *Salmo* on the fly brings all these different people together. Here you have the well-to-do aristocrats, who are usually stoic traditionalists. The nouveau riche, who just made a bunch of money on a new software company or stock market, will have been told about the most prized noble gamefish in the world and therefore they must catch it. Also, you have hard-core Atlantic salmon junkies/

passionate guides like myself who will whore themselves for any opportunity to get on a world-class Atlantic salmon river. Then there is the "bucket list brigade," who have had *salar* on their radar all their life, and want to add them to their list of species caught on the fly.

Finally, there are the spouses that have come along for the food and beautiful scenery, and are usually the ones that get the most attention from the Lodge guides and ghillies, since they are usually attractive. Usually their lack of familiarity and amateurish proficiency usually gets them the top catch. Much of this is not due to sheer dumb luck, but because of their open-mindedness and the habit of listening closely to their guides.

Conversely, the more experienced anglers often brush aside guides due to their know-enough-to-be-dangerous egos, stacked fly boxes, fancy equipment, and their "been-there, done-that" attitudes. These are almost always the most difficult pain-in-the-ass clients to guide, and present a challenge to justify and validate the techniques the ghillie is advocating. Most guides run from them with their tails between their legs, but I find them very intriguing. I always tell salmon ghillies that if you are tough enough, smart, creative, and are always thinking outside the box, you can hit a grand slam with these obstinate clients when you present a new fly technique and catch the lodge's biggest salmon of the year.

The late-night after-dinner hour at a salmon lodge when the scotch, fine wines, martinis, and fine local brews are flowing can be intriguing, even fascinating. The proverbial "When I!" tales (each discussion starts with "When I . . .") fuel the conversations about grand world travel, exploits, intriguing tales of heroism, the giants that got away, fatal encounters with wild animals—are all told in the finest British smoking parlor tradition. It is often after the clients have had a little too much alcohol that the bullshit detector starts ticking and squawking erratically. The tales of the eighteen-pounders start becoming thirty-pounders, and discordant chirps of frustration start to sound, such as "Why the hell did I spend so much money on such a world-class bucket list destination when I'm not catching anything?" I have heard that confession over and over again at just about every salmon lodge in the world . . . except Iceland and Russia.

But the mind boggling *Salmo* utopia of Russia is totally in its own fantasy land. Here, due to the rivers' extreme seclusion in pristine wilderness, and the fact that the pools are just jammed full of several spawning year classes, the competitive niche hierarchy dominance behavior pushes the fish to aggressive taking modes almost all the time. Lodge guests subsequently log in double digit hook-up days, versus the occasional one or two here and there in mainland Europe, the UK, or in the Canadian Maritimes.

## Chronic Casting Syndrome

One common denominator that must be fully emphasized is to spend more time observing and less time casting. This is a common approach the lethal brown trout angler will take in order to observe foraging predator profiles on clear waters. Unless you are employing a Euro nymphing/mine sweeping/dredge casting technique, especially on fast tannic waters where this technique is highly effective, observing your prey will allow you to notice many subtleties not revealed to sufferers of chronic casting syndrome. Just as you don't sit in a duck blind or big-game tree stand and shoot your gun constantly to attract your victim, so also stalking and observing must be applied to the salmon game especially in highly visible waters like the Bonaventure.

This will often go against the grain of what your guide or peer group would like you to pursue. Guides get paid for you standing in a river, casting like fool, for the chance of hooking a fish. There are a set number of hours in the day that you must perform the task, and as old saying, goes, "You can't catch a fish if your line isn't in the water." But this flailing works against you in the *Salmo* realm, as the fish will habituate to your continual presentation of the same fly, to the same spot, from the same point of origination.

I'm sure that a guide driving his truck to the same pool day after day, slamming the car doors and trunk shut, or dropping anchor in the same spots, day after day, conditions the fish. I have been accused of overthinking and giving too much credit to the fish's degree of perception. But the lack of thinking, common sense, and respect for these animals' wariness, is unfortunately why many people don't catch fish. Keep in mind the *salar* in those runs really don't want you there or care if you are, since they have bigger fish to fry.

Yet for whatever reason they will on the rare occasion take your fly, whether through constant irritation, aggression, or an ingrained predatory response. In my experience this is usually novel and a time when you least expect it. One story dear to my heart that describes this angler/fish habituation took place on the Grand Pabos River on Québec's Gaspé, in a *salar* episode I like to call "never say never."

It was a brutally hot and dry early September at the former Malbaie Lodge, owned by my friend Bill Greiner. Temperatures soared into the low nineties, setting early September records on what would already normally be a period of rain and cooler weather. The York, Dartmouth, St. Jean, and Grande Riviere had abnormally higher-than-normal water temperatures and negligible, trickling flows. Needless to say they were not giving up fish to the fly. To have one or two fish caught a day amongst fourteen rods

▲ A size 14 tiny treble tube fooled this beast. Credit: Lax-A

along five prime rivers, with most days having no fish at all, was simply pathetic.

Lodge owner Bill Greiner asked me if I would like to go check out the Pabos rivers since he had permits to fish those beats, but no one wanted to drive the longer distance or spend the time on rivers that were producing zero fish. To me, when a guide says, "Nobody catching fish there," it is music to my twisted ears.

"Are there fish in the pools, Bill?" I asked.

"Hell yeah—there are some beasts up to thirty pounds. You'll see them, but good luck trying to catch one. I have never seen them so dour."

This sounded like a job for thinking outside the box, which is what draws me to the sport; the Pabos system is almost purely spring-fed, and the water temperatures there must be colder than the rest. Getting in the vehicle with my trusty ghillie, I took the challenge to crack the code, which I thought must definitely be a presentation problem.

Arriving at the beat known as Arrowhead, the pool was actually loaded with salmon, some beasts in the twenty-five-to-thirty-pound range. With the water as low as it was, the moment we approached the pool, we jostled and startled the pod of fish, but the water was ice cold, just as I predicted.

"Matt, stand here and make your cast from this rock," Gordie guided me. The bubble line or current flow was totally inverted from the last time I fished it several years ago. I was already dubious since I already envisioned my line would pass through a slack eddy, creating no movement to the swing.

"This isn't going to work, Gordie. I'm going a little way up through the riffle to cross the pool and fish it from the other side, where the current is flowing."

"Oh no, you never fish this pool from the other side, no one ever does that! Austin, our head guide, always says to fish this pool from this spot."

"Well hell! That explains why no one has caught a fish from this pool all summer!" I shot back.

Atlantic salmon guides are creatures of habit all over the world no matter where you find them. They have their handful of flies that produce consistently on each of the rivers, take their lunch breaks at a certain sacred time, have you back to the lodge for dinner at a certain time. To survive four straight months of seven days a week guiding, as a ghillie you must be on a rigorous schedule. As someone who has guided up to three hundred days a year, I know the gig. But here was not a time or place to say the word "never."

I crossed the river, told my wife to man the tripod and camera, and get ready—I had a feeling things were about to explode from the lovesick *salar* in this pool. After sitting down, smoking a cigar, and just watching the fish and the current play out, I was ready to take aim and fire.

I tied on a red Francis, a prawn imitation, since it has the red and orange color spectrum suitable this time of year. On my first swing close to shore a good-sized Atlantic broke out of the school and chased the fly to my rod tip. Wow, I hadn't seen such behavior since I fished the Ponoi in Russia! When I screamed out what just happened, Gordy shouted, "Oh no, that can't be!" But surely it was, and on the third cast a twenty-two-pound kype-jawed male slammed the Francis, went aerial, and had the reel screaming into overdrive as I ran down the bank to chase it with my tailing glove. After all was said and done, I was elated and euphoric, Laurie was busy snapping away on the Nikon, and Gordie stood in disbelief.

That afternoon I brought close to two dozen fish to swipe or chase the fly, caught my brace—the second fish was a beast of twenty-eight pounds—and released them. Here was a classic example where breaking with convention saved the day: "never say never." When I came back to the lodge for dinner and my digital Nikon was full of images I was definitely an instant hero for the lodge

owner Bill. The next day everyone left the lodge with a red Francis that I individually tied for a very premium price. There was a new sense of hope in the air, versus the despair, long faces, and negative attitudes of the previous nights' cocktail hours.

## The Classic Wet-Fly Swing

This basic technique, dating back centuries and described in accounts such as the red fly of Macedonia and by Dame Juliana, is a pure coincidence of river current acting as tension against the line. The "sit-and-wait" positions *Salmo* like to hold in are perfectly suited for a "track-it-and-take-it" technique, which elicits a strike to a broadside swinging fly. When fishing blind, which occurs on many larger tannin-stained salmon rivers, this technique will cover every inch of the water from shore to shore if properly executed.

"One good strip, then one step," my Micmac Indian guide, Paul would say over and over again when presented with my overzealous double hauling to the other bank immediately upon wetting my waders. Starting close to shore and progressively working your way out to the other bank, you cast in a 45 degree angle as the line will be creating belly, leading broadside across the current to finally end up in a straight line below you. The speed of the fly will usually hook the fish by itself, resulting in a gentle

▲ Sweeping a wet fly, the author covers an entire pool and can pique the interest of fish whether they be at the head, midsection, or shallow tailouts of a pool.
Credit: Laurie Supinski

tightening of the rod in a low profile. A "slip loop" of line pinched between the fingers allows for shock absorption, if you strike too hard.

Paul's suggestion to strip off a foot of line off the reel and take a step down progressively covers all the water and every holding that they can exist in a pool. Keep in mind that Atlantic salmon tend to be suspended in the pool, hence they don't take up "tight" choice lies beside rocks, obstructions, or in gravel pocket buckets like browns do, hence *salar* only use structure for hydrodynamic flow regulation and spatial separation.

There are some important things to note when executing the wet fly drift. Make sure your cast completely straightens out and hangs below you, for often the salmon, or a brown, will move a considerable distance to hunt it down and take it just as it's turning straight upstream, the straight-line drift is completed, and the fly sweeps to the surface. This is the Leisenring lift trigger that we talked about in the brown trout tactics section. Here the fish will swipe at the fly just as it's getting away from its normal trajectory and begins to turn upstream. This is the "take it before it gets away" response predatory hunting characteristic of *Salmo*. Sometimes they will take the fly just as it hits the water and starts to swing, but mostly through the mid-swing as it is sweeping broadside through the pool and running past the snouts of the snooty *salars*.

It is important that you cover the whole pool, since the taking fish can be either higher up or toward the lower section. After covering the entire pool, switch flies and do it again.

The straight-line "hang time," just as in swinging for steelhead, can produce results by horizontally pumping the rod back and forth creates a jigging motion for a few seconds, which may entice a potential taker that was previously unwilling to commit. Where allowed by law, various intermediate sink lines can be employed if the salmon are holding at deeper depths, or this can be accomplished by using heavy wire Jackson/Bartleet hooks and upstream mending.

If a fish rises to the fly on the swing and boils to the surface, this is a good thing, especially when fishing larger tannin-stained rivers. This can either be a result of a fish refusing the fly at the last split-second for whatever apparent reason, a fish missing the fly, or the fish playing with the fly, which believe it or not happens more than we care to admit. Often they will poke at it with their noses or tails, or tail-slap it just as they do pelagic sardine prey in the ocean.

When these occurrences happen, the angler and ghillie must take a gamble and employ one of several tactics. The first would be to cast the fly immediately to the same target area and hope for a hookup, which I have experienced. Another would be to immediately change flies to another similar style upon the next cast. Size down your fly and fish something either much brighter or much drabber in color tone and hue. Or what has usually worked the best for me, is to sit down and take a break for a few minutes and let the fish think about what just happened. Often like a sulking dog that has just been refused a treat, the very next fresh cast after a short delay has a very good chance of producing a strike.

In very clear pools like you have in Québec, Iceland, or Spain, you and your ghillie can "spot fish" certain fish in certain pods and schools of pools. With a high observation point, the ghillie and you can watch the interaction of the fish in the pool. Most pods of fish stay in the bubble line main current in a carefully-maintained and tight-knit pod profile with uniform spatial separation. The potential "taker" fish will often display nervousness, trouble instigating with other members of the pod, or will change positions from the top of the pool to the bottom of the pool. These indicate the most curious sorts who are the most conducive to taking your fly. These can usually be smaller aggressive males or females that don't fit into the Alpha hierarchy pecking order. But any size fish can take your fly at any time.

In "spot drifting," the angler presents the fly above a potential target fish, swings the fly past it, and allows the fly to swing another for three yards, before picking up and repeating the process. This ensures that the "follow-and-grab" take can occur, which is common for *Salmo*. The ideal scenario is to have someone watch how your fly is presented and to watch how the fish reacts to it. If the fish shows interest by moving its pectoral fins with a slight sideward movement, or rises to the fly but refuses it, repeat the steps listed above.

We often prematurely lift the fly out of water to start another swing. This is a problem particularly later in the season when fish are sometimes slower to react and more deliberate. In some cases they have been known to take a fly at the last second even when it's moving ten feet away from them. These late fish are an incredible joy to watch and are characteristically often blown by the early hook set, since we see the fish coming in for a good distance, only to strike too quickly.

Remember that *salar* and large predator browns like prey that are moving away from it towards the surface, and can often chase these things from a considerable distance away. That is why blind fishing usually has the best hooking results; the angler doesn't force error into the presentation by either premature hook sets, or by impatience when allowing the swing to unfold and hang, which can trigger "late fish" responses. At what speed the fly is swinging can be paramount to the salmon's take. Most ocean and landlocked salmon in pools prefer a steady, deliberate, unchanged velocity. Erratic changes, stutters, and stops are

▲ *Salmo* worldwide favor calcareous rock for incubator/holding pools for depth and ledge undercuts. Credit: Lax-A

not conducive for the classic wet-fly technique. We will discuss how to use these to our advantage later.

In basic terms, the fly is speeded up by lowering the rod tip or moving it upstream. Allowing the rod tip to rise and point downstream directly will slow down the swing. Mending the rod up or downstream in a series of simple stack mends can produce speed changes and depth suspension.

But be careful with having too much unnecessary movement to your fly presentation. There is a new school of thought that twitching or jigging the fly produces more results with *salar*. As I have discussed in a previous chapter on brown trout wet fly swinging and the "Parkinson's twitch," where a steady pulsating twitching action gives much life to a fly imitating an emerging insect or baitfish, when it comes to salmon the jury will always be out on this technique. Some swear by it, others like myself have never had success with it on a consistent basis. Adding the occasional short/tight strip to accelerate the broadside swinging fly or at the final downstream straight-line, has enticed a reluctant salmon in uncertain holding lies, but more often than not, it turns them off for whatever reason.

### Meniscus Commotion: Riffle Hitch and Rubber Legs

As when discussing *trutta* tactics, I often mention the meniscus, since our so-called surface presentations often ride flush in the film or slightly below it. The impression the fly has on, or in, the surface, with its hackles, shape, tone and silhouette, most notably creates an interesting perspective due to refraction, which changes in the eye of the beholding *Salmo* when viewed from various depths below it, or from the side.

The mirror of the meniscus and how motion and light can distort it, for instance in the V-shaped wake of the riffling hitch, can rouse Atlantic salmon or brown trout into taking your topwater offering. Enter here one of the most deadly forms of fly presentation—the Riffling Hitch.

*Salmo* are generally very fond of the motion/commotion gig. They are usually the first ones to check out something and quickly verify its authenticity or appeal, although this motion may also make them quickly refuse something. Their affinity for looking up at things in the surface that create a movement, as with the riffling hitch, can be just the thing to crack the *Salmo* conundrum.

No one now at Portland Creek claims to have been the originator of the riffling fly, but here is the accepted story. Long ago, warships of the British Navy anchored off the stream, and officers came ashore to fish. They left a few old-style salmon flies, with a heavy loop of twisted gut wrapped to the straight-shanked hook to make the eye. Soft and pliable when in use, the loop enabled the fly to ride more smoothly on its course and avoided the stiffness and canting which occupied any solid attachment of this style leader to the eyed fly. Quickly realizing that a salmon hook on a gut-looped fly was likely to break free, they made sure the fly would stay on by throwing those "hitches" around the shank behind the wrapping.

—Lee Wulff, *The Atlantic Salmon*

As Wulff described it, exciting new techniques such as the Labrador "Portland Hitch," are often born out of necessity using available materials—just as poor Polish mountaineers with no money for tackle developed Euro nymphing.

This is where *salar* fly presentations get exciting, as enticing movement ups the game, rather than a monotonous wet fly swing to cover the water. Adding lifelike movement to imitate insects, crippled baitfish, swimming crustacea, squid, etc., will often elicit salmon takes when nothing else seems to work. On Portland Creek and other Canadian and Icelandic rivers, it is a religion.

Described in its simplest form, the fly and the slanted hitch/knot makes a V-shaped wake along the surface that swings against the current on an upstream trajectory. The current flow is important in order to manipulate the fly; the right amount of current acting against the tippet and fly makes this presentation lethal in the appropriate flows. Flies in slack or still water can only be V-shaped, waked by manipulating the rod movement upward to cause tension and by steering the fly through the surface.

Lee's riffle-hitch revelation happened by accident. Lee was fishing with a leader that had a thick blood knot above the fly. He hadn't clipped the tag ends of the blood knot quite close enough, and the knot created a V-wake on the surface. A salmon came up out of the depths of a Portland Creek pool known as Low Rock and struck the thick blood knot.

My first experience with the "hitch" was when I was a young lad traveling Europe directly after culinary school. I would pick up low-level cooking jobs, mainly bloody jobs such as butchering meat and cleaning smelly shellfish, which prestigious chefs delegated to young apprentices, especially cowboy Americans! Having a Eurail pass allowed access to the rivers, beaches, and mountain resorts of Europe, and there was always some kind of lodge or a resort looking for culinary help, which I targeted for experience, pay, food, and travel.

Since I flew Icelandic airlines and had a layover in Reykjavík, I befriended a chef who knew a wealthy businessman that was part owner of the famous Grimsa Lodge,

designed by architect Ernest Schwiebert. Since it was less than one hundred kilometers from Reykjavík, we took a one-day easy drive to view this beautiful river and maybe get permission to fish it. We were told to ask for a grounds-keeper/caretaker named Olafur, who might get permission to fish at the lodge if it wasn't full of aristocratic investors.

Olafur pointed us to a ghillie who was fishing during his day off, since the lodge was not heavily occupied. Having a good command of the English language like all Icelanders do, he greeted us, offered us a shot of Icelandic vodka out of his pack, and gave me a tiny size 14 double-hooked Black Sheep fly, a favorite on the Grimsa. With a gap between the eye and the tied-off thread finish, he tied on a funky-looking knot that caused a right angle from the leader to the fly. I had never seen this before and asked Gunnar, I believe his name was (forgive me, it's been years), "What sort of knot is that?—my dad taught me salmon Turle knots."

"It's a Portland hitch, made famous by your American *Lax* genius Mr. Wulff. Watch how it wakes the surface—pretty cool, eh? Don't set the hook, eh? The way the fly is hitched the *Lax* will set it by itself. The line will just tighten, and you'll be off in a battle!" Sure enough, after a good twenty minutes of casting I caught my first seven-pound chrome-silver Icelandic grilse with that Black Sheep buried perfectly in the side of its little kyped jaw.

The modern-day guru of Atlantic salmon fishing, once Mr. WULFF passed away in a tragic plane accident, is the magnificently entertaining Art Lee. Each of the pieces he has written over several decades for the *Atlantic Salmon Journal* are all masterpieces. Art's gem on this subject is the little book *Tying and Fishing the Rifling Hitch*. Its beautiful descriptions of how to fish the hitch-type fly are especially useful on the beautiful big waters of the Laxa River in Iceland.

The amazing clarity and smooth, placid surfaces of Iceland's rivers are just like one giant spring creek, and enhance the V-shaped waking motion of the riffle hitch. This presentation perfectly simulates the *diptera* and *tricoptera* hatches that juvenile Atlantics and browns see most often in this river. Without writing a mini book on the subject matter myself, here is a simple description by the always-entertaining Art Lee himself:

The way I remember where to position my hitches (my humble means of spiking the procedure to what's left of my brain) is always to hold my fly facing head-first upstream-to the right if the current is flowing from right to left, to the left if the current is flowing from left to right, and then to place my hitch or hitches on the side of the head facing the stream bank behind me. Normally, but not necessarily if I happen to be wading a lot of River criss-crossings in the course of

▲ Swifter waters can make a hook take and are a component of many successful hookups. Credit: Arni Baldurson/Lax-A

fishing a stretch of water, this is the bank from which I waded into the water in the first place. In other words, forget which the last is or which the right side is, or which the left is or which the right side of your fly is. Too complicated. Instead, just fix in your noggin the direction of stream flow, face the fly upstream, half hitch accordingly, and you can't go wrong.

The hitch technique works very well where the river speed is moderate and has a slick surface that can show the waking motion. You are basically doing a down-and-across wet-fly swing, but the fly swinging creates a V-shaped waking motion on the surface, preferably upstream of a pod of fish that will move to either side, forward, or chase it downstream to crush the fly.

On many deep and fast boulder-filled pocket water rivers like you have in the Gaspé of Québec, Russia, Iceland, and Norway, the Atlantic salmon will hold in deep pockets above and behind, or to the side of boulders later in the summer. These are difficult spots to swing a fly, so using a riffle hitch with larger flies that create more of a

wake is an ideal choice for these waters. Lifting your rod and manipulating the hitch through all the "tongue" and "slosh" eddies created by multi-surface turbulence, makes the fly is very visible as it moves around with undeniable appeal. In these situations the strikes are violent, so use heavier tippets.

When the salmon has "boiled" and shown interest in the fly but didn't take it, many guides will immediately go to the riffle hitch, which usually "seals the deal to the steel."

Lee mentioned his bafflement that the riffle hitch worked so well even in the coldest water and air conditions, a time when one would not think of using a dry fly, which is more suitable for warm water conditions. The riffle hitch has produced over and over again in very nasty, inclement, and windy situations. This is perhaps due to the water surface being stirred up and rippled by the winds and wave action, thus the riffle hitch shows up so much better against the sky silhouette.

For those who have never tried the riffle hitch, go to any trout stream, and tie on a highly buoyant pattern such as a largish elk hair caddis, stimulator, or tarantula.

If the river is flowing from the left to your right, cast downstream at a 45-degree angle, raise your rod tip to elven o'clock, and twitch and jiggle your wrist continuously to make a constant jittering motion, creating V wakes on the surface. This in all practical simplicity is what you are trying to create with the riffle hitch. If that stream has trout in it, and the water is low in summer or early fall, you can bet on it getting aggressive browns to the surface regardless of whether there is a hatch. I have taken some of my biggest browns on stillwater pools, tailwaters, and big freestone streams by using this technique. It works particularly well for brown trout during stonefly and caddis emergence, and also when large mayflies are on the water like *Hexagenia* and *Isonychia*. I often riffle hitch my articulated wiggle nymphs with lethal success, and highly recommend the riffle hitch in brown trout rivers.

Fishing the hitch entails several small details. You can perfect the speed and consistency, even if the water is less than ideal, by manipulating the rod tip. Always choose the smallest and lightest size flies you can get away with; the lightest low-water salmon hooks are ideal. You can hitch tube flies by drilling or punching a hole in the left or right side of the tube and at a right angle below (thick needles or fine nails usually do the trick). I've caught some amazing salmon on tiny greased up size 14–16 tubes. Have flies in a box that are strictly devoted to hitching and that leave plenty of space below the eye of your fly to fasten the hitch. Remember the most critical part of your hitched fly is the wing, so stiffer materials like moose mane, fox, squirrel tail, calf tail, mallard, etc., all work well. The sleekest and simplest fly bodies are perfect to push the current toward the wing and the hitch.

## The Funky Rubber-Legged Gig

Fishing for *salar* can become very boring and monotonous, especially when they are off the bite and in a passive/dormant mode. Good *Salmo* guides always push you to up your game through challenging techniques. If conducted properly, these can result in hookups regardless of the conditions.

My first encounter with the "Rubber Legs" was back in 2003, again with my good friend Bill Greiner of Malbaie Lodge in Gaspé, Québec. These rivers can be brutally tough, especially during the low water and heat wave conditions of August and September. No one is really sure who introduced the first Rubber Legs concoction to *salar*, which was originally a bass and panfish concept. When Bill told me we would be fishing rubber leg patterns on a particularly difficult pool, where the fish had been dour, I thought he was joking. He showed me a handful of seriously crappy-looking flies with chenille bodies, palmered grizzly hackle, and black-and-white barred rubber legs protruding from the sides. Obscene! This was a total affront to the established salmon fly traditions.

Bill laughed as he tied one on my leader, and told me, "We are going to fish it radically different, think of yourself

▲ The author's wife, Laurie Supinski, with a box of delectable rubber legs. Credit: Author

as fishing on *Bass Masters*. You won't believe how these fish target these flies in the big clear pools. They go on the hunt for them like a big brown or muskellunge chasing articulated streamers."

Needless to say I was shocked, but as a guide I'm open-minded to anything. It made perfect sense, since the incubator pools become sexually aggressive and niche territorial dominant areas later in the season. On the more tannic waters of the York, Cascapedia, Restigouche, Matapedia, and Dartmouth, the red/orange/white/ black concoctions seemed to work best. On the extremely clear aqua blue waters of Iceland, Labatt's Blue and Green Rubber Legs flies were the ticket.

Rubber Legs tactics resemble A. H. E. Wood's "greased line" technique, which often included an upstream cast to let the fly sink down and drift naturally as it horizontally skimmed the flanks, went broadside, then down over the pods of salmon. The "patent" technique, developed in 1929 by Col. Thompson on the Restigouche, did the same by allowing large hair-winged flies to undulate as they went downstream like a dead-drifted nymph.

Regardless, the rubber legs technique turns a lot of salmon heads, period. It will move fish on very long chases across a pool, sidewards, and downstream, often right to the tip of your rod before a last-second refusal. You will get more refusals and looks than you could possibly imagine with this technique, which is exciting in itself, since many of the followers are in crystal-clear river scenarios where the technique works best. On heavily tannin-stained rivers in Russia, Norway, Scotland, and most of the Canadian Maritimes, you are streamer stripping bright orange and red patterns and waiting for the line to tighten like a dead weight—streamer style—before strip-setting the hook.

The technique begins by casting upstream at a quartering-across trajectory and employs the same clockwork/countdown covering the water by extending the line and working the pool or run from bank to bank, except in the upstream direction. The key here is to gain the attention of the salmon and watch it turn and follow the fly downstream or across to hopefully nail it.

Slower stripping and long drift pauses and jigs, allows the fly to submerge deeper. But the highest success ratio with this technique is to have the fly skimming right below the surface or in the upper strata at a fast, pulsating pace. Stripping feverishly has been the most successful and it becomes very hard work if one choses to fish the technique all day, which I had strenuous pleasure of doing under the slave-driving guidance of my ghillie. Often salmon rivers later in the year run low with very little current, making traditional salmon wet-fly swinging or riffle hitching impossible. This definitely was one of the motivations for developing this technique. It also came

side-by-side with development of many speckled/barred/sparkling synthetic rubber leg materials in all different colors by companies like Hareline, Wapsi, and Spirit River.

## The Dry Fly

The simple matter of drawing a fish up from the depths to the top for any surface fly is more of a thrill than having the same fish take the fly well under and getting first indication of his presence by a pull on the tackle rather than by sight. In the words of Jack Young, guide on the Serpentine River, "I don't believe there is a more beautiful thing in the world than to see a salmon rise to a dry fly."

—Lee Wulff, *The Atlantic Salmon*

In a simple paragraph, this sums up the *salar* dry fly experience to many of its passionate practitioners. Keep in mind that the whole world is in love with brown trout. And perhaps 90 percent of that fan club love the dry fly. Also 90 percent of that admiration society would love to catch Atlantic salmon. But what could be a finer way to catch a regal fish that you have dreamed and desired your whole life, than for it to be on the surface, engulfing your fly, just as when you match the hatch for a *trutta*.

Here again is the nexus connection that perfectly unifies the personalities of *trutta* and *salar*—the floating fly. As a Catskill man who fished the famous Beaverkill for its beloved brown trout, Lee Wulff was a passionate about fishing tiny dry flies. When he wrote his Atlantic salmon treatise he mentioned that he caught thirteen salmon over twenty pounds on size 16 dry flies, and how exciting this adventure was in the playing of such a noble, discriminate creature.

Employing the dry fly for *salar* can be based on two different principles: the first out of practicality, the second out of pure romantic purist indulgence. In early spring, when snowmelt and heavy spring rains contribute to high water conditions, the fish do not see the fly or have any desire to come to the surface. The *salar* dry fly "itch" usually occurs as waters warm up and the flows come back down to summer levels. The fish then become pooled up and stacked in a very uniform spatial separation with individual and pod hierarchy formations. It is here where the dry bomber has the greatest impact.

Usually once the ghillies of the river start to see back-and tail porpoising of the surface, which in most places happens around July, the fish are now disposed to a surface-taking orientation and thus slowly move up the strata in the pool to maximize flow and oxygen under the bubble line. Here is where the surface curiosity of investigating pieces of twig, bark, leaves, the occasional water snake, or the eastern red spotted newt, which I talked of

▲ Keep in mind there is nothing logical about a salmon taking a dry fly, like this thirty-eight-pound specimen the author took at dusk on a Labatt's Blue Bomber; the fish is in the river system for the sole purpose of procreation. Credit: Gordie Malbie

earlier in the mystery of the Doddi Orange fly. Of course in our wildest hopeful dreams, a salmon will come up and gulp our dry fly.

A good *salar* dry fly box should have a variety of styles, colors, silhouettes, and floatability. A common misconception is that fish are color blind, but this is obviously not the case with either brown trout or Atlantic salmon, since certain rivers have certain color flies that always produce fish on a consistent basis. One theory is that this is a function of natal imprinting to certain food forms, like for instance the green Wulff surface stone, which imitates the eastern green stone fly. Other theories have to do with the clarity or opacity of the water, which tends to promote the visibility of one color over another against an open sky.

There is no doubt that bright-colored dries show up better on a darker day and thus is the logical choice to fish those flies. But the Labatt's Blue Bomber—blue deer hair with white wings—is a standard go-to dry fly that produces consistently on crystal-clear blue-green oligotrophic waters with high calcium carbonate and volcanic basalt content, pure spring water, and no tannic forest/bog influences, like for instance on Québec's Grand Riviere and the St. Mary's. Other grayish-brown-tan colors produce on river systems that have large caddis and stonefly hatches, and these colors may come closer to resembling these natural foods. So a box full of deer hair bombers, large and small high-riding hackled Wulff's, spiders, bi-visibles, very trendy mice patterns, along with Green Machines of Miramichi fame, is a good start to the dry fly game.

Since most Atlantic salmon rivers are in northern latitudes, they usually experience cold nights in the summer. Thus it is usually wise to start with the traditional wet-fly swing and save the dry fly game for later in the afternoon into the evening, as waters warm and fish start porpoising, often looking for oxygen or just out of surface curiosity. Keep in mind these are ocean creatures that travel in the high upper pelagic ocean and sea zones, and are very comfortable in that area. Unlike winter steelhead, who are totally oriented toward the bottom, the Atlantic's comfort zone is definitely near the surface—thus an ideal dry fly–taking fish.

As with very selective brown trout rising on a tailwaters, spring creeks, or long Catskill eddy pools, the salmon also exhibit compound/complex rises. Thus they will inspect the fly for usually good distances, causing anglers and guides to have a panic attacks or heart palpitations. Watching a twenty-pound salmon following a dry fly, nose up to the surface for five-to-ten feet, and then to turn downstream in a complex fashion to follow it even more till the fly gets washed over a tailout of the pool, will be cause for even the most composed angler or ghillie to change their underwear.

Keep in mind that the salmon will often come to the surface and inspect your fly, even for considerable distances, and never take it. This is the most exciting and at the same time the most frustrating aspect of the dry fly game. I've had a salmon inspect my Labatt's Blue Bomber on an Icelandic River or on the Miramichi over a dozen times and never take it. Sometimes they take it on the very first cast or two, or three casts later. Thus it is wise to fish your dry flies with very long floats, allowing upstream mending to extend a drag free float as that is what is desired and most commonly taken by *salar*. This differs highly from steelhead, which unlike the majority of *salar* surface takers, prefer more skittering and waking techniques.

But I and many other salmon anglers have caught Atlantics by skittering, waking and twitching the fly in combination with dead drifts. Or one can alternate the two different presentations or combine them on the same drift. I have often had salmon that do complex rises, only to be enticed by a skitter/twitch at the end of the drift.

One general rule applied by guides and skillful salmon anglers is that once a salmon comes to your fly you should give it a rest, to allow it to return to its holding position, only to try it again either with the same pattern, or to switch patterns in another size or color. If you are a romantic sort of guy like I am, who supposes that *Salmo* think like human beings or higher evolved animals, let them sit there and brood and sulk over what they could have had as a predatory kill, even though their effort would be totally unwarranted since they are not feeding. The eternal enigma of why salmon takes a dry will never be known other than the fact that it simply does. Theories ranging from boredom, territorial marking behavior, and predatory strike-and-destroy instinct, all fit into the theoretical mix.

The dry fly game for *salar* is strictly a "curiosity killed the cat" type of mental jousting. On some rivers it is highly effective, on others it is useless. The *salar* migratory river run goes from aggressive to passive pretty fast. The aggressive takes of the early season are replaced with no takes, or hard fought over fish, as the Ides of August and September's passive/dour attitude takes hold. Thus the dry fly is one game changer that can bring elation after many fishless encounters.

One other extremely unorthodox technique was perfected and mastered by Art Lee during the dog days of August on the Moise and Matapedia in Québec. Here he would stand at the top of the pool with a large white Wulff or massive bomber, and cast it all the way down to the tailout and strip it feverishly to the top of the pool into the riffles. This would wreak havoc on a school of salmon enjoying very placid calm waters when not even the zephyr of wind was in the air. Particularly close to darkness, he would catch some of the largest salmon in the river system, but most of the time spook everything into a frenzy and drive the school of salmon down to the lower benthos of the pool. It is definitely a technique worth trying when nothing else is working.

In closing, the cardinal rule of the dry fly is not to set the hook too early in blowing the hook set. Many guides will tell the client to loudly say, "God save the Queen" before setting the hook when an Atlantic salmon finally takes the dry. This is a three or four second pause to allow the salmon to take its mouth completely over the dry fly and start its descent downward. Once a *salar* commits to the dry fly, it does so with conviction, unlike a finicky selective trout that will spit the hook as quick as it takes it. Keep in mind these are big, cartilaginous mouths and kypes, with lots of space for you to pull it out of the mouth un-pricked, no matter how big a dry fly you have. Even with a male *salar*'s kyped "croc" mouth is closed to the greatest extent, it still has an extended, gaping mouth.

Also when setting the hook, do not lift in a high profile like you do for brown trout. Even in trout situations this type of hook set will cost you lost fish and opportunities. By gently dropping your rod and setting downstream from

the mouth of the fish, your fly will most likely be secured in the corner of the mouth with the help of the current tugging against your line.

## Road Kill Aggression

The new age of salmon angler is like everything in today's contemporary world: "bigger/better/faster/more/now," cutting-edge, breaking the mold, marching to the tune of your own drummer. There is a similar progression of an angler from fishing for brown trout in little streams as a little boy and girl, then progressively graduating to salmon and steelhead, only to return back to their first love—little streams. Each venue has its own charm and mystique once fully explored.

Very few anglers start off strictly in the Atlantic salmon / steelhead world unless they are from Europe, the Canadian Maritimes, British Columbia, or the Great Lakes. Atlantic salmon are not known as the poor man's fish, whereas the trout can be found in any tiny brook or waterway under the town bridge, from peasant farm to city rivers.

Thus new Atlantic salmon anglers come to the sport

▲ A massive *Salar* beast taken by Brett Howard in Michigan on my Rogue Roadkill Electric Candy Cane Leech.

with an open mind and willingness to experiment, much to the scorn of their stoic, tradition-engrained predecessors. The new Atlantic fly fisher has a distinct advantage in that they are not crippled by tradition! I too had a Scottish ghillie on my first encounter in the Canadian Maritimes who was about as curmudgeonly and set in his ways as Ebenezer Scrooge.

In today's world, Atlantic salmon fishermen and guides want to catch steelhead, and vice a versa. Through this process the exchange of ideas is taking place. Often good guides will fish trout in Patagonia in the winter, steelhead in the fall and sometimes spend summers in Russia or Iceland fishing Atlantic salmon. In their "guide bum/ nomadic gypsy world," they bring fresh attitudes and perspectives often associated with funky new fly designs and dastardly techniques. Streamer dudes like Brett Howard, Paul Zagorski, Brian Judge, and my crazy guiding mind are forever pushing the limits of what is too big or too unorthodox.

The "Road Kill" concept was born out of a steelhead guide's frustration of seeing twenty- to forty-pound salmon stacked like cordwood in a Québec pool on the Grand Cascapedia. When Steve Stallard, a diehard steelhead guide, had his first encounter with the dour summer fish that can drive anyone crazy, he showed them a huge clump of variously-colored pieces of marabou eight inches long by dredging a pool at the most bizarre time of day, only to get his fly hammered by a thirty-eight-pound Atlantic salmon female. It was the start of a new and unorthodox fly legacy. Over several stiff drinks, the guides were still in disbelief and eventually named it the roadkill, since dead animals are often littered everywhere along Québec highways, due to logging trucks mowing everything from moose to small animals.

Since steelhead are attracted to large, bright, gaudy intruders and Spey flies, the *salar* roadkill concept blends in perfectly with large streamers and night stalking for aggressive *truttasaurus* brown trout. But to large carnivorous brown trout, it is the predatory instinct to kill a big meal. For the *Salmo salar*, it can only be aggression and the invasion of space that triggers them to crush the fly of that size, when they are usually more busy targeting size 12 Blue Charms and Undertakers.

I had my first encounter with roadkill in 2001 on the upper Alder Island sector of the Cascapedia. It was absolutely loaded by the hundreds with giant male and female Atlantics pushing the twenty- to forty-pound mark. As a steelhead guide it drove me crazy to see that many fish, especially when they didn't want to bite anything or even look at my flies. Famous West Coast steelhead and salmon guide Jim Teeny once said, "If you spot em, you've got em." Mr. Teeny obviously didn't fish the Gaspé in early September.

After spending the entire morning throwing the traditional favorite flies with the Micmac Indian guides, who were fond of taking native hemp breaks since they had a lot of time on their hands what with not catching fish, I didn't even turn one head of a salmon. Frustrated as hell, I threw in a couple of old seven-inch-long summer steelhead string leech standbys, with my salmon flies. I picked the biggest, gaudiest, black and red pattern I called the Electric Candy Cane, tossed it up into the riffles of the pool and let it dead drift downward with slight twitches. Whatever triggered that massive male salmon to absolutely demolish it and tear the rod out of my hands, was like divine intervention. After a fierce battle the Indian guides could not believe that fish took my inaugural roadkill offering.

In hindsight, knowing that Atlantics will encounter eels and large ocean annelid worms in their predacious sea-going adventures, they targeted this black electric *Salmo* candy cane because it invaded the holy sanctum of the pool and disrupted the hierarchical salmon pecking order.

Since roadkill became the rage of the salmon guides during that week, when the crazy steelhead guides like us were in camp, the full-time local guides had no ammunition and locked us to our tying tables, where we created roadkill patterns that resembled small animals like raccoons, creepy scorpion body concoctions, and weird jellyfish/squid. Needless to say under the dour conditions, they were producing fish—and very large ones to boot— pure "money" to a salmon guide.

Several days later I was with Dave, a Micmac guide on the Salmon Branch of the Cascapedia. Since a guide was customarily obliged to offer his fly box for the first fly to tie, he did not have the latest rage of roadkill. But a more traditional concept did the trick. Dave was a master "fly in hand" tier. He took out a plastic tube and with his black thread hand bobbin secured black, orange, and yellow deer hair to make a six-inch-long Willie Gunn tube, which is perhaps the most lethal fly ever developed to imitate the Thunder and Lightning pattern.

When David pointed to the large salmon at the top of the pool in Indian Brook with giant kypes that had all the spotting and marble coloring of massive brown trout, I thought I was looking at German U-boats. I was merely shell-shocked for a while and could not cast looking at all these males. He estimated that at least seventy-five of them were in the twenty- to forty-pound range, all pent up like lovesick dogs. "Wait, let's not cast yet, let's watch them," David said, as he puffed on his hemp, while I smoked a Cuban cigar and took a sip of Spring Bank Scotch out of my pewter flask to calm my nerves. It was later in the day and the fish were getting very antsy.

Every once in a while a male would break out of the hierarchy of pool structure, swim around, and target another male in a brief jousting, kype smacking battle. "Okay, now they are stirred up, throw that tube way up into the top of the pool and slowly pulsate/ strip it down," he said. "Ahh! The Colonel Winchester Patent Method, I replied. "Something like that," David said. "Whatever you want to call it, that big hairy fly will piss one of those boys off." Sure enough after ten to fifteen minutes my rod stopped cold in its stripping/ pulsating mix, as though I had snagged against a giant rock. A massive thirty-five-pound *salar* male was doing aerial displays like an orca at Sea World—I was onto one of the biggest fish of my life-time, and forty minutes later at dusk, with the outstanding guiding from Goodman, who poured ice cold water from the Salmon Branch on my arms to stop them from cramping up in the 90-degree heat, I landed that beast.

In hindsight all of these crazy "envelope-pushing" doings centered around the aggressive color spectrum and niche hierarchy lie dominance that the Atlantics were conducting, in this phase very close to spawning. The techniques and applications worked best when they were dead drifted in and pulsated repeatedly close to the fish to provoke them into striking the roadkill. By the fly sinking and drifting in the pool, with only weight from the fly's heavy wire traditional hook, and slowly lifting or moving the rod to change the fly's direction, the large alpha male and female salmon usually looked at it repeatedly until they decided to crush it.

These roadkill flies have just globs of materials stacked and articulated on several hooks. More refined motion/ movement articulation exists today in Tommy Lynch's Drunk and Disorderly and the Double D, as well as Galloup's Sex Dungeon and Circus Peanut. They all wreak havoc on territorial *Salmo* fish—browns and Atlantics alike. I further explored the extreme influence the seven-to nine-inch-long articulated diving deer hair heads had on the migratory landlocked Atlantics of Michigan, along with the original black, red, and orange color combination of my Electric Candy Cane leech. Males up to twenty pounds in the fall of 2015–16 destroyed these unorthodox pre-sentations. Here they worked with lethal efficiency with deep, slow, pulsating, presentations right into the fish's domain—especially to the males that were jockeying for territorial courtship rights to female fish in the pre-spawn mode, like they do for giant *trutta*saurus on the Tailwater Rivers to the south. The new roadkill and "chickens" have revolutionized *Salmo salar* fishing forever.

▲ Credit: Jessica DeLorenzo

# 11. Landlocked Atlantic Salmon and Sea- and Lake-Run Browns

The future of *Salmo* lies in their new frontiers and protecting existing ones. Indigenous ocean, sea, and lake waters have changed or been decimated by civilization's influence, including climate change.

My intial experience with landlocked *Salmo salar* and sea-going *trutta* begins with some of the cleanest waters on earth, Lakes Superior and Huron. In these vast inland seas that feed the entire chain of the Great Lakes, where six quadrillion gallons and one-fifth of the Earth's fresh water is stored, has shaped up to be an exciting new frontier for *Salmo salar*. Superior's deep, icy-cold waters produce loads of plankton, the life-giving source for all salmonids. The entire food chain gorges on these tiny delectable items, but most importantly the herring, whitefish, smelt, Cisco, and alewives that become the day-to-day buffet for cruising *salar* and *trutta*.

The St. Mary's River rapids are a series of turbulent cascading pools of turquoise-blue flows over red sandstone, and you can spot the Atlantics holding mid-depth in deep pools below tumbling spill gates roaring with icy flows. Thanks to the plankton-rich waters, and a few modern visionary gurus like Roger Greil, the St. Mary's River is now a *Salmo salar* Mecca right in Michigan's heartland of the Midwest. It produces magnificently silver- and grey-sided *salar* with azure-blue cheeks. With their hunting grounds in the deep cold waters of Lake Huron, they come back in the early summer just like their oceangoing cousins to the site of their original upbringing, the "Soo" as it's called locally.

▲ Landlocked Atlantic salmon like John Spevacek's massive Great Lakes/St. Mary's strain have a fascination for small, easily-available prey like caddis and *Mysis* shrimp. Credit: Author

What intrigues me the most about these fish is central to my book—the nexus between *salar* and *trutta* and how these fish feed and behave almost identically—given the unique laboratory-like proving grounds described below.

Though there is now a documentation of natural Atlantic reproduction in the St Mary's river, the *salar* of the St. Mary's and Lake Huron are produced by Lake Superior State University's aquatic research lab in conjunction with the Michigan Department of Natural Resources hatcheries, which was spearheaded by Roger Greil. Released as smolts and fingerlings in the spring and fall, they feed on the plethora of mayfly and caddis hatches that subsequently gorge on the plankton produced by Superior. Then the *salar* migrate to the big ocean-like waters where baitfish and *Mysis* shrimp comprise their diets in the pelagic zones.

When I first started guiding for the Atlantics, I swung traditional Atlantic salmon wet flies and bomber dries with limited results. Though we would pick up an occasional fish here and there, there was something more mysterious going on in these crystal-clear pools and boulder-strewn rapids. Ranging anywhere from 5–20 pounds, the Atlantics were clearly moving in and targeting food items in the mid-strata and surface, similar to a predatory brown trout. But this predatory dilemma was still encoded in mystery.

The St. Mary's attracts massive schools of whitefish that feed on the plankton coming from Lake Superior. Locals use a fly called "the brown jewel" to catch the whitefish. It is the simplest and most primitive of all designs, nothing but brown chenille wrapped around a hook with a bit of tan/yellow hackle palmered around the neck. To discover why the whitefish were so keen on this fly, scientists seined the waters coming out of Lake Superior.

Biologists at the aquatic lab routinely checked the duration and frequency of the plankton in the biological drift behind the laboratory waters emanating from the Hydro channels by seining with large plankton nets in various water column depths. We cracked the first part of the code while observing the net contents of the seine one day at the laboratory while chatting with Roger. Tons of brown tannish caddis pupae and larvae—*Hydropsyche* cinnamon and zebra caddis—covered the nets at all depths. Could these large chrome silver beasts be actually feeding on caddis like a river brown trout? Couldn't be, I thought. These were pelagic baitfish hunters; why would they mess around with such a tiny form of prey?

Insect foraging by *salar* can be traced back to Maine and the Grand Lake strain, where the landlocked salmon, which spend equal time in the river systems as juveniles and adults, feed heavily on surface aquatic insects. At the time, I did not know this as I was concentrating on cracking the St. Mary's Atlantic salmon dilemma. The feeding movements of the Atlantics, as seen through the icy,

clear-blue waters at the Straits of the Soo, prompted me then to my fly-tying table. I came up with a sophisticated Carl Richards/Gary LaFontaine–style sparkle caddis pupa with a brown body and yellowish Antron. I suspended two droppers below the strike indicators, a caddis pupa and a *Mysis* shrimp.

On the first trial, the strike indicator went down deep within a matter of minutes, and a twelve-pound, chrome-silver bullet went aerial like a nuclear submarine's ballistic missile. Shaking its head, it had a size 12 caddis pupa firmly implanted the backside of its jaw. I couldn't truly believe my eyes and never in a million moons would I have predicted such large fish with such a different lifestyle would zero in on the food that it consumed when it was a pre-migratory smolt. In hindsight, Grand Lake, Maine-style feeding behaviors made perfect sense.

The power of the natal imprint into food forms, no matter where you relocate *salar* from their indigenous waters, is perhaps the most striking conviction of the behavioral and genetic DNA coding of the fish, despite such divergent predatory lifestyles and habitats later in life. Of particular note here is that Atlantics spend equal time in big waters as they do in rivers, so the river's *Salmo* blood bond of food and habitat is familiar to the returning salmon, and imprints as much as anything they find on the big seas.

As the summer endured, St. Mary's fish became more selective to size and pattern, and also became leader shy, just as a typical brown trout would. Also during the summer months prior to their late fall/early winter spawning, they would hunt down the schools of migratory Rainbow smelt that entered the upper St. Mary's to spawn. Smashing the surface like giant killer orcas, they eventually became very susceptible to trolled Grey Ghost–style streamers, which Canadian Soo guide John Giuliani and I experimented with, and which is typical of the landlocked salmon techniques anglers employ on Maine's Rangeley Lakes.

As more inland glacial style deep lakes in Michigan like Torch, Higgins, and Gull Lake received these Grand Lake strain fish from Lake Superior State University, their behavior was identical no matter where you found them. On Gull Lake for instance, they were fond of midge *diptera*, and the size 18 Griffiths Gnat was the key to these vexing surface-rising schools of cruising landlocked salmon.

As I write this chapter in the middle of July, anglers of all types are catching chrome-silver Atlantic salmon of the finest looking order up to fourteen pounds, just outside the ghettos by the Detroit River, in what used to be the most filthily-polluted waters on earth! Thus an exciting new world awaits this amazing fish. Despite what is going on in the big ocean waters now, there is a bright new future for

*Salmo salar* and for the average common man to embrace this most amazing of all piscatorial creations.

## The Potamodromous Magic

In the anadromous journeys, through the process of osmoregulation, the sea-run *Salmos* balance the amount of salinity or freshwater through their kidney systems. Here by frequent urination, or lack thereof, or by gulping water, they adjust their bodily fluids into homeostasis, which is necessary for the back-and-forth journeys most fish could not possibly attempt to handle.

In the potamodromous, freshwater-to-freshwater migrations of landlocked Atlantics in the Great Lakes and large freshwater sea environments, the lack of this overriding physiological necessity allows these fish to spend more time in the pre-spawn predation mode. This is not uncommon for these fish, even though technically they are not feeding, which is affected by the amount of body cavity space necessary for egg and sperm production. During

▲ When my guiding client Thomas Aufiero and I caught the twenty-six-pound twelve-ounce IGFA world record landlocked Atlantic salmon at Torch Lake Michigan in 2011, we broke a record that was held in a Swedish lake and river system. Given appropriate food supplies, like they have in this northern Michigan system along with the Lake Huron/St. Mary's River system connection, these fish can grow quite large. Credit: Author

this phase their stomachs shrink down to nothing, and since they spend more time than their anadromous cousins in this mode, these potamodromous fish are on the bite mode a good amount of time.

North America has more landlocked inland salmon than most of Europe and its indigenous range, where most of these lakes are usually sections of long rivers in Sweden, Finland, Norway, and Russia that have been dammed up by hydroelectric reservoirs.

## The Rangley Lake Legacy

The Sebago, Green, and Grand Lake systems and their rivers, is where the indigenous landlocked *salar* systems produced the strains for Rangeley Lake back in 1877. Since then, this has become a Mecca for the landlocked fly fishing angler, due to the legacy of fly fishing styles, streamers, and creators.

This amazing area of six major lakes and hundreds of smaller ponds, lakes, and river systems that eventually enter the Androscoggin and Kennebec rivers and on to the Atlantic Ocean is 99 percent primordial wilderness. During the Pleistocene Ice Age epoch 120 million years ago, the glaciers and continental ice sheets carved out beautiful mountains like Arcadia National Park and all the lake systems and river valleys. While waterfalls, dams, and other natural and man-made barriers could have trapped indigenous ranges of the Atlantic salmon, many of these high Alpine-like Lake systems in Maine and its *salar* physically adapted to the river and lake system life, rather than the oceangoing migrations preferred by the fish of the lower river systems. Eventually they became landlocked and have remained so ever since.

Here is another strong bond between the two *Salmos* where they share almost identical preferences for habitat feeding lifestyles and migrations to coincide with it. Besides their slight variations in DNA, the landlocked salmon of the Northeast from Labrador to Québec to as far south as New York and Vermont, show the ultimate behavioral *Salmo* nexus connection.

"Ouananiche," is the French-Canadian/Algonquin Indian term for *salar* that have the appearance of *Salmo trutta*, and refuse to go to the ocean for whatever apparent reasons. With their dominant *trutta*-like behavior, they outcompete the native chars like brook and lake trout in lake environments, to become the dominant apex predators.

To look at the Rangeley Lakes and the other four indigenous landlocked Atlantic strain *salar* is to look at a brown trout in its most glorified fashion. For all practical purposes, their morphology is almost identical, except for fins, tail configurations, and a few different spotting pattern differences. Due to the shorter growing seasons of the harsh Maine winter climates, which can last up to eight months, the landlocked salmon of Rangeley, and also the indigenous salmon in the Grand Lake Stream district, do not grow very large, so a four- to-five-pound mature adult is a hefty prize.

But they surely do have the capacity given the food source to do so. The twenty-seven-pound IGFA land-locked Atlantic record-breaker caught by my client was from the Grand Lake, Maine strain. Being extremely opportunistic feeders, especially in the Great Lakes, I can easily envision future fish in the thirty-pound and higher range being caught, since the diversity of food supply in Lake Huron is dramatically higher and tilts in the favor of landlocked salmon, since they are large predators of aquatic insects.

The Huron/St. Mary's system and Torch Lake have the largest population of the giant *Hexagenia* mayfly in the world, which litters the streets at night like a snowstorm. This massive food supply, coupled with the pelagic baitfish diversity, is very promising as the new home for "ouananiche."

## The Carrie Stevens/Herb Welch Landlocked Legacy

> Large freshwater resident Atlantic salmon typically change from an invertebrate to a fish diet has been reported from lakes in Finland and Sweden where European vendace (whitefish family) are the main prey species. And for lakes in Maine, USA, (Sayers et.al.1989) found that Rainbow smelt was a major food item for landlocked Atlantic salmon, although it could feed on other species. This change to piscivory prey is probably both because they are able to handle large prey and because of the high proportion of the prey that is absorbed (absorption efficiency) allowing the predator to grow quickly.
>
> —Jonsson & Jonsson,
> *Ecology of Atlantic Salmon and Brown Trout*

As *Salmo trutta* anglers could build a monument to the mayfly, so also could landlocked salmon anglers build one to honor the rainbow smelt. Possessing its own morphological beauty, there could not be a finer or more easily digestible pelagic sardine for the purpose of growing carnivorous, hunting packs of *Salmo*. Combined with the dense aquatic insect life of all sizes, such as freshwater shrimp and other gamefish and baitfish like perch, landlocked salmon have a tremendous wealth of prey and very few competing predators in colder pelagic lake environments. Although pike, muskellunge, and bass predatory dominators exist in these lake environments, they mainly constitute warm water fringe predation, as distinct from deep, cold open waters. Thus the landlocked *Salmo* pretty much has it made from an alpha dominance perspective.

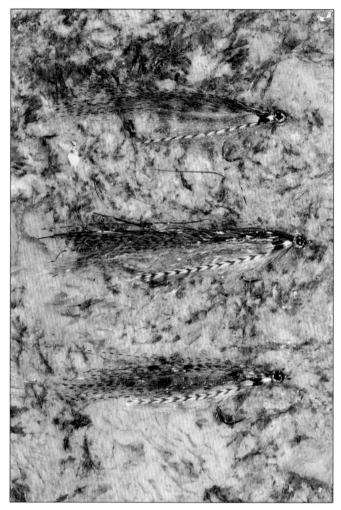

▲ The first streamers, other than some crude facsimiles from the United Kingdom, could have come from Welch at his shop in Maine, at Haines Landing on Lake Mooselookmeguntic. Credit: John Miller

Rangeley's fly fishing luminaries like Cary Stevens and Herb Welsh were to landlocked *salar,* as was Marinaro and Fox were to selective brown trout, and Wulff and Lee to seagoing *salar.* Welch's masterpiece creation, the Black Ghost, is still known today as an extremely effective smelt/baitfish/Atlantic fly pattern. Welch first tied it as early as 1919 to duplicate the Rainbow smelt. Today my *Salmo* Parr/Smelt impressions shown above incorporate new age synthetic materials.

The true first icon of landlocked salmon streamers, and streamers as a whole, was Preston Jennings, who came from the Catskills. Jennings was an introspective cutting-edge genius who explored how the fly appeared through a prism and based his color tonal combinations on his optics studies. His Lord Iris and Silhouette Minnow were directly inspired by Welch's Black Ghost.

Carrie Stevens is perhaps most beloved for being a very creative and prolific fly fisher and fly tier. She was inspired by Welch's creations and came up with dozens of patterns along the lines of the style of the day imitating the

Rainbow smelt. Her Grey Ghost pattern is perhaps the most eulogized in landlocked fishing history. Her hook partnership with Partridge of Redditch England introduced the Carrie Stevens streamer hook and her legendary innovations are well-known throughout the world.

## Sea-Run Browns

It will probably never be known whether salmonids were first stream born inhabitants in their evolutionary development and eventually sought big water oceans and lakes, or that they evolved from the big seas and eventually migrated to upper river limits. Thus we may never know how sea trout came to be. But looking at *Salmo trutta* as a whole, their habitat preferences in the oceans and seas account for only a very small number—perhaps less than 10 percent—of the population. Since browns are great adapters and migrators, it stands to reason that those rivers with easy access to the ocean and estuaries became prime predatory habitat targets for *trutta* always trying to maximize growth and prey dominance.

Iceland, the UK, Scandinavia, and Western Europe through the Baltic, all have a long sea trout history similar to Atlantic salmon. It is in the UK, Baltic, and Tierra del Fuego perhaps, where they are most appreciated and have the greatest range for sporting and culinary appeal. Several Baltic countries even allow commercial harvest of wild sea trout in the Baltic.

## Ocean/Sea/Lake Predation

Once in the vast and extremely complex sea foraging grounds, brown trout and salmon tend to favor identical food forms until the eventual return to their natal rivers. Here they almost look identical in color and shape, with similar morphology. Both have "X paramecium"–looking black marked spotting against the silver blue sheen of their scales, and their steel-grey backs serve as cloaking devices. However there are several factors between Sea trout and Atlantic salmon that significantly separate their spatial niches in the big water environment.

Sea-run browns stay closer to shore and do not venture into the vast deeper offshore waters like their nomadic *salar* cousins. Warmer waters are much more fertile in food sources, which corresponds to browns' earliest predation profiles formed in the parr stage. Again, the Jonssons in their *Ecology of Brown Trout and Atlantic Salmon*, investigate early predator feeding which establishes differences that may lead to long-term habits, whether in the rivers, oceans, or seas:

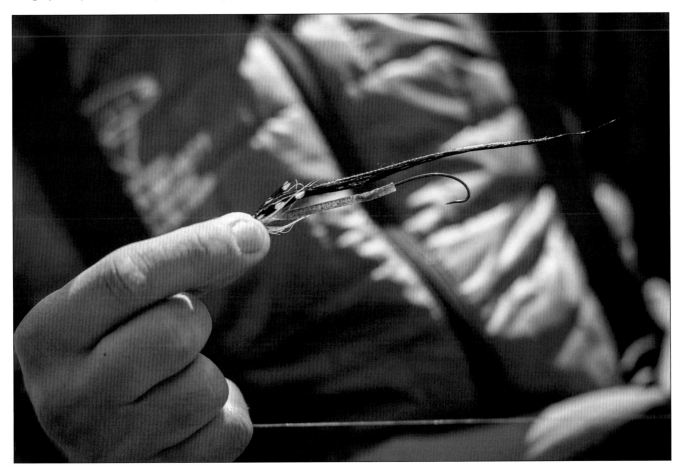

▲ The biodiversity of sea trout is greatly influenced by their ability to spend equal time in fresh and salt water, and live close to shore estuary environments that are very fertile in food forms, like this squib represents. Unusual fly imitations like the one ingested here for Ross Purnell in Tierra del Fuego are often effective on sea-run trout. Credit: Jessica DeLorenzo

When parr of Atlantic salmon and brown trout co-occur in river pools, Atlantic salmon can exhibit behavioral plasticity and adopt a more cryptic non-aggressive behavior and thereby feed successfully. (Harwood et al, 2002; Stradmeyer et al, 2008) Hojesjo et al, 2015), observed that brown trout tended to hold station by swimming actively in the central regions of pools, where Atlantic salmon parr occupied the margins and remain quite stationary on the stream-bed. Brown trout made approximately twice as many foraging attempts as Atlantic salmon but their efficiency of food capture was lower, and therefore no significant difference in food intake. Atlantic salmon fed by briefly invading the space occupied for most of the time by brown trout. This behavior has similarities to the 'sneaky' behaviors often existed by subordinate males during spawning, when gametes rather than food are the contested resource. Thus, these species can adjust the performance according to their social environment.

Thus by not requiring the extreme cold temperatures Atlantic salmon have evolved to prefer in such places as Greenland and the Faroe Islands, brown trout cruise the murkier, warmer and extremely plankton rich fertility of the near-shore pelagic areas of the Baltic Sea and Tierra del Fuego. This makes brown trout ideal candidates to forage on everything and anything.

One chief difference between the more opportunistic loner and scavenger sea-run trout versus the nomadic *salar*, is the amount of time the sea-run browns spend in the lower freshwater/brine areas of the estuaries after river spawning. Being fall spawners, they will drop down into the lower river systems and estuaries through winter and well into the spring, capitalizing on all the delectable prey items along the fertile shorelines.

Although they survive in full seawater (35 psu), anadromous brown trout feed chiefly in estuaries and near the coast. Only large individuals can occur in the open ocean (Klemesten et al. 2003). During the first couple of weeks after entering the estuary, brown trout typically stay close to the river mouth (Middlemast et al. 2009). Then, they move further away from the river for feeding, but few move longer than 100 km from the river. It has been hypothesized that estuary living close to the river mouth and longer marine migrations are alternate life history tactics in anadromous brown trout in northern Russia.

At sea, brown trout feed largely on fish and invertebrates such as *Polychaetes* (bristle worm annelids), crustaceans, and surface-living arthropods (crabs,

lobsters, water spiders etc.). An ontogenetic shift in beating niche occurs when the post-smolts reach 25 cm. From this size onwards, they become largely piscivorous and take littoral and pelagic fishes. Gobies, young Atlantic herring, and sprat appeared to be the selected food forms.

—Jonsson & Jonsson,
*Ecology of Atlantic Salmon and Brown Trout*

## Sea-Run Garbage Feeding

The qualities of being tremendously opportunistic and diverse prey feeders, and being sufficiently flexible to take advantage of feeding situations that other species are incapable of exploiting, are *Salmo* trademarks. For instance while Pacific Chinook salmon are totally hardwired to alewives in the Great Lakes and to a certain size sardine in the Pacific, the sea-run trout continues to practice the exploitation of diverse prey niches it first encountered in the freshwater streams of its youth. Feeding near sewage discharges, cattle crossings, and other questionable environmental habitat from a water quality standpoint, sets brown trout—whether freshwater or sea-run—apart from other salmonids.

This food diversity is probably why browns are more likely to take a variety of flies, and with greater regularity. What is intriguing to me, from a fly design standpoint, is the bristle worm/annelid/eel phenomenon that dominates a sea-run brown's food source in near-shore estuaries. It is no wonder that large leeches, woolly worm patterns, and other things that look extremely buggy work so well, from the Baltic estuaries to the rivers in the UK and Iceland, and finally at the tip of the world in Tierra Del Fuego. Large, articulated-motion leeches/Intruders/Wooly Worms must imitate foods that are imprinted on these large seagoing *Salmo* vacuum cleaners.

With all the modern synthetics available today, guides and anglers are having a field day concocting buggy, meaty, impressionistic, delectable flies that sea-run browns absolutely hammer. Each year, using the standard Woolly Bugger/Woolly Worm/Bitch Creek/Stone Nymph/Rubber Legs motifs, guides are creating new variations on a theme to imitate the worm, leech, and sand eel connection. In addition, baitfish imitations of the inshore areas are perfected. Here great schools of sardines, sticklebacks, Zander perch, cichlids, and deep-water sculpins, all form broad categories for fly imitations.

## Scandinavian Sea Trout Legacy

Anglers perfected the art of sea trout fly fishing on the jagged coastlines, fjords, and beautiful beaches of Scandinavia. Due to the cold waters pretty much all year round, except for the extreme heat of summer, the sea-run browns cruise the shorelines, drop-offs, reefs, and jetties

▲ The victorious net job on this sea-run brown—many a ghillie's ecstasy or agony. Credit: Jessica DeLorenzo

in a constant search for all different types of invertebrates and vertebrates.

The Baltic Sea trout is a magnificent *Salmo* that is often overlooked for others in northern Europe chasing the more coveted *salar*. Martin Jorgenson, the Danish "Global Fly Fisher," is a passionate pursuer of these stunning *Salmo* gamefish. He shares his sea trout passion here in the following passages.

## Stalking Danish Sea Trout

It's quite a special feeling, after a short drive on nice roads through a beautiful, lush countryside, to take a turn down a small road toward the ocean, minutes later parking your car just a cast away from the lazily-breaking waves.

You look out over the ocean that you are going to fish in just a few minutes. Clean beach, calm and clear water, no houses, resorts, or hotels visible, not a fence or a "posted" sign in sight, not another angler in the water, and a good chance of catching a wild, bright, silvery sea run brown trout.

Additionally, all this is easily accessible, basically free, and doesn't require special skills or gear. Just your average nine-foot 6-weight, a floating line, and a Wooly Bugger. That's what meets the angler who travels to the Danish

coast to fish for sea trout (sea-run browns) and those are some of the reasons why this fishing is as popular as it is.

The Baltic area is particularly well suited for fishing for sea trout. A clean and well-maintained environment and optimal marine conditions is the foundation for some potentially very healthy fish stocks. Coupled with a generally very good access to the water, good logistics, and facilities, makes this fishing both widespread and popular in the region.

The sea-run browns, always referred to as sea trout here, have been my personal fishing passion for a long time. These fish are your ordinary brown trout, migrated into the ocean to feed before returning to the streams to spawn. In other words, the exact same behavior seen with salmon. Like the salmon, the fish turn bright and silvery in the ocean, and will become shiny torpedoes in top condition during their salty stay.

Conditions in the Baltic—most of Denmark, south Sweden, southern Norway, and most of the other countries lining the Baltic Sea—are close to perfect for fishing for these migrating fish. Because of the conditions in the sea, mainly the brackish water and the abundance of food, the fish will often stay close to the coast rather than roam the deep ocean. The option to fish them is almost

▲ Catching a trout in an ocean, sea, or estuary is a fantastic feeling. It's not easy, it's not like the fish are queuing to be caught, and it's not like there are fish everywhere all the time. But the experience of catching a sea-run brown or silver foraging in the shallow water along most of the coastline in Scandinavia, the Baltic countries, and Tierra del Fuego, where the smell, sounds, and rewards of the beach and surf, is unlike any other. Credit: Jessica DeLorenzo

everywhere thanks to the food supply, the coastal geography, public access to most coasts, and a very limited tide. There are basically no licenses, no permits needed, and very few and reasonable limits and rules in the whole area. Sea trout fishing has become a very popular pastime in Denmark in particular.

The fishing is open year-round, literally only limited by the ice that forms on the ocean during the coldest winters. Apart from that the fish are present both during the warmest summer months and during winters, mild or harsh. And they can be legally fished in all these months, only limited by some protected areas near streams and by local rules protecting the fish that are on their spawning run, allowing you to fish them, but requiring you to release them again.

Sea trout fishing doesn't require much. In Denmark you need a cheap state license, which is a thirty-dollar-a-year license, allowing you to fish freely on the coast. Access to the coast requires nothing else. You are allowed to walk on the shore and in the water everywhere, even in front of private property, and access to the water is allowed most places, even crossing private land. A few bird sanctuaries and military installations are out of bounds, but the rest is open for you to roam.

The coast is generally well-protected, the water is shallow, and no high and steep rocks or cliffs worth mentioning keep you from entering the water.

Nearly all of the fishing in Denmark is done wading, so you need a pair of waders. Other areas in the region might require a boat. The rocky Swedish and Norwegian coasts and archipelagos aren't quite as accessible from the shore, and a boat allows you to easily move from location to location.

A nine-foot rod in the 5–7 weight range, a floating line, a rod-length leader, and a few shrimp or scud flies, hair-wing streamers or Woolly Bugger–style flies, and you are set.

Fly selection isn't big science. A really simple guideline is: colorful for the winter, large for the spring, bushy for the summer nights, and small for the autumn.

Fishing will typically be best in the daytime during the winter, peak mornings and evenings in the spring and autumn, and be best at night in the summer. These are not set rules, but a general guideline.

From there on the fishing requires patience and quite a few casts, but not necessarily much finesse or delicacy. Finding the fish is the hard part. They can be everywhere and nowhere, and success is a product of some local knowledge about locations combined with a lot of walking and casting. You will rarely see fish rising or splashing. The fish are hunting sub-surface, and seldom reveal themselves, so you find them by observing the location and probing the water with your flies. Once you find the fish, they are usually quite willing to take a well-presented fly. You can fish under most conditions from dead calm mirror-like water, to frothy and murky breaking waves. The easier fishing is somewhere in between, but the fish can be there in both calm and turbulent water.

The fish prefer mixed environments with stones and rocks mixed with sand and seaweed patches. This is found in many places, and even the most uniform and sandy beach can hide some underwater sea trout oases. Walking along the coastline in the water or on the beach while casting over interesting structures will eventually bring you in contact with a fish. Like trout in running water, sea trout are more alert and cautious in calm water and more reckless and aggressive in turbulent water. The angler can use this to his or her advantage by altering tactics and tackle.

So, from Sweden's Morrum River to Poland's Slupia River along the Baltic coast, sea trout will enter almost any coldwater river and stream to spawn. They are not far-ranging ocean navigators like the Atlantic salmon, intent to pursue extreme bounty of the eutrophic waters lying close to the coastline. Here they prey on crabs, crustaceans, squid, capelin, herring, and the multitude of shallower prey in the sea waters of the Baltic Sea. Next time you are on a business trip to Europe or on vacation, pack your *Salmo* gear and enjoy this very special fish!

### *Trutta*saurus at the End of the Earth

Tierra del Fuego—the "Land of Fire"—is at the farthest most tip of the earth before you get to Antarctica. This archipelago district of Patagonia covers an area divided between Chile and Argentina. It is a land of howling winds, stark wide open spaces, and contains the islands where Darwin came to study evolution. Its long, cool summers and moist, moderate winters is the perfect environment for *Salmo trutta* to run the area's big rivers like the Rio Grande and the Gallegos, as well as the coastlines between the Atlantic and Pacific ocean, which funnel a massive amount of biodiverse nutrients like no other place in the world. Its brown trout roam the near shore waters, and predate upon everything—shrimp, squid, and every baitfish known to both oceans—and in this way become enormous in size. The Rio Grande boasts one of the largest sea brown trout runs of approximately seventy-five thousand fish that average twelve pounds or more.

The fierce winds are so strong here that the trees, such as the Winter's bark (canelo), beech, and conifers are called "flag trees," since the winds twist them into notorious shapes. Sea lions dot the coastline along with the various parakeets, gulls, foxes, condors, and king penguins.

The brown trout of Tierra del Fuego often hit the twenty- to thirty-pound mark, and fish higher than that have been captured. Since its rivers are in low-lying tundra estuaries, they are very nondescript. The way to go here is to swing big black uglies and leech/eel types with rubber legs, using a two-handed Spey rod to help with the wind.

But due to a brown trout's slower attack speed versus a steelhead, they are able to pursue a variety of aquatic insect life and vertebrate. The swinging technique here is less of a broadside approach, and more of a downstream jigging/lifting, which slowly entices the big fish to strike your fly. Remember, these coastal fish aren't used to having to work very hard for their food, and will nail a creepy, black, rubber-legged Woolly Bugger on demand. Slow your presentations down here and adjust to the incoming tides and viscosity levels for success.

### The Dynamic World Record Brown Trout Frontier: The Great Lakes

The Great Lakes have one of the best migratory brown trout fly-fishing opportunities in the world—the latest world-record fish have come from Lake Michigan on the Wisconsin shoreline (forty-two pounds) and Michigan's Manistee River (forty-four pounds). These monsters are Alpine *Seeforellen* Lake strain brown trout, and can often forgo a year spawning to eat pelagic baitfish and increase their tremendous size. They can also be sterile triploid fish.

Whether you are targeting upstream migrating fish on New York's Oak Orchard off of Lake Ontario, or hunting them in August on Wisconsin's wild and wonderful Boise Brule, the Great Lakes offers such an incredible diversity where one can target these massive, lake-going brown trout in cities like Toronto, Cleveland, and Grand Rapids. Even in view of the Chicago skyline, silvery brown trout are caught in the wintertime as they hunt baitfish off the shorelines and power plant discharges.

The Great Lakes salmonid revolution blossomed tremendously in the early 1970s, with the introduction of the Pacific Coho and Chinook salmon in Lake Michigan. All Great Lakes states began to plant domestic and *Seeforellen*-strain brown trout in their waters in large numbers. The "Pacific salmon experiment" that Michigan embarked upon in the late 1960s was an attempt to find an apex predator to devour the over-abundant and invasive alewife pelagic baitfish, which were introduced from the Atlantic Ocean when the Welland Canal opened for freighter ship commerce. These were becoming a nuisance species, fouling up beaches with their dead carcasses. The browns found this food source impossible to resist.

In the fall of 2009, while fishing for Chinook salmon on a warm, clear sunny day, Joe Healy latched into a "brown

▲ The Great Lakes is the perfect "soup bowl" of food for this predator. Browns have the most diversified diet and also have the slowest predator attack speeds when compared to their competition: salmon and steelhead. Lake browns are the ultimate "junk yard dog" eating machines, especially *Seeforellen* leviathans from Lake Michigan, as pictured here with Michael Durkalec.

trout from hell" and his forty-one-pound, seven-ounce leviathan became the new world record! Since final DNA testing is pending, it appears that the fish was six years old and was on the first spawning migration. It just stayed out in the lake for years chowing down on baitfish and finally decided to come up river and spawn. It was a *Seeforellen*, which are known to attain leviathan sizes.

However, since the genetic diversity of the Michigan *Seeforellen* posed a problem for hatchery production, the state introduced its own wild unique Sturgeon River strain of migratory brown trout into Lake Michigan in 2010. It is a very exciting wild strain of brown trout that has the ability to go to the Great Lakes or live in the river.

Brown trout have quite the reputation for being carnivorous predators that will stop at nothing to get a good meal. The old saying that "A brown will eat anything that doesn't eat it," or "a brown trout would eat its tail," cannot be truer to

their lifestyle. Their cannibalistic tendencies have found them eating shoreline mice, small chickling ducks, and snakes, and devouring anything that swims is their daily credo.

Lake-run *Seeforellen* browns are also fond of nocturnal hunting and slowly cruise the shorelines and harbors of the Great Lakes, preferring 58 degrees to 63 degrees Fahrenheit waters that are too warm for Pacific salmon and Steelhead. As the Great Lakes continue to evolve in both positive and negative directions—predominantly from invasive species like the zebra and quaga mussels, Asian carp, exotic Mediterranean crustaceans, etc.—the lake-run browns are poised to be the species that will most likely capitalize on these food chain fluctuations, just as they have in the Baltic Sea. A Great Lakes Pacific salmon's diet is about 80 to 90 percent alewife baitfish. These pelagic baitfish have seen such drastic "up-and-down" population estimates from year-to-year that in some cases they have become almost non-existent, as is the case of Lake Huron, thus their Chinook salmon for the most part have become extirpated.

The Great Lakes have an incredibly diverse prey food chain, such as alewives, smelt, emerald shiners, deepwater sculpin, gobies, stickle-backs, and shrimp just to mention a few, and the brown will wholeheartedly eat every one of these. Along with native indigenous species like yellow perch, white perch, and walleye, these prey fish populations fluctuate drastically in numbers and balance percentages of the overall prey population. The brown does not discriminate, as it can adjust to the most abundant "entrée du jour" available in any given year. They are very fond of harbors, warm-water discharge from power and nuclear plants, sewage purification stations, and other "slum lord" areas. These areas usually feature high plankton and nutrient loads, which feed pelagic baitfish and other smaller prey species.

The lake-run browns are the German U-Boat/ wolf pack stalkers that cruise these areas to the theme from the movie *Jaws*. Recently, all the Great Lakes have become infested with the Giant *Hexagenia limbata* mayfly. A true size 2 dry when it hatches in July, they cover the roads like confetti after a parade and are known to curtail Cleveland Indian evening home games along Lake Erie and practically shut down shoreline airports. Lake Browns become ferocious topwater sippers when this hatch goes on for weeks on end with the extreme water clarity brought about by the filtering zebra mussels. As a result of the Great Lakes being cleared up from their heavily polluted days of the seventies, the giant native mayfly "wiggler nymphs" has become a stable food source for browns and steelheads alike.

So how does all this pan out in the big picture? It means you have a predator fish that will take a fly, any type of fly, anytime, anywhere, and often more than once! But, as gregarious as it may be, the brown trout is still one of the most cunning, elusive, and wary salmonids ever to evolve. Its often downright shy and coy behavior allows it to elude its ultimate predator, the angler, time and time again. That is what accounts for their huge sizes. Combine these Dr. Jekyll–Mr. Hyde qualities, and you have one hell of a game fish on the fly rod!

## Stillwater Lake Browns

Whenever you have a series of river systems interacting with smaller lakes and larger ocean/sea type systems all fused together, these create ecological waterway systems perfect for *trutta*, which are masters of migration and adaptability. Whether it be Scandinavia, Alpine Europe, Iceland, the UK, or the brown trout frontier of Patagonia, these complex systems serve *Salmo trutta* most perfectly. Here in the Great Lakes, we have several glacial lake systems that emulate the dynamics of the Scandinavian waterways, where perhaps *Salmo* as a whole evolved.

Populations can consist of migrant and non-migrant individuals. In brown trout there is a continuum from completely freshwater populations to completely anadromous populations. Lake migratory trout are often silvery, being analogous to anadromous trout and differing from their stream resident relatives that exhibit parr-like dresses. For instance in the Greana River, Sweden, there are two distinct spawning and rearing areas for brown trout, which are geographically separated by lenthic (still water lake) segments. The downstream section empties into Lake Ovregla. Resident trout dominate in the upstream sections, and 90 percent of the brown trout that migrated to the lake originate from the downstream section where density was high and growth rates low. Lake migrants had higher growth rates than non-migratory conspecifics. Peterson et al (2001) concluded that dispersal of the landlocked population and migratory and resident females appear to belong to a common gene pool adopting alternative migratory strategies. The same holds for populations that are split into anadromous and non-anadromous subpopulations of brown trout.

It was found that most brown trout became migrants when food levels were low but fewer did so at high levels. A positive relationship between density and the propensity to migrate has also been demonstrated experimentally.

—Jonsson & Jonsson,
*Ecology of Atlantic Salmon and Brown Trout*

So once again, we see adaptation and survival of the fittest molding the brown trout lifestyle and migratory patterns. In the Great Lakes and its inland glacial lakes, we have a system perfectly analogous to the ones in Sweden, Norway, and other parts of Europe. The beautifully-colored browns and the silver lake-running browns have the same genetics; privation and opportunity caused the migrations.

By migrating to rivers on their annual spawning drives and then dropping back into the lakes, they deftly hang on the same rocky, gravel-variegated, littoral shoreline areas where food items are abundant in all forms and their slow predatory speeds and cautious lifestyles allow them to sabotage and intercept available food forms at any given time. As waters warm into the summer they will venture out deeper into pelagic areas, which will cause them to adapt a more silvery, gray-backed, oceangoing appearance.

On another inland system, Torch Lake, which is a very deep, three-hundred-foot, twenty-mile long, ice-cold, clear blue Scandinavian-style Lake, and on the Finger Lakes of New York, there is a tremendous population of wild, lake-dwelling brown trout that exist in perfect cohabitation with the landlocked Atlantic salmon. Though there are several streams for migratory spawning, which a few do, most of the lake residents will find gravel shoal areas where there is current to spawn in the lake.

At first I didn't believe it until I read the research in the Jonsson book that documented similar *Salmo trutta* lake-spawning scenarios in Europe. I could not find where these fish would go to spawn in the fall to target them pre-spawn before migration. Thus in this situation, they maximize their food consumption all the way up into their last-minute spawning urges, and have once again mastered their environments, where often upstream migration can cause mortality and winter freeze-up situations.

## Landlocked and Sea/Lake–Run Tactical Diversity

There is such a tactical diversity when targeting landlocked and sea *Salmo*—both *salar* and *trutta*—wherever they are found. The techniques revolve around the following: pelagic and near-shore baitfish imitations, matching the hatch, and spawning aggression stimulations. Targeting these fish on a lakes and rivers on cloudy, overcast days with precipitation are usually ideal tactics. Strong storms and offshore winds also aid in their capture and aggressiveness to the fly, especially the dawn and dusk bite.

One of my first encounters with landlocked salmon was during a spring at the Sagamore resort on Lake George, New York. It was during my corporate food and beverage director days, and I was attending a conference there. I'd heard the stories of the landlocked salmon of Lake George and was determined to catch one, since I'd only had experience with oceangoing fish in Europe and Canada.

The old-timer locals were into traditional New England trolling with Grey and Black Ghost fly patterns on long lines below small V-shaped boats with tiny trolling motors, or large Montréal style canoes with three-horsepower motors. They would target the tiny feeder creeks that came into the lake where the rainbow smelt would school up to prepare for their spawning migrations along the shore and into the small runoff creeks and harbors, since the landlocked salmon would hone into these smolt-imprinting areas.

Many anglers waited for calm conditions to wade out just deep enough off the beach to double-haul baitfish streamers on sink tips. Since I had no boat, I waited for a nice, overcast, drizzly morning to head out and fish. Along the southern end of the lake there was a marina and a small creek entering the lake. At the crack of dawn,

▲ Landlocked Atlantics are very light sensitive, just like *trutta*. Though their seagoing relatives do not share such an affinity for darkness, perhaps being in similar surroundings and water types as *trutta* makes them photophobic. Credit: Jessica DeLorenzo

I was not the only one, as there were many other wading anglers. Small trolling boats were already plying the pre-dawn surf. Armed with a few Clouser minnows in white, chartreuse and blue, and of course the old standby Grey and Black Ghosts, I double-hauled my patterns as far as I could and slowly stripped, alternating the speed and jerking of the streamer strips. Occasionally I would see the backs of a small pod of fish moving around the marina, but nobody was hooking up. As soon as I arrived, a morning cold front storm was coming in and almost everyone vacated the premises, since it was cold and blustery, but in my opinion these were ideal conditions for the landlocked *salar*.

Being the only one left in the harbor, I took sips of cognac out of my flask to stay warm, while the waves started pounding the shore. It was then I noticed a small pod of what I assumed were Atlantics, even though there were other species of trout in the lake. Occasionally a few smelt would be jumping out of water in one area, obviously signaling that they were being hunted to the surface by a pack of ravenous larger fish. I targeted the commotion with my pattern and let the wave action sweep my fly toward shore with long, steady, jerking strips. After a few casts I noticed a small landlocked about 5 pounds become aerial-born, and it took a while for my line to tighten since I had so much line and slack from the wave interactions. There I was, finally hooked up the nice fin-clipped and stocked chrome Atlantic from Lake George, which I took back to the kitchen at the hotel and made the most killer gravlax cured salmon I ever tasted.

### New England–Style Trolling

With today's advancements in boating and fly tackle technology, trolling is by far the deadliest form of landlocked *Salmo* fishing. By trolling at a slow speed, or varying the speed if strikes are not occurring, the fish will take your fly convincingly—no hook set necessary—and immediately launch into an aerial display! Landlocked salmon will often produce better on moderate-to-faster trolling speeds, whereas lake browns like their prey moving a little slower, and will often follow a considerable distance before striking. Regardless of general standards, varying your speed and depth when the bite is off, or going deeper on calmer sunny days, will produce more hookups.

I have found the "dark fly dark day/bright fly bright day" to be unreliable in these pelagic zones where blue-green light is prominent. Thus, flies in that color spectrum with white and silver, produce very well in the spring and summer when pelagic baitfish are poised near the shore. Later in the summer and fall, choose sexual aggressive colors of red/orange/pink/black, etc.

Today's modern drift boats and power drifters with a small motor as pioneered by Stealthcraft of Baldwin,

Michigan, or any V-shaped boat able to take waves are ideal, and do not create such an alarming profile on the water as larger craft. Using today's modern Spey and switch rods, along with all the various sinking lines, from full sinking to intermediate in a variety of depth penetrating grains and stealthy colors from blue green to clear, one can fish large tandem flies emulating baitfish schools. With all the synthetic materials such as flashabou, realistic looking eyes, and all kinds of articulated movement, you can control the depth and visibility of your presentations.

With today's fish finders and GPS monitoring, which old-school New England trawlers didn't have—hell, some didn't even have motors but paddled their way around—you could zero in on the temperature breaks in the surf and spot schools of pack-hunting Atlantics or browns looking for the same smelt candy. By varying your speed with the different grains of sinking lines, T8–T20, and full and partial density compensating lines by Airflo, you can control slow-and-deep or fast-and-hot near the surface. Since the water temperatures in spring are pretty consistent, varying your presentation until you find the right mix is the key, since the baitfish schools can be scattered just about everywhere, even into the very extreme shallow waters.

### The Surf

Keep in mind that *Salmo salar* or *trutta* are still fussy, and that one must treat them just like finicky and nervous wild brown trout stream residents if you want to have consistent success. On very calm water days they will be quite spooky and see shadows and sloppy casts just as easily as a trout on a spring creek. Also bear in mind that no matter what size they are, they still have nearshore predators. In the ocean that can be a host of ravenous creatures like smaller seals, sea lions, sharks, and the list goes on. In fresh water, muskellunge and giant pike will attack lake-run brown trout and landlocked salmon in the ten-pound range with no problem. But on stormy, windy, and crashing-surf days, they and their prey are clumsy, due to the change in viscosity and murky waters, and become more aggressive. Sometimes they will venture close within a rod's length, since your presence is not noticed.

Keep in mind both Atlantics and browns in lakes or on the sea have similar lifecycles where they spawn in the late fall and winter, and hunt prey in the big open waters and estuaries the rest of the time. Thus their most aggressive periods will be when they have to make up for weight loss in the spawning process, and as they approach the shoreline spawning tributaries in late summer and fall or after spawning and spring ice-out.

In the spring, water temperatures are consistently cold throughout the shoreline surf areas, thus the fish can be anywhere. This again is the time where they must make up for lost body weight and will be hunting aggressively

▲ Maria Behety River, Tierra del Fuego. Credit: Jessica DeLorenzo

all day long. The offshore areas of spawning rivers will attract migrating spawning baitfish in spring and summer that have yet to spawn. Also the part of the shoreline that warms up the fastest, the surf shoals, will attract both predators and prey.

If you are fishing the summer surf in cold northern latitudes, where lake and sea temperatures remain consistently cold, there is heating during the day, so this becomes an early morning or dusk game.

The fall is prime time for locating schools of migrating landlocked salmon and brown trout, since they are schooling up and are ready to head toward their spawning tributaries. They are on one last surge to ingest as much food as possible prior to their upper river journey migrations, and thus in a very ravenous mood. Since the coastline has retained a good amount of heat from the summer, the coldest water will be in the shallowest areas at dawn after a night of cold air cooling.

Targeting the surf just as the sun is approaching, or in the darkest hours of predawn, is a great way to have fish close to where you're wading. Of course baitfish patterns, now trending toward the florescent reds and oranges, along with the giant Double D's, Lynch's Drunk and Disorderly, and Senyo's new pelagic series, are perfect for this

occasion. These schools are moving very close to shore in pods that often can be seen breaking the surface water. Anticipating the pods' movements is critical and casting at the area to the left or right of where you anticipate movement should produce results. Alternate the speed of your streamer stripping and where there is current allow for dead drifts of your patterns, just as a wounded or stunned baitfish would have appeal drifting naturally.

Winter is also a prime time to target the shorelines. In the seas and oceans, due to colder water absorbing more salinity, sea trout and Atlantics will seek the freshwater estuaries and fjords because of osmotic regulation in the bloodstream. Luckily, this also is where a majority of the baitfish and other annelids etc. will reside. Ice fishermen in these bays usually pick up sea trout and salmon. Wherever you have hydro and nuclear power warm water discharges, which are common along the Baltic, Atlantic Ocean, and Great Lakes region, you will find a huge congregation of predatory *Salmo* and baitfish enjoying the warmer, more fertile waters.

Certain features of the shorelines and coastal areas are worth paying attention to for locating fish. A river's "plume" or effluent is usually discolored from the type of stain and viscosity—some tannic, some sandy and silty,

▲ The rocky, jagged coastlines of Denmark and the Baltic usually form backwater eddies, where wave actions and tidal influences form accumulations of floating debris and concentrations of baitfish feeding on biological drift. These areas also often have shelves and drop-offs where *Salmo* lurk during bright light periods for refuge, like this landlocked rocky-back eddy *Salmo* that took a baitfish intruder in a Michigan ecosystem similar to the Baltic. Credit: Author

some green, etc. This will usually show up in the lake or sea either along the coastline or straight out, and can go for miles. The wave action and winds will direct how that effluent current interacts with the clearer big water. The fish would be attracted to the plume since the temperatures are usually warmer or colder depending on what season it is. The predator salmon and browns will clue in on these to hunt and will cruise along the seam, gliding in and out of the boundary between the colored plume and the clearer sea water.

It is good to concentrate on rips and channel trenches formed by river effluent. Here one can often find a good amount of current where you can manipulate your fly pattern. Offshore rocky reefs will also be areas of food and baitfish concentrations. Often, sand or rock bars exist a good distance off the shoreline and one can wade—carefully!—to these to fish these atolls.

Keep in mind both Atlantic salmon and browns migrate on high tides and full moons. Due to the interaction of their pineal gland, which is connected to their biological clock, the optic nerves, and the olfactory nerves, which signal the river system of natal origin, the smaller concentration of melatonin in the bloodstream due to full moons,

allow for around-the-clock migrations, coupled with higher tidal water levels into the estuaries pushing the fish up in a stealthy, cloaking fashion. It is often advisable to time your migratory sea-run fishing trips to periods right after full moons and high tides.

## Matching the Hatch

Landlocked salmon and lake browns relish multiple preys, pretty much taking advantage of every invertebrate and vertebrate feeding opportunity. Aquatic insect hatches in the surf are at their prime during late spring and the summers.

When landlocked salmon on Maine's lakes are in their younger year classes, they will move up into river systems like the Rapid River and feed on all the early spring hatches alongside the resident brown trout. Here they will pursue all the early-season mayflies, caddis, and stoneflies on the surface, and you'll catch landlocked salmon that look identical to *trutta*.

Lake- and sea-dwelling browns also migrate with the hatches. Often when the caddis and larger mayflies like the *Hexagenia* start hatching in the lower system, the migratory browns on their constant search for food will move up into the system. Usually other migratory fish such as rainbow trout and suckers will start the migration process as hatches correlate with upstream movement.

Most lake and sea-going *Salmo* are not extremely particular about the exact imitation to a natural fly, due to their larger predatory base foraging templates. Thus very suggestive patterns like the Wulff, Adams, and tarantula stimulators twitched and skated on the surface will produce results. In June the alderfly (*Megaloptera*), a large caddis/stonefly/dobsonfly–looking buggy creature, proliferates on New England and northern Canadian waters and is a delectable favorite of landlocked salmon and brown trout. Later into July and sometimes August, the *Hexagenia*, *Isonychia*, and white *Ephoron* mayflies will dominate in rivers emptying into lakes and coastal systems. Caddis of all different species are also estuarial, and can bring up surface activity almost instantaneously. Other significant lake-going insects such as dobsonflies, dragonflies, and larger moths will also bring on violent *Salmo* surface feeding. An amazing Orvis video shot by Simon Perkins of large brown trout leaping out of the water to take damsel flies in New Zealand is a perfect example of this: https://news.orvis.com/fly-fishing/video-damsels-in-distress-on-a-new-zealand-stream.

The larger *Diptera* order of lake- and sea-dwelling midges are significant food sources for big water *Salmo*. Their sizes range anywhere from a size 14 to 22, but the larger 14 and 16 "Black Buzzer" is very common on still-water lakes in the UK and throughout the world. "Buzzer" patterns were perfected on the British lake systems. Pods of feeding landlocked salmon and browns will migrate with the hatches and cruise the surface in a continual search for hatching pupae and egg-laying female *diptera*.

But don't ignore terrestrial insects. They are often blown off coastline cliffs and sand dunes and are carried in the wind for great distances. Beatles, ants, bees, deer flies, even hoppers, can be found miles offshore, and *Salmo* will feed on them prolifically, especially in the frothy "scum-line" temperature break demarcation zones, where a cold wall of water meets warm water and creates an upwelling effect. Baitfish will gather here to feed, which attract *Salmo*, who will eat not only the baitfish but also and invertebrate insects, which is an ideal foraging combination.

When fishing these river and lake migratory systems, the riffle hitch is an ideal tactic, the fish are not holding still in certain preferred lies, as on a river, and movement on the surface is what triggers them. Thus they tend to move around a lot and are looking for signs of prey.

## Migrations and Dominant Aggressive Behavior Tactics

The commencement of spawning migrations on a river can vary in timing based on latitudes and climate. Colder northern climates will begin to see earlier migrations starting in July and August. Wild strains have much greater run timing and success.

It was a particularly hot August years back when I traversed the entire shoreline of Lake Superior with my wife and our four-year-old son Peter in search of wild, summer-run steelhead. I was conducting research for my book *Steelhead Dreams*. Wisconsin's Boise Brule river system was a must-visit due to its legendary rainbow trout, magnificent woodland wilderness setting, and gorgeous ice cold waters. President Calvin Coolidge, an avid fly fisherman, spent his summers right in the middle section of the Brule at Henry Clay Pierce's Cedar Island luxury summer home, in what was then called the "summer White House." Coolidge's friend Clay was a rubber baron of the time, being the fourth richest man in the country.

Big Lake is a section of the river that was one giant bog-type lake, where the newly-arrived deepwater Browns found it more to their liking, even though they were a long way off from spawning in the fall. Here I had the pleasure of fishing with a legendary guide's son, Cordell Manz, who was a biologist for the Wisconsin Department of Natural Resources and knew the waters well. He explained that the lake-runs could push the scales at twelve pounds, and were aggressive critters, but pretty moody and often not on the take most the time. They got real active around nighttime and just before thunderstorms.

All this made sense, since cold pressure systems mean changing water conditions, usually rising water when it cools, which favors migration and increasing irritability. Keep in mind, most rivers are running low from summer heat waves and droughts in the early fall migration, which is an inopportune time to be running up the river.

We waited for days of stifling upper 90 degrees F weather until we saw a huge cold front brewing off of Lake Superior. Cordell informed me that it was time to get the canoe and get out there. As we launched our canoe and floated on Big Lake, we saw large browns breaking surface everywhere, which was kind of unheard-of on a bright August day. The barometric pressure was triggering their air bladder systems and obviously the best weather forecaster is usually arthritic joints and a migratory fish's air bladders.

Armed with a large articulated streamer, I cast to where the fish were porpoising and my line stopped and went dead like I had just snagged a log. A stunning kype-jawed Big Lake brown launched into the air several times, one of five others on that memorable day. Most anglers have good success on hungry browns with mouse patterns in nighttime, when the fish are less cautious. But if you can time a weather frontal system and sling some big meat at these beautiful creatures, it was lake-run trout ecstasy as good as you can get.

▲ The big browns like this hefty Ontario tributary *trutta*sauarus will take egg patterns, large stonefly nymphs, leeches, and buggers with gusto. Credit: John Miller

Swinging flies on Spey rods and two-handed switch rods is a great way to target them through the incubator pools where these fish will stage, similar to Atlantic salmon fishing. Fishing big, articulated streamers like we discussed in the *Trutta*saurus chapter, is one way to elicit a violent strike. Streamer colors in orange, black, yellow, red, also the white/gray motif of a common baitfish, is the key to success.

Nymphing is also highly effective, especially on rivers that have Pacific salmon, Atlantic salmon, and Steelhead migrations. One notable world-class system in New York off Lake Ontario's shoreline is the Oak Orchard. But when water conditions are low and clear they are just as spooky and ultra-selective as a West Branch Delaware brown trout.

Due to the extremely territorial and aggressive natures of alpha spawning fish, non-anadromous *Salmo* have been known to be caught several times in the same day. This, combined with the fact that they still are very much in the predatory eating phase, at the same time of jockeying for spawning supremacy, makes them much more game to take the fly.

## New Frontiers For *Salmo Salar*: The Great Lakes And Beyond

In October, 1836, two men took (from the Salmon River in New York) 230 salmon between 8 PM and 12, with Spears and fire-jacks, and after 12 till morning two other men in the same skiff took 200, the average weight of the entire lot being 14 ¾ pounds. We have had 1500 fresh salmon in the fish smokehouse at one time. When a freshet occurred in June they would always come up, and sometimes a few early in the spring. Any time from June till winter when there was a freshet they were sure to come. The principle time, however, was in the fall, during, October and November. 12 skiffs in one night have taken an average of 300 salmon each,

—Witness account, Pulaski, New York

Lake Ontario is the last deep cold Great Lake at the bottom of the Great Lakes basin chain. It spills over Niagara Falls, where the water finds its way to the Atlantic Ocean via this very fertile and deep lake. In the early 1660s, the

French Jesuit explorers Le Mercier and Le Moyne used Indian guides as they paddled their large Montréal birch bark canoes, filled with furs to trade and provisions to eat. They were on a mission to conquer and spread Christianity throughout the New World. Another account attests to the abundance of the salmon at that time: "One of our men took twenty large salmon, and on the way up the river our people killed thirty other salmon, with spears and paddles. There are so many of them that they were struck without difficulty." It must have been an amazing sight to see all these rivers on the New York and Ontario side all the way from the Gulf of St. Lawrence to Niagara Falls having runs of the magnificent *Salmo salar*.

Before the tragic loss the British officers of the French and Indian war and Revolution appreciated the sporting qualities of *salar* in these river systems. As they fished their traditional English salmon flies, they lobbied locals to stop the wanton killings. Whereas the sport was a leisurely pursuit of the gentleman officers, the locals utilized them as a food source and just pitchforked them to death.

According to another account, "In 1817, a dam was built on the Genesee River at Rochester, which flows into Lake Ontario. Thousands of salmon were clubbed to death, mangled with spears and pitchforks like mass frenzy, seal-like slaughters." These massive and ignorant slaughters eventually had catastrophic repercussions, as by 1891, the US Commissioner of Fish and Fisheries reported that the native salmon of Lake Ontario and some sections of the Finger Lakes had totally disappeared, though the Finger Lakes and inland Champlain and Lake George held on to a few landlocked salmon, where they thrive today.

In the constant effort to restore indigenous species, the US Fish and Wildlife Service teamed up with New York State and the province of Ontario to reestablish the indigenous Lake Ontario Atlantic salmon. It began in earnest in the 1970s and is still going strong today. Natural reproductive documentation has occurred on the Salmon River in New York, named for the once indigenous *salar*, as well as on the Credit River that runs through Toronto.

Besides the natural reproduction of *salar*, Fran Verdoliva, NYDEC coordinator for this Lake Ontario Atlantic salmon restoration, indicated that wild brown trout/Atlantic salmon

▲ A Detroit River *salar*. Once the fish of nobility, kings, and queens, now available to the common man, thanks to new *salar* frontiers. Credit: Brad Smyth

hybrids were present in some tributaries of the Salmon River. They are result of a male brown trout fertilizing a female Atlantic salmon. Though research in Europe shows that it will only survive to a certain point in their life and then die or become totally sterile, this new finding could be revolutionary for *Salmo* morphological perspective and evolution, as they are surviving to older ages.

Today, Michigan, New York, and Ontario are taking the new *Salmo* frontier limelight, celebrating victory in their attempts to colonize the Great Lakes with *Salmo salar*. It all started with the Lake Superior's Roger Greil–inspired aquatic laboratory on the St. Mary's River in Sault Sainte Marie. Raising first Penobscot mainstream and now Grand Lake strains, the returning salmon look as beautiful and healthy as any oceangoing fish returning to Russia or the Canadian Maritimes. Its vast territory of Lake Huron provides a tremendous amount of baitfish and crustacea, but without sharks, orcas, seals, and other predators. Roger Greil's Grand Lake strain, has now probably evolved to a Michigan/St. Mary's strain. Raised in the Soo and stocked as yearlings and fingerlings, these fish were responsible for my client's IGFA world record landlocked salmon at twenty-seven pounds. As of this writing, our record still stands.

Hence a new horizon is looking bright on the deep and cold waters of Lake Huron and Lake Ontario. Once a phenomenal fishery for the large King Pacific salmon, introduced into the Great Lakes in the 1960s to battle the Alewife baitfish overpopulation on Lake Huron, the King salmon did such a tremendous job of eating the prey that they basically ate themselves to death and destroyed the entire alewife population. Today the Lake contains Emerald shiners, perch, sticklebacks, smelt, whitefish, and herring. Coupled with these food forms are *Misys* shrimp and massive populations of giant *Hexagenia* mayflies, which occur all summer. All these are ideal prey forms for the *salar's* multi-faceted appetite.

Introducing them to river tributaries like the Au Sable and other tributaries, made perfect sense and is now starting to see fruition. Further investigation shows that the *salar* are also infiltrating the cold Canadian river systems that have tremendous opportunity for natural reproduction.

All of this could not have come at a better time. It is unfortunate that the indigenous Atlantic salmon population of the North Atlantic and Baltic Sea have hit all-time lows, except for places like wilderness Russia and the always fruitful Icelandic rivers. Exploring new frontiers is necessary to preserve a tremendous legacy of what could be civilization's king of all fish and new waters to explore for their regal destiny.

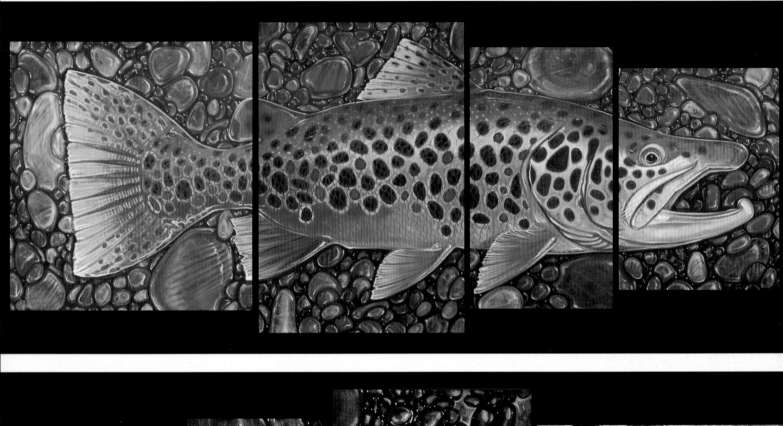

▲ Derek DeYoung's *Salmo* tetraptychs.

# 12. The Artisan, the Forager, and the Future

**B**rown trout and Atlantic salmon have inspired mankind for tens of thousands of years with their beauty, bold wild spirit, fascinating evolution, and life's journey—a true love affair since before the early cave drawings of Neanderthal man in Europe. Watching them jump waterfalls beguiles an angler and inspires artistic creativity and ingenious fly impressions to fool them. Countless artists, fly tiers musicians, chefs, and foraging naturalists have walked the river's ecosystems and forests, and have celebrated the *Salmo* in their various ways. In this chapter, we view the tremendous artistic and culinary contributions of *Salmo*, and look into the future for civilization's founding fish.

## Mark Susinno

http://www.natureartists.com/mark_susinno.asp
http://www.wildwings.com/

▲ Credit: wildwings.com

**Derek Deyoung**

https://www.derekdeyoung.com/

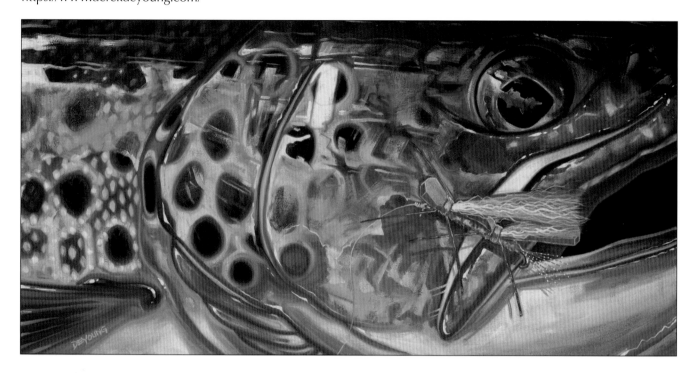

**David Ruimveld**

http://www.davidruimveldstudio.com/

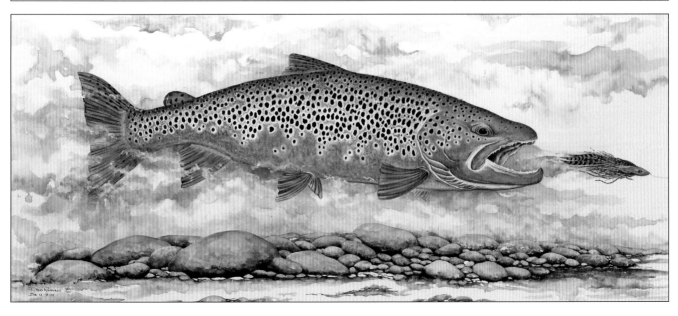

**Duane Hada**

http://www.rivertowngallery.com/

## The Culinary Passion for *Salmo*

My angling philosophy on brown trout and Atlantic salmon is 99 percent catch-and-release. They are noble survivors of a constantly-changing earth and the delicate, unstable ecosystems where they thrive. Ocean populations of *salar* are diminishing at an alarming rate. Wild brown trout fisheries are losing rivers and streams in their indigenous range of Europe as their populations, size, and existence are threatened through habitat destruction, corporate aquaculture greed, and pollution—both biotic and abiotic—along with urban sprawl. Many wild populations are on the verge of vanishing forever.

We must protect every possible genetic contributing individual fish in wild or hold-over fisheries. But on strictly put-and-take rivers where there isn't the remotest chance of a brown or Atlantic surviving (and I seriously mean acknowledging "remote possibility" being a cause for live release and possible survival and natural reproduction), there are exceptions that will allow harvest.

Being a classically-trained chef, I believe one of *salar's* chief downfalls is the fact that their flesh has been loved to death by millions of chefs and food connoisseurs throughout the world. Poaching, grilling, smoking, curing, and sushi have all taken the Atlantic salmon to new gastronomical heights. But the complications of aquaculture farming in their indigenous habitat at the Norwegian fjords, UK firths and river esturaries, and Canada's vast maritime aquaculture bounty, and now spreading to distant Pacific waters of Chile, are implicating diseases and genetic interbreeding flaws that are doing micro-specific damage to indigenous genetic populations.

The responsible new trend in organic, closed-containment separation from the wild, is the aquaculture of the eco-friendly future—thus separating farmed fish from indigenous wild stocks by using cold inland lakes, mining quarries, constructed modern metallic holding and feeding facilities, which is the responsible new wave for *Salmo's* survival and gastronomical enjoyment. Organic vertical infused feed systems of purple corn, crushed krill, sardines, etc., that duplicate the wild forage and taste as well, will be critical to the future. Thus the taste of responsible aqua-cultured fish will taste as good, if not better, than the

▲ The Author's culinary passion for Salmo extends to his fight for organic/closed containment and conservation-minded aquaculture to preserve wild fish.
Credit: Author

highly-prized wild variety, minus the damaging price of harvesting the last surviving wild populations.

People always ask me for the most delicious way to prepare salmon and trout. That is a tough question to answer. *Salmo* as a whole have higher healthy omega-3 fat concentrations, which lends their flesh a taste distinct from the lean, white flesh of other fish. You either love the flavor of *Salmos* or disdain them. Thus grilling, poaching, and grill/ light smoke hardwood infusion are tasty ways to enjoy this fish. Cooking to "medium rare," leaving a significant raw center/ pink flesh in the middle, retains much of the fat content and gives you an amazing taste. My favorite method is grill/smoking in this style, and making a French-inspired sauce to coat the fish platter, using responsible farm-raised salmon or trout from closed containment ecosystems. Here is an easy and delicious recipe that is sure to impress guests.

▲ The author with his signature *Salmo* dish.

## Grilled Cedar-Planked Salmon/Trout with Dijon/ Dill Beurre Blanc Sauce and Wild Caramelized Mushrooms

### Ingredients:

- Atlantic salmon,
  sea-run browns (or steelhead, Pacific salmon) fillets— pin bones removed—leave skin on when grilling

Prepare cedar planks by soaking them for two hours in a bin of water with cheap wine and some sea salt in the water. Grill medium-rare on cedar planks, throw soaked apple/cherry/hickory chips on flames for a tinge of smoke flavor if desired, or plain directly on grill—baste fish with olive oil and cracked pepper prior to grilling. One hour before grilling put fillets in baking dish, basting with white wine and squeezed lemon to take any fatty taste off. Don't overcook fish—medium rare pink inside!

### Dijon /Dill Beurre Blanc Sauce

Use deep sauté pan.

### Ingredients:

- Two packs of fresh dill
- One pack of fresh Tarragon
- Fresh lemons
- Shallots, two bulbs
- Garlic
- Bottle of chardonnay (cheap)
- Pint of heavy whipping cream
- Stick of unsalted butter
- Dijon mustard
- Pack of wild mixed medley mushrooms
- Pack of shiitake mushrooms
- Pack of regular white sliced mushrooms
- Balsamic vinegar
- Virgin olive oil
- Cooking sherry

**Prep Sauce:** Chop and mince the tarragon leaves and one pack of dill leaves. Mince/slice shallots, mince garlic as much as desired, and throw all into sauté pan with half a bottle of wine. Reduce until ingredients are simmer-cooked in a shallow pool of wine liquid. Then add pint of heavy cream. Reduce until ½ to ¾ is boiled off, should have ingredients visible, then shut heat off and whisk in ¾ stick of butter—BUT DON'T SEPARATE BUTTER-SLOWLY MELT IT. Then add 2 to 3 tablespoons of Dijon Mustard and whip with whisk. Add a few squeezes of fresh lemon, cracked pepper to taste, and garnish with lots fresh dill leaves. Keep in sauté pan and make sure no heat on it so it doesn't separate.

### Caramelized Wild Mushrooms

### Ingredients:

- Virgin olive oil
- Washed mélange of wild mushrooms, or just morels
- ¼ cup or more of chardonnay
- cracked pepper
- ¼ cup balsamic vinegar
- ¼ cup of sherry

Coat a large sauté pan with ample virgin olive oil, bring to heat and add remaining ingredients. Sauté/stir until caramelized. If too tart/citric from wines, sprinkle with a tinge of sugar during caramelization.

Serve as pictured above, on large serving platter. Pour sauce amply over fish with caramelized mushrooms on top. Garnish with sprigs of fresh dill and wedges of lemon. Serve family style. BON APPETIT!

## Foraging the River Ecosystem's Wild Edibles: Fiddleheads to Mushrooms

We are often oblivious to the magnificent wild flora and fauna while exploring new *Salmo* waters, or when we are enjoying the local rivers we have come to love. *Salmo* often live in stunning wilderness that still retains the wild goodness of the earth that early civilizations of natives learned to harvest for food and medicine. To make your experience on these waters so much more special, learn the harvestable items that can add to your dinner table.

Take a hike along the small springs and brooks that enter your main *Salmo* streams and rivers. It is here in the glens, ravines, forested valleys and slope areas that have the bounty of the wild. All the wild forage edibles live in wet, damp, cool places near rivers and their spring aquifer sources. With a combination of mixed deciduous and conifer forests that border on open fields and old orchards

▲ Walking the rivers, we often ignore the wild delectable flora beckoning us to explore. Credit: Jasper (upper left); Alan Bergo (middle right); Author (both bottom right)

for organic matter and light, if you start finding ferns and mosses you are definably on the right track.

In the spring the ferns and wild flowers soak in the warming rays of the sun and use the stored winter snow moisture. Morel mushrooms are the delectable choice of early foragers. Look around dead elms, poplars, aspens, and anywhere ravines have dead barked tree shavings. Newly-burnt soil and abandoned orchards are choice places.

In those areas you will also find the fiddlehead ferns, wild ramps, and garlic. Also as for a spring salad, wild chickweed, wood sorrel, poor man's pepper, garlic mustard, watercress from the spring brooks, pennycress, and violet leaves make a nice mix for a balsamic salad with local goat's cheese or a gorgonzola dressing. Walk up the brooks and spring aquifers and add watercress for a nice tart and crispy touch.

As the spring into summer progresses, look for wild edibles after thunderstorms that give a nutrient electronic shock to the organic soil, along with moisture that fuels the mold/fungus nutrients. In combination (hardwood/conifer) forests and along wet damp ravines and ferns, also look near conifer spruce, cedar, and pine needles along with decaying organic mosses and leaves, where you will find white and red chanterelles, Boletus or "the king of mushrooms," oysters, chickens of the wood, beefsteaks, and many more luscious fungi.

Also don't forget all the wild raspberries, blackberries, and strawberries, abandoned plum trees, and other fruit like wild grapes, raspberries, and blueberries, that can be found often by rivers that can you can pick and eat at the same time. Take a porous foraging bag with you to harvest these wonders as you allow their seedlings and spores to repopulate the soil. Along with tasty wild edibles, there are also toxic plants and mushrooms. Your best bet is to join a local foraging and/or mycological group, along with night classes available at your local community college or adult education classes, whose members and students have plenty of local foraging experience. Also consult the many books and field guides to foraging in the wild by Skyhorse Publishing, which will give you authority and comfort to discern the edible from the potentially poisonous and harmful varieties.

Being a former corporate hotel food and beverage director and chef, my passion for the culinary arts runs as deep as my love for fly fishing. Chef Alan Bergo from Minnesota, a chef of my liking who writes the famous blog foragerchef.com, is a true master forager who brings the wild to comfort cuisine dishes and amazes everyone with the bounty of the land that fly fishers all too often ignore. Here is his famous fiddle head salad, which goes great with spring asparagus.

## Fiddlehead Salad with Spruce Tips, Peppermint, and Pecorino

▲ Credit: Alan Bergo

One of the most interesting parts of this is the rough, salty pieces of cheese, it's important they're in chunks, so resist the urge to grate it.

Also, make sure you have a species of spruce tips that have a nice flavor, since the bitterness can vary considerably between species. I've been commissioning Amish in Wisconsin to pick them for the Salt Cellar; they don't know what species they are, but they know what bitter tastes like.

Serves two as a side dish.

### Ingredients

- 2 cups shucked fava beans, still inside the green shell
- 1.5 cups fiddlehead ferns, stems trimmed
- 1 tablespoon ramp bulbs, sliced (*shallots or green garlic would be a good substitute too*)
- ⅛ cup extra virgin olive oil
- Fresh squeezed lemon juice, to taste
- Kosher salt and fresh ground black pepper, plus additional salt for the blanching water
- 1 tablespoon spruce tips, picked into ½ in pieces
- 1 tablespoon wild peppermint (commercial spearmint or peppermint can be substituted)
- 1 ounce pecorino Romano cheese, highest quality available, broken into rough ½-inch chunks

### Method

1. Bring a few quarts of salted water to a boil. Blanch the fava beans for 2 minutes, then shock in ice water, drain, peel, and reserve. Next blanch the fiddleheads for no less than 1 minute, then shock in ice water, drain and reserve.

2. In a small sauté pan, heat 1 tablespoon of the extra virgin olive oil and the ramp bulbs; do not color the

ramps, you just want to remove the raw flavor, cook them for 2 minutes or so on medium-low heat, then reserve.

3. When you want to serve the salad, combine the peeled fava beans, fiddleheads, ramps and remaining ingredients and toss in a salad bowl. Double check the seasoning for salt and pepper and adjust as needed, then serve immediately.

## The Future

There is no question that *Salmo* had been loved nearly to death. Since they evolved from the Eocene Ice Age, which created a new world aquatic order, the first brown trout, and later Atlantic salmon, were destined by divine creation to be civilization's founding and most-adored fish.

From the moment Cro-Magnon man saw the first beautiful red-spotted *Salmo trutta* pecking tiny mayflies on the surface in the brook outside his cave, to the runs of the salmon that adventured up the rivers throughout Europe, Canada, Iceland, and the UK, and sustained life for many clans of Neanderthal hunters and gatherers, they have formed a strong bond with mankind.

Managing *Salmo*, both brown trout and Atlantic salmon, for the future will take near genius intuition, a humble respect, and the foresight to overcome changing conditions due to direct encroachment, climate change, and man's abuse of the habitats where *Salmo* have thrived for millions of years. Sustainability of fish populations and habitat degradation, over harvesting, ocean and river temperature and water quality regimes—both human and natural climate change induced—all impose serious implications that must be addressed if *Salmo* is to survive for the millennia to come.

Just as *Salmo*—the proverbial "Atlantic trouts"—have continually evolved to overcome massive changes in civilization's industrial and urbanization development, all the while dealing with constantly-changing climate and ecosystem turmoil, so too must mankind plot out a journey to allow the fish to do what they have done best without man's interaction. *Salmo* are the eternal underdogs that continue to baffle scientists and anglers alike for their resilience and ability to recover, even when their future looks perilous.

Roman Moser, as an innovative tier and angling conservationist-thinker, sums up *Salmo trutta*'s future in its indigenous European waters:

▲ Live release is the only way *Salmo* will survive the onslaught of climate change and civilization's encroachment. Credit: Arni Baldursson/Lax-A

▲ Roman Moser, the Lee Wulff/Tom Rosenbauer of Europe is the "canary in the coal mine" for Europe's indigenous *Salmo*. Credit: Albert Pesendorfer

it is estimated that only 20 percent are available for the fishes' survival.

Population growth and the resultant density of new home construction have reduced the aquatic living space for the brown trout more and more.

With global climate change there is been a trend for warmer early winters and colder springs, almost as if Arctic and Antarctic weather takes its good time in reaching temperate latitudes at the onset of winter transition into summer.

*Salmo* has survived climate change multitudes of times, and their genesis took place during a very tumultuous period of change. They have shown through millennia they can handle and adapt to change. We have seen this for sea- and lake-running brown trout as well as resident browns that will feed year-round and grow to amazing sizes like the Muskegon 'trutta saurus' taken by my Geno Kelly.

Since sea browns can tolerate much warmer water temperatures close to shore than Atlantic salmon, changing variability in water temperatures including the rapid onset of them recently, has less impact on migratory Browns.

As for Atlantic salmon, droughts, floods, temperature

After World War II the world was still in order for the brown trout in Austrian and German waters. Natural river banks, very few hydroelectric dams and the eutrophication from the untreated discharge of household water into the waters where the brown trout of the Danube lived, as well as those of the Atlantic branch, allowed them to amass great numbers as well as weight. Every little meadow brook held these red-spotted trout, and I can remember how we boys could grab *Salmo Trutta* from under the creek stones with our bare hands.

But what is the situation like today? I consider it depressing.

In free-flowing stretches all fish, not only trout, come in contact with agricultural run-off (pesticides), waste material from treatment plants (pharmaceuticals, cleaning chemicals, antibiotics, estrogen) as well as water from factories and industry. Even the recently-discovered micro plastic is not helpful to the growth of young fish. Because of these factors basic nourishment, namely the number of water insects, is severely diminished. In comparison to previous years

▲ Russia and Iceland cannot be the only last bastions of wild *Salmo* if they are to survive. We must explore new frontiers and nurture the resources we already have. Credit: Mark Danhausen

extremes and anomalies such as warm winters and cool summers, can totally flip the fine-tuned biological clocks of these thirty-million-year-old masterpieces. As the Jonssons point out in their book, the traditional migratory and resident behavioral cycles will all be in a topsy-turvy state. This could delay or accelerate spawning success, confuse food foraging with fluctuations in hatch and baitfish availability, implicate exotic invasive species, and other complications. Floods and droughts can effect egg hatching and alevin emergence. Low flows and rapidly-changing water temperatures can affect the growing seasons and migrations of smolts. Droughts can delay upstream spawning migrations, and severe winters can kill holdover adults in river systems and estuaries. Overall, so much uncertainty to think about.

In conclusion, the encouraging aspect of *Salmo* is their incredible ability to adjust and maintain dominance in spite of everything, as I mentioned throughout this book. They have survived greenhouse gases, Ice Age lockups, world wars, ecological pollution travesties, and all types of climactic and celestial catastrophes, and are the ultimate survivors. They have the watchful conservation shroud of the Atlantic Salmon Federation (ASF), the North Atlantic Salmon Conservation Organization (NASCO), Trout Unlimited (TU), and the Federation of Fly Fishers (FFF), and you further add the reader, chef, naturalist, and passionate *Salmo* angler, to all lobby and watch over them.

Given the fact that *Salmo's* mothership, the earth, is 70 percent water—both fresh, salt and subterranean—and that *Salmo* can adjust to all of it, gives them an encouraging chance at survival as civilization's most adored and divine piscatorial wonder, as they embark on a new and exciting unknown journey with all of mankind.

# THE NEXUS FLY MASTERY: NEW AGE PATTERNS FOR *SALMO*

**Courtesy of Stacey Niedzweicki and John Miller. Visit www.brownatlanticnexus.com for detailed fly recipes, pattern history, presentation, and tyer.**

▲ Nexus Crustaceans

▲ Drakes and BWOs

▲ The Euro nymphing bethos invasion

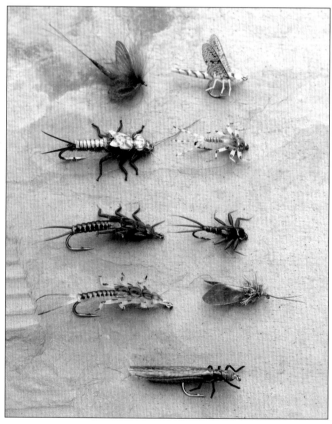

▲ Frosty/Hemingway New Age Realism

▲ The para-visibles

▲ Big, meaty game flies

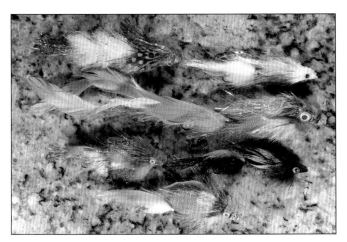

▲ Tommy Lynch's drunk and disorderlies

▲ Modern foam terrestrials and stones

▲ Graeme Ferguson's "Taste of Scotland"

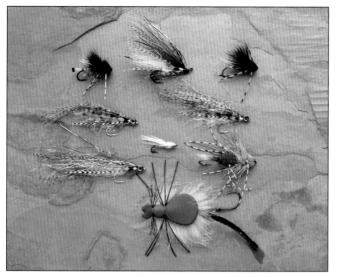

▲ *Salmo* fusion delectables

▲ Author's nexus mayfly synthesis

▲ Nymphs and emergers

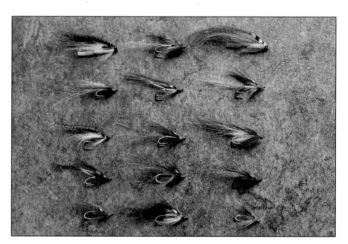

▲ *Salar* supremacy: Caledonia fly style

▲ Author's WMDs, or weapons of midge destruction

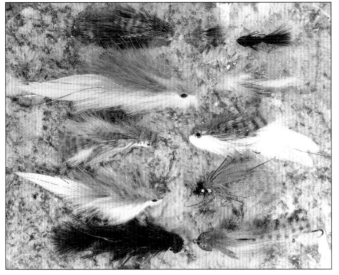

▲ The sculpin evolution/revolution

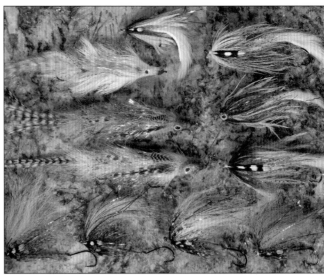

▲ Senyo's *salmo* synthesis

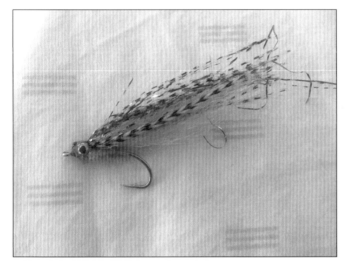

▲ Author's super sac fry

▲ Double deceivers: Motown and Angler's choice

# Acknowledgments

*M*y *Nexus* book has been truly one of the most unique and daring undertakings in my authorship/writing career. I have always insisted and personally challenged myself that my writings will forever be remembered as being thought provoking, controversially stimulating, and cutting edge into new frontiers about the way we view our piscatorial angling passion.

There are many reasons why authors write books and articles. Many do it for fame and fortune or to elevate their professional careers. Many have a serious affection and fervor they have been blessed with on a subject matter where they share their viewpoint/ concept/ theories with the world. With me and my book, it was a pure obsession and passion for the *Salmo*, which is mankind and civilization's founding fish, that has held a mesmerizing emotional and romantic grip on me since a young boy, when I caught my first brown trout at the age of six on a small spring creek in the gentle rolling Allegheny mountains of southern New York state. Later, at the age of nine, on a river along my dad's farm off the Baltic Sea in Poland, my first Atlantic salmon and sea trout came into my hands and immersed my eyes into the beauty of these masterpieces of creation forever.

When I first conceived of the strong "connection /nexus" of these fish by my fifty-four years of perpetual pursuit and more so by my intense streamside observation, angling and guiding for them, I asked many great minds and talents from the scientific, angling, photographic, authorship, artistic, and culinary worlds to be a part of my journey. The overwhelming support, contributions, and graciousness they all bestowed on this project is truly humbling. I am proud to acknowledge and forever be grateful to them.

To Dr. Bror Jonsson, "Salmo Godfather" from University Oslo, Norway; Dr. Bob Bachman, brown trout/ *trutta* PhD thesis visionary; and to the true pioneer of amazing fly-fishing minds and talents , the one and only Tom Rosenbauer, from Orvis for writing the introductions.

To all the world-class angling, author, and editorial talents that have written such great and much appreciated endorsements for the book: Kelly Galloup, the streamer Einstein and "*trutta* Buddha" from his Slide Inn Mecca on the Madison in Montana. Ross Purnell, the gallivanting world traveler and connoisseur, and editor–in-chief at *Fly Fisherman* magazine, for all the support over the past decades and for allowing us to live the dream through his travels. Bob Linsenman, angling author and poet laureate extraordinaire of all things fly fishing and the natural world

who is a true creative writing treasure. Henry Ramsey, modern dean of Pennsylvania's gentlemanly hatch-matching legacy and fly tying. Jason Randall, the great technical mind and authorships of all things trout, that gives us a perspective from the trout's viewpoint. Glen Blackwood, the masterful eye for literary excellence, modern and vintage book connoisseur, collector, and aficionado at Great Lakes Fly Fishing Company in Rockford, Michigan, a book emporium of the utmost bibliotheca treasures. Ed Shenk, living dean and sculpin master of the Cumberland Valley limestoners and good friend. Beau Beasley, Mid-Atlantic trout seeker, Project Healing Waters mentor, author, and visionary and entertainer par excellence. Arni Baldurson, the ultimate *Salmo salar* "whisperer" and gallivanting, world-traveling adventurist. And a special thank you to the "Lee Wulff" of Europe, the honorable Roman Moser of Austria, who is a fly-fishing talent of the highest order; folks like him only come our way once in a lifetime. Thanks for all your support starting with my *Selectivity*, and your future vision in the *Nexus*.

I am proud to feature, showcase, and in some cases introduce, these amazing artistic photographic visionaries and talents, some of whom you have seen in the past and others whose talents you will be seeing for many years to come. Photographic Director John G. "Bugsy" Miller, from the hallowed Delaware and Catskills, for his epic insect and natural world class photography. Dave Jensen, master Alberta and New Zealand guide and *trutta* shutter master, www.flyfishalberta.com. James Haswell from Michigan, for his excellent historical perspective, assistance with global outreach on fly tying, and classic artistic salmon patterns. The amazing Stacy Niedzwiecki, friend and finest Great Lakes photographer and website builder par excellence. Legendary *Salmo salar* shutter master Gilbert Van Ryckervorsel from Holland and Nova Scotia, where he has his amazing art studio www.salmonphotos.com. The amazing eye and talent, Jessica De Lorenzo of Pennsylvania, www.delorenzo-photo.com. Albert Pesendorfer from Austria. Hermann Schmider of Black Forest, Germany. Andrew Steele Nisbit of Buffalo, New York, @andrewsteelenisbet-instagram. Mike Tsukamoto, www.mikescatchreport.com. Rich Felber from Michigan, *trutta* hunter extraordinaire. Patrick Fulkrod from South Holsten River, Tennessee, tailwater guide specialist and shutter bug, www.southholstenrivercompany.com. Jim Klug, the ultimate professional camera work and world destination adventurist, www.yellowdogflyfishing.com. Kevin Feenstra, the amazing underwater diving photographic eye of this master guide/fly tier and talent, www.feenstraoutdoors.com. Robert Chiasson of the Margaree River, Nova Scotia. Laurie Campbell of Scotland. The Catskill Fly Fishing Museum archives. French Ministry of Culture. Jack Flaherty. To the master historical interpreter of the fly fishing journey, the one and only Paul Schullery. The living legend of Salmo salar, Art Lee, who has delved into the spirit of Atlantic salmon more than any other living soul. I have read and have been mesmerized by his writings in the Atlantic Salmon Journal for decades. The Polish fly fishing shutter master, Arek Kubala.Fran Verdoliva, who is NYDEC keeper of the Salmon River salar restoration. Mark Danhausen and Pete Humphries, the gallivanting two-handed "fishy" spey duo. Paul Marriner, world-class author and publisher. Craig Fellin, the passionate Big Hole, Montana river keeper, and lodge owner par excellence, www.bigholelodge.com. The "fishy biologist" Michael Durkalec of the Cleveland Metro Parks system. Martin Joergenson, Scandinavian sea trout expert and proprietor of www.globalflyfisher.com. Brian Fleschig, trout educator, guide, and instructor, www.madriveroutfitters.com. Andrew Vanderwall, leviathan trutta stalker of the Au Sable. Doug Danforth, bug shutter master.

To all the passionate brown trout and Atlantic salmon stalkers that have shared their multi-faceted talents in fly patterns, photographic images, and insights into the world of Salmo. Mike Schmidt, passionate fly designer of www.anglerschoiceflies.com.Tommy "truttasaurus Buddha" Lynch, who was a brown trout in a former re-incarnate life and one of the most talented trutta stalkers I know. Terry Lawton- author and Britsh trout/salmon guru.-www.terrylawton.co.uk .Torrey Collins, master tight-line nympher from Conneticut-www.farmingtonriver.com .Nanda Sanise, Euro-nymph lady extraordinaire. Joe Goodspeed, Thomas & Thomas Fly Rods. Aaron Jasper, troutsman extraordinaire. Larry Halyk, Ontario fly fishing biologist and world traveler. Vince Wilcox, master fly creator and keeper of the Au Sable River. Eric Richrads, Perry County, Pennsylvania mountain man and "trutta Buddha," who understands the karma of wild brown trout, The Pennsylvanian David Rothrock, traditionalist gentleman of all things fine in the Pennsylvania trout legacy. Rich Strolis, Chasing Shadows fly tier and truttasaurus hunter. The keeper of the historic Au Sable of Michigan, author, guide, and owner, Josh Greenberg, www.gateslodge.com. Tommy Baltz, fly tying master, guide and modern dean of the Cumberland Valley Limestoners. Brian Judge, Pennsylvanian "truttasaurus stalker" and always on the hunt for nomadic waters. East Coast innovator Mark Sedotti. The ultra-creative modern Dame Juliana. The elegant and beautiful Linda Bachand, may your creative hands continue to spin classic salmon patterns. John Holsten, master truttasaurus guide and hunter of the White River. Montana Fly Company for their amazing portfolio and innovations, www.montanafly.com. Jon Kestner, seasoned Michigan guide and fly company owner, www.guidefitter.com. Daniel Podobed, creative east coast fly designer, www.eastcoastflycompany.com. Bill Chase at Angler Sport Group. Marcos Vergara at Hareline Dubbin. Boris Cetkovic, creator of realistic fly patterns and materials at www.frostyfly.com. The lovely Ann Woodcock, directo, www.fishpal.com. Fiona and staff at Orvis UK in Edinburgh, Scotland, for your wonderful reception and hospitality.

To the true visual artistic interpreters of Salmo: the amazing talents of Michiganders Derek Deyoung, www.derekdeyoung.com. David Ruimveld, www.davidruimveldstudio.com, Pennsylvania's Mark Susuinno, www.wildwings.com, Arkansan Duana Hada, www.rivertowngallery.com. To culinary masters that forage the woods for epicurean delights, Chef Alan Bergo, www.foragerchef.com.

To WNY trout hunter, Nicholas Sagiebene, www. http://www.adventureboundonthefly.com. To Josh Miller, Dusty Wissmuth, and Derek Eberley. Neil Sunday, Pennsylvania's new age brown trout legacy unfolding, John Field, to one of the finest casting gurus and authors. To Dave Karczynski the Polish princem editor-at-large, English professor, and fly fishing world adventurist and author. Scottish fly tying wonders, Ryan Houston, Colin McDonald, Paul Hankin, and Graeme Ferguson. Kiki Galvin, fly guide goddess of the mid-Atlantic. Colby Trow, Mossy spring creek river keeper of www.moseycreekflyfishing.com. Ken Collins, Grand River trout stalker, www.grandrivertroutfitters.com. Michigan's Ethan Winchester, www.boyneneoutfitters.com, and video master Spencer McCormick, for their northern passion of Hemingway country and its stunning brown trout rivers. Steve Galletata of the majestic Big Horn, www.bighornangler.com and Capt. Brad Smyth, urban salar guide at www.ifishdetroit.com.